Fly By Knig

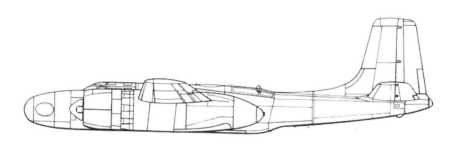

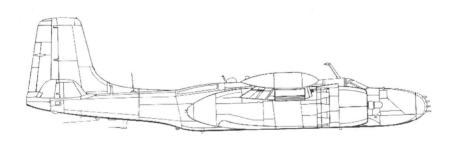

Fly By Knights

*Air Force A/B/RB-26 Air Commando
Missions in the Vietnam War*

Edited by ROGER D. GRAHAM

McFarland & Company, Inc., Publishers
Jefferson, North Carolina

Frontispiece: *top*, Fly By Knights (photograph by Roger D. Graham). *Center:* B-26B (courtesy Andrew W. "Andi" Biancur). *Bottom:* A-26A (courtesy Andrew W. "Andi" Biancur).

ISBN (print) 978-1-4766-8680-6
ISBN (ebook) 978-1-4766-4683-1

Library of Congress and British Library
cataloguing data are available

Library of Congress Control Number 2022033305

On the cover: *top* Fly By Knights patch worn on the right shoulder of pilots' flight suits; *bottom* photograph of A-26 pilots and navigators (in black flight suits) in front of an A-26 at Nakhon Phanom RTAFB, Thailand, circa 1968–69 (USAF).

Printed in the United States of America

*McFarland & Company, Inc., Publishers
Box 611, Jefferson, North Carolina 28640
www.mcfarlandpub.com*

To all of the unforgettable USAF B-26, RB-26, and A-26 combat aviators who lost their lives while flying those remarkable attack bomber aircraft during the Vietnam War (see Memorial chapter).

To all American military veterans and members of their families—in all wars—who bear the burden and pay the price for freedom in the United States of America.

And, to all of the loving and supportive members of my immediate family: Dianne, Kimberly, and Ryan Graham, and Kristi (daughter), Bill, Colette, Averi, and Chase Visage.

Table of Contents

Acknowledgments

I would like to thank everyone associated with A/B/RB-26 training and combat operations in the Vietnam War era, in whatever capacity, who have contributed stories and photographs for publication in this book. Even though more than 50 years have passed since those combat flight operations took place, their remarkable stories and photographs bring this tumultuous period of American history alive for the reader. Their memories have not faded. The A/B/RB-26 aviators loved flying this classic American combat aircraft, and they considered themselves honored and privileged to fly and fight for freedom, and for our great country. A special thank-you to Frank Nelson for sharing his stories and photographs, and for locating and retyping 609th Special Operations Squadron Historical Reports in a legible format; to Bruce Kramer, Jack Williams, Joe Kittinger, Al Shortt, Jimmie Butler, Richard "Rick" Fulwiler, and Donald Vogler for sharing their photographs; to Franklin "Hawkeye" Poole for sharing his videos and photographs; and to Jim Boney of the Air Commando Association, who shared many great articles and books in the Air Commando library that helped make this book possible.

Also, I would be remiss if I did not acknowledge that this book would not have become a reality without the proactive encouragement and support of my wife, Dianne Graham, who never wavered in her conviction that this is a book that needed to be published for the entire A/B/RB-26 community, and for the American public.

Southeast Asia

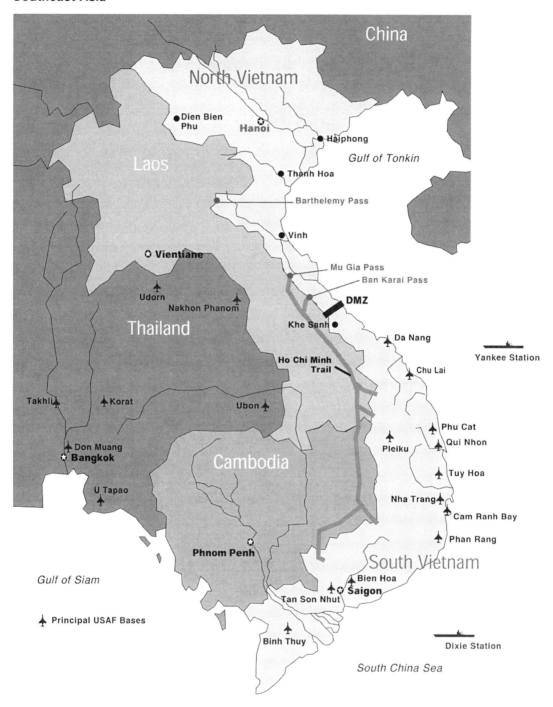

Map of Southeast Asia (reprint courtesy *Air Force Magazine*).

Introduction

Overview of Book

The goal of this book is to document—through the individual stories of American patriots who were there—the rich history of A/B-26 aircraft and crews during the Vietnam War era. I should say A/B/RB-26 aircraft, but that description simply becomes too long and cumbersome, and maybe confusing, to readers unfamiliar with classic American military aircraft. The "A" stands for Attack; the "B" stands for Bomber; and "RB" stands for Reconnaissance Bomber. All three versions of the aircraft (B-26, RB-26, and A-26) were flown by courageous combat crews during the Vietnam War period. The Douglas A-26 Invader (not to be confused with the Martin B-26 Marauder) is the only USAF combat aircraft to see combat service in World War II, the Korean War, and, finally, the Vietnam War. This book will cover Operation Farm Gate at Bien Hoa Air Base, South Vietnam; Project Big Eagle at Nakhon Phanom Royal Thai Air Force Base (NKP), Thailand; and Nimrod combat operations out of NKP.

The inspiration for writing this book crystallized at the A/B-26 Reunion at Hurlburt Field, Florida, in October 2009. A book titled *The Nimrods* about A-26 combat operations in 1966–69 out of Nakhon Phanom Royal Thai Air Force Base had been published in 2007. That book, written by Roger D. Graham, contains many stories about A-26 Nimrod missions that he had personally experienced in 1967–68. *The Nimrods* was well received, but a new book concept emerged during the A/B-26 Reunion dinner at the Soundside Club. During the open session following dinner, Roger Graham challenged the attendees to contribute their stories to this new book effort. Holding his hand in the ice bucket, as is the tradition to discourage long-winded speeches, Roger reminded attendees that there were many amazing stories told at each reunion, and that we needed to write and contribute those stories to this new book effort to memorialize the incredible A/B-26 Vietnam War story for everyone involved, and for the American public. As reflected in "Truck Killer," appearing in the July 2010 issue of *Air & Space Magazine*, aviation enthusiasts and the American public remain interested in this story.

Brigadier General Harry "Heinie" Aderholt and his wife were present at that A/B-26 Reunion dinner as honored guests. Never one to shrink from a patriotic challenge, Brigadier General Aderholt immediately suggested that an article be written for publication in the Air Commando Association newsletter seeking individual stories from pilots, navigators, scope operators, photographers, maintenance and armament personnel, family members, and anyone affected by A/B-26 combat operations in the Vietnam War. That article was written and published, and it resulted in many of the stories you will read in this book. Regrettably, "Air Commando One," as Heinie was affectionately

1

known by the Air Commando community, passed away on May 20, 2010. He was recognized as the key USAF Air Commando commander and leader during the Vietnam War. He is sorely missed.

Readers are encouraged to note from the outset that this is not just another dry historic treatise written by a single writer; it is a book filled with the stories and photographs of a wide cross-section of pilots, navigators, maintenance and armament personnel, scope operators, photographers, and family members. Most of the stories appearing in this book were written some 40 years after the last A-26A Counter Invaders flying out of Nakhon Phanom Royal Thai Air Force Base, Thailand, were retired from service in November 1969. However, you will find that the memories of these storytellers have not faded with time.

One of Winston Churchill's more famous quotations is that "there is nothing more exhilarating than being shot at without result." Having survived untold thousands of antiaircraft rounds being fired at them in

Colonel Harry (Heinie) Aderholt, commander, 56th Special Operations Wing, NKP (1967–1968) (USAF).

combat, all living A/B-26 crewmembers would readily agree with that quote. Unfortunately, in war, sometimes the good guys do get hit, and sometimes they are lost in combat. We honor their memories, and we honor their families.

Origin of "Any Time Any Place"

The origin of this well-recognized Air Commando motto dates back to World War II. In 1943, General Henry "Hap" Arnold (commander of the Army Air Forces), with the enthusiastic support of President Franklin Roosevelt, established the 1st Air Commando Group to provide air support to U.S. and British air and ground attacks on the Japanese in the China-Burma-India theater of operations. The 1st Air Commando Group, consisting of 523 volunteers and 348 aircraft (troop gliders, light planes, C-47 transports, B-25 bombers, and P-51 Mustangs), constituted a formidable force. General Arnold selected Lieutenant Colonel Phil Cochran and Lieutenant Colonel John Alison to lead the Air Commandos. General Arnold's parting words to Cochran and Alison were "To hell with the paperwork; go out and fight." Brigadier General Orde Wingate of the British Army was another key figure in unconventional warfare against the Japanese in Burma. President Roosevelt had been introduced to Brigadier General Wingate at a conference in 1943 and was most impressed with Wingate's plan for renewed attacks on the Japanese in Burma. In early January 1944, a successful glider operation was conducted; however, a training accident produced both British and American casualties. To restore confidence and morale, Wingate dispatched the following message from headquarters: "Please be assured that we will go with your boys any place, any time, any where." The 1st Air Commando Group and British allies quickly recovered and went on to execute a successful campaign against the Japanese, and the motto of the USAF Air Commandos was born. The motto was shortened to "Any Time Any Place" by the Air Commandos in the Vietnam War and is still in use by USAF special operations forces today.

Formation of the 4400th Combat Crew Training Squadron

Political and foreign affairs events often drive military events, and such was the case in the early 1960s. In early 1961, the Cold War between the United States and the Soviet Union entered a new, more intense phase. Following the Soviet shootdown of U-2 pilot Francis Gary Powers, Nikita Khrushchev made a speech that intensified the East-West political conflict. Khrushchev announced Moscow's support for communists engaged in "wars of national liberation" and declared that the Soviet Union would "help the peoples striving for their independence" through the overthrow of pro–Western governments in those brushfire wars. President-elect John F. Kennedy knew that Moscow was already supporting a communist insurgency in South Vietnam. The United States had supplied economic and military aid to the South Vietnamese since the 1954 partition that produced two nations—North Vietnam and South Vietnam. Following a comprehensive review, President Kennedy directed that the U.S. military develop counterinsurgency forces capable of resisting Soviet-backed guerrillas in such conflicts. It was a daunting task. In the early 1960s, the United States was well prepared for nuclear war with jet bombers, ICBMs, and nuclear submarines, but it was ill-prepared to meet counterinsurgency warfare threats in remote parts of the world. In response, General Curtis LeMay directed officers at Tactical Air Command (TAC) to form an elite unit able to conduct such missions.

On April 14, 1961, TAC officials activated the 4400th Combat Crew Training Squadron (CCTS) at Hurlburt Field, near Fort Walton Beach, Florida. The unit was an all-volunteer organization with an initial strength of 124 officers and 228 enlisted men, and they were soon known by their "Jungle Jim" nickname and referred to as "Air Commandos." General Curtis LeMay and other military officers (including Colonel Benjamin King and Colonel Robert Gleason) recognized early on that propeller aircraft would be better suited to the counterinsurgency role than jet aircraft. Consequently, the CCTS was initially equipped with eight B-26 bombers, eight T-28 fighters, and 16 C-47 transports. Since those aircraft had been manufactured during World War II, maintenance and armament crews faced a major challenge in maintaining and safely arming these aircraft.

Role of A/B/RB-26 Combat Operations in the Vietnam War

In the early 1960s, the role of B-26 bomber aircraft was to act as a tactical bomber aircraft conducting a variety of combat missions: interdiction against predetermined targets, close air-support of friendly ground forces, air cover, and escort of friendly supply vehicles and other forces as they traveled in the vicinity of enemy forces. Although the numbers of RB-26 aircraft available in South Vietnam were relatively modest in the early 1960s, those specialized reconnaissance aircraft and crews performed a valuable role in aerial photography and intelligence. Following the loss of some B-26 aircraft and crews in the early 1960s due to wing spar failure, the USAF awarded a contract to On Mark Engineering Company of Van Nuys, California, to "remanufacture" 40 B-26 aircraft to strengthen the wings and make other significant improvements before the aircraft were returned to combat duty. Those 40 remanufactured aircraft were initially designated as B-26K aircraft, and then redesignated as A-26A Counter Invader aircraft to satisfy Thai officials who did not want bomber aircraft based on their soil. Four of those B-26K aircraft were "loaned" to Belgium in 1964 to resist aggression by Simba rebels in the Congo. Later, those aircraft were returned. The 40 A-26A aircraft were used in armed reconnaissance combat operations out of Nakhon Phanom Royal Thai Air Force Base, Thailand, from 1966 to 1969.

CHAPTER 1

Operation Farm Gate

Deployment to Bien Hoa Air Base, South Vietnam

The story of Operation Farm Gate is an important story in U.S. military history, and it is a story of true American courage in combat that has not received the recognition that it deserves. In the early 1960s, as military conditions in South Vietnam continued to deteriorate, President John Kennedy and his administration decided that action needed to be taken to assist the government of South Vietnam in resisting escalating communist aggression. On October 11, 1961, President Kennedy directed that Secretary of Defense Robert McNamara "introduce the Air Force 'Jungle Jim' Squadron into Vietnam for the initial purpose of training Vietnamese forces." The mission was to be covert, and the Air Commandos were to maintain a low profile in-country and avoid the press. The initial deployment package was quite modest: 155 airmen, eight T-28s, and four modified SC-47s. The unit later received B-26s from a repair facility in Taiwan, where they were being "rebuilt" for the mission.

The unit was officially designated as Det. 2A of the 4400th CCTS, code-named "Farm Gate." On November 5, 1961, the detachment departed Hurlburt Field for Southeast Asia. Their destination was Bien Hoa Air Base, located approximately 15 miles north of Saigon. Upon their arrival, Farm Gate personnel were greeted with very austere conditions at Bien Hoa. The base had been built by French forces, and the airfield was in bad condition. Living conditions for the crews and support personnel also left much to be desired. The deployed airmen lived in "hooches" reminiscent of World War II barracks. The airmen slept in open barracks in bunk beds surrounded by mosquito netting. And it was hot, and very humid. There were large fans operating 24 hours a day, but there was no air-conditioning … true "Jungle Jim" conditions.

From that modest beginning, Farm Gate personnel and aircraft steadily grew as the war in South Vietnam expanded. A total of 27 B-26 aircraft were taken out of storage at Davis Monthan AFB, Arizona, between March and September 1961 and reconditioned at Hill AFB, Utah, for use by "Jungle Jim" crews in South Vietnam. The initial "announced" main mission of Farm Gate personnel was to provide training for Vietnamese Air Force (VNAF) personnel. To that end, B-26 aircraft displayed South Vietnamese markings, and a VNAF observer was included in the aircrew of B-26 crews operating out of Bien Hoa Air Base. However, as the war intensified, the mission of U.S. B-26 aircrews, in reality, became actual combat strike missions against Viet Cong communist forces that were terrorizing and killing South Vietnamese civilians in hamlets across South Vietnam. The Vietnamese observer sat in the "jump seat" behind the navigator seat, and the American B-26 pilot and navigator, sitting side by side in the cockpit, actually flew the aircraft and conducted the strike missions.

Navigator George Rose, who flew with pilot John Cragin, arrived at Bien Hoa Air Base on December 3, 1963. By that time, Detachment 2A had been redesignated as the 1st Air Commando Squadron. According to George Rose, the majority of targets bombed by B-26s were marked by forward air controllers. The next most frequent targets were in defense of strategic hamlets. The B-26 crews also flew escort for friendly truck convoys, trains, and Ranch Hand Spray C-123 aircraft, and would attack any Viet Cong forces impeding those efforts. On one of those daytime missions, Captain George Rose took a couple of photographs of Captain John Cragin in the pilot's seat, and the target area they had just bombed.

Although the Farm Gate B-26s and T-28s flew combat missions under both daytime and nighttime conditions, the B-26s were particularly effective at night (when the Viet Cong usually attacked outlying hamlets). The VNAF had no nighttime air strike capability, making B-26s the aircraft of choice when South Vietnamese hamlets would come under attack at night from Viet Cong forces. The B-26 crews were regularly scheduled for nighttime alert duty, and when called upon, would race to their aircraft and fly to the location directed by command personnel. B-26 crews typically worked with USAF or VNAF C-47 flareship aircraft, and with South Vietnamese ground controllers within the hamlets. If communications with the hamlets proved difficult, a last resort was for the people in the hamlet to light a "fire arrow" pointed in the direction of the attacking Viet Cong. After a first pass (usually using napalm), the forward air controller (air or ground) could direct the remaining B-26 attack passes (using napalm, rockets, bombs,

Captain John Cragin, B-26 pilot, during daylight mission in South Vietnam (courtesy George Rose).

View of white phosphorus bombs on target following B-26 strike in SVN, 1964 (courtesy George Rose).

and guns) based upon an estimated bearing and distance from the napalm strike. This was a very demanding mission for B-26 pilots because they were making dive-bombing passes at night, at low altitude, based upon limited visual contact with the ground and directions from FAC personnel. Having a navigator flying in the right seat of the B-26 was a real advantage. The navigator could verify the target, set up the armament switches, and tap the pilot on the shoulder if the B-26 was getting too low on an attack pass (yelling worked too).

Operation Farm Gate at Bien Hoa Air Base, spanning the dates October 1, 1961, to July 28, 1963, involved the earliest U.S. Air Force combat operations in the Vietnam War.[1] Initially, the purported purpose of Farm Gate operations was training and support for the South Vietnamese Air Force. However, operations quickly evolved into direct involvement of U.S. aircraft and aircrews. At its peak, the number of B-26 aircraft assigned to Farm Gate stood at some 18 aircraft. The crews suffered significant combat losses during that period, but they inflicted even more severe losses on the enemy. At the beginning of Farm Gate in 1961, U.S. military forces in South Vietnam numbered approximately 5,000; however, in the 1964–65 time frame, U.S. military forces in South Vietnam had grown to some 500,000. President Johnson ordered more detailed planning for direct action against North Vietnam, possibly including Farm Gate aircraft and three B-57 squadrons to be transferred from Japan. However, B-26 aircraft were taken out of that planning process because of wing failures and aircraft/crew losses in 1963 and 1964:

> But even if the plans had been implemented immediately, it would have made little difference to Farm Gate: time had finally caught up with their B-26s. The heavy underwing loads used by Farm Gate imposed high negative G forces on the wings when taxiing the aircraft on the

bumpy airfields in Vietnam, and the structures were becoming increasingly fatigued. After a B-26 had lost a wing during a mission on 16 August 1963, strict limitations were imposed on the stressing allowed during missions. But when Captains Herman S. Moore and Lawrence L. Lively were killed in a B-26 on 11 February 1964, the decision was taken to withdraw the B-26 from combat altogether. Moore and Lively had been flying in a fire power demonstration at Eglin AFB range 52 when the left wing of their aircraft separated during pull out from a strafing run. When news of this second accident reached Vietnam, one B-26 was airborne on a strike mission. The crew was given orders by radio to return immediately to Bien Hoa, making sure not to put any undue stress on the aircraft on their way back. From this day on, the Farm Gate B-26s were, for all practical purposes, grounded.[2]

First Air Commando Squadron, Bien Hoa Air Base (1964) (USAF).

Farm Gate

Maury Bourne

In the early 1960s, the USAF was well-prepared to fight a global nuclear war. We had a fleet of intercontinental bombers, transports, and fighters superior to any other force on earth. But we were not prepared to fight a guerrilla war in third-world countries.

By 1961, President John F. Kennedy had committed American counterinsurgency forces to prevent the fall of third-world countries to communism. The First Air Commando Wing was formed to fill the requirement for air support in those countries fighting against communist guerrillas. In the coming years, Air Commandos would serve worldwide in many countries and in many different circumstances, but our greatest challenge would prove to be the Vietnam War.

The First Air Commando Wing was a great outfit. It was all-volunteer, from the

Farm Gate crew: Mike Styer (left) and Maury Bourne (courtesy Maury Bourne).

colonels in command to the young, enlisted men working as mechanics, medics, clerks, and bomb loaders. We had Air Commandos serving all over the third world as advisers and trainers, often on the edge of combat, and sometimes right in the middle of it. Most of those operations took place in secret, and from the start the First Air Commando Wing operated as a shadow outfit unknown to most Americans, and little more than a rumor even within other branches of the USAF.

In guerrilla warfare, the requirement for strike aircraft is best described as "close air support." This need is met by slow-moving aircraft capable of making visual contact with small friendly ground units and working closely with those units to strike enemy positions. The only aircraft suitable for this type of work were mostly left over from World War II and Korea. The B-26 and the T-28 were selected to fulfill that role. Both of those aircraft were old and no longer operated by the USAF. B-26 and T-28 airframes were located in boneyards and weed lots worldwide, given various degrees of overhaul, and sent off to war.

At that time, both the B-26 and the T-28 operated as "the Sixth Fighter." The Sixth Fighter was the original home of the B-26, and all following B-26 squadron designations—the 602, the 605, and the 609—were all descendants of the Sixth Fighter. The B-26B became the early workhorse in the Vietnam War.

I enlisted in the Aviation Cadet program in 1960 and was one of the last of the young men given the opportunity to win a commission and a flight rating in the USAF with only a high school education. In the spring of 1963, I arrived at Hurlburt Field (Eglin AFB Aux. Field #9), the "Home of the Air Commandos." I was a 23-year-old navigator with the rank of first lieutenant and was assigned to the Sixth Fighter Squadron. When I first sat down in the right seat of a B-26, my flight experience as a navigator

B-26 operating out of Bien Hoa Air Base, VNAF Markings, 1962 (courtesy Jack Williams).

consisted of about 40 hours in the back seat of a Northrop F-89 and about 700 hours over the Pacific Ocean as a navigator on an RC-121 early-warning aircraft. Nothing in my previous experience prepared me for the job ahead. My memory of B-26 operations is from the perspective of the navigator. The things I remember, the things I write about, the stories I tell, are all from the viewpoint of the man who rode in the right seat.

Every B-26 pilot I ever flew with was older than me, had more flight experience than I had, and outranked me. The pilots typically were older and more experienced than the navs. I don't know if this was by design, or by accident. In my memory about 75 percent of the navs were first lieutenants and younger than about 27, while 75 percent of the pilots were captains 28 to 35 or older. A few of our pilots had flown in the Korean War.

Most of us were teamed together as a crew, but from time to time crewmembers changed and it was common to fly with several different men over a period of time. I don't remember any effort on the part of the commanders to form crews. It was evident from the start that crews would team up, and over our training period pilots and navs just naturally found a partner to fly with.

We deployed to Bien Hoa AB, South Vietnam, in the summer of 1963. Bien Hoa was designated "detachment two," and our code name was "Farm Gate." Bien Hoa AB was located about 10 miles north and east of Saigon. We lived in structures called "hooches" that usually housed six men. A hooch had a wooden plank floor, a corrugated iron roof, screen-wire walls, and four overhead fans that ran night and day. We slept on GI cots with a mosquito cloth over every cot. Concrete walks connected the hooches and led to the latrine, showers, chow hall, and the officers' club. I don't remember ever seeing an air conditioner in SVN.

At that time, our total fixed-wing strike capability in SVN consisted of about a dozen flyable B-26s, a handful of T-28s, and a very limited number of AD Skyraiders flown by the SVN Air Force. Between us, we covered the air attack requirements from one end of SVN to the other. At nighttime, only the B-26 was deployed. The primary base for the B-26 was Bien Hoa AB, but in time a few aircraft were based at Da Nang to cover strike requirements in the north.

My first pilot was Captain Dick Fields. Dick had come from an F101B Voodoo squadron and was a fighter pilot to the bone. We got along well from the start. Dick made it plain to me. "I'll do the flying. You do the navigation." That proved to be a good plan. We did have our encounters. One of the secrets of a two-man aircrew is their ability to fight, argue, and yell at one another, and still remain friends. That just seems to be natural behavior of alpha males when you strap them into a narrow hellhole of an attack bomber, send them off to war, and instruct them to do their best not to get killed.

Dick would fly an additional combat tour in A-1E Skyraiders but would die in the crash of a civilian aircraft. That occurred after I had left the USAF and I never learned the details.

The B-26B was a great airplane. It carried lots of fuel and lots of ordnance and flew like a fighter. We carried six cans of napalm under the wing, a dozen bombs in the bomb bay, and .50-caliber machine guns in the nose. We flew right on top of our targets, usually in direct radio contact with friendly forces. The navigator served as navigator, copilot, flight engineer, and radio operator. One of his primary jobs was to look out the window and take note of anything the pilot might have missed. I soon found that my biggest challenge was to constantly harangue pilots who seemed to be determined to die young and take me with them. No doubt that was an overreaction on my part, but at the time it was the dominant thought in my life. Dick Fields often complained that his right shoulder was chronically bruised from my beating on him during low-altitude pull-ups.

In time, I learned to ride easy in a B-26. I learned to trust the men I flew with, grit my teeth, and just hang on for the ride. No matter what anybody ever tells you, sitting in the right seat of a B-26 in combat is a scary job.

The biggest problem with the B-26B model was that they were old. They had flown in several wars in several lands, and by the time the Commandos took them over they were pretty well worn out. We had a very dedicated group of maintenance men who worked on them night and day to keep them in flying condition, but with few spare parts and limited maintenance facilities, it was an uphill battle. As an old armorer sergeant recalled: "The B Model was a maintenance nightmare. It would be just sitting on the ramp with no one around and suddenly decide to start dropping bombs on the ramp. We considered it a minor miracle if all six guns fired during a mission." In my estimation, one of every three B-26s returning from a combat mission came home with a red X in the logbook.

It was common to turn on the master switch and smell the musty smell of overheating electrical circuits. The vacuum-powered flight instruments were old, and wildly precessing gyros were normal. Devotion to needle, ball, and airspeed kept many a pilot right side up and brought many a B-26 crew safely back home.

Because our aircraft had been flown by so many different air forces in so many different roles, no two were alike. Mystery antennas were common and oddball switches and circuit breakers appeared here and there. Chopped-off cable bundles and strange placards were commonplace.

The legendary Pratt and Whitney R-2800 engine that powered the B-26 had the reputation of being a cast-iron engine. It was tough. But nothing lasts forever, and cylinder changes and complete engine changes were never-ending. Nonflying aircraft always littered our ramp, and any nonflying aircraft was always in danger of being used as a parts supplier in order to keep another aircraft in the air. Spare parts were always in short supply, and every B-26B I ever saw had at least one empty hole in the instrument panel awaiting a "part on order." Some aircraft had several empty holes.

Most of the problems that we had with our engines were not with the basic engine itself but with the systems that made the big radial do its work. Fifty-rpm mag drops were found only in the dreams of young pilots and old maintenance sergeants. It became the practice not to notice the distinction between a 75-rpm mag drop and a 100-rpm mag drop. After all, who can really read a shaky needle on a 20-year-old instrument? "Just listen to the engine" we were told. If it sounds smooth, it's good to go. If it's a bit rough, just lean her out a bit and burn off the plugs. It was considered good practice to check her again before takeoff.

Communication between the pilot and navigator on intercom was always difficult, and on some aircraft, impossible. There was so much noise in the cockpit that screaming directly into the ear of the man sitting next to you was usually a waste of time. But with an experienced crew, a lot of talking was not needed. If the navigator paid attention and "stayed on the same page" with the pilot, cockpit requirements were usually evident. Hand signals were common.

Our communications radios were vintage World War II. Only in 1963, they were 20 years older. They were push-button and crystal-tuned and had only five channels. They were full of static when they worked at all and picked up engine ignition noise constantly. Much of our attempt at radio conversation was with a SVN soldier or forward controller and was in broken English or shrill, high-speed Vietnamese. Communications were not the best.

Our navigation aids were nonexistent. A single low-freq "coffee grinder" ADF was standard equipment on the B model; however, there were no ADF radio installations in SVN. It would pick up random commercial local radio stations, but our inability to identify the location from the spooky music and the strange language made the unit useless. I never bothered to turn it on. There was a VOR station somewhere in the Saigon area, but none of our aircraft had VOR receivers. There was a radar site at Tan Son Nhut, but it was of little use outside the local area. It was of no use at all when we were working at low altitude. The pilots I flew with seldom if ever talked to the radar site. For the most part we navigated by dead reckoning, the time-honored art of time, distance, and compass heading. Basically, the same system used by Christopher Columbus (except that Columbus wasn't traveling at 200 mph).

My personal experience was that I had very little problem when we flew to the south of Saigon. The flat delta country, with several rather large towns, made map-reading relatively easy. I thought that going south in good weather was even easier at night. The moonlight on the Mekong and Saigon Rivers, the well-defined coastline on the South China Sea, and the lights of Me Thou, Can Thou, and Soc Trang made navigation easy.

Going north up into the Central Highlands and into Three Corps and High Corps was an entirely different story. North of Saigon the mountains began to rise and towns became few and far between. At nighttime, very few towns in the interior were large enough to give positive identification. It was probably just my imagination, but it always seemed to me that the farther we went north, the higher the mountains got, the darker the night, and the more likely it was that the weather would be bad. I remember a time or two on my earlier missions when I attempted to locate a target by getting airborne out of Bien Hoa and trying to fly directly to the coordinates on the frag order. That was always a mistake, particularly at night. I came to believe that the area between Bam Me Thou and Da Nang was the blackest place on earth.

My preferred navigation plan when we left Bien Hoa and headed up anywhere north of Da Lot was to pick up a heading of about 070 degrees as soon as we got airborne. This would put us on a nice long leg and hit the coast about Phan Rang. Following the coast north was easy, particularly in the moonlight. The trick was to pick an easy-to-identify point on the coast that was abeam of your target area. From that firm fixed position, a carefully flown compass heading to the west of no more than 40 or 60 miles would usually put you very near the target. Of course, everything we did was complicated at night and particularly in bad weather. But for the most part, we found our targets by dead reckoning, and very little else.

We did not have what could be described as "good targets." My idea of a "good target" would be a locomotive pulling a dozen freight cars loaded with war materials, or a truck convoy, or an enemy bomb dump, or a hydroelectric dam, or an antiaircraft installation, etc., etc. On a rare occasion we did have trucks, or boats, or gun installations, or hard structures as targets, but for the most part our targets were only glimpsed fleetingly, and strike effectiveness was usually based on crew judgment or by verbal evaluation from the forward observer. In a land like Vietnam with rural villages everywhere, rugged mountains, and endless forests, we all too often placed our ordnance in locations that were verbally described to us by an observer on the ground or in a small spotter plane. The phrase "hit my smoke" became one of the working-day instructions given to a B-26 crew. Often this instruction was on a static-ridden radio and was something like, "You see smoke? You drop bomb four clicks north smoke," and perhaps followed by, "No, no … you hit my smoke *other* side big tree!" At nighttime, flares were used to mark targets. A flare would give off a bright glow and was easy to spot. It was usually orange but sometimes white or red or random other colors.

One of the tactics of the South Vietnamese government was to develop the "strategic hamlet" program. Under this plan, small villages throughout the country become fortified, and home guard units were organized to defend against Viet Cong attacks. These scattered, small fortresses were supported by the U.S. and often contained advisers from U.S. Special Forces teams. The intent of this program was to give the locals the ability, as well as the determination, to defend themselves against communist infiltration and attack. During the Farm Gate period, this program was in full swing, and defense of these strategic hamlets often fell to Air Commando strike aircraft. The communists were not dumb. They avoided scheduling their attacks on pretty, sunshiny days when aircraft held a clear advantage. Consequently, B-26s were regularly called out on the darkest nights and the foulest weather to defend those small fortresses. Some of my most vivid memories from that period of my life are of night scrambles in bad weather to defend a strategic hamlet. The central highlands seemed to be our most frequent destination on those nights, and just to locate an obscure village in a mountainous area in scattered thunderstorms was a next-to-impossible task. Nonetheless, I seemed to usually manage to blunder onto the scene, often after considerable roundabout searching, guessing, and backtracking.

Often the coordinates of a target would be given in "army grid coordinates," the same coordinate system used since World War I by forward observers to direct cannon fire. We had no previous instruction or experience with this system and had to figure out how to use it on the go. Often this grid information was relayed on poor radios by panicky voices on bad nights. The navigator's chore was to first plot out this position on strange army charts, convert the information to latitude and longitude, transfer the information onto our sectional charts, and give navigation instruction to a confused, mad, and hopelessly lost pilot in a noisy, storm-tossed aircraft on the blackest night that ever was. My memory is of usually having the wrong army chart, forgetting how to plot the strange system, and a flashlight that wouldn't work. The fact that the coordinates given for the location of the target were as likely to be incorrect as correct did not help matters.

Many times, we would be assisted on these nights by flare ships. Flare ships were either C-47s or C-123s also flown by Air Commandos. Flare ships would operate at higher altitudes than B-26s, and often had navigation capability with a VOR or TACAN site in Saigon or with radar coverage. Of course, flare ships also had their navigation problems and would often be attempting to locate the target area with no more help than we had.

But as a rule, a flare ship on location was a blessing to B-26 crews. Even if contact with the village could not be made, a flare dropped at almost any location within several miles would give the observer on the ground a marker from which he could direct the aircraft to his location.

On many occasions, I experienced this wonderful system at work when the flare ship was operating above a solid overcast, and the B-26 was operating below that same solid overcast. Few things are as memorable to me as desperately searching along a long mountain valley beneath the weather and experiencing a soft orange glow slowly pushing into the darkness.

Suddenly, a flare would pop out of the overcast and appear wondrously in an adjacent valley a few miles away. Such a randomly dropped flare would enable the ground observer to direct the flare ship directly over the battle area and enable the B-26 to follow happily behind. Flares were a wondrous sight, illuminating vast areas of countryside and, in fact, turning night into day. Few things were as comforting to a B-26 navigator as seeing a flare pop out of a solid overcast a mile or two in the distance. I'll always have a special place in my heart for the men who dropped flares over the valleys, jungles, and rice fields of South Vietnam.

Once we had made visual contact with a village under attack, and established radio contact with someone in that village, it was a whole new ball game. The pressure was no longer on the navigator and it was all the pilot's show. We were often told, and I believe it to be true, that nothing was as effective at discouraging the enemy as a B-26 suddenly appearing out of a stormy night. There's nothing like that first can of napalm on a black night to get everybody's attention.

As always, radio communication was difficult at best. The Vietnamese defenders of fortified villages devised a practical and very effective way to direct strike aircraft toward enemy positions. This became known as the "fire arrow." A fire arrow was a long board that could easily and quickly be moved about by two men. Four or five flare pots were placed on this board and it was positioned to point directly at the location from which the attack was coming. An additional two flare pots could be quickly positioned on either side of one end of the long board to complete the fire arrow. Once a fire arrow was in place, a B-26 pilot knew to deliver his ordnance at some point into the darkness to which the arrow pointed. Once in place, the only information a pilot needed was a distance, usually expressed in "klicks." Even this information was of secondary importance. A napalm delivered into the night along the shaft of a fire arrow anywhere beyond the perimeter of the village was a good thing. In the course of a battle, the fire arrow often would be repositioned several times, and on at least one occasion, I remember the use of two fire arrows in the same village. One thing notable about night attacks—it was easy to see the gunfire arcing up at us. This gunfire was usually small-arms fire aimed at the sound of our aircraft. On occasion, we would encounter fire from heavier guns, but the use of modern antiaircraft weapons in South Vietnam was still in the future.

As often as not, we would make two or three strikes, go into orbit for 15 or even 30 minutes, and be called back to begin the attack all over again. This was the beauty of the B-26: fuel to hold in a target area, and plenty of ordnance to deliver when the need arose again. Even without any radio contact at all, a fire arrow was perfectly easy to understand and a far better way to communicate than gargled and unintelligible radio traffic.

But the successful defense of these little hamlets was not always the case. I hate to admit it, but on more than one occasion I failed completely to find a strategic hamlet that was under attack. I distinctly remember being called out on one of my first night missions. Dick Fields and I were still flying as a crew and we struck off out of Bien Hoa for what should have been an easy location no more than about 45 minutes to the north. Rain showers were scattered everywhere and Dick tried to get radar vectors out of Saigon. This was a lost cause, and we ended up in heavy showers after making several abrupt heading changes that were supposed to keep us in the clear. I was trying to do air plot on a knee board while lightning flashes revealed ragged thunderstorms dead ahead. I was mad because Dick would not maintain any heading I gave him, and he was mad because every heading I gave him put us back in a thunder cell. Dick was convinced that we had overflown the target area, and I was just as convinced that we were still a good five minutes out. We argued about that as well as two men sitting only 12 inches apart and directly between two 2,000-horsepower Pratt & Whitney radials in the middle of a thunderstorm can argue. After burning up fuel for two hours, staring into a black void until our brains ached, and arguing ourselves hoarse, both of us finally admitted that we were hopelessly lost and went back home. (I know this sounds very "unprofessional," but damn it, that's the way life was back then.) I am proud to say that on many other occasions Dick and I were dead on target and carried the battle for those poor lost souls who were desperately trying to defend their families and hometown against the onslaught of a communist guerrilla attack.

The eventual failure of the Strategic Hamlet program gave an early and ominous hint to the decade of war that lay ahead.

On many days, our targets were easily seen enemy soldiers, or at least described to us as "enemy soldiers." Often we would be clearly taking ground fire, leaving no question as to the validity of our attack. That was not always the case. Some of the strikes that I rode on, and was active in identifying, later came to leave questions in my mind. I know that this was also true of several of my squadron mates. We moved on. We understood that ambiguity was all part of the fog of war.

But those questions sometimes remained. Even after almost half a century, there are certain very distinct memories that continue to rummage through my mind. This is not to suggest that I am in any way "burdened by guilt," or suffering from some fashionable "syndrome." It is simply my way of stating that I am a moral man, and that I am quite capable of examining and reviewing the actions of my life. I know that many of my fellow Air Commandos also have these memories. But we have no regrets.

When I first came to the Commandos, I had pilots brag to me that the B-26 was "built like a railroad bridge." The one thing we had total faith in was her structural strength. In fact, the B-26B had been overstressed for many years by heavy pullouts and rough runways. Maintenance had been sparse, and inspections of aircraft structure had been limited. Unknown to the men who sat in the cockpit, the aircraft were starting to come apart in high-speed, high-G bomb runs. That stark truth was not evident at first. B-26 combat losses were attributed to other causes, but the fact was, wing spars were failing. In time, we all came to understand that truth. For some of us, it was too late.

We continued to fly in spite of all challenges. We flew day and night. We flew between rain squalls and without navigation aids of any kind. We flew with rough engines and ground fire, and with aircraft systems that were chronically inoperative, leaking, smoking, malfunctioning, and failing.

Those of us who flew the B-26B in the Vietnam War under the code name "Farm Gate" were proud beyond all reason. That was the most invigorating period of my lifetime. I still get goose bumps, just remembering those days. I would do it all over again.

Vietnam Memories

The B-26 Invader

Bruce Kramer

My daughters and wife have asked me to recall some of the experiences that I had during my time in Vietnam. It is now 2009, over 45 years since I was there. I don't know how well my memory will be, but I thought that I might jot down some of the exciting, and maybe some of the not so exciting, flights. As most everyone has heard in the past, flying is a series of dull and boring takeoffs and landings, and interspersed are a few moments of stark terror. This was my experience, especially in Vietnam.

I think I should go back and give a brief explanation of how and in what circumstances I even ended up in Vietnam.

I entered the Air Force in July 1960 as an aviation cadet, a flight training and commissioning program that was discontinued shortly after I was fortunate to have applied and have been accepted. I was 19 years old, did not know anything at all about the military, but wanted to fly. The pilot program had already been discontinued so I was accepted into the navigator training located at Harlingen AFB, almost as far south as you can go in Texas. I soon found out that the weather in South Texas in late July is not only hot, but very, very humid. The program turned out to be a boot camp–type experience for almost a full year with a lot of calisthenics, marching, square meals, yelling, and even some classroom and flying training. I was too proud to quit so I eventually graduated in June 1961, receiving a commission as a second lieutenant and the wings of a navigator.

Since I was in the middle of the class ranking, I was assigned to Mather AFB in Sacramento for radar bombardier training. Again, I was in the middle of the class ranking at graduation, did not receive the RB-47 assignment that I thought I wanted, but was assigned to Langley AFB as a line navigator in a KB-50 tanker squadron. I believe that the Man Above was looking over me because, not only did I receive great navigating experience, but I met and married my wife in Newport News.

In the spring of 1963 while I was TDY (temporary duty station) in the Azores, a TWIX came through requesting applications for assignment to B-26s in Vietnam. The KB-50s were being deactivated and the squadron was to be eventually equipped with C-130s, which I knew spent the vast majority of their time TDY. I figured I could get an overseas assignment out of the way, and at the same time, get the assignment of my choice when I returned to CONUS.

I reached Eglin AFB Aux #9 (Hurlburt Field) for crew assignment and B-26 qualification in May 1963. I can't recall whether we individually had any choice as to assignment with a pilot, but I don't think it would have made much difference anyway since we didn't know each other. Tom Johnson and I were crewed together. He had been in the Utah National Guard, flew F-84F fighter bombers, and had been recalled to active duty during the Berlin crisis. During civilian life, Tom flew fire bombers during the summer, usually TBMs. I have to say that Tom was probably the best stick and rudder man that I ever flew with (that's excluding myself, of course, since I eventually went to pilot training after I returned to CONUS). As you will see later, being a good pilot also requires common sense and good judgment. There's an old saying that you have to know when to "hold 'em" and know when to "fold 'em."

In late August, I flew commercial aircraft to San Francisco and a civilian contract carrier aircraft to Saigon. While I traveled in style, everyone else flew first class in a windowless C-135 facing backward in canvas seats. I arrived at Tan Son Nhut late in the evening so I stayed overnight in the Majestic Hotel in downtown Saigon. It was just like out of *Casablanca*—wide-open verandas, open rooms, slow rotating overhead fans, bidets, and no air-conditioning.

The next morning I caught the regularly scheduled USAF Blue Bus (while I was at Bien Hoa, the VC never attacked the "bus"). By the time I got to Bien Hoa, several weeks after everyone else, the members of my group had received their orientation flights and were established in their "hooches." As I recall, our "hooches" were some 20 feet long and 14 feet wide, holding about 10 people. Each of us had a military cot, with mosquito netting, a small table, and a locker.

Each building was open-sided, with louvered sides that could be raised or lowered to allow air to circulate, and with screens to keep out the bugs (didn't work). As well, the rats were ever present. At night, you could hear them scurrying around. If you left out food, forget it because it would be gone the next morning. We had a wooden frame over our bed from which was suspended the mosquito netting, which, in turn, was tucked under the mattress. To get into bed, you first sprayed with DDT to kill whatever had gotten inside, then you loosened one side, slipped into bed as fast as you could, then retucked the net under the mattress again. We had overhead fans that kept the air recirculating. We had one common bath/shower room, with warm water, one small officers' club with liquids of choice and some card tables (I learned how to play bridge, others learned how to lose Washingtons), and one common chow hall. Once a week, we could BBQ our own steak, it always had SOS (chipped beef, or shit on a shingle) available (don't knock it, I liked it on toast, especially after a late-night mission when you had missed dinner), and it was open 24 hours.

The day after my arrival, I was scheduled for my orientation flight. One of the squadron officers, the operations officer as I recall, had to go to Soc Trang, south of Saigon on the Mekong River, pick up a T-28 pilot, and fly him up to Ban Me Thuot, where he would pick up a T-28 that had had mechanical problems. Anyway, he told me not to worry about anything, just look at the map and he would show me the prominent sights. The aircraft assigned was a C model B-26 with a glass nose as opposed to the B model with the hard nose with 50-cal guns, either five or eight. The C model had been equipped to photo-recce and map South Vietnam.

Flight line at Bien Hoa Air Base (courtesy Bruce Kramer).

After takeoff at Bien Hoa, we flew south into the delta toward Soc Trang. He said that I would become familiar with the area very soon. The delta is very flat, with numerous canals, few roads, and a scattering of small huts with occasional larger communities where canals crossed. These larger communities normally contained a triangular stronghold with embankments where the residents gathered when attacked by the Viet Cong. He told me that the majority of our work would involve providing close air support (CAP) for these "forts," when attacked, usually at night.

After arrival at Soc Trang and a stop for a Coke, the pilot asked me to climb into the nose section since he wanted to chat with the T-28 pilot as we flew north. In addition, the T-28 pilot didn't have his head set, so I "volunteered" to loan him mine. If anyone has seen a B-26, you know that the prop is almost even with the guy in the nose so the noise level is extreme, to say the least. Imagine the situation—there I was, couldn't see either of them and couldn't hear. We took off, climbed about 30 feet to clear a line of palm trees off the end of the runway, then descended to about 10 feet off the ground—believe me, I had a bird's-eye view of everything. We proceeded north over the delta, climbing slightly when we had to clear houses or trees, eventually into the mountains with large mahogany trees, and I received a very good look at them too. Of course, as soon as we took off, I didn't have a clue as to where we were. For all of this trip, there I was, sitting in that glass house at ground level, in a war zone, so all I could think of was someone throwing a rock at us as we drove by. We arrived at Ban Me Thout, landed on a PSP runway, dropped off our T-28 pilot, and returned to Bien Hoa, where I was cleared for combat flights.

The very first combat flight with Tom was over the western border of Vietnam with Cambodia near Tay Ninh. As I recall, it was in a rubber plantation and the ARVN were in a pretty good firefight with a large group of VC. We were to provide CAP, armed with the typical load of six cans of napalm, about 4,500 pounds of hard bombs (usually 260-pound fragmentation bombs for antipersonnel), and our guns. We dropped the napalm, dropped the frags, and finished with the guns. Tom normally liked to use the nose guns and then the wing guns.

The aircraft carried insignia for the Republic of Vietnam and we were officially flying training flights for student pilots. Of course, the "student pilots" were 19-year-old airmen and most could not speak or understand English. They rode in a jump seat located immediately behind the navigator's position on the right side of the cockpit. I know what it felt like to ride back there because during training at Hurlburt, the instructor pilot rode in the right seat and I rode in the jump seat. I believe that the seat was designed initially when a 75 MM cannon was installed, requiring a gunner to load ammunition. I always tried to be courteous to these Vietnamese because I'm sure that they were scared, couldn't understand what was being said or done. They couldn't tell us they were airsick or that they needed to have a bowel movement. The seat was back far enough that they really couldn't look out and more than one of them filled up a glove while we were flying—poor guys.

Several nights after that day flight, we were scheduled

First Lieutenant Tom Johnson, pilot (left) and First Lieutenant Bruce Kramer, navigator (right), Bien Hoa (1963) (courtesy Bruce Kramer).

for our first of many nighttime airborne alerts. The activity was very heavy at this particular time and B-26s were almost always needed every night. There were regularly two airborne alerts every night. The first aircraft took off at 2200 hours (military time) and flew until 0200 hours unless he expended, at which time another aircraft, previously cocked for a rapid engine start and launching so there would always be an aircraft airborne. A second B-26 was launched slightly before 0200 hours if the first plane had not expended and flew until 0600 hours. This could have had something to do with subsequent wing spar failures; an aircraft that had not expended would land with the unexpended ordnance.

Tom and I were both first lieutenants, but very junior. Guess who regularly ended up with the 0200 to 0600 hour alerts? Believe me, we could find our way around the delta at night but wouldn't recognize it in the daytime as being the same country.

I'll never forget the first night attack we made. We worked under flares dropped by C-47s out of Tan Son Nhut. They were called the "Dirty Thirty"—USAF pilots with VNAF copilots who flew a great number of missions every month. The C-47s were supposed to fly about 1,500 feet above our dive-bomb-perch altitude. The flares were a million candle lights and were suspended from a small parachute. While the flares burned, the hot air would rise into the canopy and keep the flares suspended. After they burned out, they often continued to float around in the area in which we were working. We tried to keep a watch out for these "ghosts" but it wasn't uncommon to hit one now and then.

This first night attack was in the delta and the "good guys" were inside the fort and the "bad guys" were on the outside trying to get inside. On this particular occasion, the VC had a heavy machine gun for antiaircraft, something we never again experienced at night. I had seen TV war movies showing antiaircraft tracer fire streaking into the air; being on the receiving end was a "learning experience." Even though we flew without lights, our aircraft could be seen when we would go to rich mixture and pull power coming off the target. The blue flame from the unburned fuel would stream out of the exhaust stacks and flow back over the wings. The tracers were spectacular to say the least. They would climb rapidly and then arch in our direction and then flash by us. Since there were tracers every five rounds, that meant there were a lot of rounds doing the same thing. Fortunately, we made several bomb runs and were not hit—they, on the other hand, were not so fortunate. Whenever an enemy gun was fired, there were very distinctive muzzle flashes, which gave Tom a very good aiming point. Soon, there were no muzzle flashes, not even rifle fire—AK-47s had muzzle flashes as well, which we used to locate ground troops that were firing at us.

Not too long after our first night mission, we were again in the delta, at night, doing our thing. As I mentioned above, it was important for the flare ship to be above our dive-bomb-perch altitude. As normal, we dropped napalm first and then bombs if required. Napalm drops necessitated multiple low-altitude passes directly over the target area as directed by the ARVN located within the fort. Often, we dropped on runs parallel with the dirt embankments of the sides of the fort, most of the time within 25 to 100 meters. It would not do to drop one inside the fort. After we expended our napalm, if required, we climbed to our perch altitude for our dive-bomb runs. Again, it was very important to understand exactly where the ARVN wanted the bombs. Sometimes the ARVN would shoot a flare in the direction where they wanted the bombs or they would communicate with us through the flare ship. Tom was flying the aircraft and my responsibility was to do radio work, monitor the engines, to be sure the weapon panel was set in the proper fashion in case we wanted to drop single or multiple bombs, relay airspeeds and, most importantly, read off altitudes during the bomb run so he could drop at the proper height above the ground. Tom would be concentrating on keeping the aircraft in trim and aligning the pipper on our bomb sight with the target. Our drop points were all based upon dropping at a specific airspeed and a specific altitude above the target. One serious problem was that the pilot could get target fixation, which meant that he concentrated so hard on keeping the pipper on the target without a slip and would be oblivious to the navigator's signals that we were at the drop altitude. There have been numerous occasions of this happening. In fact, Tom did this on one occasion and I grabbed his arm and shoulder, shaking him to pull out. We pulled out very near the ground: seeing the ground at night that close was not pretty.

Continuing the story as started above. After we dropped several bombs, Tom pulled the aircraft into a climb and started a slow left-hand turn, so we could look over the left wing and determine where the bombs had hit and if they had exploded (we had trouble with duds). As we approached our perch altitude, Tom would increase the bank angle to approximately 90 degrees and let the nose fall to level off at the correct altitude. As it happened on this particular run, we had pulled up into a climb and into approximately a 75-degree bank. We looked back and all we saw was C-47. How we missed a collision, I will never know. We flashed up in front of his starboard engine and the nose. I can vividly recall looking into the cockpit seeing both of the pilots very clearly. They had their red cockpit lights on and I could clearly see the copilot's eyes; in fact, I can still see them today. We could not have been more than 20 feet away. This may have been as close to death as I ever was in Vietnam. This particular C-47 flight was an all-VNAF crew and they somehow allowed their aircraft to descend below our perch altitude. After we gathered our wits about us, Tom "suggested" in words I'd rather not put on paper that they climb up to their proper altitude. Apparently they weren't looking outside because they never saw us.

Tom had a concern that he might be incapacitated somehow (wounded, injured, etc.) while we were flying and he thought it was important for me to be able to get the airplane back onto the ground in a fashion that we could walk or crawl away from after the plane came to a halt on the ground. We wore parachutes but since the airplane did not have an ejection seat, exiting the aircraft involved jettisoning the canopies and bailing out over the wing. As far as I know, only one person got as far as actually bailing out and he hit the horizontal stabilizer, which didn't do him much good. We lost a number of aircraft after Tom and I arrived in-country. Most of the aircraft, if not all, that were lost were not due to battle damage but due to wing spar failure resulting in the loss of a wing. Those aircraft were all World War II vintage and had been used extensively in Korea, some had been used by the French in Indo-China, and then by the CIA in Taiwan with Air America. Air America had a maintenance facility in Tainan in southern Taiwan and we flew the aircraft there for heavy maintenance. I had occasion to fly up to Tainan with Tom on two trips.

Tom decided that I needed to learn how to land the B-26, and I was agreeable since I wanted to eventually go to pilot training. Because the engines were powerful, the pilot had to be careful to maintain sufficient airspeed on final approach in case of engine failure. If the airspeed was too low and an engine failed, the other engine would roll the aircraft over out of control, again something that you do not want to do when close to the ground. There was a small airfield about 20 miles north of Bien Hoa called Phuoc Vinh.

This was a rubber plantation airfield owned by a French family but was being used by an Army Special Forces A Team. With Tom's instruction, I learned to fly into an overhead traffic pattern, lower the landing gear and flaps, and fly a haphazard base turn and final approach. We never actually touched down, but even a go-around was a learning maneuver for me in case the approach was not good and I would have had to go around. We went to Phuoc Vinh on several occasions and I'm sure that the Special Forces and the French wondered what we were doing. I also taxied the plane, using brakes and differential engine power to steer, so I was fairly confident that once on the ground, I could have maneuvered the plane to a stop, good enough to walk away from.

Phuoc Vinh, where Tom tried to teach me to land, was on the edge of what was called "D Zone," a large area approximately 25 miles square and heavily timbered. The ARVN had allegedly evacuated all of the "friendlies," so, in theory at least, any people remaining were assumed to be "bad guys." We sat alert on the ramp during the day, as opposed to the airborne alert at night. The daytime alert aircraft were loaded with different types of munitions than the night alerts. Often, if we had not launched on an actual mission, we would be sent to D Zone, generally near sunset, to expend our munitions rather than download. We always had a spotter plane to mark our targets during the day. On one day, we launched at near sunset and upon arriving in D Zone, we were tasked to burn up some large stacks of rice that had been harvested and were in the process of drying. The stacks were located in an elongated clearing, running generally north to south, and about 150 yards wide by 500 yards long. We also noticed a small "hooch" on the eastern side, about halfway up the clearing, but underneath large trees that surrounded the clearing. We could only see the "hooch" when we were down low where we could see under the tree line. We decided to drop napalm on the rice, which required low and rather slow passes. We had dropped several cans on piles in the center and western edge with good results. There were several piles on the eastern edge so we performed the same maneuver. As we were driving along, I suddenly noticed this fellow under the tree line about 150 feet in front of us but only about 75 feet to our right. He had a large "long gun" and I remember that it looked like a BAR (Browning Automatic Rifle). Before I could say anything, I noticed very distinct muzzle flashes and my thought was "Oh s---." As we drove by, low and slow, he emptied the entire magazine. I'm sure that he was like the elk hunter that has the large set of antlers in his sight close in front of him. I'm sure he was already considering the accolades from his boss for shooting down an armed mercenary, an enemy of the people, until he watched us loop around and rain bombs and guns on his last position. We also burned down his house for good measure. Once-in-a-lifetime opportunity and he failed. I really don't know how, though; he put 10 rounds into our airplane but didn't hit anything important, nor did he hit the cockpit. It certainly gave the sheet metal people something to do after we returned to Bien Hoa.

There was a railroad that ran from Saigon, up to Bien Hoa, and then eastward about a hundred miles to near Phan Thiet and then northward up the coast to Da Nang. As a sideline, a spur ran from Phan Rang northwestward to Dalat, a mountain city located at 4,900 feet elevation, which was a cool tourist attraction for the French. Of course, the VC were always mining the tracks and knocking the train off the tracks. It was politically important to try keeping the train running. We were often tasked to follow the train as it left Bien Hoa toward Phan Thiet. We circled over the train as it trundled from stop to stop. Since we didn't have communication with the crew, I don't know what our role really was. I can remember on one occasion that it stopped out in the middle of nowhere, no station, and people came out of the jungle and were standing around and apparently visiting. No one seemed to be concerned so we flew several low, very low, passes over them and everyone just stood there, watching us and waved to us, so we decided it wasn't an emergency. On another occasion, the train was going along, pushing several flat cars in front of the engine to take up the blast of a mine. Anyway, all of a sudden, the flat cars, followed by the engine, just kind of laid over on their sides. It was a mine, but what could we do except call someone and tell them the train just ran off the track? I don't think anyone was hurt since the engineer and fireman crawled out of the engine and stood around, obviously wondering what they should do now.

As I mentioned earlier, our maintenance facilities were limited and the Air Force contracted with a company called "Air Asia," which was located in Tainan, Taiwan. Tom and I had the opportunity to take planes up there on two separate occasions. The first time we flew up was with two other B-26s. Our first hop was from Bien Hoa to Clark AB, Philippines. After leaving the NDB at Phan Thiet, the flight was about 600 miles over water. Our navigation equipment consisted of a fixed-card ADF. The gyro attitude indicator and compass (powered by a vacuum system) was almost unreliable due to aircraft unusual attitudes during delivery of the various munitions. Even though we attempted to cage the gyros, they normally tumbled, which meant that the pilot relied upon the needle, ball, airspeed, and vertical velocity to fly instruments. The navigation on the over-water leg consisted of using the "whiskey compass" to hold the flight planned heading. On one other occasion, another crew overflew Luzon and never saw the island. They finally called Clark for a DF steer back to the base. After that incident, 13th Air Force required us to fly in formation with an aircraft that had navigation capability. Horrors of all horrors, Tom and I had to fly formation with a C-124 on our last trip from Tainan; how embarrassing could it ever be. The C-124 even cruised faster than we did, which meant that every 20 minutes or so, we had to increase power to catch up with him. When we finally reached Phan Thiet, Tom increased power and we passed under the C-124, pulled up into a barrel roll in front of him, and went to Bien Hoa by ourselves. The aircraft commander even remarked how good we looked.

After reaching Clark on the first flight to Tainan in the three-ship formation, we all ended up in the "stag" bar at the CABOOM (Clark Air Base Officer's Open Mess). There were six of us and a few of the locals eventually told us to key down our noise level. Well, one thing led to another, and a major eventually asked one of our lieutenants to step outside to discuss that our behavior didn't meet the conduct criteria of the club. All we had been doing was playing "dead bug" and banging down the dice cup. Of course, we all had received defensive tactics training at Hurlburt and there was no doubt of the outcome of any "fisticuffs" if the discussion got that far. Did I mention that we all probably had had too much to drink? As we arrived outside, our trained mercenary assumed the position—feet slightly apart and at a 45-degree angle with left hand about head level in front of his body (to deflect the opponent's thrust) and the right hand at chest level (to strike the opponent). I'll never forget the look on that major's face, almost like "what a stupid idiot." He threw an overhand looping right hand that hit our poor lieutenant directly on his nose. Our Commando just fell over backward, still holding the posture position, but with blood spewing from his nose. At the same time, he's yelling to us that "He broke my nose! He broke my nose!" We tried to encourage him to get back up, but to no avail. Since no one else wanted to take on Major "Nose Breaker," the fight was over and he turned around and went back inside.

Talking about instrument flying, Tom kept up his instrument approach requirements by flying GCAs at Tan Son Nhut. They also had an NDB approach requiring directional flight using aural null bearing outbound, followed by a procedure turn to intercept another aural null inbound. I'm amazed at how well Tom was able to fly instruments using rudimentary needle, ball, and airspeed. Every once in a while, the fog would sit in heavy at Bien Hoa with a 500-foot ceiling, plus or minus, and we would pick up the river at Saigon and fly north until a jog left followed by a U-turn by the river. In the middle of the U-turn was Bien Hoa.

About this time, Tom was getting kind of worked up about our getting more than our share of the early morning alerts. One morning after ginning around for about three hours with no indication of our being needed, he suggested we go back to Bien Hoa and provide "wake up" service, something to the effect that "if I have to be up, other people should be as well." About 10 miles out from Bien Hoa, to the east, he asked the tower for a low pass down the runway. After permission was granted, we went to climb power, lowered the nose, and we were on our way to Bien Hoa. I think we were somewhere in the vicinity of 425 mph (not a misprint, everything was in mph, not knots), faster than we should have gone. We also didn't go down the runway; we offset to the north several hundred yards and passed directly over all of the hooches. One more slight deviation as well, we were a bit low. As we flew by the squat French water tower, which was probably no more than 50 feet high, I looked up to see the top. I don't think Tom had really thought through the entire fly-by and resulting ramifications. When we eventually landed and taxied in, we were met by Lieutenant Colonel "Robby" Robinson, our 1st ACS CO. He ordered me to leave and he and Tom had a chat, probably only one-sided. I don't know what was said, but I don't think it was an "attaboy."

I think it was in January of 1964, not too long after the "wake-up fly-by," Tom and I were scheduled as the umpteenth crew for night alert. There was a lot of activity and so we were called out at about 0400 to preflight and cock our airplane. Tom was in no mood to do anything and said it would be just a waste of time to preflight since we would never be needed. We went into the alert mobile home and sacked out. Sure enough, we were needed and it took us about 15 additional minutes to get airborne. I had been upgraded to instructor navigator in the B-26 and the C-47. Within a day or two of this incident, I was sent TDY to Nha Trang (Army Special Forces Headquarters). Our C-47s were flying support for the Army Ranger teams in outlying small bases. This was not an unusual thing for navigators to do. I was up there for several weeks and when I got back to Bien Hoa, Tom was no longer in the Air Force and he was gone. I really felt a sadness when I realized what had happened and, to this day, I still miss him. After you have a relationship as we did, not being able to even say goodbye gives me pause to think about him. For all of his impulsiveness, he was a good pilot and he taught me much about airplanes. I heard later he went to Los Angeles and was flying a radio station traffic helicopter.

While at Nha Trang, I became friends with the sergeant major. At one point, the Special Forces folks were scheduled to make their quarterly parachute jump to maintain currency and to get jump pay. I don't recall the specific conversation but somehow I let it be known that I would like to jump from the C-47 as well. The sergeant major arranged for several days of PLF training, which entailed jumping off of a 10-foot or so tower into a sand pit and practice landing. I was all set to go. The morning of the scheduled jump, I was all ready to go until the Army lieutenant colonel in charge at Nha Trang somehow discovered what the sergeant and I had arranged. He came out to the airplane and ordered that I was not to jump. He didn't have an objection; his concern was what would happen if I broke a leg or, possibly, something worse. Here he was, dependent upon the Air Force to resupply his folks and he didn't want to take the risk of the Air Force coming back at him if I was hurt somehow. Whining didn't help—I didn't jump. To this day, I'm still disappointed.

Sometime in February 1964, a B-26 at Hurlburt had structural wing failure and two were killed. As a result, the Air Force grounded all B-26s. However, "Colonel Joe" Kittinger, then a major, did not interpret the order as a complete cease-and-desist order to not fly, but only an order to not dive-bomb or put the aircraft into stress maneuvers. Accordingly, "Colonel Joe" somehow obtained a Norden bombsight and installed it in the glass nose of a B-26C. I flew five sorties with him using the Norden sight. My records show that the first flight was February 29, 1964, and the last sortie was March 7, 1964. We didn't have the controls for directional control or a bomb release button, which meant that I verbally told "Colonel Joe" directional changes (three degrees right, two degrees left, etc.) and verbal instructions to drop the bombs. We had agreed that we would drop a three-bomb string, one early, one on target, and one long. Amazingly, we became very accurate. Eventually, 2nd Air Division or 13th Air Force discovered what we were doing and clarified that the grounding meant exactly what it said and there was no ground for confusion. It was okay as far as it went though. I think I may have been one of the last, if not the last, bombardier to ever drop bombs at actual targets using the Norden bombsight.

Not long after that experience, orders were given for a one-time flight of all of our B-26s to Clark AB. On April 1, 1964 (April Fool's Day), we flew to Clark. My records show that we logged 4:55 from Bien Hoa to Clark. We left the airplanes at Clark and

B-26s flying to Clark Air Base, 1964 (courtesy Bruce Kramer).

returned to Bien Hoa. My records also show flights on a C-47 on April 9 and 13 and training flights in B-57s at Clark beginning on May 7.

In mid–May 1964, we were ordered to fly the B-26s on a one-time flight to Okinawa where they were to be shipped by water back to CONUS for remanufacture into A-26Ks by On Mark. My last flight was eventful, however. As I recall, we were lead for a flight of four. I don't recall the exact spacing on takeoff but I would surmise that it was about a minute or so. We started our takeoff and everything seemed normal until we were airborne with the gear coming up. All of a sudden, smoke was very obvious and it was coming from the emergency hydraulic reservoir located behind and slightly higher than the pilot's seat. The pilot (I can't recall his name—he was associated with a special weapons development section in 2nd Air Division) reported the emergency and began a climbing left turn to downwind. Of course, the other aircraft were on a staggered takeoff so we had to extend slightly before making a base turn. In the meantime, we determined that the reservoir had been overfilled and hydraulic fluid was leaking onto the VHF radio—radios at that time had vacuum tubes, which were hot in temperature. At the pilot's direction, I used the fire extinguisher on the source of the smoke. We shut down on the runway and evacuated the aircraft after shutting down the engines and turning off the electrical power. We stood around for a few minutes until "Pedro" and the fire trucks arrived. My last flight in a B-26B was logged on May 15, 1964, for 10 minutes.

1st Air Commando Group

Vietnam 1963

JACK WILLIAMS

Near the main gate at Hurlburt Field is a static display of airplanes flown by the Air Commandos. In front of the A/B-26 Douglas Invader is a plaque inscribed as follows:

Dedicated to the men of the 4400th Combat Crew Training Squadron (Jungle Jim) and to their commander, Brigadier General Benjamin H. King.

In the spring of 1961, the 4400th Combat Crew Training Squadron (CCTS), code named "Jungle Jim," was formed at what was then known as Eglin Air Force Auxiliary Field 9 (Hurlburt Field). The initial unit was composed of 124 officers and 228 airmen, and had 32 aircraft: 8 B-26s, 8 T-28s and 16 C-47s. C-46 and U-10 aircraft were added shortly before the unit was expanded and designated the 1st Air Commando Group.

Each man initially assigned to this elite, all volunteer unit was required to declare that he was willing to fly and fight for his country either in or out of uniform, and to agree that his country may be required to deny that he was a member of the U.S. Military.

In May 1962, the name of the 4400th was changed to 1st Air Commando Group, and is the present day predecessor of the USAF Special Operations Command. During 1961–1963, Jungle Jim Detachments were deployed to Mali, South Vietnam, Panama, Thailand and Laos.

It is to the revered memory of those American Patriots, both living and dead, that volunteered for the dangerous missions envisioned for the 4400th CCTS/ 1st Air Commando Group, that this plaque is proudly dedicated. 13 October 2002.

I was part of the April 1963 rotation to Bien Hoa Air Base, South Vietnam. Each rotation had four B-26 crews, a crew being a pilot and navigator. Our three months of training to transition to the B-26 consisted of low-level cruising (25 to 50'), bombing, strafing, and aerial photography. My transition was from B-52 EWO (electronic warfare officer) to B-26 navigator. Our navigational instruments were a magnetic compass and an ADF (automatic direction finder). There were no ADF stations in Vietnam at the time. We flew low to make us a more difficult target. Hurlburt was an interesting place. While there I overheard two permanent party members discussing some magazine photos of a B-26 shot down in the Bay of Pigs invasion in Cuba. They both agreed that that B-26 had been at Hurlburt. Toward the end of our training we had a formal dinner at which our squadron leader spoke. He explained our presence in Vietnam. When the French were defeated at Dien Bien Phu, the Catholics fled to South Vietnam. The Catholic Refugee Organization went to Cardinal Spellman to request protection for the Catholic refugees. Cardinal Spellman (he had married John F. and Jackie Kennedy) contacted then–Senator Kennedy, who sponsored the first legislation relating to Vietnam. I was initially assigned to fly with Captain Andy Mitchell. Captain Jerry Campaigne reported in and they assigned the captains to fly together. I was then assigned to fly with Mike Newmyer. Mike Newmyer is an excellent pilot and a good friend. He and Gay had gotten married the Saturday night before we reported to Hurlburt, as did Peg and I. The end of our training was marked by a speech and a parade. We stood in formation dressed in our 1505 (khakis, with short-sleeved shirt). I could not hear much of the speech but there was a lot of talking in the ranks. A voice behind me said, "You guys had better keep quiet." Another voice said, "What are they going to do to us? Send us to Vietnam?" A few giggles and we marched past the reviewing stand. We then all dashed back to our home bases, where we signed in and out the same day and reported back to Hurlburt to begin our 165-day TDY (temporary duty) in Bien Hoa.

Bien Hoa is located about 25 miles north of Saigon. We flew B-26 Douglas Invaders with VNAF (Vietnamese Air Force) markings. The A-26 Douglas Invader had flown in World War II and Korea. The French used them against the Vietminh, and the Chinese Nationalists used them against the communists. The A designation was changed to B during the Korean War. The gun turret, top and aft of the bomb bay, was removed but the gunner's compartment remained. Three wing pylon stations were added to each wing. We carried 14 .50-cal guns, eight in the nose and three in each wing. We carried 500 pounds of napalm, or occasionally 500-pound bombs on the wing stations. Our internal load usually consisted of about 4,000 pounds of frag cluster bombs. She had about 5½ hours' endurance. Our runway was 5,300 feet of PSP (pierced steel planking). We lifted off at about 128 knots and used about 4,500 feet of runway. Our missions were strikes, escorts (boats, trains, and motor convoys), air cover for ground and airborne operations, and weather reconnaissance.

Our day began with a short briefing in the briefing room. This was the only place on base with air conditioning. Next we went to base ops and waited for a "frag" order. The "frag" gave us a location to meet a FAC (forward air controller). We flew to our assigned destination and contacted the FAC. The FAC marked a target for us and told us to bomb his smoke. We confirmed. Bombing runs were commenced at 3,500 feet. Once on target, Mike never took his eyes off the target. We set the arming switches, set the props to 2,400 rpm, throttles to 32 inches, manually charged the nose guns, and went into about a 60-degree dive. At about 1,000 feet I tapped Mike on the shoulder to remind him it was time to begin our pullout. We pulled about 4 or 5 Gs on pullout. We dropped one bomb at a time. Our strafing and napalm runs were made at 25 to 50 feet and again we dropped one at a time. When our weapons were expended, we were expected to do IBDA (initial bomb damage assessment). That required overflying the target at 1,200 feet at 180 knots and taking photos. This was not our favorite pastime. The folks on the ground were very often in a very bad mood by that time.

Night missions were a little different. We over flew the hamlet to see the "fire arrow," which was pointed in the direction from which the attack had come. Someone in the hamlet told us by radio how far away the VC (Viet Cong) were in "klicks" (kilometers). We flew in the direction of the fire arrow to where we estimated the VC to be and began our bomb and strafing runs. Vietnam could be very dark at night. When in the dive you felt as if you were suspended. The only noticeable movement was the unwinding of the altimeter. You then pulled out and flew through your ricochets. Every few rounds was a tracer so it was a spectacular sight. One night we had support from a gunboat in the Mekong River. The combined pyrotechnics rivaled any fireworks demonstration I have ever seen.

There was a SFC (sergeant first class) who used to salute and say something like, "Good morning, Lieutenant Fuzz." I would return the salute with a "Good morning, Sergeant Snorkel" and we would both grin. One day he and another sergeant showed up at my tent with two cases of C rations. This was a gift that was greatly appreciated. The Vietnamese government allowed each officer a maximum of $100 per month. We were officers on TDY (temporary duty) and received about $3.50 per day for meals. That was enough to cover three meals a day. The problem was that we paid $15 per month for maid fees, $10 for base operations cleanup, and $5 for the flower fund. That left $70 per month for laundry soap, toilet articles, entertainment, and food. I preferred to eat my one meal a day at supper. The C rations were a godsend. We could exchange our dollars for piasters (the local currency) on base at the rate of 72 ps to $1.00. Most of us used the black market. We took the bus to Saigon. We then walked up Tudor Street to the Modern Tailor Shop. It was not hard to find. The base pay line was lined up on the sidewalk in front. Inside we asked to "see a Vietnamese shirt." We were escorted into a room and a guy came in carrying two cardboard boxes: one was full of ps and the other of dollars. The exchange rate varied from 86 to 92 ps to $1.00.

We were not the only unit on base. We had a group of VNAF airmen who flew with us. On every mission we carried a VNAF airman who sat on a pull-down seat behind the navigator and the hydraulic fluid reservoir. We were ostensibly there to advise the VNAF. Our advice was simple: "Don't touch anything." We did not carry the aircraft forms with us. In the event of a crash, the VNAF airman was flying the airplane, and we were along to give him advice. One little guy who flew with us filled five barf bags on one mission. He never complained, just kept puking. There was a VNAF fighter squadron on base equipped with A-1 Sky Raiders—a newer and better airplane than the B-26. Each morning at 0830 the VNAF pilots dashed out to their airplanes. They started their engines and revved them up, scarves flying in the prop wash, every man a tiger. At 0900 they switched off their engines and went back to base ops. There they played ping-pong until 1530, when they again dashed to their airplanes. This time only half would start. The lucky pilots whose engines started flew off into the wild blue yonder and were not seen again until they landed at 1615. We could not figure out what they were doing for 45 minutes. Some of the guys removed their gunnery film and developed it. They were dropping their bombs into the South China Sea, the Mekong River, or on a Montagnard Village.

En route to Bien Hoa, I met a C-123 navigator who described the B-26s as "snake-bit." He was right. The "snake" was that paragon of cost-cutting, Secretary of Defense Robert McNamara. Money was saved by not repacking the parachutes, not installing transponders in the airplanes, and by returning to base with any unexpended ordnance. Landing with 3,000 pounds under the wings resulted in a large negative g-force that severely weakened the wings. Mitchell and Campaigne had been "in-country" less than two weeks when they lost a wing over the target. Captain Bob Binderim was flying their wing and saw the accident. He said, "The wing came off, they did a snap roll and went into the ground." Remedial action consisted of installing positive and negative g meters. We were instructed to pull no more than 1 g. When you fired the nose guns the g meters were pegged in both directions.

Colonel Finan and I went to Tainan, Taiwan, to bring back a B-26 that had been rebuilt by CAT (China Air Transport). It looked new and was just beautiful. We flew back via Clark AB and landed at Bien Hoa in late afternoon. I found myself on night alert with George Phillips. I found George and told him about the "new" B-26. George had already preflighted another B-26, which we flew that night. The next day, John McClean and "Skip" Bedal flew the "new" B-26. They lost a wing over the target and we lost two more good guys.

Flying low level in Vietnam was hot. The B-26 had no air-conditioning and no air circulation. You could lose 15 pounds in a five-hour mission. I wore a survival vest over my fatigue jacket. In the outside pocket I kept a bottle of water purification tablets. I sweated the label off of that bottle. I made the mistake of giving our maid an unopened box of laundry detergent. She probably sold it since it was a full box and washed our clothes in the local soap, which was made from or with fish oil. This time we not only were sweating but we itched and smelled like two dead fish. From then on the maid got just enough soap to wash for that week.

We used to joke that we endured hours of monotony interspersed with moments of stark terror. We made a pass in the delta. Just as we pulled up it got dark. The windshield was covered with mud! Mike looked at me and said, "I thought those were trees?" I replied, "Nope, rice plants." We stopped on the runway and used the water in our canteens to wash off enough mud to see to taxi in. There were several times that I saw B-26s parked with tree limbs hanging out of the bomb bay but no one else brought home mud on the windshield. Other notable moments came when we found that one B-26 would not pull out of a dive with the bomb bay doors open. On some you had to waggle the wings to get the ordnance to fall off. Then there was the time that a wing man called us on the radio to tell us the arming propeller on our starboard 500-pound bomb was turning! We hit the "salvo" button and said, "Thanks."

We had just touched down with a full load when in the blink of an eye we were on the left side of the runway with dirt flying everywhere. A few hundred feet in front of us was a large hole that was dug to reinforce the point where the runway joined a taxiway. I asked Mike if he could get back on the runway. He said, "No, but I can straddle that hole." Straddle it we did, carrying six cans of napalm under the wings. Mike went back with the ground crew to inspect the area. The nose wheel missed the hole by 2½ inches. The right main tire came so close that dirt spilled into the hole. Mike could put a B-26 anywhere he wanted!

A good mission was called a "Zap" mission. Most of the time we never saw the target and never paid much attention to the results. We got a call late one afternoon from an ARVN (Army Republic of Vietnam) battalion commander asking for an immediate air strike. His battalion was pinned down by the VC near Ca Mau. He feared that once it got dark the VC would annihilate his battalion. We got to his position just about dusk and made radio contact. The ground troops marked the target for us. Unfortunately, we began having engine trouble. We had fluctuating fuel pressure (prelude to a fire) in both engines. Number one was running rough and number two was backfiring. Our problems were obvious to those on the ground. We made one or two passes and dropped everything we had, including six cans of napalm. We struggled to 1,200 feet and called Paris Air Control at Saigon. We gave them our position, altitude, and heading. We were only about 60 miles from Saigon but they could not find us (a transponder would have been helpful). We knew we were on our own. We limped back to Bien Hoa and landed. The battalion commander was on the phone and thanked us for saving his battalion. They counted over 200 VC KIAs. We got an Air Medal for "over-flying a known enemy position." After all, we were only advisers.

ZAP patch (Good Mission) at O Club (courtesy Jack Williams).

There were some stories that were hard to understand. One such story involved Larry Granquist. Larry and his pilot, Howard Purcell, were flying out of Da Nang. This was some sort of easy mission and Sergeant Raphael Cruz was riding along in the gunner's compartment. The engines were running when the base intelligence officer, Neil McKinney, approached the airplane and asked to go along for the ride. Howard turned to Larry and commented something to the effect that McKinney was bored and that Larry had plenty of flight time. Howard asked Larry to let McKinney go in his place.

Left to right: Bob Seaton, Atis Lielmanis, Jack Mezzo, Woody Halsey, and Bob Dutton (courtesy Maury Bourne).

Larry agreed, got out, and McKinney took his place. They took off and the plane was never seen again. No one had any idea what happened. Some speculated that they flew into a "box" canyon and could not get out.

The first B-26 was lost in December 1962. This was about a month after eight B-26s were stationed at Bien Hoa. The airplane was shot down by ground fire. The pilot (James O'Neill) rode the plane down and was killed. The navigator (First Lieutenant Johnson) and the VNAF observer bailed out and were rescued after a few days of wandering around in the jungle. Later, Howard Cody, pilot, and Atis "Atie" Lielmanis, navigator, were lost in November 1963. They bailed out of their shot-up B-26. Neither parachute opened. They had not been inspected or repacked for about a year. Atie got his first ride in a B-26 with Mike and me.

It was a memorable nine months with some great guys. They were courageous men who would defend America anytime, anywhere, under any conditions.

Night Scramble Mission

Andrew "Andi" Biancur

A portion of our mission with the 1st Air Commando Group at Detachment 2A, Bien Hoa, South Vietnam, in the early days of the Vietnam War was to maintain one B-26 and two T-28s on 24-hour alert to support ground operations in the III and IV Corps Districts (the southern half of the country).

On 13 September 1963, my navigator, Wells Jackson, and I had settled ourselves in the alert trailer for a good night's sleep—a luxury since it was only one of two air-conditioned facilities on the base. We had preflighted our aircraft # 43–2890 with little hope of being launched that night.

Sometime around 2200 hours, we were aroused and given a mission to support a Special Forces outpost deep in the delta somewhere south of our base at Soc Trang in danger of being overrun by enemy forces.

Following an immediate launch, we headed south and as Saigon faded to our rear, we realized there was no moon and we were flying under a high overcast into the total darkness with little or no references. There were absolutely no visible lights anywhere to be seen.

Fortunately, we were informed by Paris Control at Saigon that a C-123 flare ship was also being launched from Tan Son Nhut Air Base in support of the same mission but with no estimate of its arrival over the target.

We had previously worked at night under flare ships and understood the possibility of the dangers of night blindness and vertigo brought on by flying in darkness under the light from the flares. In all, such operations brought limited success at best in delivering ordnance.

Upon arrival over the coordinates of the target, we were able to gain contact with the A Team on the ground through the use of a PRC-10 radio we had grabbed on our way out of the trailer—something we did only when an airborne FAC was not assigned to a strike mission.

The only visible lights in the totally black environment below us were two small, contained fires some distance apart. They would have to serve as our only ground reference until the flare ship arrived to further illuminate the site.

We initially elected to orbit the area awaiting the flare ship, believing the sound of an aircraft overhead would deter any further actions by the attacking force. Some 15 minutes had passed when we received a panic call from the camp stating that the attack had resumed and they were very close to being overrun. The directions we were given were strike at the fire 400 feet from the point of the fire arrow illuminated by fire on the ground. In haste, and presumably under great pressure, the speaker did not provide directional information.

I rolled in on the target and fired several 50-caliber rounds at the target. Because of the shallower-than-normal dive angle and lack of ground references, the tracers showed my aim a bit long and the rounds went slightly over the target. As we passed over the target, I clearly saw it as a fire arrow and immediately feared I had hit the wrong target and had killed the forces we were trying to protect.

No sooner had that reality sunk in than an excited call came that we had hit the attackers coming over the wall of the compound. The message continued with praise for the finest shooting the caller had ever seen. We had not only killed several of the enemy but they were in full retreat across the surrounding rice paddies.

After this one pass, I elected not to make any further attempts until the flare ship arrived. And, upon its arrival a short time later, its drop of the first set of flares stabilized the situation on the ground for the troops and cleared the entire scene. The enemy had erected their own fire arrow, pointed at the compound, in hopes that any U.S. airstrikes would hit the friendly compound. Thankfully, that did not happen.

We continued to orbit the area under the flare ship for the next hour prior to returning to Bien Hoa Air Base, realizing for the umpteenth time that we had in fact, been far more lucky than good, and that we had not killed any friendly forces.

Captain Miles T. Tanimoto

A Hawaiian Hero's Tale

Kenneth J. Alnwick

A graduate of Mid–Pacific Institute and the University of Hawaii, Captain Miles Tanimoto began his career as a rated Air Force navigator at Mather AFB in Sacramento, California. In that capacity, he rose from a lieutenant student trainee to one of the most respected young navigator instructors in the Air Force's Navigator/Bombardier Training Program. As both mentor and teacher, he introduced his students to the art of aerial navigation in the classroom, in simulators, and in flight. His classes ranged from basic navigation skills to somewhat esoteric subjects such as "High Latitude/High Speed Celestial Navigation." Throughout his tour at Mather, Miles was consistently rated as an excellent instructor who was held in high esteem by his students, peers, and supervisors.

However, lured by the promise of adventure and President Kennedy's call for small elite forces to counter communist-led insurgencies in the third world, Miles left the routine training environment and arrived at Hurlburt Field in Fort Walton Beach, Florida, in early 1963—while his wife, June, and son, Lawrence, returned to Hawaii until Miles could find a home for them in Fort Walton. As a son of Hawaii, Miles was in his natural element, swimming and spear fishing in the waters of the Gulf of Mexico and in the bays and bayous of Fort Walton Beach. Having volunteered for "*extra hazardous duty at the convenience of the government,*" Miles was assigned to the 6th Air Commando Squadron, which flew both the single-engine combat version of the T-28 and the World War II twin-engine B-26, manned by a pilot and a navigator—who also performed copilot duties in the side-by-side cockpit. After initial qualification training, Miles was paired with me to form a first lieutenants' "new-guy" crew. I was an Air Force Academy graduate who had flown the C-121 and C-135 as a MATS pilot. Neither crewmember had prior tactical experience and learned together how to work as a team and how to shoot guns and rockets and drop bombs, without damage to ourselves or to our flying machines.

It was an exciting time as pilots, navigators, and ground crews from throughout the Air Force banded together under the Air Commando banner. In addition to training in special operations tactics and procedures, there were classes in marksmanship, hand-to-hand fighting, and foreign languages. The squadron was a tight-knit group bound together by the lure of fighting for a cause and the promise of adventure—and, of course, the Commando's Aussie bush hats.

We deployed to Bien Hoa, South Vietnam, in June of 1963 and returned to the U.S. that November as the Commando B-26s were placed under severe flight restrictions due to wing failures and other structural defects within the World War II–era B-26 fleet. Upon initial arrival at Bien Hoa as part of Operation Farm Gate, the crew had been assigned to the unique and challenging B-26 photo reconnaissance mission, flying a specially modified, plexiglass nose, RB-26L aircraft in support of Captain Jimmy Ifland's Farm Gate photo reconnaissance requirements. The photo package included a forward-looking KA-1 36-inch camera in the nose, plus panoramic and split vertical cameras aft of the cockpit.

Miles (left) and Ken in Hawaii en route to Bien Hoa, South Vietnam (courtesy Kenneth J. Alnwick).

The aircraft could also carry 52 high-intensity photoflash cartridges in the bomb bay for night operations. Missions were flown out of Saigon, Bien Hoa, and Da Nang, and included visual low-level target acquisition/surveillance and photo reconnaissance during daylight and darkness over hazardous jungle and mountainous terrain. For precise low-altitude photos, because of line-of-sight issues from the left seat position, Miles Tanimoto had to crawl into the nose and relay aiming instructions to me. The aircraft was relatively easy to fly, with good handling characteristics. Our team also participated in early Air Force experiments with infrared night photography, which required that a photo technician pour liquid nitrogen over a photosensitive plate in the bomb bay area. We also tested an airborne SHORAN navigation system. Neither of these worked very well, but the primitive IR system became a precursor to the sophisticated systems of today.

Perhaps our most exciting mission took place in Area C, east of Saigon. That night we were equipped with a rack of 54 white phosphorus high-intensity photo flares, suitable for night photography. Captain Jimmy Ifland was in the converted bomb bay, tending to the IR and the flares. On that night, we were the only B-26 working in that area when we got a call that a village in our area was under attack. When we were over the village, we were told by the Special Forces commander that the VC were assaulting the wire and that the villagers had positioned a fire arrow pointing in the direction of the attack. Since our only weapon was the rack of photo cartridges, we dropped down to 500 feet perpendicular to the fire arrow, set the timer for a two-second delay, and salvoed all the cartridges on the unsuspecting VC. Our Special Forces partner said that all the VC had fled and asked if we had a new weapon system aboard. When we got back to Saigon, we were told that we had lit up the entire western sky. Perhaps I could have put our crew in for a medal, but I was not sure that HHQ would have been too pleased with our unauthorized/unconventional mode of attack. However, for at least one mission, we were the only B-26 photo-attack aircraft in the theater.

One of the most bizarre events that the team experienced in Vietnam occurred one night in Saigon, when they found themselves in the middle of the coup against President Ngo Dinh Diem and his subsequent death. Amazingly, the day after the coup, there was the sense that a great cloud had been lifted from the city as the streets and thoroughfares of Saigon were festooned with Vietnamese and Buddhist flags that fluttered side by side from surrounding buildings, and street venders and soothsayers again surfaced to ply their trade. This was, in my opinion, a crucial tipping point in the sad history of this ill-fated country as the infighting among a succession of corrupt and inept generals led their country to its now inevitable fate.

One month later, Miles and I were on our way back to Hurlburt Field. During his tour, Miles had flown over 90 combat missions and was awarded the Air Medal with two Oak Leaf Clusters, the Republic of Vietnam Campaign Medal, the Republic of Vietnam Gallantry Cross, and the Vietnam Service Medal.

Upon his return from Vietnam, Miles settled his family in the Fort Walton area and began to familiarize himself with the newly refurbished On Mark version of the interdiction/strike B-26s. Subsequently, he was selected to be an instructor navigator for the newly established 602nd Fighter Squadron. Miles was also central to the development of the new camera system that had been installed in the two RB-26s dedicated photo platforms. After a short interlude at the Squadron Officers School (where he excelled), Miles also created a reconnaissance training program for the squadron's navigators. He designed the course, wrote the training manual, and then taught the course. Before the squadron and their families moved to England AFB in Louisiana in mid–December 1965, Miles was designated as the Wing Navigation Standardization Officer and Flight Examiner, a distinct honor for any aspiring aviator. In addition, along with his fellow B-26 navigators, Miles attended the USAF Air-Ground Operations School to become one of the first aviators, other than fighter pilots, to become qualified as forward air controllers and authorized to guide air-to-ground attacks. In June 1966, eight B-26s, now designated A-26As to accommodate their Thai hosts, deployed to Thailand on a six-month trial basis. Because of his reputation for solid performance and meticulous planning, Miles was selected as the lead navigator for establishing the headquarters for this classified operation. June and her children, Lawrence and Janis (born at Eglin AFB), went back to Honolulu, while Miles and a small, advanced party proceeded to Nakhon Phanom Royal Thai Air Base to prepare for the arrival of their squadron mates and aircraft. The base was only a short distance from the Mekong River and there was already a mixed bag of Commando aircraft operating from the base and its pierced steel planking runway. Not surprisingly, the base was not markedly different from the Commandos' previous accommodations at Bien Hoa, SVN. On 11 June, following a brief orientation, the A-26s were declared ready for combat.

As before, pilots and navigators were teamed together for combat missions. Miles was teamed with Major Henry Welch from Waycross, Georgia (I had gone on to teach at the Air Force Academy following a six-month tour in Laos). Their mission was to interdict North Vietnam's infiltration and supply routes along the Ho Chi Min Trail, which ran through Laos along the North and South Vietnamese borders and the Laotian border and then on into South Vietnam. Missions were flown almost exclusively at night to avoid the North Vietnamese formidable anti-air defenses. Once in their operating area, based on intelligence from observers on the ground or other means of command and control, the Nimrods could instigate their own attacks or direct other strike aircraft to promising targets. Crews flew just about every other night searching for telltale indications of movement or concealed fortified positions along the heavily traveled routes. Dive-bombing, rocket attacks, or close-quarters strafing attacks were employed against their elusive moving targets and AAA fixed sites. On several missions, including one over North Vietnam, Miles and Major Welch were cited for heroism for attacking into the teeth of North Vietnamese antiaircraft positions and destroying them.

On 26 July 1966, the night of his final mission, Miles was filling in for a fellow navigator. His pilot was Major Glen Duke, a former T-28 pilot, who also had been in the Farm Gate program in South Vietnam in 1963 and, more recently, on assignment in Laos. As the crew flew north on their assigned mission, they were diverted by ground control to search for a suspected North Vietnamese helicopter patrolling the Ho Chi Minh Trail. After a lengthy but futile search, they headed back to NKP.

But fate was not on their side that fatal night. Due to an aircraft fuel systems failure, their aircraft crashed on their final leg home. Miles and Glen lost their lives in that crash.

Miles welcomes Bob Dutton and other commandos to NKP (courtesy Kenneth J. Alnwick).

In recognition of his gallant efforts as the unit's lead navigator, the Air Force awarded Miles the Air Force Commendation Medal, his fourth Air Medal, the Distinguished Flying Cross with One Oak Leaf Cluster, the Purple Heart Medal, and an Air Force Honorable Service Citation

Captain Miles Takeshi Tanimoto now lies in repose in the National Memorial Cemetery of the Pacific, overlooking the City of Honolulu and the Diamond Head National Monument (Plot H556).

Recollections of an Old Man

Photography from RB-26s and T-28s

Jimmy Phillis

I read some time ago on the Air Commando Association webpages about how the original Jungle Jim program was formed with all volunteers. I will start with the story of how I came to volunteer. I was stationed at Westover AFB in Massachusetts for my on-the-job (OJT) training as a photographer. When I finished the training and completed the tests, I was contacted by someone who told me he was looking for volunteers for a new outfit that was being formed. This set off alarms right away because I had always been told to never volunteer. I told him I wouldn't be interested in it and he told me he was sorry to hear that because I was to be the last person asked about it and that if they got no volunteers they would go to the test scores on the OJT program and take the highest score. Since I had just passed the OJT tests with the highest score they had recorded, I volunteered.

From there I went to Hurlburt Field in Florida. We had training shortly after I arrived including an hour of calisthenics, followed by a mile run, and weekly swim classes just outside the base in the inner canal. We were given a portable photo lab consisting of inner and outer tents and wooden sinks and pumps to pump water from a pond nearby. We had to set it up in the woods off base. I believe we set it up and operated out of it for three days, eating K-rations and putting pills in the pond water in our canteens to purify it. (I still don't think the water was that great after that, but it was something different anyway.) I slept in a hammock that had a plastic roof on it and mosquito netting on the sides; that's when I found out the netting didn't do much good if your arm was against it while you slept. My arm looked like an enlargement of pebble grain leather when I rolled out the next morning.

Then we went to Stead AFB outside of Reno, Nevada, for what they called survivor-school training. Lots of fun that place was. I remember being crowded into a boxlike little cell in a fetal position and kept there so long that when they pulled me out my legs had the circulation cut off so long they wouldn't work to hold me up for several minutes. They finished it off by dumping us off in pairs up somewhere in Donner Pass, with rations for two men for one day, and given maps and a compass to get from point A to point B in three days. When they picked us up at the end of that little hike, they had sweet rolls and an orange on the bus, and the best SOS I had ever tasted when we got back to the mess hall. Could be that I was a little hungry.

After we passed our operational readiness tests, it wasn't very long until we were on planes and headed some place. I didn't know where, but someone said it was to be a place called Vietnam. Hell, I had never even heard of it. Much later, we landed at an airfield with a very rough runway. Turned out it was a place called Bien Hoa, and we landed on PSP. What a shocker! The next few nights we were sleeping on old canvas army cots in what I think they called 10-man tents. We were reminded to shake our boots out every morning to be sure that they didn't have a scorpion or spider or snake in them before we put them on. They made a makeshift shower for us that consisted of a black iron pipe with holes drilled in it every few feet, sitting on A-frames, and they had pallets on the ground for us to stand on. Not exactly the Ritz, but at least we could get wet and wash some of the grime off. Within a week or so they had us moved into tents on wooden floors, and they constructed real shower tents where eight or 10 people could shower on concrete floors. We never did see a shower tent with hot water.

I think the first flying missions I was on were flying the coast in a C-47. My place was sitting in the doorway with one foot on each side of the door with a K20 camera in my hands. We photographed every boat that we saw along the coast. I remember once seeing a ship with a hammer and sickle on it and when we happened on it everyone in the plane started running back to the doorway. The crew chief on the plane came unglued and the plane started to shutter. A dozen or so people tend to make the plane a little tail heavy, and a half mile offshore at 300 feet altitude is not a good place to practice a stall recovery.

We finally got our B-26s and T-28s. I found out my place in the B-26 (the photographer's position) was behind the bomb bay. They had a handle overhead inside the bomb bay that you could grab hold of and pull yourself up until you could swing your feet through an opening and get yourself into a compartment with a seat facing the rear of the plane, and a panel with lots of knobs and buttons in front of you. Ours was one of two RB-26s that we had. It had the plexiglass nose on it with two cameras in the nose, a 24" telephoto camera mounted in a forward oblique position, and a 6" wide-angle camera mounted under the other camera pointing straight down. The bomb bay had, to the best I can recall, two K36 9" cameras mounted with one angled left and the other angled right to give an overlapping strip, and an infrared camera that we really didn't use that much. Then in the tail behind the panel containing the switches and interval meter in my compartment were two 9" K17 cameras, one mounted vertical and the other on the oblique to the right. I had a cozy little place … if you like seeing where you have been instead of where you're going.

I usually carried a couple of extra magazines with me, not the reading kind; these were film backs for aerial cameras, about 8"×20"×20", probably weighing 40 pounds each. I remember one time we were on a mission along with some of the other B-26s and during the slack time the pilot started a mock dogfight with one of the other B-26s and shot him with our forward oblique camera, followed abruptly with an unexpected victory roll. After that, he called back and asked if I was all right. I told him I was but that I would appreciate it next time if he would give me some warning. I was glad he didn't hesitate at the top of the roll. If he had hesitated, I would have had those magazines floating around in the air.

Another mission we had someone on the ground firing up at us and we could see tracers from a machine gun coming up at us. The pilot called back and asked if I wanted to swing around and get some pictures of that. I think my response to that was "not no, but hell no." Later, we did have one of the B-26s come back with a malfunctioning camera and found a bullet had made a direct hit and lodged in the film magazine on one of the K17s in the tail of the plane.

The biggest scare I had over there was on the way back from a mission when the navigator came over the intercom and said, "Fire in the cockpit." Then came the longest minute in my life as I proceeded to tighten every strap on my parachute and make sure the pistol in my shoulder harness was outside the straps ... all the while with my hand on the handle to the plexiglass door on the side of my compartment. I made up my mind then that I didn't want to leave a perfectly good airplane. Luckily, he came back and said we were okay. I'll leave the sky-diving to someone else. The jungles are not a place I would like to hike out of.

I remember that we had some very good pilots and navigators in our bunch. I remember once hearing talk on the radio from one of our group saying he was going to try to put a canister of napalm through the doorway of a little shack that was their target. I can still see that canister tumbling end over end through that door and exploding and blowing the back of that hut off. Of course, I also remember once at Da Nang seeing a B-26 after it came back from a mission and they cleaned out a pile of leaves and twigs that stood about three feet high out of the engine nacelle.

I also remember one flight where we were out looking for one of our B-26s that had crashed into a hillside. We flew by it and from my position looking back I could see through almost a tunnel of forest the wreckage of one of our own planes. I don't think the pilot or navigator could see it because of the angle we were flying as we passed it. That jungle was thick.

I also did a lot of flying in the T-28s. I was assigned to a pilot in a T-28 who told me he was previously in the reserves and was one of the original test pilots in T-28s in World War II. He knew everything the plane would do and how to make it do it. He would point out what we were to photograph, then point the plane at what seemed like a straight-down vertical dive until it would almost stall, then kick the rudder and dump out the air brake and we would zoom down and take the picture, and he would pull out and that 10-pound camera would suddenly weigh 70 pounds and be wedged on my lap. I saw 6 Gs on the G-meter and experienced my first blackout with him, and he also showed me what -3 Gs and a red-out was.

Oh well, enough of an old man's ramblings for now. I haven't talked that much in a long time.

Charley's Foot

One .30-Cal Bullet

Charles H. "Chuck" Holden

Was it really 47 years ago? Seems like last week. October 19, 1963, Bill Cody and I formed up in the mass briefing room for the start of another day's activities at Bien Hoa

Chuck Holden before an antiaircraft round struck his foot during a mission (courtesy Charles H. "Chuck" Holden).

Air Base, Republic of South Vietnam, as we had done most days since our arrival in July. We had trained together as a crew in the Douglas B-26, at Hurlburt Field, Florida, and had flown almost all of our combat missions together since arriving in-country, TDY, with Det 2a (EBF) of the 1st Air Commando Group. The drill was an early morning mass brief of intel, weather, current situation, ongoing efforts, etc., followed by handing out sorties for the day. Bill and I were scheduled to support an ARVN heliborne assault by the 21st ARVN Division near Loc Ninh, Chuong Thien province, in the delta. As we left the briefing, we were approached by the group commander of the 34th Tac Group, to whom we were ostensibly attached, and informed that he would fly the mission instead of Bill. I didn't even know if he knew how to fly the aircraft, much less employ it, but he was a "full colonel" and I was a very junior 23-year-old first lieutenant navigator.

The Douglas B-26 was crewed by a single pilot in the left seat and a jack-of-all-trades in the right seat. The nav generally performed the usual duties of copilot, plus tried to keep track of where we were and where we were going, and most importantly, tried to keep the six or eight .50-cal Browning machine guns in the nose charged and firing when employed. Needless to say, since you may or may not have a set of flight controls in front of you—depending on which tail number you flew that day—trust and confidence in your crewed pilot was a big deal.

Colonel Coleman O. Williams and I exchanged some introductory chitchat as we proceeded to the mission brief. I happened to notice that he wore an "iron" class ring. As a good Texan, I knew that a solid class ring, with no stone mounted and with a shield and crossed sabers, was obviously from Texas A&M. As I remarked that my dad had also graduated from Texas A&M, and "What class did you graduate," he icily informed me that he was a graduate of the Citadel. So much for ingratiating chitchat. As I said, I was a very young first lieutenant.

The mission itself was a disaster. Friendly losses were 41 killed and 84 wounded (including 23 Americans), and the loss of one U.S. Army H-21, as described on page 184 of *The United States Air Force in Southeast Asia, The Advisory Years to 1965* and on page 26 of *The United States Air Force in Southeast Asia, 1961–1973, An Illustrated Account*, both from the Office of Air Force History. Our normal tactic in single-ship attack was to approach the target in a shallow dive, strafe the target area with the .50 cals, level off at 50 feet, and deliver the napalm. This time the guns did not work. Not one fired despite my frantic efforts to recharge them and to curse their forebears, as well as the gun plumbers that had serviced them. One U.S. Army H-21 helicopter was down and the ARVN were being cut to pieces in the open paddy. We came around and did it again. Someone once said that the definition of insanity is doing something over and over, expecting a different outcome. On about the third or fourth pass, Joe Holden—no relation but a good friend—attempted to cover us with a flight of T-28s. Great effort, but the Viet Cong pretty well had our range at that point. I actually saw the guy pop up out of a spider hole, put the butt of a BAR (Browning Automatic Rifle) on the back edge of the pit, and cut loose. He got nine rounds into the aircraft, nose to tail, and received a 500-pound can of napalm in his face. I got one of those rounds through the floor and through my left foot. There was a little excitement in the cockpit, and we called it a day.

My combat boot seemed to be containing most everything and the only thing that really hurt was the front of my leg where it had slammed into the bottom of the instrument panel from the upward force of the bullet. Besides, we had other problems: no hydraulics and other unknown damage to the aircraft. We had expended all the napalm but still had six 500-pound bombs in the bomb bay, and maybe no gear. So, we needed to get rid of them. One of my jack-of-all-trades duties was to hand pump the bomb bay doors open, with the emergency system, then, after jettisoning the bombs, pump the doors closed, and finally, if there was enough left in the system, pump the landing gear down. At least that part was maintained better than the guns, and it worked.

Coleman O. landed at Tan Son Nhut, no flaps, no brakes, and no rudder control, and kept it on the runway. We were met by assorted crash and medical personnel and I was hustled off to the clinic. I thought it was the worst day of my life—little did I know.

This should be the end of the story—but it is actually only the beginning.

After an operation and a couple of weeks in the U.S. Navy Hospital in Cholon, in Saigon (where I had a ringside seat for the overthrow of President Diem), I returned to Bien Hoa in a cast and on crutches. I immediately began a campaign with our resident flight surgeon to get back on flying status. I was a bit of an oddity as I was the only B-26 crewmember at that point to have the Purple Heart and still be alive. Verne Bergstrom, another B-26 nav/jack-of-all-trades even came up with a logo for Charley's Foot: a highly stylized rendition of a skeletal hand with the upraised middle digit. Seemed appropriate. By the last week of November, without cast or crutches, I was cleared to fly. The effective date for the order was 24 November 1963.

Bill woke me up in our hooch at about 0630 hours on the morning of 24 November. Something big was going on, and the crews were alerted early. The operations duty controllers didn't realize that I was back on flying status as of that day, so they had assumed that Atis was going with Bill. He said, "Atis is already up and dressed, so we'll go, but it is going to be a big day, so you and I will take the next one after I get back." Howard "Bill" Cody and Atis Lielmanis both received the Air Force Cross for that mission, but they did not come back. The bare bones of the engagement are described on page 196 of *The

United States Air Force in Southeast Asia—The Advisory Years to 1965, Office of Air Force History, 1981. That was my flight, but somebody screwed up the notification and I lived. One .30-cal bullet.

Coleman O. departed Bien Hoa about this time and I never forgot his farewell at the bar. Standing on the bar, he proclaimed that he was "a regular, permanent colonel, had a beautiful wife, owned a Beech Bonanza, and didn't give a damn"—then did a backflip off the bar. I thought it was a life to aspire to.

On the completion of my tour in SEA and return to Hurlburt Field, I flew a lot with Dick Klopfer, who introduced me to the joys of fishing for king mackerel and dolphin on the Miraboo Maru—and weekend cross-countries. Dick also knew that I had not been selected for pilot training on my recent application.

In the late spring of '65, he announced that Don Shirky, another B-26 pilot that was with us at Bien Hoa and now instructing in pilot training at Laredo AFB in Texas, had invited us down to Laredo to attend a class graduation. The speaker was now Brigadier General Coleman O. Williams.

We checked out a B-26 and headed to Texas. Don jumped us in a T-Bird (T-33) as we got into the local flying area and a couple of turns proved we could turn inside him, but not climb with him.

At the Dining-In that night, Coleman O. did not know of my presence, nor, I think, did the wing commander. At the conclusion of his speech, which leaned heavily on his recent combat tour and our mission together, I shouted from the rear something to the effect, "That's not how I remember it, General." This brought down the house and a warm reunion followed. As the mess adjourned and BG Williams, myself, and the wing commander strolled to the bar, Coleman O. asked whatever happened about going to pilot training. I replied that I had been non-selected upon return from Bien Hoa, but had another application in. The wing commander, who had just recently taken over the wing after a tour at ATC HQs, immediately asked for my service number. Back at Hurlburt, a month or so later, I received a call from an NCO at ATC HQs, who asked, "Lieutenant, *when* you are selected for pilot training, where would you like to go?" Naturally, I thought Laredo would be just great. One .30-cal bullet.

And last, but not least, I did complete pilot training, got a fighter, flew more tours, traveled the world, and was well on my way to a medium to mediocre career. In the late summer of 1977, I was working on a very black and sensitive project, basically reporting out of the chain of command to a two-star. He called me in when I was passed over for promotion to lieutenant colonel, as befits an uneducated aviation cadet. He stated that he could do a lot of things in the Air Force, but he couldn't get me promoted to lieutenant colonel if I didn't have a college degree. I said I didn't know it took a college degree to get this job done for him. He threw his shoe at me.

How do you get a degree in seven months? I contacted several colleges that military members were using for "bootstrap," submitted all my records, assignments, training, awards, etc., and requested an evaluation. I was contacted by the director of military admissions at one college and his first question was, "Were you the navigator of the B-26 that they brought into the ward at the clinic in Saigon in October of 1963?" He had been in the next bed when I arrived on the ward.

I got all the help I needed and had a degree in May of 1978, followed by promotion to lieutenant colonel the same month. One .30-cal bullet.

I finished my Air Force career in November 1989, just short of 30 years, as a regular, permanent colonel; I have a beautiful wife and a Beechcraft Bonanza, but I never did perfect the backflip off of a bar.

One .30-cal bullet.

Mission with "Jumping Joe" Kittinger

GEORGE ROSE

I did know "Jumping Joe" Kittinger[3] during my tour in B-26s at Bien Hoa Air Base, South Vietnam. When I arrived in-country on December 3, 1963, Major Joe Kittinger was the commander of the B-26 Section of the 1st Air Commando Squadron. I recall flying a memorable mission with him.

The mission, as I remember it, was an afternoon mission. We were armed with napalm on the external stores, 250-pound fragmentation ("frag") bombs internal, and of course, our .50-caliber guns. We made contact with our forward air controller (FAC) in the assigned target area. The FAC was having a problem finding a good target for us (i.e., bad guys), so Joe suggested we fly low and slow over the area to draw enemy fire and we did. After drawing enemy fire, the FAC was able to mark the target and Joe delivered all of our ordnance on the marked area, starting with the napalm, then the frag bombs, and then strafing with the .50-caliber machine guns. The FAC was pleased with our effort.

Captain John Cragin (left) and Captain George Rose (courtesy George Rose).

On our way home, we buzzed the tennis court on the An Loc rubber plantation. If there had been a lob tennis ball, we could have hit it. We landed back at Bien Hoa. Mission complete.

B-26—Bien Hoa, South Vietnam—1963–64

Joe Kittinger

I made my solo flight in the B-26 on 25 May 1954 while stationed at Holloman AFB, New Mexico. During the next four years I accumulated over 400 hours in the aircraft while being assigned to the Fighter Test Section. I transferred from Holloman in April 1958 to Wright Field, where I was assigned to the Aero Medical Lab until March 1963, at which time I volunteered and was transferred to the 1st Air Commando Wing at Hurlburt AFB, Florida.

When I arrived at Hurlburt I had a total flight time of 4,600 hours, of which 3,300 hours were in single-engine jet fighters (F-80B, C; F-84 E, G; F-86 A, E, F, H; F-89B; F-94B, C; B-57; F-100 A, C, D, F; F-104). In addition, I had flown the T-6, P-51, and the P-47. I volunteered to fly the T-28, which was the closest thing to a fighter that was assigned to the Air Commandos. I thought that with my extensive fighter time I would be selected to fly the T-28. WRONG! You guessed it; I was assigned to fly the B-26.

My checkout commenced soon after I arrived at Hurlburt. I was crewed with Gary Pflughaupt, who was an absolutely outstanding copilot and navigator. We breezed through the process to get combat ready in the B-26 and had a ball doing it. All of our instructors had already had a tour in Vietnam. They were good.

In September 1963 Gary and I arrived at Bien Hoa. We were still assigned to the 1st Air Commando Wing at Hurlburt. We were the last TDY B-26 crew sent to Vietnam (Farm Gate) as from

Air commandos—Joe Kittinger, far right (courtesy Joe Kittinger).

B-26 aircraft (courtesy Joe Kittinger).

then on all of the replacement B-26 crews would be PCS for a one-year tour and not Air Commandos. Gary and I were to be there for six months. The day that we arrived I was made the operations officer for the B-26s at Bien Hoa. There were also six RB-26s at Tan Son Nhut, Saigon, that performed all of the photo recce missions.

We were tasked to fly by a FRAG order received each day from 7th Air Force Headquarters in Saigon, usually at about 2 a.m. on the day of the missions. Occasionally, additional missions would be requested by 7th Air Force for unseen contingencies. We had about 14 B-26s assigned to our detachment and usually we would have eight to 10 aircraft available. The B-26s were old and tired. They were quite a collection from all around the world. Some of them had been used by the CIA and flown from Taiwan over China. Some had been flown by mercenaries in support of the French at Dien Bien Phu.

At Holloman, I had been approached and offered an opportunity to fly the B-26 as a mercenary to support the French at Dien Bien Phu, but fortunately had turned it down to continue my Air Force career.

Every B-26 was painted differently. Some were all black, some were various degrees of camouflage, and some unpainted. None had any USAF insignia or identification and all had the roundel of the South Vietnam Air Force. Some had six .50-caliber machine guns and some had eight. All had numerous patches all over the aircraft from bullet holes, etc. None of the cockpits and switch locations were the same. The R-2800 engine had a high-tension ignition system, which was very susceptible to humidity, which resulted in the crew chiefs having to change the spark plugs continuously. It was a rare day when the mag drops were within limits during the pre-takeoff engine checks, but we would go anyway.

Our crew chiefs, engine mechanics, armorers, and gun plumbers were outstanding. There were no "unions." Everyone pitched in and did what was needed to keep the aircraft ready to fly. Frequently when visiting the flight line I didn't know what the individual skills were because all of the men on the flight line pitched in to do whatever task was required to prepare the B-26s for combat. Checklists were very seldom in sight as all of these Air Commandos were very professional and knew their trades and didn't need a checklist for tasks they performed routinely every day.

The rules of engagement required on every flight that we carry a Vietnamese airman in the jump seat. We could not fly unless one was in the jump seat. None could speak English and none wanted to be there. The political reason that they were on board was for us to teach them to fly the B-26. What a joke. But if that was the game we would play it. We had a very sharp Vietnamese Air Force sergeant that spoke very good English that scheduled the jump seat occupants.

To indicate just how ridiculous the observer rule was, I'll relate about an event that took place in Soc Trang. At that remote airfield in the southern part of Vietnam, we had a detachment of T-28 fighters (Air Commandos) stationed there. Of course, they had the same rules of engagement that we, the RB-26s, the C-47s, U-10s (all Air Commando aircraft) had requiring an observer for any flight. One night at Soc Trang the enemy started mortaring the air field. Two fighter pilots ran to the runway and took off in the T-28s to respond to the enemy action. As soon as they became airborne, the enemy ceased their firing and withdrew. When this response was reported to 7th Air Force, a court-martial was proposed for the two Air Commandos because they took off without an observer. However, the charges were soon dropped and the pilots were awarded well-deserved Distinguished Flying Crosses.

Three-quarters of our flights were in the daytime in support of the South Vietnamese Army. On half of our flights we worked with a FAC flying a 0–1/L-19 with a USAF pilot and a Vietnamese observer who usually was in radio contact with a ground unit. Other times we were directed to hit a target (approved by the Vietnamese observer in the back seat of the FAC aircraft) that the FAC would mark with a smoke rocket. Occasionally, we would provide support for the air infiltration of South Vietnamese Army units being airlifted initially by H-21s and later the Huey helicopters. Usually on these missions we would fly very low immediately in advance of the lead helicopter hoping to draw fire, which would locate the enemy. As the helicopters hovered and discharged the troops, we would fly in a low tight left turn to provide immediate support if needed, but mainly to be seen by the enemy to discourage them from firing at the helicopters. Communications were by VHF or FM radios. We wanted to be seen to deter any resistance. If there were two B-26s on the mission after the initial pass, one would climb up to 2,000 feet and be prepared to immediately roll in for a strafing pass or to drop napalm while the other stayed low and buzzed the landing zone. After the troops landed, we would hang around as long as the fuel lasted to provide any support that they might need.

Usually our ordnance was four to six 500-pound cans of napalm and 12 110-pound fragmentation bombs in the internal bomb bay. We could also carry four 500-pound bombs or two 1,000-pound bombs in the bomb bay instead of the frag bombs. The machine guns were loaded with 300 rounds of ammo for each gun. We always had a full load of fuel.

We also had a night mission, which was in support of the Strategic Hamlet program. As the sun set, the Strategic Hamlet would close the gates and not allow anyone out until sunup. Anyone outside of the hamlet was considered as a VC (enemy). If the hamlet was attacked, they would call on an FM radio provided by the Army and we

Napalm canisters (courtesy Joe Kittinger).

would be scrambled from Bien Hoa. When we arrived they would set up fire pots in the shape of an arrow indicating the direction of the enemy. Usually we would see the gun flashes from the enemy outside of the walls of the hamlet. We would drop our ordnance on the enemy and then fire our guns. It was very effective and much appreciated by the inhabitants in the hamlet under attack.

Sitting on night alert was interesting. We had a trailer that was air-conditioned, one of two buildings having air-conditioning at Bien Hoa. We would preflight the aircraft at sunset and prepare the aircraft for a rapid departure. We would put the Vietnamese observer in the back bedroom of the trailer. On two occasions when it came time to takeoff on a scramble alert, the Vietnamese observer had escaped from his room and was long gone. We solved this problem by having the observer give us his boots as soon as he entered the trailer. They were very much afraid of walking bare booted at night because of the possibility of stepping on a poisonous snake. When we were scrambled, we would throw him his boots so he could run with us to the aircraft. The boot trick worked.

In October during a dive-bombing run, the pilot reported that he could not pull out of the run. He said that something was wrong with the aircraft and he thought that he had "bought the farm." The aircraft was grounded and the maintenance troops did all of the checks of the flight controls, cables, bomb bay door spoilers, etc. We also communicated with Hill AFB at Ogden, which was the Air Force Prime depot for the B-26, for any suggestions that they might have. When all of the checks were completed, I did a test flight of the aircraft. I made over 20 dive-bomb runs and had no difficulties. I had another test pilot make another flight on the aircraft and the aircraft performed perfectly. We cleared the aircraft for flight. Before every flight I would personally brief the pilot on the previous problems that we had with this aircraft and then after the flight I would debrief the pilot to make certain that the problem had not reoccurred. Ten uneventful flights were subsequently made before its final flight.

We had a B-26 that had taken a direct hit in the right-wing spar with a .50-caliber bullet that we could not repair at Bien Hoa. An engineer from the depot was sent to Bien Hoa to make a temporary repair on the combat damage to allow us to fly it to Tainan, where a permanent repair could be made. The depot for the B-26 was the Air America Maintenance facility at Tainan, Taiwan. Everyone was very suspicious of the makeshift patch that the Ogden engineer had made on the aircraft. I asked the engineer if the patch was safe enough to make the ferry flight to Tainan. He said, "Of course." I replied that if he was so sure that the patch was okay, would he be willing to fly in the aircraft to the depot? He said yes, so I scheduled myself to fly the mission to Tainan. The first leg of the flight was to Clark AFB, Philippines, where we spent the night. At Base Operations the next morning, I received a request to call the squadron at Bien Hoa. Before I had departed Bien Hoa, I had informed the maintenance officer and the scheduling officer to not fly the aircraft that we had encountered the recovery problem with as I was planning on asking the depot for any recommendations that they might have regarding the aircraft with the recovery problem. Unfortunately, in the heat of the moment, someone substituted the problem B-26 for a flight. During a dive-bomb run, the aircraft did not pull out of the run and our two crewmembers and the observer died. I was devastated and thoroughly aggravated that my order had not been followed. We never did determine who substituted the aircraft or why it was used in spite of my order. Some losses in combat are not attributed to enemy fire.

I had a close relationship with Major Hayes, the U.S. Army commander of the Huey helicopter unit also stationed at Bien Hoa. Soon after we met, Major Hayes shared with me some recent helicopter losses that they had encountered on an infiltration mission of Vietnamese Army troops. It appeared that the VC knew just where and when the infiltrations were to take place. He and I came up with a plan to reduce their losses. The day before the mission, he and I would fly an Army L-19 over the landing zone at 5,000 feet but not loiter over the area to indicate an interest. If required, 30 minutes later we would again fly over the area from a different direction. Our observations led us to devise a plan of attack for the next day's mission. Since I was the operations officer and scheduler of the pilots for the missions, I always signed myself up as the pilot for the mission. If the landing zone was to the south of the village, I would precede the helicopters and drop napalm and fire the .50 calibers to the north of the village hoping to deceive the enemy to assume that the landing zone was to the north of the village. These tactics worked because the enemy actually had several infiltrators attached to the South Vietnamese Army Headquarters that were passing the actual battle plans to the VC in the field. They not only knew the time and date of the infiltrations but the actual location of the landing zones. Our tactics worked as we always changed the written instructions for the missions, which confused the VC. During all of the missions from then on that we supported with the B-26s, the Army did not suffer a single loss of a helicopter. Hayes's unit always requested the B-26s for aerial support of their infiltration missions because it worked.

Occasionally, 7th Air Force in Saigon would substitute South Vietnamese fighters to support the infiltrations. This just didn't work out because of communications problems and the diversionary tactics that we had worked out could not be implemented by Hayes. The unit lost a helicopter on an infiltration mission supported by the Vietnamese Air Force. I drove into Saigon and made an appointment with the Operations Officer at 7th Air Force Headquarters. I explained to the general the diversionary tactics that the Army unit and our B-26s had devised. I showed how successful we were using our tactics. The general was visibly upset and chided me in saying that "The Army doesn't tell the Air Force how to fly." He just didn't get over the fact that our tactics worked because we worked together to defeat the enemy.

Soon after this discussion, General Joe Moore was assigned to command 7th Air Force, and overnight the cooperation between the Army and the USAF was greatly improved. The enemy was the VC, not the U.S. Army. Being stationed at the same airfield greatly simplified the cooperation between Major Hayes and myself and having the L-19 available to reconnoiter the landing zones was a great advantage in planning the missions. We had an effective and efficient way to perform close air support for the Army and it worked. It was a great feeling after every infiltration mission when there were no losses of Army helicopters; after all, we were on the same team fighting the same enemy.

I always reviewed the next day's missions every day to make certain that no new wrinkle had been scheduled. On 31 October, I noticed a rather unusual mission that was scheduled for 1 November. The only instruction was for the B-26 to arrive over Saigon at 2 p.m. and report in to Combat Operations at 7th AF. I never scheduled any of the crews to a mission that I had not flown first. This was one of those questionable missions so I scheduled myself for the flight.

On 1 November, I arrived over Saigon exactly at 2 p.m. and witnessed South Vietnamese Sky Raiders and T-28 fighters bombing the President's Palace in downtown Saigon and Navy boats on the Mekong River. I also noticed that barricades had been installed on the Tan Son Nhut Airport. I immediately called Combat Operations and reported the bombings. They instructed me to fly about 10 miles northwest of Saigon and report back any troop movements. Apparently, the 7th Command Post was concerned about a Division of the South Vietnam Army located to the northwest of Saigon that might be moving to assist the president in fighting the coup. There was no unusual activity that I could see, which I reported back to 7th Air Force. For the next three hours, Combat Operations vectored me all around Saigon asking me to report all ground movements and aerial bombing. It was quite obvious that a coup was taking place and that the USAF/7th Air Force had known prior to the event that it was going to start on 1 November. That was why they had scheduled a B-26 to be airborne at that time to act as an aerial observer to the attacks on the government/president of South Vietnam. After about four hours of flight, I was getting low on fuel and told the Combat Operations that I had to land. They then told me that I could not land at Bien Hoa as the runway was closed to all traffic. They instructed me to stand by while they coordinated removing the barricades from the runway at Tan Son Nhut so I could land there. Upon landing, I was met by a South Vietnamese Army jeep with a .50-cal gun mounted on it and escorted to the parking ramp. We could hear machine-gun and rifle firing close to the airport. We could also watch the Sky Raiders and T-28s dive-bombing targets in Saigon. We were right in the middle of a battle.

We walked to the new officers' club that was having its grand opening that day. The club was packed. As instructed by the 7th Air Force Combat Operations before we

Snapshots taken by Maury Bourne in Saigon the day after the Diem coup (1963) (courtesy Maury Bourne).

landed, I called the command post by the telephone in the club letting them know where they could contact me. We ordered something to eat and after a lengthy wait we finally received our hamburgers and a simultaneous announcement over the loudspeaker for Major Kittinger to answer a call. I was directed by the Command Post to take off ASAP to find a missing U.S. Army helicopter. We ran back to our B-26, which had been refueled, and had to wait for about 15 minutes before an armed South Vietnamese lieutenant would allow me to start the engines. I had to wait another 15 minutes before the South Vietnamese jeep showed up to escort me to the runway. I had to wait another 15 minutes while they coordinated removing the barricades from the runway. The Command Post directed me to a U.S. Army helicopter landing strip about 100 miles north of Saigon and gave me a VHF radio frequency to contact the site. When I arrived over the site I buzzed the site, called on the radio, and was informed that the missing helicopter was on the ground there with an engine problem and would remain there overnight. This I reported back to the Command Post. I returned to Saigon and flew top cover for another two hours before I was instructed to return to Bien Hoa. When I arrived at Bien Hoa, I was informed that the runway was closed. By this time, I was tired of being screwed around with. I told the tower to clear the damn runway as I needed to land. I then buzzed the tower; that got their attention and they quickly cleared the runway so that I could land.

A funny incident occurred that evening when I entered the hooch where I lived. It was rather late and there were no lights on in the hooch. As I was slowly walking by Barney Cockran's bed, I kicked a machine gun that Barney had placed by his bed. He immediately jumped up and tried to find his machine gun. He thought that he was being attacked. The next day we laughed about the incident but at the time it was not funny.

The next day we received absolutely no information. We repeatedly called the Command Post at 7th AF and were told to "stand by." Nothing moved on the base and the gate was barricaded. The only way that we could find out what was happening was to ask the VNAF sergeant in charge of the observers what new information that he heard on the AM radio. The runway and taxiways were all barricaded. The following day all was back to normal and we started flying our regular missions.

The coup against President Diem was a complete failure. His assassination was the beginning of the end for the government/leadership of South Vietnam. The subsequent leaders of South Vietnam got progressively worse. The U.S. was to blame for this assassination, as none of the generals/leaders of the South Vietnamese military would have caused this coup without the approval of the U.S. It was obvious that the USAF knew what was being planned; hence, the B-26 was on station when it started.

We had a unit in Saigon that was doing some research in conjunction with the new concepts, weapons, etc., for the war in South Vietnam. I was approached by an Air Force colonel from the unit and asked to do a flight test on a ground proximity fuse attached to a 500-pound bomb. I had known the colonel when I was in Flight Test Section at Holloman and he knew that I was trained in conducting flight tests. We needed a ground proximity fuse for the bombs so that the bombs would detonate before ground impact to provide a more destructive bomb directed against standing targets. The normal bomb that detonated upon ground impact would make a hole in the ground and, of course, destroy buildings, etc. Thousands of ground proximity fuses were left over from Korea and World War II that were available for our use. However, there had been some problems of premature detonations soon after being dropped. This next-generation ground proximity fuse had been modified and my flight test was initiated to determine if the fuses were safe for our use.

I established a plan for the test and started the drops. I had a FAC to give us a general target area and another B-26 with a photographer to record the drops. I would drop the 500-pound bombs with the proximity fuses installed, and the FAC, the other B-26, and myself would estimate how far above the ground the bomb would detonate. I dropped the bombs singly and in a 25-degree dive-bomb run.

Bombs dropped from aircraft are very safe because of the arming mechanism installed on the bombs. The arming fuse on the front of the bomb has a small propeller mounted on the fuse that after turning several hundred times allows the bomb to be armed and detonate upon impact with a normal bomb or a signal using a ground proximity fuse. The propeller is prevented from turning by a wire running through the propeller. The arming wire attached through the propeller is routed to an electrical solenoid that retains the wire if armed. Just prior to dropping the bomb, the pilot arms the solenoid, which retains the wire when the bomb is dropped. Immediately after this wire is pulled from the fuse, the propeller starts turning, and several hundred feet from the aircraft the bomb is armed to explode on signal or on impact with the ground. The bomb is absolutely safe until the arming wire to the fuse is pulled.

On the second flight test, one of the bombs detonated before it got close to the ground. This caused some concern because it appeared that it detonated too soon. I called the colonel and explained that we may have had a premature detonation of one of the ground proximity fuses and invited him to be on the next tests as an observer in the photo chase B-26. He agreed. The next day, on the third bomb drop, the 500-pound bomb detonated just below my aircraft and caused several hits on my aircraft. It was a very close call and we and the colonel agreed that the ground proximity fuses were not safe and needed further modifications. I was delighted that the colonel had witnessed the failure of the fuse. That ended that test. Later, a three-foot pipe was inserted into the nose of the 500-pound bomb that detonated the bomb three feet from the ground. It was an improvement over the ground-impact bomb for certain missions. We were always trying to improve our effectiveness. In September we received a plastic additive to add to the napalm mix that improved the performance of that weapon. War is hell and every warrior agrees with that statement. However, if we are at war we always want the most effective weaponry and tactics against the enemy whose goal it is to kill us. Given a choice, it's better to win than to lose that battle.

Our B-26s were tired. The aircraft had not been designed to be a fighter bomber, the way that we were using them. In combat, when getting shot at or when pulling up in a dive-bombing pass, the aircraft was frequently stressed above its design limits. After many missions where the wings were overstressed, some failed. There were at least two losses of B-26s in combat in Vietnam that were attributed to ground fire that were suspect wing failures. The easy way to avoid any embarrassment was to assign enemy ground fire to explain a loss. Finally, in February of 1964 at a night firepower demonstration at Range 52 at Eglin AFB, the wing came off a B-26 on a strafing run. There was no doubt this time as to the cause of the failure. As a result of this failure, all B-26s worldwide were grounded, including ours in South Vietnam.

It's hell to be in combat and to have your aircraft grounded. No one could tell us what was next. Necessity is the mother of invention. So after a few days we came up with a plan on how to get back flying combat missions in our B-26s. Obviously, we would have to devise a way to deliver ordnance without dive-bombing or to put any Gs on the aircraft. One of our clever navigators who had also been a SAC bombardier came up with the idea of dropping bombs from the B-26 in straight and level flight. Since there were no Norden bombsights available, we had to improvise. The result was a sighting device, which we titled the "Flintstone Bombing Sight." It consisted of a wire horizontally attached across the forward edge of the bomb bay with another wire mounted vertically through the bomb bay. The navigator would ride in the back of the B-26, and at an altitude of 1,500 feet above the target the bomb bay doors would be opened. The FAC would mark the target and the pilot would fly the aircraft toward the smoke. The navigator looking through the open bomb bay would give the pilots instructions on heading changes to get the inbound

"Flintstone" bomb sight used after straight and level bombing imposed (courtesy Joe Kittinger).

heading along the line of the vertical wire in the bomb bay. The pilot would select the proper switches and the navigator would give the pilot a countdown as to when to drop the bomb on the designated target. Usually, the first bomb would not be right on target but usually on the second pass the navigator would go to school on the first bomb, and subsequent bomb drops were usually right on. These missions were not much fun but at least we were hurting the enemy and it was better than sitting on the ground. We had a helluva time getting 7th Air Force to approve our "Flintstone" missions but we finally got the go-ahead. I flew the first "Flintstone" mission and I think that there were three other flights flown before the aircraft were permanently grounded. The B-26 was no longer an Air Force aircraft that could be safely flown on a routine basis; they were all quickly retired and flown to Clark AFB, in the Philippines.

My last B-26 combat mission out of Bien Hoa was on 7 March 1964. I had flown 92 combat sorties and had accumulated 358 hours of combat.

The following was the departure song that we sang at Bien Hoa for those returning to the ZI (zone of interior) at the end of their tour.

> "Give my regards to Saigon,
> Remember me to Madame Knew
> Tell all the girls down at the Tudor Bar that my tour here is through
> Tell them I am returning back to the ole ZI
> Tell them to kiss my ass,
> Yes, kiss my ass,
> Yes, kiss my ass, goodbye"

On 10 March 1964, Gary and I headed back to Hurlburt.

After returning to Hurlburt I made a recommendation that we change the title of the navigator crewmembers to that of copilot. That's what they were. The navigator's purpose is to navigate. The navigator sitting in the right seat of the B-26, and later on in my career the back seater in the F-4, were a helluva lot more than just a navigator. They were the copilot assisting the pilot in flying the aircraft and in combat an extra set of eyes looking for targets and ground fire. They were there to assist the pilot in the event of an emergency, knowing the boldface items on the checklists, knowing the mechanics of the aircraft systems. They were the ones that called out the altitudes during dive-bombing runs to remind the pilot of the calculated altitude to release the bomb. Sometimes the pilot got so engrossed in the target and obtaining the right dive angle and airspeed in the dive-bomb run that he forgot when to drop the bomb and recover from the dive; the copilot reminded him. Safety of flight was greatly enhanced by these intrepid airmen in the right seat of a B/A-26 and the back seat of the F-4. They deserved to be called copilots because that is what they were. I guess I was the only one that felt this way as my suggestion was not accepted. Perhaps the pilot's "union" would object.

Loss of Aircraft and Crews Due to Wing Failure

The tragic loss of B-26 aircraft and crews due to wing failure brought Farm Gate B-26 combat operations out of Bien Hoa to an unexpected early conclusion. The first reported loss of a B-26 and crew due to suspected wing failure took place on 8 April 1963. On that date, Captain Andrew Mitchell, pilot, Captain Jerry Campaigne, navigator, and a VNAF observer were killed in action during a strafing run approximately 33 miles northeast of Pleiku (left wing came off due to unknown causes). The crews and maintenance personnel were aware of structural fatigue problems associated with heavy ordnance wing loads while taxiing over rough taxiways, and due to wing stress during pull-ups from dive-bombing passes, but wartime air support demands led to continued B-26 combat operations in South Vietnam. A second aircraft and crew loss during a combat mission on 16 August 1963, killing Captain John McClean, pilot, First Lieutenant Arthur Bedal, navigator, and a VNAF observer, led to more aircraft flight restrictions. Finally, when a third B-26 was lost on 11 February 1964 during an air show at Eglin AFB, Florida, killing Captain Herman Moore, pilot, and Captain Lawrence Lively, navigator, during a strafing run at Range 52 (left wing separated from aircraft coming off of strafing pass), a decision was made to ground all B-26 aircraft until a "fix" could be found for B-26 wing spar fatigue deficiencies.

War Story

Andrew "Andi" Biancur

On 1 April 1961, following the guidance of President Kennedy, the Air Force established the 4400th Combat Crew Training Squadron (CCTS)—code named "Jungle

Jim"—to counter the increasing terrorist attacks by communist guerrillas in South Vietnam, supported by North Vietnam. A detachment (Det. 2A) of the 4400th was subsequently established at Bien Hoa AB in South Vietnam. Using the code name Farm Gate, and beneath its training cover, its mission was to stop communist guerrilla forces in the south. Farm Gate was a highly classified mission committed to providing close air support to Vietnamese ground forces and to attack the Viet Cong.

In January of 1963, I was assigned to the 4400th CCTS for training in the Douglas B-26 Invader. Following that training, I, along with my navigator, Second Lieutenant Wells T. Jackson, arrived at Det. 2A on 1 May 1963. When we became competent in performing the various required combat tactics, we were further assigned to a Deployed Air Strike Team (DAST). The DAST generally consisted of two B-26s paired to operate from various airfields in South Vietnam for temporary periods in support of ongoing operations. It was while assigned to a DAST that Wells and I found ourselves at Da Nang AB in August 1963.

On 16 of August 1963, I was fragged on an interdiction mission to a mountain valley target in I Corps. For whatever reason, Wells was replaced by First Lieutenant Woody Halsey as a crewmember for that mission. We also carried a Vietnamese observer (name unknown). We departed from Da Nang AB in B-26 #44–35822 shortly after 1300 hours and proceeded to our target in Quang Ngai Province.

The second B-26, #44–34681, flown by Captain John McClean (pilot) and Lieutenant Arthur "Skip" Bedal (navigator), also drew a target in the mountains southwest of Da Nang and departed at approximately the same time. (I cannot recall if we went as a two-ship formation or were later directed to the same target.)

Regardless, both of us wound up working the target as a two-ship formation, under the direction of a Vietnamese Forward Air Controller (FAC), flying an O-1 aircraft. We had each made a pass or two on the target located in a north-south valley in a fairly rugged narrow mountainous area. I had pulled off the target and was up on a left downwind ("the perch") heading northeast when McClean began his run to the southwest. Shortly after he began his run, the Vietnamese FAC yelled over the air the words: "His wing come off!" I glanced to my left and caught sight of the wing section flipping through the air. I immediately caught sight of the remainder of the aircraft tumbling out of control and heading for the ground. I yelled for them to get out but, of course, it was impossible because of the adverse "Gs" and lack of time. The two large sections of aircraft impacted the jungle some distance from one another. I immediately broke off the attack and called Paris Control (the tactical control agency) to report the incident. We remained in the area flying air cover over the site until we were relieved by—what I recall to be—two T-28s.

It is my opinion that the wing separated from the aircraft as a result of structural failure and not enemy action, for the following reasons. First, McClean was positioned early on his ordnance delivery run. At that point, the only force active on the aircraft should have been increased airspeed. He was well above the altitude where he would normally have initiated a pullout causing increased "G forces." Second, there was no visible explosion or fire associated with the aircraft, only the two sections trailing fuel vapor. Third, I believe that if there had been hostile ground fire, the FAC would have yelled some other words. Fourth, the entire time we remained over the area, even on our low passes initiated to determine if there were survivors, we never experienced hostile fire. Fifth, the photos we were shown later, taken by photo reconnaissance aircraft and ground-recovery assets, showed the wreckage pattern to be indicative of wing separation at altitude.

A-26/B-26 Historical Notes

Tom Smith

I have reviewed my pilot logbook from the Vietnam War period and lament not doing a daily journal or being more precise about mission data. Frank Hayes, my B-26 navigator, also kept a record and tracked coordinates for assigned targets. We flew together on most of my missions except for my initial area checkout and several times when he was unavailable. In addition, we crosschecked our logs to validate mission data. Therefore, our story conforms to our personal records.

Frank Hayes (left) and Tom Smith (right) at Bien Hoa (courtesy Tom Smith).

Our Military Air Transport Service (MATS) Boeing C-135 landed at 1300 hours on 30 July 1963 at Bien Hoa Air Base, South Vietnam, 25 miles west of Saigon. MATS had an idea that it was safer to fly facing the rear; that was confusing too. When we stepped out on the ramp, the heat was staggering. I was packing a Category 5 hangover from the previous two nights in Honolulu and Okinawa and I blame my initial disorientation on booze and flying backwards into an oven. An old comrade from the past, Frank Defonce, met me and sensing my dilemma rushed me to the Detachment bar. Unbelievably, here, tending bar was one of the seven wonders of the Orient. Gloria was unfazed by the thermometer and a frothy blue ao dai covered her more Occidental than Oriental configuration. It can happen, thank God. Another surprise was the price of drinks. Everything was a dime! Hard liquor was abundant, but the beer department stalled out after the local Vietnamese Ba Mi Ba. The preservative formaldehyde used in the brewing process singed your lips and flamed the stomach. I was considering my third—a death wish with this brew—when I heard aircraft overhead. I rushed out and could not believe the sight and sound. There were a pair of B-26s flying overhead with what sounded like screaming turbo-prop engines. I had no idea that B-26s with that engine configuration existed. It was very exciting until I inquired and found out that many of the maintenance and fuel access panels were missing and the high-pitch noise came from the air rushing over the open spaces. So this explained the screaming turbo-prop noise and was the beginning of learning a lot of things I never knew before.

Well, we got off to a flying stop in combat ops. One of our first assignments was to ferry a bird from Clark Air Base, Philippines, to the Air Asia maintenance facility at Tainan, Taiwan. We were to move a plane with multiple grounding Red X maintenance write-ups. It had fire damage and while grounded was cannibalized for parts.

Maintenance put it together just enough for this one flight. It was a recon/bomber glass-nose B-26C. Canopy operation was dubious and worried me since most of the route was over water. We were reluctant to go, given the condition of the plane, but also anxious to complete the mission. After takeoff, we rendezvoused with a Douglas C-124 Globemaster to buddy with on the route. I think they were along to witness our plunging into the Philippine Sea. The entire route was studded with rain and thunderstorms. On top of that, I was unfamiliar with good reference points for flying tight formation on such a huge plane. Therefore, being close to "Old Shaky" and all those moving parts in heavy rain was a very hairy situation. It was hard to tell if turbulence was only weather or wake turbulence or prop wash or a combination of all three. There were times when we wondered if this ragtag machine was going to hold together. The canopy would not seal and it was almost as wet inside as out. Welcome to monsoon country.

Well, we made it to Tainan, Taiwan, and our destination Air Asia was an amazing maintenance facility. Surprisingly, they had a whole line of modified B-26s painted black and configured for a variety of ELINT, SIGINT, recon, and covert combat operations mostly directed at Red China. We had several company minders (Air Asia employees) and they provided some examples of Tainan operations. One interesting mission they described was to drop "observers" out of the bomb bay from 400 feet. On landing, they discarded their chutes and harnesses and took up a route out of the country to return and report what they saw along the way. Problem was that strangers stood out and movement was restricted. Red Chinese military were numerous and vigilant and not easy on itinerants. The first thing they did on stopping a person was to strip them down and check for abrasions and bruises revealing the effect of chute opening. Therefore, the "observers" wore heavy padding and prayed for good fortune.

We flew back to Clark Air Base on a China Air Transport (CAT) Republic C-46. The ship had plush seating, stewardesses, in-flight cocktails, and meals. We did not expect these accommodations and were hardly dressed for the occasion. We stayed over at Clark to await military transport back to Saigon. In the meantime, we took a swing through Angeles, the local "ville" near the base. It was full service as you may recall. Frank had already done some shopping in Taiwan. He had bought a stack of medical books for one of our mates that aspired to go to med school on returning to the ZI. Now, here at Clark and Angeles he would complete his wish list. Frank has siblings that are fathers and nuns in the Catholic Church. They were aware of Philippine art and had requested decorative mahogany religious artifacts and artwork. Therefore, he bought crucifixes and carvings of an arrow-pierced Saint Francis of Assisi and an assortment of paintings on black velvet of a suffering Jesus that looked like Elvis Presley. What's more, crewmen had added a range of pornographic paraphernalia that was available only in the Philippines. None of these items came packaged and it was a chore to be discreet while tending and transporting them. You can imagine the scene.

We got into Saigon too late to make it back to base and so we had to lay over at the Metropole Hotel. Trouble was the only room was on the third floor. We humped our personal gear and all of Frank's booty up to the room. It was hot and tight in there so we decided to step out. A minor problem surfaced as there was a coup in town and the streets were to be empty between 7 p.m. and 7 a.m. Yeah, right. The first shadows of evening saw us zigzagging our way to the bars on Tu Do Street.

Next morning is when the fun began. In 1963, there was no U.S. military transport to any base outside of Saigon. You were on your own. Of course, we needed to find a taxi big enough to handle the load and willing to make the trip. We really needed a truck, but no such luck. The most common cab was a midget four-seat Citroen. We flagged one and tried the load, but there was no room left for us. Now, again, we were stuck on the curb with pedestrians gawking at our peculiar mix of gear. Eureka, a Simca taxi arrived. This car was one-third larger than the Citroen and looked like it would handle our load, and the driver saw a good fare in the 25-mile trip to Bien Hoa. We loaded up. I was in the back with most of the stuff and Frank was up front with the medical books under his feet. There was light at the end of the tunnel.

We left Saigon and were on the highway about midway to base when we heard explosions and machine-gun fire. Off to the side, we saw a flight of three Vietnamese Douglas A-1H Skyraiders hammering targets near the road. Almost at the same time, the left rear tire blew out. The driver was more concerned for his car and stopped. We were more concerned about being overrun by the VC. We thought the VC would not be compassionate with our predicament or us and shouted for him to drive on. He agonized about bumping along and destroying his tire. He stopped again. I pulled my .45 from my survival vest and racked in a shell. This action was as much to defend us as to impress the driver. He responded by seeing the urgency and went ahead a mile or so until we were clear. We all hopped out, changed the tire for another one of dubious service, and added the ruined tire to our load. We went a little way when the replacement tire failed too. Now, what are we to do? Some tense moments passed until a farm truck came along. The cab driver negotiated for us and we stacked our strange load onto the bed of the truck. The farmer's partner was an old woman: it was always hard to judge their age. We paid off the cabbie rather generously given the roll of events and got in the truck. The old woman never stopped grinning and sat atop the eclectic stack all the way to Bien Hoa. Maybe Frank's artwork amused her. It was like a chapter from *Tales of the South Pacific*. We made it back on 25 August 1963 and started combat operations the next day. Most of our missions were escort and armed recon for planes, trains, and automobiles ... really!

Generally, we finished each mission with an airstrike on a designated target or in the free-fire area northwest of the base called Copperhead Alpha. I got a night checkout on 4 September. The Vietnamese Air Force disdained night ops. They had all the war they wanted and preferred daylight operations. That left most of the night fighting to us. Too bad; night combat ops were safer anyway. Our airplanes were Vietnamese and so identified—most of the time. The insignia placards were removable. We always carried a Vietnamese "trainee." About one-half of our total flying was at night. Some of it was escort in hot areas, but mostly our night mission was outpost defense. Daily, we launched one ship at 2200 hours and another at 0200 hours. Other crews were designated as backup for the airborne alerts should they have mechanical problems or expend their entire ordnance and need a replacement, or if additional targets developed.

Following my initial checkout on 4 September, we flew a helicopter escort on the seventh, and on the eighth, we were put in the schedule as backup for the airborne alerts. The weather was rotten and operations canceled the normal scheduled alert missions. Everybody breathed a little easier. Weather recovery was tough at Bien Hoa. Our planes had an eight-channel VHF radio—A through H—for voice communications, and one ADF radio for navigation. This was a Vietnamese base and language was always a struggle, so there was no GCA. If we were stuck up with weather, we had to divert to Saigon's Tan Son Nhut Air Base, where they had an American on duty to provide GCA service.

One time, unbelievably, we did an RDF—using the aural null—when thunderstorms rendered the ADF needle useless. Back to the story. An outpost between Bien Hoa and the South China Sea, near Vungtau, came under attack. Ops assigned a crew to the target. As time went on, the overcast and rain worsened. Shortly, another crew deployed. It rained even harder. The first crew recovered in the sorry weather and returned talking excitedly about the hazards with weather, communications, flares, and antiaircraft fire. At 0200 hours, we were called to depart. The target was about 50 miles east. We got a call sign, Whiskey Dan, precise target coordinates, and an aircraft loaded with 12 internal bombs, two external 750-pound cans of napalm, and 14 .50-cal machine guns. Eight guns were in the nose and three in each wing. That was a lot of ordnance and allowed us remain on the target for some time. The prospect of a protracted stay on target was a bummer given the weather.

We took off climbing and turning and found that the base of the clouds was 800 feet. The terrain was level all the way to the target; therefore, we stayed low and visual and tolerated the heavy rain. We did time and distance navigation to target and contacted the Douglas C-47 flare ship forward air controller (FAC). They were circling the target between 3,000 and 4,000 feet, staying in the clear. The controller spoke broken English and it was tough to make sense of the situation. We were uneasy about being able to pull this off given the setup; it would have been a relief to cancel, but how could we go home without firing a shot? What the hell, we decided to take a look-see. There was an outpost under attack and they had a fire arrow indicating the direction of attack. These fire arrows were small cans filled with sand and gravel soaked with diesel fuel and ignited. The cans rested on a platform that rotated to show the axis of attack. Flares dropped through the undercast were both startling and revealing. We were truly in a pickle having to run an airstrike within 800 feet of the surface in the rain. Circling the descending flares, we spotted the fire arrow. The FAC was talking to the defenders and jabbering at us trying to describe a target he could not see in an unfamiliar language. It was my third night mission and Frank's second. Overconfidence was not our problem. Whiskey Dan was worried. We armed the guns and got ready for business.

It felt like we were inside a light bulb that kept turning on and off as flares illuminated, drifted, and then went out. The fire arrow was our anchor. It was the only light on the ground and even it went off when it was behind us or we passed through a heavy shower. On top of this, the canopy seals were poor and old and water poured in during heavy rain. The FAC requested ordnance at a certain distance along the fire arrow. They did not want bombs. We could not deliver them anyway because of our low-altitude situation. That left the napalm, which we delivered at 25 feet above the ground, and guns. They requested a certain distance and we complied with a short burst. As our tracers impacted, corrections were made for our next pass, and so on. Communications were a nightmare and I felt remorse for shooting so much until I took a good look and saw how the enemy gunners on the ground were hosing us too. I remember feeling better knowing the enemy was where the FAC said he was and fighting back. The cockpit was smoky and smelled strongly from the cordite powder in the ammunition. It was also wet inside, poorly ventilated, and hard to breathe (when you thought about it), and the smoke burned your eyes until long after the firing stopped. I mention the eyes because with so much ammo, we made multiple passes and the irritation was a nuisance. Pull-ups were especially dicey, as we had to avoid the ground and then the flares. The flare ship generally dropped three flares per pass so there was all manner of debris drifting around the

Tom Smith (pilot) and Frank Hayes (navigator) were thankful to be able to walk away after landing this B-26 that was shot up during a mission (courtesy Tom Smith).

target area. The flares hung below small parachutes and were a real collision hazard—illuminated or not. A steep pull-up would plunge you into the overcast with the great prospect of upset if not corrected promptly and accurately. You only did that once. Vertigo was a problem too with an uncertain horizon and constantly changing levels of light, precession of the instruments from Gs, and continual turning.

Finally, thank God again, we expended all of our munitions—"Winchester" we called it—and took a heading for home base. We caged the gyros and waited for the instruments to stabilize. The weather had not changed a bit, but we had. The mission seemed impossible an hour earlier, but we made it. I was proud of our performance and persistence. My confidence soared thinking back and then looking ahead. We were going to make it back to base.

We returned home to Hurlburt Air Force Base, Florida, in January 1964 and continued as a crew. A nighttime counterinsurgency air power demonstration was scheduled on 11 February 1964 at Eglin AFB, Range 52. Frank and I were to fly the B-26B and demonstrate night tactics and weapons delivery capability of the airplane. The target was a range bunker. We would attack with rockets, bombs, napalm, and guns. I noticed the show date was on my birthday. As we were just back from Vietnam and had been away for all holidays in 1963, I asked to be relieved from this flight and stay home for my birthday. Honoring the principle of crew integrity, when they removed me, they did likewise with Frank. Captain Stan Moore, who lived across the street, took my place and Captain Larry Lively replaced Frank. On show night, just after our dinner, blue USAF vehicles begin to arrive at the Moores' house. Both Stan and Larry died as their plane crashed into the target bunker.

The accident investigation revealed extensive corrosion in the wing area adjacent to the engine nacelles. B-26s were grounded immediately following this accident. Looking back, wing failure was likely responsible for three aircraft losses during my Vietnamese tour of duty. Following each loss, ordnance loads were restricted or lowered and G limits were imposed. However, following inspections, these limits were lifted and the plane was cleared for unrestricted operations.

Over the entire history of the B-26, it proved to be an outstanding ground-attack aircraft. The accidents were tragic, but the plane would have new life as the B-26K. Forty aircraft were transported to the On Mark Engineering Company in Van Nuys, California, and were remanufactured and modified so extensively that they became new aircraft. In 1964–1965, they would fly counterinsurgency missions in the Congo, and a year later, return gloriously to the fight in Southeast Asia first with Big Eagle and later as Nimrod night fighters.

Air Force Contract to Remanufacture 40 B-26 Aircraft

Although the tragic loss of B-26 crews due to wing failure resulted in the grounding of B-26 flight operations, Air Force officials recognized that the B-26 was a valuable aircraft for rapidly expanding counterinsurgency combat operations. B-26 crews had performed a valuable combat role in South Vietnam, and immediate action was needed to restore the B-26 to flight-worthy condition. Consistent with Air Force military aircraft procurement practices, the Air Force quickly contracted with On Mark Engineering Company of Van Nuys, California, to produce a YB-26K prototype aircraft that would resolve the wing spar failure issues, and at the same time, produce a much-improved aircraft for counterinsurgency combat operations. The prototype contract was awarded for a bargain price of $577,000. The Air Force was not disappointed with On Mark's performance. The YB-26K aircraft entailed updated 250-hp Pratt & Whitney R-2800-103W radial engines with larger propellers with square tips; the wing spar failure problem was fully resolved through redesign and complete rebuild of the wings; 165-gallon fuel tanks were added to the wing tips; and four weapons hard-point pylons were installed underneath each wing. The vertical stabilizer and rudder were enlarged, and the cockpit was adapted for dual controls (both for the pilot and navigator side-by-side positions in the cockpit). Improved updated communication and navigation avionics were installed, including FM, HF, UHF, and VHF radios, and ILS, LF ADF, TACAN, and VOR navigation capability. The nose of the aircraft retained the eight .50-cal machine-gun arrangement.

Following the success of the YB-26K flight test program, the Air Force ordered 40 B-26s converted to the B-26K standards. The Air Force awarded the $12.6 million production contract to On Mark, and the 40 aircraft were converted in 1963 and 1964. The production B-26K differed from the prototype in some significant particulars: the Pratt & Whitney engines were changed to the R-2800-52W from the R-2800-103W; the prop spinners installed on the YB-26K were deleted; and the six .50-cal machine guns mounted in the wings were removed. However, the B-26K still maintained the desired combat firepower: eight .50-cal machine guns in the nose section; 4,000 pounds of bombs carried in the bomb bay; and up to 8,000 pounds of mixed ordnance carried externally on eight wing pylons. The technical specifications[4] of the 40 "remanufactured" B-26K aircraft were as follows:

TECHNICAL NOTES:

Armament: Eight .50-cal nose machine guns, eight wing pylons capable of carrying 8,000 lbs. of mixed ordnance, and 4,000 lbs. of bombs internally in bomb bay

Engines: Two Pratt & Whitney R-2800-52Ws of 2,500 hp (maximum with water injection)

Max. Speed: 323 mph/281 knots

Range: 2,700 statute miles/2,346 nautical miles

Service Ceiling: 30,000 ft.

Span: 71 ft. 6 in.

Length: 51 ft. 7 in.

Height: 19 ft.

On Mark Engineering
History

Robert B. Denny

The company and people that produced the A-26 Counter Invader have a rich history that can be traced back to World War I.

Corliss C. Moseley

Major Corliss C. "CC" Moseley, son of the sheriff of Boise, Idaho, fought in France during World War I. He flew the Nieuport mostly, but also the Spad. His specialty was downing German observation balloons at the crack of dawn. You can imagine the pilot's condition at 0400 hours after a night of toasts to those who were lost the day before. The average life span of a World War I pilot was three weeks.

He went on to win the first Pulitzer Prize air race in 1920.

After that, he helped found Western Air Express, then was part of a group which bought and modernized the Grand Central Airport in Glendale, California. Grand Central quickly became the main air terminal for the Los Angeles area and continued until Mines Field was turned into LAX. During that period, air travel was the domain of the rich and famous, and Moseley made the most of his airport's patrons, entering LA's social inner circle. This would become an important piece of the puzzle in the birth of On Mark Engineering.

During the late 1930s, Moseley started several civilian pilot training schools, which continued throughout World War II. It was during this period that Moseley became friends with General Claire Lee Chennault and his ace operations officer (XO), David Lee "Tex" Hill. Hill was the leader ("Shark One") of the American Volunteer Group

Lieutenant C.C. Moseley, smiling because he is on the ground in front of the Nieuport 17. Note the hole in the upper wing from the blown cylinder. The rotary engine appears to have instantly frozen! (courtesy Robert B. Denny).

Flying Tigers in China just before the U.S. entered World War II and continued as XO of the 75th Fighter Squadron after the All Volunteer Group (AVG) transition to an Army Air Corps unit.

Lieutenant C.C. Moseley with the Verville-Packard racer (courtesy Robert B. Denny).

Robert O. Denny

Meanwhile, Robert O. Denny, an All-American track athlete from Kokomo, Indiana, left college shortly after Pearl Harbor to join the Army Air Corps. After training, Denny was assigned to the 75th Fighter Squadron, the unit that replaced the AVG Flying Tigers at the Kunming fighter base in China. Denny flew the P-40 for Chennault and Hill.

He was shot down while strafing a convoy, which turned out to be transporting Japanese soldiers. Their small-arms fire disabled Denny's engine and he was forced to

Grand Central Airport and Cal-Aero Technical Institute (courtesy Robert B. Denny).

Grand Central aircraft during the later years of World War II (courtesy Robert B. Denny).

belly land the airplane into a rice paddy. Incredibly, Denny evaded Japanese capture, being hidden by Chinese farmers for several weeks. The "blood chit" and "pointy-talkie" that were issued those pilots undoubtedly saved his life. He returned, uninjured, to his unit and flew for the 75th for a few more months. He then served several other flying and command assignments in Southeast Asia, relating to the air transport over the "Hump," until he rotated back to the States. Thereafter, he flew transport for senior officers and served as an advanced instructor in Texas and California.

Robert O. Denny and his P-40 at the Kunming Fighter Base, China (courtesy Robert B. Denny).

Around Christmas of 1944, while visiting in Southern California, Tex Hill and his wife, Maizie, introduced R.O. Denny to Major Moseley's daughter, Marquita. They were

Overhauling the Douglas B-26 Invader in the Grand Central Hangar (courtesy Robert B. Denny).

married that next summer. Denny retired as a major and went to work for Moseley at Grand Central. During this time, Denny learned the aircraft modification and overhaul business and made contacts with many of the finest aircraft engineers, managers, and craftsmen in Southern California. One of the many jobs that Denny oversaw as president of Grand Central was overhauling Douglas A/B-26 aircraft.

After about five years, Denny decided that working for his father-in-law wasn't what he wanted long term. Through Moseley, Denny had met many of the LA area's high-society people. When he and wife Marquita decided to strike out on their own in the aircraft overhaul and modification business, Denny went looking for an investor. He found one in Mr. William H. Doheny, the grandson of E.L. Doheny, one of the founders of the Southern California oil industry. Doheny agreed to put up the money to build a first-class facility from scratch at the Van Nuys Airport. The site chosen was the "back 40" of a structural steel company, just south of the California Air National Guard base, and right next to the Van Nuys control tower.

The Birth and Growth of On Mark

Denny and Doheny formed the On Mark Engineering Company. The company name comes from their wives' names, Onnalee and Marquita. The company was started in a storage building in Burbank that had been used to store part of Doheny's collection of rare Ferrari race cars. *[Author's note: I clearly remember walking into that building on Winona Avenue and seeing what seemed like dozens of bright red Ferraris. I watched as they moved several out onto a trailer under their own power. The sound is still amazing to me.]*

On Mark facility (courtesy Richard E. Fulwiler).

The Van Nuys facility was completed and opened in 1954. For the next 10 years, On Mark produced A-26-based civilian executive aircraft conversions of increasing sophistication, departing more and more from the original A-26C design. All aircraft were certificated in the Limited category and thus could not be used for compensation or hire. Key modifications introduced along the way included:

- Full instrument panel and copilot controls with state-of-the-art avionics
- Metal cockpit roof panels
- Additional windows, including panoramic windows for passengers
- Deluxe hand-crafted leather and naugahyde interiors, fabricated and installed by On Mark craftsmen
- An air-stair door in the belly (replacing the gunner's hatch), later replaced by an air-stair door on the starboard side aft of the wing root.
- The so-called "103-inch nose," an extended fiberglass nose, which could hold baggage and weather radar
- Aft ring-spar replacing the carry-through spar and opening up the cabin substantially
- Permanently mounted 165-gallon tip tanks
- DC-6 brakes and wheels, including Bendix Hytrol anti-skid feature
- DC-6 engine package, with the 2500-hp R-2800 CB16/17 engine and a specially cut-down reversible propeller, the Hamilton Standard 43E60
- Redesigned cowling and air intake to minimize effects of icing
- Anti-icing systems on wings and control surfaces

The On Mark hangar in about 1959. Note the military aircraft being overhauled, the executive "Marketeer" model, and an old Beech E-50 Twin Bonanza taken in trade for one of the executive aircraft (courtesy Richard E. Fulwiler).

- Increased area vertical stabilizer with vortex generators on the critical side to reduce single-engine air minimum control speed (Vmc) with the increased power output
- A completely redesigned fuselage featuring stand-up cabin, pressurization, and cockpit windshield and side windows from the DC-6
- Wing spar cap to increase the bending moment capability of the wing
- Two special aircraft were built for the CIA and had rear cargo drop doors. At least one is referred to as the Blue Goose (maybe the Goose is really two aircraft). These aircraft were probably contemporaries of the B-26K; they may have been built between the time of the YB-26K and the production of the B-26K.

The B-26K Counter-Invader

In the early 1960s, On Mark was working on a counterinsurgency aircraft, which would be an upgraded B-26 which would use the DC-6 engines, propellers, and wheel/ brake sets it had introduced into its civilian line. A series of catastrophic wing failures

On Mark Engineering Van Nuys, California
Douglas A-26 Invader based conversions.
The B-26K / A-26A

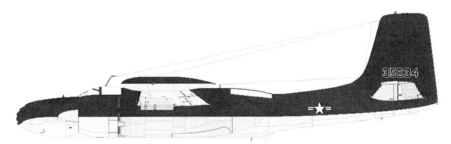

YB-26K Counter Invader (prototype) 44-35634

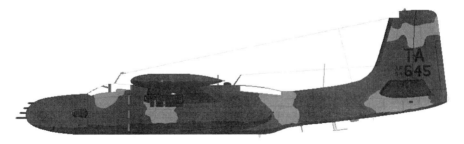

B-26K / A-26A " NIMROD " (64-17645) with 609th S.O.S., NKP Thailand, 1969.

Richard E. Fulwiler 2012

Drawings of prototype and converted A-26A combat aircraft (courtesy Richard E. Fulwiler).

Photograph of the YB-26K, probably taken at the time of Air Force evaluation flights during 1963 (courtesy Richard E. Fulwiler).

Another view of YB-26K prototype aircraft (courtesy Richard E. Fulwiler).

on the original B-26 being used in Southeast Asia caused the Air Force to ground its B-26 fleet. The problem was a combination of structural fatigue and the stresses generated by "rolling pullouts" while releasing ordnance from wing mounts. The Air Force needed a medium attack aircraft capable of more than the single-engine AJ/A-1E.

On Mark's experience and reputation, combined with R.O. Denny's connections with the military, provided the opportunity to produce this new aircraft. Implementation was accelerated, and the YB-26K made its maiden flight in January 1963. Production of the B-26K began in early 1964. *[Author's note: I recall meeting Capt. Dan Grob. He was involved at around this time and may have been the Air Force acceptance test pilot.]* Production continued through mid–1965, at which time the specified 40 aircraft had been completed and accepted by the Air Force.

Richard E. Fulwiler and Martin J. Simpson

The author connected with "Rick" Fulwiler in 2011 while researching the A/B-26 and On Mark. Rick is undoubtedly the world's authority on the technical details and aircraft histories of both civilian and military modifications made by On Mark. Rick pointed me to Martin Simpson's incredible website dedicated to the A/B-26 Invader. Martin has extensively researched the A/B-26 in all respects, making him the world's authority on the Douglas-built Invaders. Simpson and Fulwiler have collaborated to produce an online reference for the Invader, the results of which can be viewed on the website https://napoleon130.tripod.com/index.html.

In conclusion, I am proud of my father's role in founding On Mark Engineering Company, and in On Mark's crucial work in "remanufacturing" 40 B-26 aircraft into the A-26A aircraft so effectively flown in combat out of Nakhon Phanom Royal Thai AFB in 1966–69.

B-26 to A-26

How Could We Not Love It?

John Sodergren

The only other bomber I flew was the B-25 in Aviation Cadets. The Mitchell was a gentle airplane that helped keep 100-hour pilots from doing themselves in.

I soloed in an Aeronca Champ as a teenager in 1953, and I received my USAF wings in 1958.

My total hours are approximately 20,000. I have shoeboxes full of pocket-sized logbooks that I hope to total "someday," but I stopped totaling after getting my ATP at 10,000+/-.

I checked out in the B-26 at Hurlburt Field in the spring of 1963, and then went to Bien Hoa under "Farm Gate," arriving in July and returning to Hurlburt in January

1964. George Rose presented an excellent overview in *A-26 CLASSICS #6* of the operation at Bien Hoa. Who comes up with those names? "Farm Gate" was part of "Jungle Jim," a name with much more pizzazz.

As most know, the old B-26s were grounded when a wing separated from one during a firepower demonstration at Eglin AFB in February 1964. I had the unpleasant duty of escorting the widow and the body of the navigator on a train to Arlington.

While waiting for our "K" models to arrive, I checked out in the C-46, and then in the "K." The "K" did not have a mission at that time, so we had a great flying club with an awesome airplane to fly anywhere we wanted in between training.

I will be forever grateful to the USAF for loaning me an airplane to fly into Navy Dallas on the first leg of a cross-country to take my tests for AAL. On December 27, 1965, I started my 30-year career with AAL. Soon after, flights to Navy Dallas were forbidden. I have around 400 hours in the A/B-26.

As to comparable airplanes, only the B-25 was similar to the A-26s vs. B-26s. The B-26 was a little more agile, but it had World War II instruments and navigation aids, such as suction-driven gyros and an ADF. We became quite proficient with "needle, ball, and airspeed" instrument flying when the flares went out as we were pointing at the sky pulling "Gs" after dive-bombing when the gyros tumbled. Navigation was a map in our navigator's lap with ground radar pointing us in the general direction of the target until we saw the firefight.

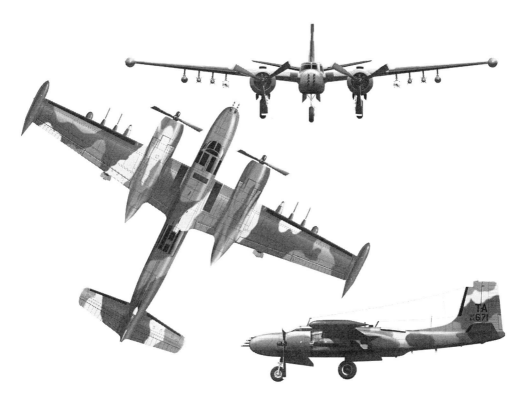

Three views of the A-26A Counter Invader aircraft flown by Nimrod crews (photo real illustration courtesy of Harry Whitver. During the Vietnam War, Harry Whitver served as a U.S. Navy combat artist in the Pacific: see his art works at *whitver.com*).

When we got the "K" models, or "A-26A," we were as giddy as the kids who got new Schwinn bikes at Christmas! Electric gyros! VOR! Tacan! Anti-skid brakes! Reversing props! Bigger engines with ADI! And the wings stayed on, too! Wow! I guess you could say we *loved* our new airplanes, and I give a Farm Gate tip of my bush hat to the Nimrods who did the airplane and themselves proud.

At this point, I am supposed to say what I liked and did not like about the '26s, but I think my paragraph above covers it. I will add that in spite of the problems with the "B-26," we enjoyed flying it. At that time, in the early days of the war, it was, along with the A-1, the best plane available for that environment. Besides, it was such a pretty airplane. How could we not love it?

Here are my thoughts on maintenance. All I can say, as a nonmaintenance person, is that our mechanics, armament guys, and the others did a great job of keeping these relics in the air. My apologies to the sheet metal men who repaired one of our airplanes when I joined the Paul Bunyan Club and harvested a bit of jungle during a poorly executed napalm run. My navigator, Dave Dennis, yelled, "You are too steep!" And he was right.

My favorite story? I shall refrain from relating my "The Spin" story that scared the heck out of us, and instead narrate "The Bridge" incident instead:

We always had a B-26 deployed to Da Nang. On this occasion, we were following a FAC to a target. When we arrived near the area, he said he wanted us to take out a bridge. Oh boy, a *real* target, not just another splinter mission, that is, bombing smoke from the marker rising above the jungle.

In those days of 20-20 vision, I had the eyes of an eagle, but we could not see the bridge that the FAC marked with smoke. Then he said it was a *rope* bridge, but we still could not see it. He finally pointed out a big tree and said that the rope was tied to the tree! As I recall, I had 500-pound bombs on our wing racks and not the usual napalm, so I bombed the tree. I am ashamed to say that it took *two* bombs to cut the rope.

My final thoughts on the Invader? I would have to say that of all the airplanes I have flown, I enjoyed the few hours I had in the A/B-26 above them all. Maybe it was the combination of the adrenaline flowing, my comrades, or the satisfaction of a mission well flown. I guess this airplane, being associated with the most exciting days of my life, makes it so special. And besides, as I said above, it was so pretty, so how could we not love it?

NOTES

1. See "The Vietnam War Almanac," OPERATIONS, *Air Force Magazine*, September 2004.

2. "Project Farm Gate," Air Commando Association, Mary Esther, Florida; http://www.specialoperations.net/page3.html Note: A third B-26 was lost in combat northwest of Pleiku on 8 April 1963 reportedly due to wing failure during a strafing run, killing Captain Andrew C. Mitchell III (pilot) and Captain Jerry A. Campaigne (navigator).

3. Joe Kittinger became one of the legendary Air Force pilots and combat leaders of the Vietnam War era. His nickname, "Jumping Joe," originated with his record high-altitude balloon parachute jump exceeding 100,000 feet in the early 1960s. (See YouTube video showing that amazing feat.) (See also *Come Up and Get Me*, an autobiography of Colonel Joe Kittinger, University of New Mexico Press, 2010.)

4. See generally, www.nationalmuseum.af.mil/factsheets/factsheet.asp?id=301.

CHAPTER 2

Big Eagle

Project Big Eagle

In the spring of 1966, U.S. military commanders were becoming increasingly concerned about the flow of communist military supplies from North Vietnam to South Vietnam by way of the Ho Chi Minh Trail in Laos. According to the Geneva Accords of 1962, Laos was supposed to be a neutral country, and all foreign military forces were supposed to withdraw from Laos. However, the "Secret War in Laos" became a major battleground in the power struggle between North Vietnam (supported by the Soviet Union and China) and South Vietnam (supported by the United States and its allies). Communist military forces, principally the North Vietnamese Army (NVA), simply ignored the Geneva Accords and remained in Laos in large numbers supporting communist Pathet Lao forces in northern Laos and using the Ho Chi Minh Trail in eastern Laos as their primary transportation conduit to flow troops and supplies to Viet Cong and NVA communist troops and battlefields throughout South Vietnam.

By this time, the remanufactured B-26K aircraft were ready for deployment back to the Vietnam War. General McConnell, chief of staff of the U.S. Air Force, decided to deploy eight B-26K aircraft and crews to Southeast Asia on a trial basis. Rather than deploy the B-26K back to South Vietnam, the decision was made to deploy the eight B-26K aircraft to Nakhon Phanom Royal Thai Air Force Base (RTAFB), Thailand, to test the effectiveness of the B-26K in combat in Laos. No doubt, USAF planners had not forgotten the effectiveness of B-26 aircraft and crews in interdiction and close air support roles in the Korean War, and the fact that B-26 crews had established a distinguished record in nighttime combat operations in South Vietnam. Nakhon Phanom RTAFB (simply known as "NKP" to American military personnel) was selected as the logical basing choice for the B-26Ks because of its advantageous tactical location in Thailand. NKP was situated close to the Mekong River in northeast Thailand, only 40–50 miles from the Ho Chi Minh Trail in eastern Laos. Because of that key location, NKP became the key Air Commando and prop airbase in all of Thailand. Not only would combat aircraft based at NKP be able to defend Thailand against any communist attacks, they would also be able to attack communist forces in Laos and North and South Vietnam. One diplomatic concern was quickly resolved: the B-26K bomber aircraft were redesignated A-26A attack aircraft because Thai government officials did not want bomber aircraft based on their soil (attack aircraft defending Thailand passed the diplomatic test).

Only the A-26A pilots, navigators, and armament and maintenance personnel who flew to Thailand on a six-month TDY (temporary duty) assignment in support of Big

Flying an A-26A training mission at England AFB, LA; note white helmets (courtesy Al Shortt).

View through the A-26A's gunsight crosshairs (training mission—no ammo) (courtesy Al Shortt).

Eagle can really appreciate the excitement and the magnitude of that deployment. First, extensive training and preparation had to take place back at England AFB, Louisiana. The pilots and navigators had to become proficient at flying the aircraft, and at conducting practice bombing and strafing runs on the bombing ranges near England AFB. The armament crews had to become familiar with the varied types of ordnance to be used, and most importantly, their associated arming and safety features. The maintenance crews had to learn how to maintain the remanufactured aircraft at home, and then take that knowledge and capability with them as they relocated to the new and challenging environment of northeast Thailand.

The Big Eagle contingent arrived at NKP in June of 1966. The event was not carried in the local or U.S. news, but it was nevertheless a big event for everyone involved. USAF military officials showed up to welcome the A-26A crews as they landed and departed the aircraft. Fortunately, some astute USAF photographer captured the event on film. The photos of the aircraft landing and rolling out on the NKP runway are superb. The expressions on the faces of the pilots and navigators tell the story of the excitement of arriving at NKP. The "bush hats" and uniforms of the greeters, and the PSP (pierced steel planking) taxiways, tell the story of that time period in U.S. military history.

Weather was a major factor in the Big Eagle deployment. The wet monsoon (rainy season) in Thailand and Laos extends from late April through October each year. Since the A-26A contingent arrived at NKP in June of 1966, they arrived in the middle of the wet monsoon season, causing them to experience a somewhat slow start to the combat

Big Eagle: Arrival of A-26A Counter Invaders at Nakhon Phanom RTAFB, June 1966 (USAF).

Big Eagle: Rollout after landing at Nakhon Phanom RTAFB, Thailand, June 1966 (USAF).

Pete DiMaggio, navigator (left), and Joe Maynard, pilot, NKP, June 1966 (USAF).

Joe Maynard being greeted at NKP, June 1966 (USAF).

trial period. For the most part, upon their arrival, the dirt road network of the Ho Chi Minh Trail was impassable due to heavy rains. However, the Big Eagle crews immediately began flying orientation and familiarization missions along the Trail with the assistance of FAC (forward air controller) pilots already assigned at NKP. Nighttime combat tactics had not been developed yet, and daytime attack missions were sporadic and dangerous. There were hundreds of NVA antiaircraft guns all along the 1,300-mile length of the Ho Chi Minh Trail. The first loss in combat took place on June 28, 1966. On that date, during a daytime familiarization mission, Captain Charles Dudley (pilot), Captain Anthony Cavalli (navigator), and Captain Thomas Wolfe (FAC pilot occupying the A-26A jump seat behind the navigator) lost their lives during a strafing run on a communist antiaircraft gun position. That tragic loss taught the Big Eagle crews that taking on gun positions on the Trail in daylight hours was not to their advantage. Communist truck drivers on the Trail also learned that daytime operations were not to their advantage. The result was that almost all communist truck resupply activity on the Trail in 1966 shifted from daytime to nighttime operations. The A-26A and general U.S. military response in 1966 followed suit.

As the months passed in late 1966, the A-26A flight and support crews became more proficient in their combat roles. The dry season (lasting from November to the end of April) saw truck traffic and combat activity on the Trail increase dramatically. The Big Eagle crews refined their nighttime combat operations with the various

Big Eagle greeting party, Nakhon Phanom RTAFB, Thailand, June 1966 (USAF).

FAC pilots and crews. The FAC crews were also Air Commandos based at NKP and used the radio communications call sign Blind Bat or Lamplighter (C-130s), Candlestick (C-123s), and Nail (O-2s). Optimally, the FAC crews would find and mark targets (either with high-intensity flares or ground "logs") and direct the A-26A pilots to strike a target on a certain azimuth and distance from a specified location on the ground. Once the initial attack had taken place, the FAC pilot could adjust the target parameters for the A-26A crew as needed. The following Big Eagle assessment appears in *Foreign Invaders*[1]:

> At first the A-26s were not all that successful. There had been relatively few night-time armed reconnaissance missions flown along the Trail before the arrival of the Invaders, and the tactics were still in their infancy. But things improved as the months went by, and in December 1966 the A-26s claimed a total of 99 trucks destroyed or damaged during a total of 175 missions in *Steel Tiger*. This translated as 80 per cent of the total USAF claims for the month, in only seven per cent of the sorties. The results achieved by Project *Big Eagle* were therefore good enough for the USAF to decide to base A-26s at NKP on a permanent basis, keeping the AC-47s for use in South Vietnam. Replacement crews had started arriving in November, giving them some time to absorb the experiences of the [Big Eagle] TDY crews before these left. There had been two additional A-26 losses by the end of 1966 … but several replacement and reinforcement aircraft had also arrived at NKP, bringing the strength up to twelve Invaders by early January 1967.

On Mark A-26—Nakhon Phanom, Thailand—1966–67

JOE KITTINGER

In 1961, when the Air Commandos were first organized, I feel certain that if there were sufficient numbers of P-51s or P-47s available that those aircraft would have been included in the inventory as well. However, there were no P-47s in the inventory and few P-51s.

In 1962, the Air Commandos initiated a contract with the On Mark Corporation in Van Nuys, California, to modify and rebuild the B-26. The first test flight of the B-26 "K" model was in January 1963. The modifications included installing R-2800 52W engines with paddle-bladed propellers and a low-tension ignition system that was not susceptible to magneto drops in humid conditions, full prop reverse, DC-6 wheels and brakes, a new wing spar with strengthened and modified tail and wing sections, tip tanks to increase fuel capacity and loiter time over targets, a completely

Jack Blount (left) and Joe Kittinger (courtesy Randy Ryman).

modified modern cockpit with excellent night lighting, eight forward-firing 50-caliber machine guns and four external store racks on each wing. Two items that were requested by the Air Commando test pilots for the new B-26Ks were air-conditioning and nose gear steering. Both were disapproved by armchair nonfliers. The nose gear steering would have saved a few aircraft when landing on short wet PSP (steel planking) runway and one of the engines not going into reverse at the same time. The air-conditioning would have been a welcome addition in the hot, humid conditions in the air over Laos and Vietnam, and it only would have cost $3,000 per aircraft. Forty aircraft were ordered into production in November 1963. The designation of the aircraft was later changed from the B-26K model to the A-26.

My first flight in the B-26K was on 5 January 1965 at Hurlburt AFB, Florida. In September 1965, I was transferred to England AFB, Louisiana, and assigned as the operations officer of the newly formed 603rd Air Commando Squadron flying in the first B-26K aircraft. We had a pretty good idea that we would be going back to Southeast Asia and that our missions would be flown mostly at night. In our training we emphasized flare drops and night ordnance delivery. Our night tactics range was at a bombing range at the U.S. Army facility at Fort Polk about 70 miles west of England AFB. We had a daytime gunnery range just a few miles south of England.

In May of 1966 we were informed that we would be deploying eight A-26s to Nakhon Phanom, Thailand. I immediately volunteered to lead the eight-ship formation to Thailand. Much to my surprise, I was selected to lead the formation. I was elated. I immediately asked Gene Valentine to obtain the maps for the trans-Pacific flight and to start planning the route. Gene did an excellent job of assembling the maps and preparing the flight plans. One day, the wing commander, Colonel Vollett, called me up to his office, where he asked me if there was anything that I needed for the deployment. I said, "Yes, sir, I would like to have First Sergeant Carlos Christian assigned to our deployment." Vollett replied, "No, Carlos is one of the best soldiers in the Wing and I can't do without him." I replied, "Well, you asked me and I told you what I needed." However, later that day, after asking Carlos if he wanted to go, Colonel Vollett agreed to sending Carlos as the first sergeant of our detachment. Carlos provided the detachment with his invaluable leadership of the enlisted men. Carlos had been with the original Air Commandos in Burma and was an outstanding Air Commando and Air Force NCO.

In preparation for the trans-Pacific flights, our aircraft were modified by installing an 800-gallon fuel tank in the bomb bay and a 55-gallon drum of engine oil in the observer's seat behind the navigator's seat. There was a selector valve on the tank that allowed the oil to be directed to either the left or the right engine oil tank and a hand pump to move the oil from the drum to the engine. Every hour the navigator would turn the crank on the hand pump enough times to transfer one gallon of oil into the selected oil tank. With the 800-gallon fuel tank, we had more fuel capacity and longer flying time than the regular fuel tank.

On 9 June 1966 we departed England AFB escorted by 2 KC-97s, one from the Georgia Air National Guard and one from the Tennessee Air National Guard. Each KC-97 carried the needed spare parts for the overseas flights and several crew chiefs to maintain and service the aircraft. Of course, we placed our best crew chiefs on these aircraft. During the flight to Travis AFB, California, we checked out the 800-gallon fuel tank and the oil resupply system. The flight to Travis was uneventful.

The next morning we departed for Hickam AFB, Hawaii. I assigned four A-26s to each KC-97. I led the first flight of four behind the Georgia ANG KC-97. The other four A-26s followed the Tennessee ANG KC-97. The second KC-97 and four A-26s stayed about one mile in trail of the lead KC-97. For air traffic control purposes we were handled as one flight. Both of the KC-97s had navigators aboard with sextants and Loran Navigation systems to assist in the navigation challenge from Travis to Hickam. Each A-26 also followed the progress of the flight (with Gene Valentine's maps) in the event that the KC-97s made a mistake on the navigation challenge. Our aircraft did not have any HF radio capability so we depended on the KC-97s to communicate to the appropriate air traffic control centers. The flight was long, uneventful, and fun.

After a 10-hour, 35-minute flight, we arrived at Hickam. At Travis we had decided that for the landing at Hickam that the two flights of A-26s would be led on to the initial approach by the KC-97s, which would be separated by one mile. We rolled onto

A-26 aircraft and crews over Pacific en route to Big Eagle assignment, 1966 (courtesy Joe Kittinger).

the initial approach and our leader from the Georgia ANG started a descent so that we would be at 500 feet over the approach end of the runway for the pitch up for landing. The copilot of our KC-97, a brand-new second lieutenant, thought that his aircraft was on the final approach and lowered the landing gear. Pandemonium ensued. Aircraft went in every direction as the KC-97 violently decelerated. It was amazing that we did not have a midair collision—but we didn't. The second lieutenant was named Lieutenant Fuzz at the bar that evening and retained that title from then on.

After each landing for the remainder of the flights across the Pacific, our crew chiefs would fix any maintenance discrepancies, refuel the aircraft, and prepare the aircraft for the next day's flight. During the entire voyage, we did not have a single abort because of the professionalism and hard work by our crew chiefs. They were Air Commandos and damn proud of it.

We took off the next day (11 June) for Wake (5:30); followed the next day (12 June) to Midway (4:50); followed by the next day (13 June) to Guam (6:05); followed by the next day (14 June) to Clark (6:15).

We had two unusual incidents at Wake and Midway. At Wake Island the aircraft commander of the KC-97 from the Georgia Air National Guard, "Black Jack Gannon," got into a heated discussion with the U.S. marshal and I had to mediate to keep him out of confinement. It worked. "Black Jack," an Alleghany Airlines pilot when he wasn't flying for the Air National Guard, was a real character that kept us laughing the entire trip. And then the next day we headed off for Midway Island. There was a very extensive Notam (notice to airmen) informing the pilots that albatrosses (gooney birds) were

A-26 crewmembers taking a break during Pacific island-hopping, 1966 (courtesy Joe Kittinger).

a protected bird and that they would frequently encroach on the runways and taxiways and that they had the "right of way." On taxiing in following the landing at Midway, a gooney bird ran into the propeller of my number two aircraft. It decapitated the bird. When we walked into base operations, we were confronted by rangers from the U.S. Department of Agriculture, the guardians of the gooney birds at Midway. The pilot had to fill out a dozen different forms. The ranger commenced to give us hell for killing a gooney bird. We just sat there patiently until he ran down. I then asked the ranger what would happen tomorrow if one of our 10 aircraft killed another gooney bird. He said that the aircraft commander would have to return to Base Operations and fill out the proper forms. I informed him that procedure would not work as we were a 10-ship formation and none would return to Base Ops in the event that a bird was struck. He did not appreciate my position but I could not have cared less. I suggested that I fill out the forms and leave the areas blank that I could not fill in. I would sign the forms and he could fill out the blank spaces if we hit a gooney bird the next day. He did not like that idea. As I was leaving, I told the ranger that he and his people had better be out there the next morning and remove all of the gooney birds near the taxiways and runways so that we would not hit any of their birds during our taxiing out and takeoff. For the rest of our stay, we were constantly entertained by the gooney birds. Most of the entertainment was watching the young gooney birds trying to learn how to fly. When taking off, albatrosses need to take a run to allow enough air to move over the wing to provide lift. The beginning aviators would run like hell and crash. It was hilarious. There were hundreds of these birds all over the island trying to learn to fly; it was a constant joke. Once the gooney birds learned to fly, they were then albatrosses and were the most graceful bird in the sky.

When we arrived at Clark, I briefed our flight crews and support personnel that our next flight would be over South Vietnam into Nakhon Phanom. Charlie Day (one of the best crew chiefs that I ever knew) approached me after the briefing and said, "Sir, don't you think that we should have our .50-caliber guns loaded for the flight over South Vietnam?" I thought that was a great idea, but we had not planned on this contingency and had no .50-caliber ammo with us, which I explained to Sergeant Day. He said, "Sir, let me take care of that problem." I agreed. An Air Commando can accomplish any task—just get out of the way. Somehow, Sergeant Day scrounged 20,000 rounds of .50-caliber ammo and with our crew chiefs (not gun plumbers) loaded all 48 .50-caliber guns—ready to shoot if needed. He also scrounged an additional 25,000 rounds of ammo that he loaded into the KC-97s.

We had to delay the next day because of weather, but on 17 June after a five-hour flight from Clark, eight A-26s and two KC-97s landed at Nakhon Phanom (NKP), which we called "Naked Fanny." We were met on the flight line by Colonel Curto, our detachment commander, Lieutenant Colonel Al Howarth, our squadron commander, and the other Air Commandos of our "Big Eagle" Detachment—and a cool can of beer. We said "goodbye" to the crews of the two KC-97s, who departed that day headed back to the ZI. We thoroughly enjoyed our transit across the Pacific and the great pilots and airmen of the Georgia and Tennessee Air National Guard. They were real professionals.

The next two days were used to prepare the aircraft for combat, which included removing the 800-gallon ferry tank and the supplemental oil systems. We had been told that most of our missions would be accomplished at night on the Ho Chi Minh Trail (HCMT) in Laos. Some really smart tactician at 7th Air Force Headquarters decided that our first flights would be over the Trail in daylight with a full ordnance load. The first mission was flown by Colonel Curto, who experienced no problems. The second flight, which took off a few minutes after Colonel Curto, was shot down over the HCMT and the crew lost. What a beginning. First day of combat, second flight in combat, and a loss. That got our attention.

From then on we concentrated on developing the ordnance loads and tactics for servicing the HCMT at night, even though we still did occasional daylight missions, usually late in the day, sometimes with a FAC.

We were developing tactics and ordnance loads for a night interdiction mission that was new to the Air Force in Vietnam. The B-26 had been used at night in Korea but we were trying to stop truck traffic on the main logistics artery into South Vietnam using ordnance better designed to stop trucks. We also had a much better and safer aircraft in the A-26.

The Ho Chi Minh Trail running down eastern Laos was the centerpiece of the Laotian war because of its importance to North Vietnam as a lifeline to its troops in South Vietnam. The Trail network winds south from the Mu Gia pass in between North Vietnam and Laos. In addition, arteries of the HCMT wind south out of Laos into Cambodia, where they reach the Saigon area provinces of Tay Ninh, Phuoc Long, and Binh Long. The HCMT was not a single road but rather a honeycomb of routes, passing through country that was alternately limestone karst, triple-canopy jungle, and grassland. Military historian John Prados says there were "five main roads, 29 branch roads, and many cutoffs and bypasses, adding up altogether to about 12,000 miles of roads."

Ho Chi Minh Trail showing typical dirt road, karst, and numerous bomb craters (courtesy Joe Kittinger).

There were four identifiable interdiction points on the HCMT that we monitored/serviced: Alpha, Bravo, Charlie, and Delta. These were sections of the HCMT that had been bombed repeatedly to the point that the craters, etc. made truck traffic through these checkpoints hazardous to the enemy. These "choke points" were about 100 miles east of NKP and south of Mu Gia pass. The tactic was to try to catch trucks driving through this area and drop ordnance or to use the 50-caliber guns to stop and destroy the vehicles.

FACS flew over the HCMT during the daylight hours looking for trucks that were parked in the jungles adjacent to the HCMT. Fighters were usually available, on call to respond to the FACs if they found a lucrative target or a truck park. Usually the trucks did not move during the daylight hours because of the FAC surveillance of the Trail. They did move at night, which made them our target. We closely monitored the daily intelligence reports of missions made during the day so we would know where the trucks had been and the locations of the enemy guns. During this period of time, the SA-2 missiles had not been deployed this far south. The A-26 did not have any radio/electrical means to detect if the aircraft was being tracked by the radar system associated with the SA-2. One of our SAC navigators suggested that the radio compass receiver (ADF) might detect the SA-2 radar at the upper limits of the radio frequencies. Some of the navigators believed in this rumor and religiously monitored the high frequencies of the radio compass (ADF) receivers during the missions over the HCMT. It made them feel safer so why not?

We always carried six night flares on a rack on each wing. We also carried a full load of .50-cal ammo—with no tracers. Tracers at night provides the ground gunners

A-26 wing munitions configuration showing CBU canisters and flare racks (courtesy Joe Kittinger).

an excellent target. In the A-26 we could select either the left bank of guns (four), the right bank of guns (four), or all guns. We would load the guns so that if we charged the guns once, two guns in the bank would fire, and if we charged the guns twice, we could fire the other two guns. This gave us the capability of selecting two, four, six, or eight guns, depending on how many times we charged the guns and what bank of guns were selected. Frequently, we would select just two guns for exploratory probing of the target area, but if we had an identifiable target we could really service it by selecting all eight guns—that was a serious amount of bullets directed into the target.

We experimented with a variety of ordnance attempting to determine the best ordnance to service the target. The CBU bomb/weapons were the most effective to kill trucks. We tried every bomb and CBU available trying to get the best kill ratio on the trucks. We dropped thousands of three-prong steel tire penetrators on the HCMT; regardless of how it landed, one prong was up and ready to penetrate tires. We loaded them on the closed bomb bay doors and released them by opening the bomb bay doors over a suitable stretch of road making up the HCMT. I still have one in my collection.

On about half of our night missions on the HCMT, we worked with a C-130 aircraft that dropped flares on the known interdiction points and any other suspected truck parks. The call sign for these C-130s was "Blind Bat" and the aircraft operated out of Ubon in Thailand. When over Laos at night the C-130 pilot did not turn on the red rotating beacon or navigation lights, but he did turn on four white lights on top of the aircraft that we could see when flying above the C-130. These white lights also enabled us to see where the aircraft was during our dive-bombing runs on the targets as we would release the ordnance at an altitude below the C-130s. We would coordinate the drop of the initial flare by having the C-130 delay dropping the flare until we were in position to roll in immediately after the flare ignited. The best chance of catching a truck in the open was on that initial flare. We had our highest percentage of kills on that first flare. Only on about 25 percent of the time would a target be discovered on the first flare and ordnance be delivered. There were a lot of exploratory drops of flares seeking a target. The C-130 also dropped a device that we called a "log." The C-130 would drop a "log" to hit near a choke point. On landing the log would ignite and burn bright red for about an hour before it went out. When the C-130 departed after they had dropped all of their flares, the log would mark the choke point for servicing. Frequently we would drop ordnance on the log with no flares trying to catch an unexpected truck in the open. After the departure of the C-130, if any ordnance and fuel was available, we would drop our own flares working the Trail.

Our rules were that we could not claim a truck killed (destroyed) unless it burned. Frequently, we would destroy the truck with a direct hit but the truck would not burn; therefore, we could not claim it as a kill—only as damaged. The trucks used diesel fuel, which is not as flammable as gasoline. Frequently, the truck would be completely surrounded by fuel but even with firing .50 cal into the wreckage we could not ignite the diesel. The jet fighter generals at 7th Air Force did not believe the effectiveness of the Nimrods and constantly challenged our kills whereas the jet fighters were claiming kills that did not burn. The Nimrod pilots were able to deliver munitions on any target with much more accuracy than the jet fighters, mainly because the A-26s were much closer to the targets and would roll in to deliver the ordnance at least 10,000 feet lower than the jet fighters and drop the ordnance at a much lower altitude. The A-26s were also delivering ordnance at least 250 mph slower than the jet fighters. The Nimrods flying at a much lower altitude were able to better identify the target and keep it in sight as they rolled in on the ordnance delivery pass. The airborne FACs all knew that the Nimrods were far superior when it came to ordnance delivery on the targets—day or night. Those are the facts.

The quarters at NKP were luxurious with two-men trailers (air-conditioned) with a bedroom at each end with a shower and toilet between the rooms. They were a far cry compared to the hooches (no air-conditioning) we lived in at Bien Hoa. We had shutters on the windows in the trailer. The maids knew that if the shutters were closed that the men were sleeping. The system worked. Since we flew at night we had a "happy hour" at the officers' club that started at 4 a.m. It was always fun to watch the frequent visitors come into the officers' club for breakfast and find pilots and navigators drinking alcoholic beverages for breakfast. We never did tell them that that we had been flying all night and that this was our relaxing/downtime.

In addition to the nightly missions on the HCMT in Laos we also had a mission to support guerrillas in northern Laos. These guerrillas were led by Thai mercenaries hired by the CIA. The call signs were "Tallman" and "Red Hat." After takeoff we would proceed north from NKP towards a Tacan (a navigation system) situated in northern Laos. We would contact either "Tallman" or "Red Hat" by our radio and they would give us a position heading and bearing from the Tacan to the enemy position that they wanted serviced. We would go to the stated position and drop a flare. The ground FAC would then give changes to where he wanted the next flare dropped. After the next flare he would describe just where the target was located. Usually, we would make the first pass on the target with the guns to determine if we knew exactly where the target was. If we were not right on the target, the ground FAC would give us changes, such as 100 yards to the east of where we had fired the guns, etc. We would then climb up, drop another flare, and service the target with CBUs or bombs. Usually, we would get secondary fires and explosions when the CBUs fell with much merriment from the ground FACS. It was a fun mission working with the Thai guerrillas as they really got excited. At the conclusion of a mission, Tallman told me that he was coming out of the woods for a rest. I asked him to stop by our base and that we would have a party for him. He said that he would. I really wanted to meet this warrior that I had worked with for several months. Unfortunately, it was not to be. A few days before he was to be lifted out of the jungle, when coming back through his own lines following a reconnaissance mission, he was shot by one of his own men who mistook him for the enemy. A few weeks later, I was brought an ancient Hmong rifle that "Tallman" was bringing as a gift to me. I still have the rifle and the memories of the missions that I had with that brave warrior.

One afternoon in September, our squadron commander, Lieutenant Colonel Al Howarth, took off for a late afternoon recce mission near the "Delta" interdiction point. I took off just at sundown going to replace him on target. As I crossed the Mekong River, which was just a few miles east of NKP, I heard Al call on the radio that he had been hit and was heading west. I called him and told him that I was heading towards him. A few minutes later, he called and reported that they were bailing out of the aircraft. After about 10 minutes, I saw the smoke from the burning aircraft and proceeded to the wreckage. I climbed up to 8,000 feet so that I would not give away his position to any enemy in the vicinity. I quickly established communications with Al on his survival radio. The sun was setting. I had already called Cricket, the airborne command and control aircraft, and reported the shoot down and the approximate location. I expected to be getting a call back from Cricket informing me that a rescue effort was under way. When I didn't hear anything I called and asked Cricket the status of the rescue. They reported back that the rescue would take place the next morning. I said, "Bullshit—let's pick them up now before the enemy picks them up." Al had flown far enough to the west before they had bailed out that they were probably out of a known hostile area. Cricket said to "stand by." Finally, I was told that a helicopter was being diverted to the area but that they were not certain that they would attempt the pickup that evening. I again said, "Bullshit, let's get them out—NOW!" Finally, the helicopter came up on the radio and asked me if there was any enemy activity in the area. I said, "Hell no. Just watch me." I turned on my rotating beacon and navigation lights, slowed down, and extended my landing lights and turned them on. I flew at 500 feet above the jungle with all of my lights on to demonstrate to the helicopter that there was no enemy ground fire in the vicinity. Finally, after I trolled over the area for about 10 minutes and there was no ground fire, the helicopter decided to attempt the pickups. That's when we discovered that there were three Nimrods on the ground. All were picked up and returned to NKP. After all were picked up, I headed to the HCMT and flew my mission. I think this was one of the few night pickups in Vietnam and Laos. Picking up a downed crew at night does have the advantage that it is easy to pick up the source of ground fire at night, and the helicopter has the advantage that the enemy can only hear and not see the pickup.

Also in September on a rainy night we suffered another loss when one of our aircraft ran out of fuel while on the final approach on a GCA. Both of the crewmembers were killed. The pilot had cut it too close on the fuel. Not all losses in combat are caused by enemy action.

In October I had a takeoff before sunset and headed for the Alpha choke point. It was still light when I arrived and I was instructed to contact a FAC, which I did. He informed me that he had a known position of a 23-mm gun position that had been shooting all afternoon at the fighters. He said that he knew exactly where the gun was located. He fired a smoke rocket at an opening about 50 meters from the Trail and told me that the gun was 50 feet short of where his rocket hit. He very accurately described the location of the gun. I could see the target. I armed up all eight guns and rolled in for the run. About 2,000 feet from the target I started shooting my guns at the gun position. Simultaneously, the enemy guns opened up on me. There was a solid stream of red tracers converging on me. My aircraft was severely shot up. Both generators were inoperative, the hydraulic system was destroyed, and the aircraft was difficult to fly. I knew that we were in trouble; however, I also knew exactly where that gun was so I pulled up off of the target, climbed to 4,000 feet, and set up my CBUs on the external wing stations. I could not drop the bombs in the bomb bay since I did not have any hydraulic pressure to open the bomb bay doors. I rolled over and started my dive-bomb run, which was a challenge because the aircraft was slow to respond to control inputs because of the extensive battle damage. But I was determined to destroy that gun position and I knew the exact location. At the right altitude and dive angle I dropped all of the CBUs, much to the delight of the FAC as I completely destroyed the gun site. Now I had to fly the wounded aircraft home. Unfortunately, there was a complete line of thunderstorms surrounding NKP so I had to head for Ubon Air Force Base about 100 miles south of NKP. Major Piper, the wing intelligence officer, was my navigator; he was completely calm and a joy to have with me in this very shot-up A-26. With no generators, electrical or hydraulic systems, we had our hands full. I gave him my flashlight, which he held on the standby flight instruments so that I could fly instruments. It was a completely black night with no moon. We flew in and out of the clouds and with Major Piper's accurate navigation we found the Mekong River and then saw the green rotating light of Ubon Air Base, which was home for an F-4 fighter wing. I had no radios and no external lights since the electrical system was shot up. We flew to the opposite side of the landing pattern of the F-4s, dodging rain showers and lightning. Finally, I saw an opportunity to make a landing. With no hydraulics we had to extend the landing gear using the emergency system. We also had no flaps. I landed and, using the emergency brakes, slowed down and turned off the runway. A maintenance crew close to the runway heard the A-26 tires hit the runway and called the tower. The tower had no idea that an aircraft had landed on their runway. After I had cleared the runway, I shut down both engines and thanked that grand lady for getting us safely back on the ground. Pretty soon, the crash crew headed our way. There was no fire going on the aircraft so the fire crew just stood by. Pretty soon an armament crew showed up. I asked them if they wanted me to help them download the .50-cal guns. The sergeant said quite indignantly that "they knew how to download 50s." My final remark to the armament crew chief was "that if they needed any help that we would be at the officers' club." With that we were driven to the officers' club. We immediately ordered two martinis apiece to debrief the mission and to give thanks for our survival. After we had consumed our second martini, I received a call from the armament sergeant asking me rather meekly if I could help them download the 50s. I told him no. They had had their chance for us to help them, which they had turned down. We had two martinis and were in no condition to assist them. I suggested that they call the armament section at NKP and ask for instructions on how to download the guns. It had been a hairy mission that attested to the ruggedness of the A-26, the professionalism of my copilot/navigator, and some luck. However, we did kill the 23-mm gun position that had caused our problem.

In August, Dick Secord, an Air Commando (major) who was now working as a liaison with the CIA, showed up at NKP to coordinate some proposed special missions near the HCMT. I was the contact with Dick on these special missions. Dick was in charge of the insertion of a seven-man team into the jungle close to the HCMT where they would monitor the truck traffic and personnel movement along this highway.

A week later an Air America helicopter landed at NKP and the mercenaries were quickly transported to a compound where they were placed in isolation. Dick briefed me and the helicopter crew on the tactics that we were to use. A helicopter makes a lot of noise and is quite visible even when flying low. The concern was that we did not want the enemy to know that we were dropping off mercenaries into their area. The challenge was to drop them far enough away from the enemy so that they would not be detected on insertion but not so far away from the HCMT that they would take an extreme amount of time to find a protected observation post from which to watch the traffic on the HCMT. Dick had selected an insertion location that would fit the bill. On this first mission I was to stay about 10 miles behind the helicopter and at altitude to be prepared to provide firepower if needed. I was not to fly close to the insertion point to assure that my aircraft would not compromise the insertion. Once the team was on the ground and in position they made periodic radio calls to their command post and provided real-time intelligence about the traffic on the HCMT. Usually, these teams stayed in the jungle for 10 days or so before they were lifted out by the helicopters. Sometimes they were discovered and suffered losses. It was not a very safe venture, but effective.

About a month later Dick and his helicopter with mercenaries were back for another insertion. This time a visiting colonel from Intelligence from 13th AF was to attend the briefing. As usual Dick was in civilian clothes and had no signs of rank. On this mission Dick wanted me to go about 10 miles away from the insertion point and drop some bombs and napalm as a diversion to mask the low-flying helicopter as it approached the insertion point. I would save the internal bomb load and the .50 cals to be available in case the helicopter or mercenaries needed my firepower. I thought it was a clever diversion. The visiting colonel made a big mistake. He said that he thought I should drop my ordnance closer to the insertion point. Dick replied, "Colonel, that's the dumbest idea I have ever heard, and, Colonel, we have already planned this mission and do not need any comments or suggestions from you." The colonel was rightly embarrassed and got quite red in the face. At the completion of the briefing, as we were walking out of the briefing room, the colonel asked me if Dick was in the Air Force. I told him, "I thought so." He then asked did I know the name of that colonel? (He assumed he was a colonel, not a major, because of his attitude. What major would talk to a colonel in that manner? Dick Secord, that's who.) I quickly walked away. That was Dick Secord. A very intelligent fighter pilot who didn't hesitate to express his thoughts. He rose to the rank of major general in the Air Force and had a very illustrious career. I flew four of those insertion missions for him and his mercenaries.

We should have been deploying U.S. forces and South Vietnamese Army units in great numbers starting in 1963 to stop the logistics train that the enemy had established on the HCMT in eastern Laos. I feel that we essentially lost the war in South Vietnam because the North Vietnamese operated with impunity along the HCMT supplying their army and guerrilla units with the supplies needed to engage our Army and the South Vietnamese Army. Starting in June of 1966, the small numbers of the A-26s available for the night interdiction mission on the HCMT were unable to stop all of the movement of supplies using the HCMT. The North Vietnamese used carts, bicycles, horses, and manpower to move supplies that the A-26s could not detect. For sure, U.S. and South Vietnamese ground forces could have stopped all of the enemy transport system on the HCMT. Not to have U.S. forces stopping these supply lines through Laos was a conscious decision that lost the war. In 1963 we had sufficient proof and intelligence that the North Vietnamese were supplying their forces by a logistics system running through Laos. We could not understand why we didn't deploy our U.S. Army forces into Laos to stop this constant flow of munitions and supplies to their forces in South Vietnam. We did the best that we could with the small numbers of A-26s, but our efforts stopped a very small portion of the supplies being moved at night.

We did have some fun. Sergeant Christian came to me one day and said, "Colonel, we have thousands of empty Pearl beer bottles that we have no way of disposing." (The price for a bottle of Pearl Beer was 10 cents, so that's why it was so popular at NKP.) I had an idea. I informed Sergeant Christian to bring a pickup truck load of empty Pearl beer bottles down to the flight line for my late afternoon mission. We opened the door in the rear of the aircraft, aft of the bomb bay, and loaded the empty Pearl beer bottles onto the closed bomb bay doors. The aircraft leaked beer all the way out to takeoff. After takeoff I flew to the east into North Vietnam and found a straight section of the road and dropped down on the deck. Low to the ground at a very high speed, at a suitable location, I opened the bomb bay doors and dropped the empty Pearl beer bottles. After landing back at NKP, Sergeant Christian and the flight line crew met me at the aircraft and we all sat there and laughed about what would be the reaction of the North Vietnamese when they found the empty beer bottles. I made several of these beer drops on roads in North Vietnam. I always flew very fast at a very low altitude. The aircraft did smell like a brewery after each mission. We always thought that the best use of Pearl beer was to drop the empties on the enemy in North Vietnam. These missions were a morale booster for the men.

In November, a U.S. Army ranger came to NKP and showed us the new gyro-stabilized night vision scope. I immediately thought that this might be a means to see trucks at night on the HCMT. I borrowed the system from the Ranger and on the night of a full moon I scheduled a special mission to determine if the scope would help to locate trucks. Since I was going to ride in the rear of the A-26, I scheduled one of my best pilots, John Wolfe, to fly the mission. I took with me an AR-15 rifle and 12 clips of ammo. We took off at 2200 hours and proceeded to the HCMT. When we arrived close to the HCMT, John opened the bomb bay doors, which gave me an unobstructed view of the ground, which was brilliantly illuminated by the full moon. John flew from south of the Delta choke point at about 1,000 feet above the ground to a point just short of the mountains south of the Mu Gia Pass. We made this run four times but I could not locate any trucks. Flying that low to the ground at night was an interesting experience. After an hour of flying and testing the night vision scope without sighting any trucks, I asked him to climb up to 2,000 feet above the ground and still fly down the HCMT. Just for the hell of it, I loaded up the AR-15 and shot 10 of the ammo clips through the open bomb bay doors at the Trail below. We wondered what the enemy thought as they saw and heard the AR-15 bullets striking the jungle adjacent to the Trail from an aircraft above.

I then told John to close the bomb bay doors, strapped into my seat in the rear compartment, and told him to go ahead with his normal night interdiction mission. Riding in the rear compartment as John delivered ordnance from the wings and bomb bay was a thrill that I would not like to repeat. This one flight that I made with the night vision scope did not indicate to me that it would be a viable tactic from an A-26. As far as I know, there were no further tests of this scope. I returned the scope back to the Ranger with my thanks. That was the one and only time that I ever rode in the rear compartment of a B- or A-26.

The first week of December saw the arrival of the new wing commander, Colonel Heinie Aderholt. He had been the vice wing commander at Hurlburt in 1963, where I worked for him on several special projects. He was a great leader of men and a warrior. Heinie was to the Air Commandos what Robin Olds was to the fighter pilots: a leader of warriors. Upon his arrival, great improvements were made at NKP and the morale was significantly improved.

A week before Christmas, Bob Hope and his group of entertainers landed at NKP in a C-130 to put on a show for the troops. All of the squadron commanders were lined up at the ramp of the C-130 to welcome Bob. When I shook his hand, I said, "Mr. Hope, I have about 50 men working on the flight line preparing our aircraft for the night missions and these men will not be able to attend your show." He said, "Do you have any transportation?" I said, "Yes, sir, I have my Jeep right here." He then replied, "Let's go visit your men." Bob personally talked with all of the engine mechanics, bomb loaders, and gun plumbers on the flight line and discussed where each man was from in the States, etc. After about 30 minutes, the director of the show finally found Bob on the flight line and said, "Mr. Hope, we must leave now to start the show." Bob thanked all of the men for their service to our country and wished them all a "merry Christmas." It was a very generous gesture on his part to spend that time on the flight line. I know that the men appreciated his consideration. I do remember that his group of entertainers consisted of Les Brown and his Band of Renown, Phyllis Diller, Jerry Colona, Anita Bryant, and the current Miss America. It was a helluva show put on by a great American entertainer.

Finally, in January 1967, my TDY tour at NKP was over. The newly arrived Nimrod pilots and navigators that would serve a year at NKP were trained and performing in a very effective and professional manner. Our Air Commando maintenance personnel had been replaced by the well-trained ground crew who would also be at NKP for a year.

The Loss of Nimrod 32

Harlan "Gene" Albee

The loss of Nimrod 32 early in Big Eagle operations brings up sad memories. This was a day mission, an area orientation for Captain Chuck Dudley and Lieutenant Tony Cavalli, on a bright, hot, sunny day—in two black airplanes. This was my fourth combat mission in A-26s out of NKP, and I was a month shy of my 24th birthday.

Big Eagle crewmembers at NKP, 1966: (left to right) Gene Albee, Frank Gorski, Bill Tuthill, John Mitchell, Hank Welch, Frank Hayes (USAF).

Frank Gorski and I were flying lead of a two-ship armed recce mission (Nimrod 31 and 32, if I remember correctly). We were over the Ban LaBoy Ford, just south of Mu Gia Pass. Chuck Dudley, Tony Cavalli, and Tom Wolfe (a FAC pilot) were in Nimrod 32. It was an orientation mission for Chuck and Tony with Tom providing the area detail. As I remember, in the mission brief Tom had said he had spotted a typical Russian gun emplacement at the ford and wanted to get a closer look at it. As briefed, Chuck requested lead. Frank and I took high station in a tactical combat formation and watched as he rolled in on the area. We rolled out to turn a 90/270 back to the area when we heard Chuck yell into the radio, "I'm hit!" Frank turned back toward the area and Nimrod 32's left engine was starting to burn. We saw the canopies jettison but saw no one get out of the aircraft. Then the left wing struck the ground, cart-wheeling the aircraft into a ball of fire.

The real gun emplacement was in the trees, and what Tom had seen was a decoy. It was a flak trap. I never forgot that lesson.

We took on-scene command and called for "Sandy" and "Jolly Green." We circled the area, dropping the small antipersonnel bombs we were carrying into the tree line. The fire continued to burn very hotly—deep orange with black smoke—and soon there was very little of the wreckage remaining. The end result was obvious, and Frank called "Sandy" and "Jolly Green" off. There was no point in endangering anyone else. There would be no rescue that day. We stayed in the area until bingo fuel, then returned to base. That was our first of three losses that year.

Frank Gorski was like a big brother to me. He was generally quiet in manner and had a wry sense of humor. He was a pilot's pilot—competent in every way and in firm control of the aircraft and the mission. When we'd go out on the Trail, he'd sing quietly, "Oh my darlin, Oh my darlin," nothing more. When the weather was bad he'd say we were "probing through the murk."

I remember one particularly lousy night as we were on GCA final, lightning struck very close to the airplane. The strike was so bright Frank couldn't see the artificial horizon—it was just a dot on the instrument. Frank got the airplane on the ground but the PSP was very slick from the mud and rain. When we went into reverse, one prop reversed, the other didn't, and the anti-skid failed. Here we are in the middle of the night racing down the runway sideways with no brakes and each engine doing its own thing. Somehow we got straightened out, but both of us were pretty shook up. We de-armed, taxied to the parking area, and shut down. As the crew chief was chocking the wheels, one tire blew out, knocking him about 10 feet away. Frank then proceeded to lock the flight controls and grabbed the air brake lever instead of the control lock lever. If you remember, they were right next to each other. That episode shook both of us.

In 1994, we were at the Air Commando reunion at Hurlburt, and I learned from Gene Valentine that Frank worked for Boeing in Seattle. I did too but didn't know about Frank. We got together in Seattle after that and I joined the unit that Frank was in. It was the aircraft maintenance training unit. Frank was in the 737 mechanical training instructor, and I was a 757/767 avionics instructor.

In 1996 Frank contracted cancer of the larynx. He underwent chemo and radiation treatments, and after a while, he recovered. But apparently the chemo drugs affected his liver, and after a few short years, he died from it. He was 69 at the time.

Jack Bell, another A-26 navigator, is a quiet sort. He was flying with Lieutenant Colonel Al Howarth, the squadron commander, somewhere near Tchepone on the night of December 14, 1966, when they were hit by AAA. I met Jack after many years at the 1994 reunion. There were four of us who came to the 6th Fighter Squadron (Commando) directly out of aviation cadets (one of the last classes). The other two were Dan Konopatzke and Edgar D. Crooks. Al Howarth was able to set the airplane up for bailout according to the book. Jack got out first followed by the jump seat guy (Captain Harold Cooper getting his first familiarization "dollar" ride). Howarth had to physically help him up and out, and then bailed out himself. All three were picked up by Jolly Green helicopters at night. I heard that Howarth got the McKay Trophy for that mission. At the time, I was in a jetliner rotating back to the States. Chuck Wheelahan related the story to me.

We had a lot of experience in our group. Frank Gorski had been a Waterpump T-28 pilot earlier in the war. Chuck Wheelahan flew B-26s with Farm Gate. The ops officer was Joe Kittinger. I saw Joe on the internet a few weeks ago as the chief communicator for a high-altitude parachute exit from a balloon. We nicknamed him "Joe Balloon" because he had pioneered high-altitude balloon exit in the early '60s. As ops officer, he was probably the most likely "combat" leader, but Frank and Wheelahan knew as much as anybody. For navigators, I suppose Frank Hayes and Frank Blum had the most experience of anybody along with Miles Tanimoto, my early mentor. Miles flew with Major Glen Duke and both were killed in a crash when they ran out of gas short of the field at NKP.

The Big Eagle evaluation period proved that A-26s were effective in nighttime dive-bombing operations against trucks and truck convoys taking enemy supplies south on the Ho Chi Minh Trail. We paved the way for Nimrod combat operations for the next

Big Eagle: Captain Frank Blum, Captain Miles Tanimoto, Captain George Glenn Duke, Captain Welch (USAF).

three years. I am a proud A-26 veteran, and I never forget the men we lost in combat during that incredible experience.

Three Stories

1st Air Commando Wing, 603rd Maintenance Sq. England AFB, Louisiana, 1966–1967

ED PARKER

As a ground crew member with the 1st Air Commando Wing, 603rd Maintenance Sq., my stories may not be as exciting as those of pilots or navigators, but to us ground support guys we loved our jobs, and for myself I would do it all over again.

The Taster

I was heavily involved in the day-to-day maintenance of the B-26K redesignated to A-26A for missions in Thailand. We spent our time maintaining the small number of 26s remaining in the U.S. while the others were deployed to NKP, Thailand.

Most of the aircrews as I recall were mostly "jet jockeys" who were not particularly happy to be flying "vintage" twin-engine reciprocating airplanes left over from the two previous wars.

As former "jet jockeys" know, when you preflight a jet aircraft, whether it is a bomber, fighter, or whatever, if there is a drip or spot under the plane anywhere it can be an issue. A drip or even a puddle under an A-26 was nothing to worry about and in fact if there were no spots under the engines you might wonder if it was low on oil or hydraulic fluid. We had a lieutenant colonel who was transferring over from flying B-52s and as you can imagine he was less than thrilled about being assigned to A-26s, which I could understand. We used to see him getting out of the crew van to prepare for another training flight and someone would say "here comes the taster," and "yes" he tasted every drip or drop under the plane. One day his "IP" came out early and told me to pour water through the pilot's relief tube so I did as *ordered*, being the good Air Commando I was. When the crew arrived and "the taster" began his preflight, you can imagine what happened. As the crew chief, it was my job to accompany the pilot as he did his preflight inspection and as we approached the left rear side of the bomb bay doors, there was a puddle on the ground under a small vent. The "LC" placed his finger on the drip as it came out of the "*unidentified*" vent, tasted it, and then made a face and spit. He turned to me and asked me what the hell was leaking from the vent he was pointing to. I informed him it was a "relief" tube vent and I thought for a minute he was going to hit me. Instead, he turned to the IP and said, "I bet you thought that was funny?"

The Tug Races

During this time we also used to take our aircraft to Eglin AFB to use Doolittle Field or Hurlburt Field in Florida for short-field takeoff and landing training. A lot of these training flights were at night and the ground crews found themselves with a lot of time on their hands while the planes were up. Hurlburt Field seemed to be the place where the Air Force sent all their old "tugs" used for towing or moving aircraft. These old tugs had two smaller front tires and if memory serves me correctly they had a set of small dual tires on the rear of the vehicle. These vehicles had a fair amount of power since they were used to move all sizes of aircraft. The ground crew guys used to use the taxi way between Doolittle Field and the runway and "drag race" the tugs. In what I remember to be the "race of champions," I was determined to win, so I had my tug revved up to maximum RPM. When I dropped it into gear (they were automatics—and naturally the old parts in the "rear end" did not hold up), the tug died a quick and painful death. Being young airmen and knowing this was probably a "punishable" offense, we did what any red-blooded young airman would do: we buried the tug in the "sands of Hurlburt Field." We used to go back and forth so much between Louisiana and Florida there was a tendency just to leave our equipment in place on the parking ramp area awaiting our next TDY. On our next trip down, since no one had mentioned the missing tug, we just reported it missing when arrived. The "statute of limitations" has expired … right?

Sinclair's Smile

In early 1967, I had the opportunity to accompany an A-26 and the pilot to Tinker AFB for a Memorial Day weekend air show. One of the maintenance crew (Airman Sinclair) was from a small town near Tinker and I offered to let him go in my place, and the squadron commander said why didn't we both go? When we landed at Tinker, the A-26 was going to be a "static" display only, so after we prepared the plane for display the pilot told us to disappear until Tuesday morning. When we came back Tuesday morning for the trip back to Louisiana, we introduced the pilot and copilot to the parents of Airman Sinclair. As we taxied out for takeoff, the pilot asked him if his parents would be hanging around until we took off, and Sinclair told them "yes," they would be at the end of the runway watching us leave. We took off and the pilot called the tower and requested a flyover for the parents of the airman and they said they could not officially approve his request. He took that to mean okay but they would not be responsible. We did the usual turn and "downwind" approach and I swear if the wheels had been down we would have been on the ground. When we hit the end of the runway the pilot did one hell of a pull-up and rollover. I suspect that the smile on Sinclair's face may still be there today.

My main regret from those days is that I was reassigned to Nha Trang, Vietnam, as a flight engineer on EC-47s and did not get to go to NKP with the A-26s, and for that I am truly regretful. The EC-47s served a vital service and I am proud to have been a part of that team but the A-26s will always have a special place for me.

Project Big Eagle

Randy Ryman

---

1 June 1966—We have orders. The orders are issued from HQ 834th Combat Support Group, England Air Force Base, Louisiana. The orders read in part:

> Following personnel, organizations indicated, TAC, this station, will proceed on or about 6 June 1966 from this station, to APO San Francisco 96310 for approximately 179 days in support of project Big Eagle as directed by SAWC (Special Air Warfare Center), etc. etc.

We were about to be on our way. Now, the big question, where the hell was APO 96310? We would learn that it was to be Nakhon Phanom, Thailand. No one knew a damn thing about it. So, for the next several days, we speculated since nobody we knew had any knowledge of the place. We assumed, being Air Force, that aircraft would be our mode of transportation.

6 June 1966—Once again, we arrive at the flight line. This time, hopefully, it would be the real deal. The day is bright and sunny. On the ramp in front of the processing facility there are two C-130 Hercules transports in nice shiny aluminum skin. They glisten. That is to be the way we travel to Thailand. We are split into two groups, one group on each plane. My group is assigned to tail #21800. Major Welch is to be our en route OIC. Our gear is loaded on the plane on pallets and tied down with cargo netting. We have web seats along the side of the plane. This is going to be some trip!

Finally, we are off. We are told the next stop is to be Travis AFB, California, where we will refuel, change aircrews, and continue on. It is about a six-hour flight to Travis. It is a beautiful day. I have a seat beside one of the windows where I can look out at 20,000 feet and watch the world go by below. During the flight, we can walk around the cargo area, talk, and do anything we want to pass the time. On the rear ramp of the plane is a pallet of containers, which I recognize as containing GE mini-gun pods. The mini-gun is the little brother of the Vulcan cannon. The mini-gun is just a miniature

Randy Ryman (right) loading 50-cal guns at NKP (courtesy Randy Ryman).

that fires 7.62-cal rounds at an astounding rate of 6,000 rounds per minute. This is the same weapon that is installed on the AC-47 "Spooky." Spooky has three guns, side firing, which we are told can put a bullet in every square foot of an area the size of a football field in one pass. I had the opportunity to see a "Spooky" fire at one of the ranges at Eglin on a cold December night last year. It's impressive. Based on the cargo we have on board, I assume that we will shortly be at war.

When we arrive at Travis, Major Welch gives us a short briefing before deplaning, again explaining that we are to tell no one of our destination or discuss anything about our mission (seemed odd, since none of us knew what our "mission" was anyway). He also tells us to stay close to the terminal area, as we will be departing shortly. He tells us that when it is time to return to the aircraft, they will announce, "All personnel on Big Eagle 1800 report to the aircraft immediately." He uses the tail number of the aircraft so we will know which group is called. We go into the terminal, and immediately begin getting strange looks. We are wearing our fatigues, with the traditional cowboy hats and bloused boots and blue scarves. No one else is dressed like us. We're different. At the time, most other Air Force personnel are traveling in their dress blues or khaki uniforms. We seem to be the exception. Some of the guys are questioned by some officer about why we are wearing fatigues. They refer him to the major. No more questions are asked.

After about a half hour, we learn that there is a problem with the aircraft, a hydraulic leak or something that has to be fixed before we continue. The first group leaves. We will follow when the repairs are complete. We will end up waiting at Travis six hours for the repairs to be done.

Finally, after hours of boredom in the terminal, our flight is called. We take off in the darkness. Our next stop is Hawaii, 11 hours away. After we are in the air, many go to sleep, some sleeping in their seats, others sleeping where they can. There is also a card game that has started in the rear of the plane, a game that would pretty much continue for the duration of our flight to Thailand. I crawl up on a pallet of duffel bags, make myself as comfortable as possible, and drift off to sleep to the drone of the engines.

Day 2—When I awake the next morning, we are still airborne and it is just getting daylight. We are arriving at Hickam AFB, Hawaii. I get to a window to get a look outside. We are coming in over what is apparently Pearl Harbor. I can see a submarine surfacing, coming in. We descend into Hickam and land. The major again gives us the "Stay near the terminal area, we'll only be here about an hour" speech, and that we'll be served breakfast and get an in-flight box lunch to take with us on the next leg. Even though it is early morning, it is very warm. We eat breakfast, see what we can that is in the immediate area, take a few pictures, and prepare to reboard the plane. We are each given an in-flight box lunch to take along. I have a couple pictures taken in front of the aircraft, then we reboard for the flight to Wake Island, our next stop. It will also be a long flight. We are presently flying west, ahead of the sun in early morning. Although I don't realize it, it will be daylight for a long, long time.

Again, we are winging our way across the vast Pacific Ocean, this time in daylight. I feel wide awake despite our sparse sleeping accommodations aboard the plane. Breakfast was good. We have perfect weather for flying. CAVU conditions. I peer out the window from my 20,000-foot vantage point. Nothing to see below but ocean—and lots of it. I walk around the plane and look out other windows. Nothing but water in all directions, to the horizon. I am impressed. I while away the hours in conversation with others, milling around the plane and generally trying to amuse myself. The card game in the rear continues. At one point, I spend some time in the rear of the aircraft talking to Gilbert "Gib" Handley. He is a weapons type I met at England AFB while we were being trained to work on the A-26 guns. Nice fellow. Gib had been in the Navy prior to joining the Air Force. He was submarine qualified. He was the only Air Force type I ever saw that wore the dolphins on his uniform, signifying that he was submarine qualified. He told me once what was involved in earning the dolphins medal, but I forget the details, except that it was a medal worthy of respect to those who wore it. Gib is a person who doesn't say a lot, but what he does say is to the point. I study the containers that hold the mini-guns on the rear ramp. Fiberglass and aluminum, about the size of a coffin, which I suppose is how they got their nickname. At one point, to make conversation, I say to Gib, "Those things are nice enough to be buried in," to which came the reply from him, "You just might get your chance." I change the subject.

After 36 years, I in no way remember everything that happened on each leg of the flight. But some high points do stand out and I will recount them here. The leg from Hawaii to Wake Island was long, approximately eight to nine hours. About an hour or two out of Hawaii, I once again crawl up on the stack of duffel bags and decide to get some nap time. Despite the surrounding noise, I sleep for several hours.

I wake up again. By the light shining in the porthole windows, I can see it is still daylight. I walk around again, looking out the windows on all sides. Again, nothing but water below, to the horizon. No land, no ships, just thousands upon thousands of square miles of water. I wonder how long it would take someone to find us if we had to ditch. The Herk has exits on top of the fuselage. We've been told that there are life rafts installed on the aircraft. That's some comfort. I decide it's time for lunch, and I open the box lunch we had been given at Hickam before we departed. Inside, along with the sandwich and snacks, is a ring of pineapple sealed in a clear plastic bag. I love pineapple. I will save that for dessert. I will never forget that pineapple ring. It had to be the sweetest pineapple I ever had. Stands to reason, I guess, coming from Hawaii. It was the highlight of that flight leg. After I finish lunch, I look around again. I become mesmerized with the size of the Pacific Ocean. I wonder how the hell those guys in the little boats, bobbing around down there hundreds of years ago, ever found anything! They spent months at sea. I have a newfound respect for Columbus, and all the others who struck out for the unknown. I am amused at the saying I heard once about Columbus. "When he left, he didn't know where he was going, when he arrived, he didn't know where he was, and when he got home, he didn't know where he'd been." That has a lot more meaning now.

After several more hours, we begin a descent. We must be arriving at Wake Island. I know nothing of this place, except that it was involved in World War II. I remember reading something about it in high school. We descend closer and closer to the water. From having seen it from 20,000 feet for hours, it seems to be getting *real* close. It seems that we are right on the wave tops now, and I hope we'll be seeing land soon. Bingo! The edge of the runway passes under the wing, and I hear the wheels screech when they make contact with the runway. Reverse the props, hang on for a sudden slowdown. We're back on hard ground, somewhere in the vast Pacific Ocean.

We pull up at the terminal. We are the only aircraft there. Again, the major gives the "Don't go too far, we'll only be here a few minutes" speech, and we depart the aircraft. It's hot but refreshing. The air on the plane was getting pretty stale, not to mention the other 36 or so guys who have also been cooped up in the plane for the past two days without showers either. We are taken to a chow hall, but it certainly didn't deserve that word. It was more like a nice dining room. We have table service, apparently by the locals who work there. The food is good. I don't think at this point anyone would complain even if it weren't.

During lunch, we are still speculating about what lies ahead. We finish lunch and decide to explore what we can of the place. Some of us go to look at the ocean, which is all around us. I marvel at how clear the water is, lapping on the rocks. You must be able to see 20 feet deep. I've never seen water that clear. We go back inside the terminal. There is a jukebox inside that has already been fed and is playing. Why people save space in their brain to remember things like this, I'll never know. But the song I remember hearing is "Baby, I'm Yours," by Barbara Lewis. I never forget it. Each time I hear it now, I am taken immediately back to that terminal at Wake Island. Strange.

After about an hour, we are ready to depart. We have again changed aircrews. The aircraft is refueled and is ready to go. We are given another in-flight box lunch, and we're off for Guam, which I'm told is about a six- to seven-hour flight. It is midafternoon or slightly later—hard to tell—the sun is overtaking us. At some point, we will cross the international date line, if we haven't already, and time will really get screwed up. What the hell. Who cares what time it is, anyway.

We wing our way toward Guam. The flying is getting pretty routine. I remember little about this leg of the flight. In fact, I don't remember anything about the stopover in Guam, except that we were there. It is now dark, as it would be for most of the rest of the flight. Little to do but sleep. Maybe that's why I don't remember much of it.

June 9, 1966—It is the wee hours of the morning. We land at a place called Mactan Island, in the Philippines. I haven't a damn clue where we are, but it is hot and humid. I am groggy, having been sleeping most of this leg. Whatever this place is, it is sparse. We are fed breakfast in a field tent, which is set up close to the ramp where the aircraft is parked. Looks like the accommodations are going downhill. A2C Fred Lovell is on our flight. Fred was at Hurlburt when I arrived there almost a year ago. Fred is the "old-timer" who had been in almost three years. Seems that every time there was a promotion, Fred was behind the door. Walt and I have been in scarcely a year and a half, and we have been E2Cs for six months. Fred has done a tour in the Philippines. He seems to know where we are. Way off in the distance, we can see the glow of lights. I ask what that is, and Fred says it is Manila. I was also introduced to another new item that night. I kept hearing this noise coming from the bushes, sand, or whatever was around us. Someone asked what the noise was, and Fred said, "it's a f--k you lizard." Turns out that it was the GI name for some form of gecko lizard. Seems that when it made a noise, it seemed to be saying, "F--k you!" And so it went.

We depart for our final leg of the journey. The mystery of where we were going would finally be solved. It was about a four- or five-hour flight to Nakhon Phanom, taking a route over Vietnam to get there. We would learn later that we had drawn some antiaircraft fire when we passed over Vietnam, but we were too high and it was too small to reach us. It is daylight again. We seem to be flying over endless miles of jungle below. Finally, we begin our descent into NKP, as Nakhon Phanom was called for short. We circle the area, and everyone wants to get a look at our new home. All I see out the porthole is jungle. Someone points out what seems to be a small clearing, and says, "That's it!" Can't be. That isn't even big enough to set down a C-130. As we got closer, it did get somewhat bigger. Apparently they knew they could land there, because I heard the distinct sound of the flaps and gear coming down. As the wheels make contact with the runway, I hear something I'm not used to hearing. There is a terrible "roaring noise" coming from the runway. Turns out that the runway at NKP consists of PSP, or "perforated steel planking," steel planks with holes in it, locked together to form a runway. And it's noisy as hell. Props into reverse, and stand on the brakes, more so it seems than before. The runway here is only 6,000 feet. No room to get carried away on your rollout on landing, or you'll be back in the jungle. We taxi to the ramp, and everyone is preparing to collect their baggage and get off the plane for the final time. Once again, Major Welch is going to say something before we get off. This time, A2C Fred Lovell beats him to it. We're all tired from the trip, and ready to get the hell off the airplane and at least sleep in a bed tonight, assuming they have them at this place.

As the aircraft comes to a stop, and the rear ramp lowers, Fred is the first one off the plane, even ahead of Major Welch. Fred turns around and announces, mimicking the major, "OK, fellas, I'd like you to stay right around the terminal area, and don't go too far away, 'cause we're only going to be here about six *months*!" After hearing the "we're only going to be here a few minutes" speech from Major Welch at every stop we made the last few days, this seemed absolutely hilarious, and the entire group broke out in laughter, including the major. What a way to break the ice after a long, tiring trip. Did I say ice? Forgive me. This place was like a sauna. Hot and humid. This would take some getting used to. We collect our gear, which consisted of a duffel bag stuffed full of uniforms and a set or two of civvies, and we're off to be assigned our barracks, or as we would learn to call them, the "hootches."

Setting Up Shop at NKP

RANDY RYMAN

Nakhon Phanom RTAFB, Thailand, as a base, was a far cry from what we had left in Louisiana. In June 1966, this place was pretty sparse. Our contingent boosted the base population to about 1,500. Dirt roads, PSP runway and ramp, and dust everywhere, except when it rained, and then it was mud, and lots of it. We are assigned to wooden "hooches" at what was at the time the edge of the base. There was no perimeter fence. There were trip flares strung around the perimeter. The first week was interesting. During the night, we would see the glow of a trip flare going off in the jungle. We wondered what it was. Could have been a dog or other animal tripping it, or it could have been a person. At night, we would peer out into the darkness and listen for any activity. There were also a squadron of Huey helicopters stationed on base. At night they would fly around the perimeter with their xenon searchlight they would use to cover the ground and check for activity. There were sandbag bunkers built outside of our hooches. We were not allowed to have weapons. There were two conex lockers on base, and we were told that in the event of an alert, we were to run to their location and draw M-16s. I believe there were only about 400 available, so only the fastest 400 troops would get weapons. I only remember once or twice that this happened, and I was one of the lucky ones that got there before they ran out of weapons. Nothing ever came of either event, though, and we turned the weapons back in each time.

After arriving, those of us in the munitions group, including the ones who got training on the A-26, worked in the bomb dump. Our eight A-26s would not arrive until June 18. I think they were supposed to arrive sooner, but as we would learn later, it seemed that each plane had developed some kind of problem that required at least one overnight stay at Hawaii.

Walt and I worked the night shift in the bomb dump, receiving bombs and stacking them for future use. We were entering the monsoon season. There is no rain like the monsoons. I never realized it could rain so hard for so long. Rain or not, we worked in it. Wearing the Air Force–issue poncho did little to keep us dry. Besides, it got in the way of everything we had to do. We finally abandoned them and just got wet and muddy. One night I particularly remember, Walt and I were taking some 260-pound frag bombs from the revetment. We had a rough terrain forklift in the revetment, using the forks to roll the bombs on for removal. This night, it had been pouring and continued to do so. As we rolled one of the bombs onto the forks, it slipped sideways, fell through the forks, and just disappeared into the ooze and muck beneath. We had to get a chain and feel through the mud to secure the chain to the fin, and literally drag it out of the mud in the revetment. It was not particularly fun work. Munitions continued to arrive daily. The Thais were contracted to haul the munitions from the deep-water port south of Bangkok, where they had arrived by ship, all the way north to NKP. We were stockpiling munitions for what was to come once we started flying missions.

At our hooch area, we had a common shower room and latrines located in the middle of the hooch compound. The first few weeks after we arrived, hot water was a scarce commodity. New hooches were being built right in our compound by Thai civilians. There was one chow hall located next to the flight line behind the A1-E "Sandys." All buildings were just wooden structures with screens and no windows, and no air-conditioning. We ate off metal trays in the chow hall. The snack bar was also a combination BX. It was a small building with various sundries we needed such as shaving cream, razors, deodorant, etc. The one thing I remember most about it was the large steel vats with ice-cold beer outside. That was refreshing in the heat.

The base was also a launching point for combat control teams. They would be dropped somewhere into the jungles across the river and report back by radio of any activities taking place, and living off what they could find. They would be gone about a week at a time before they would be picked up and brought back to NKP for a couple days' rest. These guys were the toughest of the tough. One night, Walt and I were sitting at the snack bar taking a break, and three or four of these combat controllers were over at another picnic table. They pretty much kept to themselves. While we were talking, and keeping our eye on them, we noticed a commotion going on. One of them drew his knife and was obviously after something beside their table, which was located next to another building. In a minute, one of them came up with what was obviously a snake. What happened next really got our attention. The guy with a knife put the snake on the picnic table and proceeded to slice and dice it right there on the spot. It appeared to me that the way he was working, he had done this before. The snake was skinned and cleaned, chopped into bite-size pieces, and they casually went back to their conversation and beers, eating the pieces of the snake raw. Walt and I decided then and there that these guys were not the ones to make trouble with!

June 18, 1966—We are told that the A-26s would be arriving today. There is to be a great welcoming party when they get here. Everyone in the Big Eagle detachment is to go to the flight line for the party. We are a very close-knit group. All told, there is about 150 of us in the detachment, including aircrews. We arrive at the flight line and await the arrival of the planes. Someone who has been in the radio room comes out and the word spreads that they are about 40 miles out. We await in anticipation of their arrival. Finally, someone shouts, "There they come!" pointing off in the distance. The first flight of four A-26s, along with their C-97 "mother ship," are approaching. What a beautiful sight. The C-97 coming with two A-26s flying formation off each wing tip. The C-97 is the escort ship, carrying the crew chiefs, mechanics, spare parts, tools, etc. for the flight over.

The formation makes a low pass over the base to the cheers and waving of everyone on the flight line. They pull up steeply and get into trail formation and start the downwind leg for the runway. The C-97 continues on, making a wide orbit to land after the A-26s are down. The runway is 6,000 feet of PSP. The remaining four ships fly over with their escort and file off into the landing pattern. The 26s taxi to the ramp and are lined up side by side. As one taxis to the ramp, it is sporting a red scarf flying off the antenna above and behind the cockpit. This would be no other than Joe Kittinger. As the planes are being parked, a tug comes out onto the flight line pulling several flatbed trailers. On the trailers are vats of iced-down beer for everyone. Unbelievable. Beer on the flight line. This is my kind of Air Force! The aircrews are handed cold beers as they climb down from the planes, and the party is on! For the next hour or so, there is much rejoicing going on. Everyone has arrived, safely. We help ourselves to beer, officers and enlisted alike, and generally have a good time. People are even smoking around the aircraft. That was a no-no.

Dominico Curto was our detachment commander, at least for the moment. He was of Cuban descent. He flew in the Korean War, and was a "loco ace," having shot up a large number of locomotives. He was a full-bird colonel. Colonel Farmer was also a full-bird colonel and was the base commander. It was becoming obvious in the days previous to the arrival of our aircraft that Colonel Farmer wasn't a fan of the Air Commandos barging into his base. This day was no exception. As we were celebrating on the flight line, here he comes in his staff car to put us in our place. He was obviously not amused at the beer drinking going on, let alone the smoking. Several of us were standing under the wing of one of the aircraft, some with beer in one hand and cigarette in the other. Roy Woodall was the first one to receive Colonel Farmer's wrath. He walks up to him, and before Roy could muster a salute, said, "Airman, don't you know better than to be smoking around an aircraft?" "Yes, sir!" Roy replied and promptly extinguished the cigarette on the PSP, as did the others who were smoking. Surprisingly, I don't recall him saying anything about the beer, but the best was yet to come. We had just seen Colonel Curto smoking a cigarette on the other side of the plane, which was where Colonel Farmer was heading. We followed to see what would happen.

When Colonel Farmer got to the other side of the plane, sure enough, there was Colonel Curto, beer in one hand and cigarette in the other. Colonel Farmer did blow a gasket. "Dammit, Curto, I just gave one of your men hell for smoking around the aircraft and damned if you aren't here smoking too." I could tell this was going to get ugly.

Colonel Curto got right back in his face, and said, "Now you listen here. The rest of our group just got here. Everyone has arrived safely, and we're going to enjoy it today. Now you go on about your business." Colonel Farmer left, and as I remember, was saying something to the effect that he (Colonel Curto) "hadn't heard the last of this." He left, and the party continued.

Over the next couple days, the aircraft were reconfigured for combat operations. For the long flight over, auxiliary bomb bay fuel tanks were installed in addition to wing ferry tanks. In addition to removing the ferry tanks, other things had to be checked and inspected.

June 25, 1966—During an orientation flight over Laos, we lose our first plane. I was still working in the bomb dump at this time. Bad news travels fast. We learn of the loss. Sketchy details come in, but aircraft #650 has apparently been lost to antiaircraft fire. Captain Charles "Chuck" Dudley, pilot, Lieutenant A.F. Cavelli, navigator, and Captain Thomas Wolfe, observer, are lost. The next morning we arrive at the flight line with ordnance, and there is an empty spot on the ramp where 650 used to sit. It was right at that moment that I realize that this is the real deal, and they are playing for keeps. From the information we got, Captain Dudley was flying a daylight familiarization flight with another A-26 about a half mile off his wing at about 3,200 feet when he was bracketed by 37-mm AAA. The other pilot reported that one instant the plane was there and the next instant it was engulfed in flames. The only transmission reported from the stricken aircraft were the words, "We've been hit." They could not discern whose voice it was. The aircraft rolled over and impacted in the jungle. No one was seen to exit the aircraft prior to impact. It is a sad day for Project Big Eagle. It would not be the last.

Within about a week, those of us who were trained on the A-26 back stateside were reassigned to the flight line. This was a positive move as far as I was concerned. It was probably as close to the action as I would get, and I felt like I would be directly contributing to the effort actually getting to work on the planes. There were enough people in the bomb dump to keep up with the munitions deliveries, but more were needed to load the aircraft. We learned that the primary role of the A-26 was to interdict truck traffic on the Ho Chi Minh Trail where it came through Laos. One of the primary targets was a place called Mu Gia Pass. Our missions would be flown from dusk to dawn, for better protection under the cover of darkness. Walt and I worked loading the planes during the day, preparing for the night sorties. The goal was to fly 8–10 sorties a night. Now being down to seven aircraft, some would have to be "turned around" during the night for another sortie. It was hard work and long hours, but it had a purpose, and no one complained. Everyone worked together. Walt and I worked as a team. We learned to load about anything that the A-26 could carry. The normal armament configuration was frag or GP bombs in the bomb bay. On the outboard stations of each wing, MER (multiple ejection racks) were installed for carrying the MK-25 magnesium parachute flare. The pilots would take their own daylight with them. The MK-25 produced an enormous amount of light. The flare canister contained a timer, which would be preset for a certain delay after release. After falling for the prescribed amount of time, an ejection charge would kick the flare from the canister, the parachute would deploy, and the flare would light, illuminating a huge area on the ground to daylight conditions. I had seen these used at the firepower demo at Eglin.

The idea was that the A-26 would loiter over the target area and periodically drop a flare, then swoop in under it just as it ignited, and take out anything that happened to get caught in the light. Each aircraft carried 12 flares, 6 on each MER. Inboard of that would be combinations of napalm, GP (general purpose) bombs, white phosphorous bombs, 2.75" rockets, with various warhead configurations, frag clusters, CBU-14s, etc.—anything that could be used to inflict the maximum amount of damage on the enemy.

I took to loading the aircraft like a duck to water. I really enjoyed it. Walt and I worked as a team for some time. We hand loaded the bomb bay, up to the 260-pound frag bombs. We would roll a small trailer in between the bomb bay doors, with the bombs lying on the trailer, then each of us would get an end and hoist it up into place.

Walt didn't like the flight line as much as I did, and eventually he returned to the bomb dump. I chose to stay on the flight line. I was paired up with Staff Sergeant Gerald Salazar. We were primarily "gun plumbers." Other load teams would take care of the hard ordnance, and we worked as a team on the guns of all the aircraft. Eight .50-caliber guns per plane and seven planes kept us busy just maintaining the guns. It was something we would get very good at.

Back to Yesteryear

LINDSEY JACKSON

This is my story…

Being black in the Air Force in the '60s was not easy. There were still people who

Sergeant Lindsey Jackson (courtesy Lindsey Jackson).

really thought blacks were dumb. I always knew that I wanted to go into the Air Force. I joined the Civil Air Patrol in New Jersey when I was 15 and enjoyed it, so going into the Air Force was the right thing to do. I completed basic training in August of 1962, then went on to Sheppard AFB for maintenance (aircraft) school, where I graduated on December 22, 1962. I went from there to Scott AFB, Illinois, arriving January 1, 1963, as a ground crew member on a C-54. This was the general's aircraft. That is where reality set in.

I was not allowed to work on the aircraft—only to polish the darned thing. My crew chief (CC) thought I was too stupid to work on the aircraft. I made friends with the flight engineer, an E-8. We hit it off for some reason so when the general went flying on short trips, the flight engineer made sure that I would tag along. Being fresh out of maintenance school, all the gauges were still new to me. Had I known what I know now, things might have been different.

After polishing the damned aircraft for a while, I saw a message on the bulletin board: "WANTED AIR COMMANDOS. MUST HAVE A FIVE LEVEL AND BE AT LEAST AN E-4." Well, I said what the hell! I had just taken my five-level test and missed it by one point. At that point I was so down that I did not give a **** what happened. I applied anyway. The general asked me if I was crazy and after talking to (head) doctors, I began to think I was a little touched. I still had only one stripe but someone was looking out for me. In October 1963 I received my orders to report to Eglin Field #9. I was happy—and a little scared. I had no idea what I was getting into.

The first person I met was Master Sergeant Carlos "Chris" Christian, first sergeant (FS), who said, "Welcome to the Air Commandos!" Later when I met Major Joseph Kittinger, I asked him if he was the one who jumped out of a gondola in 1960. When he replied, "Yes," I realized that I had gotten into something special. I was assigned to the B-26 section, where I was in charge of making coffee until then-Lieutenant Rosa said enough of this **** and I was finally allowed to work on an airplane. I worked under some great people: E. Hunter, C. Day, G. Kinkade, L. Hunt, K. Floyd, and G. Allenbrand, to name a few. They took me under their wings and taught me the ropes. We had a lot of fun, too, like when Colonel "Heinie" Aderholt attended a party down by the water. Carlos (FS) and I were standing there and each of us knew what the other was thinking. We just couldn't help ourselves, so we scooped up Heinie and tossed him into the water. The only thing he said was "LET ME GET MY WALLET OUT!"

Now for some of the bad things. I made some enemies…. I remember one day I was refueling an aircraft and joking with a couple of the pilots when TSGT Piontek (CC) came up to me and said get the **** off the plane. I had no idea what or why he said that, so I left. A little while later, the FS Carlos said the commander wanted to see me. I thought I was in trouble, but this time it was Piontek who was in trouble. He was being sent to crew another airplane and I was going to be assigned to another crew chief. Things just got worse. The new CC (Staff Sergeant Johnson) was never around on the weekends when we did most of the flying because he was in North Carolina with his girlfriend, or wife, I never knew which and could care less. This went on for about four months until Colonel Curto, wing commander, asked where was the CC and I told him that he was in North Carolina. So the "old man" asked if I was checked out (on the aircraft) yet. I said, "No." He got his chute, I got mine, and off we went—me in the left seat, Colonel Curto in the right seat. We did three touch-and-goes and taxied back to the ramp. As I was walking away from the aircraft, Staff Sergeant Johnson said, "You can't fly that plane and I'm going to have you court-martialed!" He did not realize that he was almost ready to meet his maker because if it wasn't for the wing commander, I was going to knock him into the next world and beyond. The old man tapped him on the shoulder and asked him where he had been. He told the commander some cock-and-bull story. The old man told me that I was now the official crew chief of that airplane—not bad for an E-3. This did not set too well with Staff Sergeant Johnson. After that I never saw much of Staff Sergeant Johnson and I started to take care of the plane by myself. When my airplane went into the docks for maintenance, I tried to go with it so I could learn everything about it to make me a better crew chief. We were transferred to England AFB, Louisiana, in 1965.

Mainly because it was my airplane, the wing commander usually always took me with him on trips to Florida. On one trip, we left on Friday and were planning to return on Monday. I preflighted the plane on Monday, put the cover over the windshield because of the heat, and went to eat. When I came back, the cover was just hanging on. I thought, "Oh well, I guess I didn't tie it down tight enough and the wind blew the cover off." Damn … was I wrong! We took off headed back to England AFB. When we landed, we reversed both engines. Although both engines went into reverse, when we attempted to un-reverse them, the left one came out and the right did not. The **** hit the fan and the old man gave me the dirtiest look and I knew that I was in trouble. When the plane finally stopped, I got my butt chewed out for about an hour. At that point I had no idea what the hell had happened. We called the tech rep from On Mark to help find the problem. I changed the prop, prop governor, and the engine. The damn thing did the same thing. I just knew I was going to lose a stripe. Something told me to go into the cockpit and look down to the left and there was a panel loose. I knew I did not remove it. I took the panel off and to my surprise there was the problem … someone had swapped the cannon plugs (right onto left and left onto the right) so the signal for reverse (going in) worked, but the faulty signal caused only the left engine to come out of reverse. So I switched them back and did a full runup. It worked perfectly. The old man came and I went for little ride to make sure it worked down the runway at full speed and then reverse. When we got back I told him what I thought happened. After that, no one was allowed to work on my plane unless I was there.

Now for Big Eagle…

Then we found out we were going to Southeast Asia (SEA) somewhere so I was finally going to fight and kick ass and take some names. There were long days getting the plane ready—a special fuel tank fitted into the bomb bay, 55-gallon oil drums into the cockpit, etc. It was a long trip across the pond; this was my first trip out of the country. Yes, I was scared, not knowing where we were going or even what to expect when we got there. We headed to SEA (Thailand). We had to change our aircraft designation from B-26 to A-26 because bombers were not allowed in Thailand. Where in the hell are we going? Where the hell is NKP (Nakhon Phanom)—out in the damn boonies, PSP runway, wet, and hot as hell. We thought we were there to fight, but guess what? We couldn't get any ordnance to drop. So, we took whatever we could scrounge up and put it in the bomb bay—beer bottles, three-way spikes, or anything else we could find to drop on the Viet Cong (VC). Things were going fine for about three months, then we lost an A-26 to antiaircraft guns. That was a bad day in my life because I knew who was flying and looked forward to them coming back. My job was non-commissioned officer in charge (NCOIC) of the arming and de-arming area where pilots would run up their aircraft before a mission. One day while a pilot was running up his aircraft, my poncho got caught in the prop wash and up I went and landed in a big puddle of water. I was mad! I made up rules to follow to prevent anyone from getting hurt. Everybody thought it was a joke until a pilot did not follow my instructions and the wing commander chewed his butt out. From then on, no one was going to change my rules and everyone had to follow them—like it or not.

One day when I arrived in my area, there was a C-130 which had three flat tires. I asked the person in a flight suit whose plane it was. He told me it was his. I told him that

I was not going to be responsible for anything that happened because I had five A-26s going out and they were hot. He said okay. I launched them without any delays. The next day, the wing commander asked if I knew who the person was that I was talking to yesterday. I said "No," so he informed me he was the Pacific Air Force (PACAF) commander. I almost had a cow! (Lesson for today: be kind to anyone you do not know.) Another time when the wing commander came back from a mission and opened his bomb bay, a big bomb fell out. I yelled, "Colonel, you just laid an egg on the ramp." I never saw someone get off the aircraft so fast. He grabbed me by my collar and hauled butt away from the aircraft. Of course, the explosive ordnance device (EOD) people came and took care of the bomb. Another fun time was when the ground control approach (GCA) went out and we couldn't fly. We had a party to end all parties: guys falling on the booze table, sleeping on top of the lockers, stealing the base commander's car and putting it someplace where it was not supposed to be. The next day we all had hangovers that wouldn't quit … but life goes on. The saddest part is when I was told that I was going home. I did not want to go but orders are orders.

I got transferred to Otis AFB, Massachusetts, about a year later to be a crewmember on an EC-121 headed back to SEA. No thanks, I elected not to go. I got out of the Air Force in 1970. I worked various jobs and in 1973 joined the MA ANG as a security policeman. I pissed off the commander when I held a job up because of job discrimination. While attending the Non-Commissioned Officer (NCO) Academy there was a job which I thought I should have. I was told I did not qualify although I did because I held a 7 level in security police. I ended up with a better job, or so I thought. Not quite, so I quit.

We moved from New Hampshire to California. I went to work as a private investigator (PI) until the boss went to jail for selling drugs. I had a bad feeling about him from the beginning. Next came work at the unemployment office in the San Fernando Valley, then an oil refinery in Newhall, California. My family moved to Oregon, where I worked for the Job Corps as a counselor, started my own PI agency, and started a Civil Air Patrol (CAP) Squadron in Roseburg, Oregon, in 1983. Then we moved to Portland, Oregon, where I worked for the USDA Forest Service and Army Corps of Engineers and continued my involvement with CAP. In 1985, I joined the Oregon Air National Guard as a corrosion control supervisor until I was selected to be a recruiter in 1988. I retired from recruiting in 1995. We moved to Arizona, where I joined the Arizona Rangers and quickly became the internal affairs officer. In 2009, I officially retired from the CAP as a lieutenant colonel and moved to Texas to enjoy my retirement.

I greatly credit the Air Commandos for making me the person that I am today.

NOTE

1. *Foreign Invaders*, Dan Hagedorn and Leif Hellstrom, Leicester: Midland Publishing Ltd., page 159, 1994.

CHAPTER 3

Nimrod Combat Operations Out of NKP

The Nimrods

The Nimrod concept of operations flowed directly out of the Big Eagle deployment experience, and out of continuing training conducted at England AFB, Louisiana. Except for USAF Air Commando and Special Operations combatants who fought in the Vietnam War, and the A-26 pilots and navigators who flew the incredible A-26A Counter Invader in the "Secret War in Laos" in 1966–69, few Americans are familiar with the Nimrod story. The A-26 Nimrods had the highest respect for forward air controller (FAC) crews during combat operations, and routinely teamed up with FAC crews to locate and strike targets. Even today, we are proud of that common heritage, and we are truly humble about our "certain brotherhood" that served during the Vietnam War.

The A-26 Nimrods had clear and strong leadership, and the crewmembers had all the training and courage you could ever hope for in a combat squadron. The Nimrods had a real passion for flying. And they had one thing more—once they started flying combat missions out of Nakhon Phanom Royal Thai Air Force Base, Thailand, their shared sole purpose was to help win the Vietnam War.

The A-26 Nimrod crews operated out of Nakhon Phanom (NKP) RTAFB, Thailand, from 1966 to 1969. They were called the Nimrods because their call sign for radio communications was "Nimrod" and a specified number (e.g., Nimrod 31 or Nimrod 35). According to Genesis in the Old Testament, "Nimrod" was "a mighty hunter before the Lord." If you consult a dictionary, the term "Nimrods" means hunters. That is a perfect definition for the combat role A-26 crews were assigned in the Vietnam War. The Nimrod crews were hunters. Each A-26 crew could act as its own FAC, or an A-26 crew could team up with other FACs (air or ground) to locate and strike targets. Nimrod crews often teamed up with FAC aircraft

A-26 100 mission patch (courtesy Franklin Poole).

with the call sign Nail (O-1s), Candlestick (C-123s), and Blind Bat or Lamplighter (C-130s). A-26 crews were most effective when they teamed up with other FAC aircraft because if another FAC aircraft could locate and mark the targets, the A-26 crews could focus their time and efforts on taking out those targets.

The Nimrods had the privilege of flying a "classic" U.S. Air Force combat aircraft. In the September 2007 issue of *Air Force Magazine*, the A-26 Invader is displayed as an Airpower Classic aircraft (see page 136). That designation is well deserved. The A-26 is reportedly the only U.S. Air Force combat aircraft to have seen service in three wars: World War II, the Korean War, and the Vietnam War. The A-26s that were flown in combat out of Nakhon Phanom RTAFB in 1966–69 were the end of the line for this classic aircraft. Douglas Aircraft Company manufactured a total of 2,446 A-26 aircraft during World War II. Commander of the Army Air Forces, General H.H. ("Hap") Arnold, was a strong A-26 advocate because he believed the improved performance of the A-26 over its predecessor (the Douglas A-20) would enable the A-26 to replace obsolete A-20, B-25, and B-26 (Martin Marauder) medium bomber aircraft. The A-26s and their crews experienced their greatest test during World War II as the 9th Air Force flew them into the intense flak environment of Central Europe. During the Korean conflict, B-26 crews were credited with 55,000 combat sorties and the destruction of hundreds of enemy vehicles, railway cars, and locomotives. After experiencing wing failures pulling out of dive-bombing passes early in the Vietnam War, the Air Force awarded a contract to On Mark Engineering Company of Van Nuys, California, to remanufacture 40 A-26 aircraft according to certain specifications. The wings were substantially rebuilt and strengthened by the installation of steel straps on the tops and bottom of the spars. Each aircraft was fitted with two Pratt & Whitney 2,500-horsepower R-2800-52 water-injected engines with fully reversible automatic feathering propellers. Eight new under-wing pylons were added to carry various munitions and stores. Eight .50-caliber forward-firing machine guns were added to the aircraft nose section. The top and sides of each aircraft were painted in a dark green jungle camouflage pattern, and the bottom of each aircraft was painted black. Without the crucial On Mark modifications, Nimrod crews could not have carried out the demanding dive-bombing missions over the Ho Chi Minh Trail.

The Nimrod mission in the Vietnam War primarily centered on attacking and destroying enemy truck convoys, troops, and supplies as they left North Vietnam, traveled through Laos, and engaged in troop deployment and resupply operations supporting North Vietnam Army (NVA) and Viet Cong (Vietnamese communist guerrilla) forces operating in Laos, Cambodia, and South Vietnam. The Nimrod armed reconnaissance mission also included combat close air support flight operations in support of U.S. Marine and U.S. Army combat units operating in South Vietnam, and in support of Royal Laotian and Hmong combat units opposing NVA and Pathet Lao (communist) forces in Laos.

In the spring of 1964—in order to furnish communist forces with hundreds of thousands of tons of weapons, ammunition, food, and other necessities vital for guerrilla operations and major battles—the Hanoi high command set in motion a vast and ambitious scheme to turn the Ho Chi Minh Trail into a modern logistical system. Consequently, the Trail was vastly enlarged and improved with sophisticated antiaircraft defenses, underground barracks, workshops, hospitals, storage facilities, and fuel depots. "Throughout 1964, an estimated ten thousand North

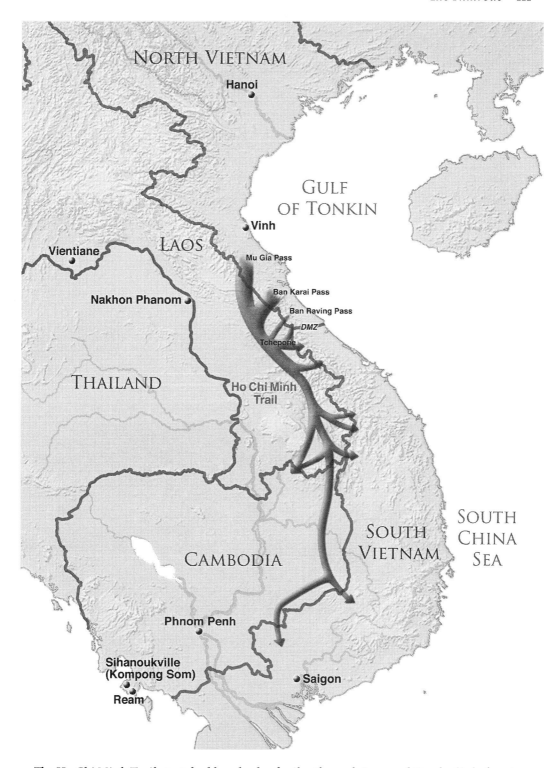

The Ho Chi Minh Trail stretched hundreds of miles through Laos and Cambodia before terminating in South Vietnam. Mountain passes allowed access to that beleaguered country (*Air Force Magazine* map by Zaur Eylanbekov).

Vietnamese troops went south … a trickle compared to the numbers three years later, when they were pouring into South Vietnam at the rate of twenty thousand or more per month."[1]

Beginning in 1966, in an effort to avoid detection and U.S. air strikes, almost all North Vietnamese truck convoy activity occurred at night. Hence, the Nimrod A-26 combat crews operated almost exclusively at night. Due to the rugged terrain, frequent bad weather, and heavy antiaircraft defenses, the nighttime dive-bombing missions were extremely demanding. A-26 crews routinely teamed up with U.S. forward air controller aircraft, and when possible, they loved to combine air strikes with B-57 (call sign Redbird and Yellowbird) strike aircraft. However, on many nights, A-26 Nimrod and AT-28 Zorro aircraft operating out of NKP were the only attack aircraft working with FAC aircraft in Steel Tiger. A-26s were uniquely well suited for nighttime attacks on truck convoys and enemy troops because of heavy and diversified armament loads (eight wing stations, bomb bay, and eight .50-caliber machine guns in the nose section), and because ample aircraft fuel reserves enabled A-26s to loiter in the target area five hours or more. Generally, the most effective weapons against trucks were M-31 and M-32 incendiary bombs (nicknamed "funny bombs") and finned napalm canisters because they could be delivered with accuracy and they covered a large area on the ground. Napalm (both

The A-26A with full ordnance load and Mekong River in background (1968) (USAF).

finned and unfinned) and .50-cal machine-gun bursts were also very effective in close air support missions and in strikes against antiaircraft guns. Hard bombs, frag cluster bombs, 2.75-inch rockets from pods, and bomblets from CBU canisters were generally effective against AAA and enemy troop positions. Typically, A-26 crews made multiple dive-bombing passes on a target until it was destroyed. The more passes a crew made on a target, the more intense became the AAA response. Sometimes attack crews alternated passes on trucks and AAA sites to suppress enemy AAA fire.

Steel Tiger was the primary area of operations for the Nimrods. Steel Tiger was a military code name for a combat area comprising much of the Ho Chi Minh Trail, a vast network of roads and trails in eastern central Laos extending several hundred miles from North Vietnam north of the Demilitarized Zone south through Laos to South Vietnam and Cambodia. The Ho Chi Minh Trail passed through terrain in Laos that was alternately limestone karst (jutting mountainous terrain), triple-canopy jungle, and grassland. The North Vietnam name for the Trail was the Truong Son Strategic Supply

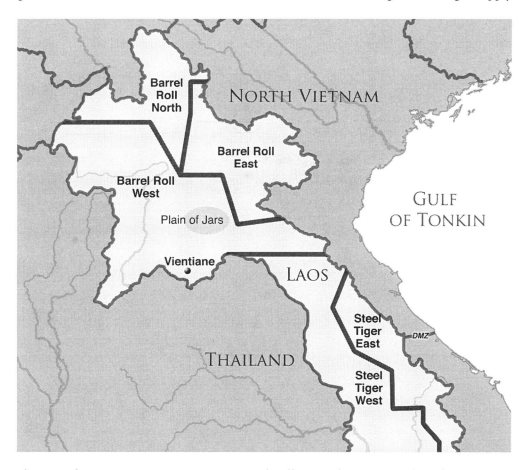

This map shows air operations in Laos. Barrel Roll in northern Laos and Steel Tiger in the south referred both to operations and geographic designations. Steel Tiger East, also called Tiger Hound, was considered an extension of the fight in South Vietnam. Air operations, both south and north, were conducted by 7th Air Force, employing aircraft based in Thailand and South Vietnam. SAC B-52s also operated extensively in Laos (*Air Force Magazine* map by Zaur Eylanbekov).

Route (named after the long mountain chain that separates Vietnam from Laos). Until President Nixon acknowledged in 1970 that U.S. aircraft had been, for several years, engaged in flying interdiction missions along the Trail in Laos, the war in Laos was considered by both sides to be the "Secret War in Laos."

Barrel Roll was the other major area of operations for the Nimrods. Barrel Roll covered a very large geographical area in northern Laos, extending from the Plain of Jars eastward to the North Vietnam border. While we only had to fly 40 or 50 miles east of NKP and the Mekong River to reach the hot combat areas in Steel Tiger, we needed to fly more than 100 miles north just to reach the combat areas in Barrel Roll. Although we didn't give it much thought while we were flying missions, Hanoi was only about 100 miles east of Sam Neua, located in the northeastern part of Barrel Roll. In Steel Tiger, we generally operated from the Mu Gia Pass on the North Vietnam and Laotian border, south past the DMZ, and further south to Saravanne. We also flew combat missions into parts of North Vietnam and South Vietnam adjacent to Steel Tiger and Barrel Roll.

There were many outstanding squadron commanders of the 609th Air Commando Squadron/Special Operations Squadron in the 1966–69 time period. Lieutenant Colonel Bruce A. Jensen, the squadron commander from January 1967 to August 1967, was killed in action on his next-to-last scheduled combat mission over Northern Laos on 27 August 1967. He was followed by Lieutenant Colonel Howard L. Farmer (27 August 1967 to 1 January 1968); Lieutenant Colonel Robert E. Brumm (1 January 1968 to 1 July 1968); Lieutenant Colonel John J. Shippey (1 July 1968 to 1 November 1968); Lieutenant Colonel Atlee R. Ellis (1 November 1968 to 5 November 1968); Lieutenant Colonel Robert L. Schultz (5 November 1968 to 1 July 1969); Lieutenant Colonel Robert W. Stout (1 July 1969 to September 1969); and Lieutenant Colonel Jackie Douglas (September 1969 to November 1969). The A-26 squadron commanders led by example: they took the same risks and flew the same demanding combat missions as the rest of the squadron. They inspired teamwork, and they aggressively fought to win.

Two other giant USAF combat leaders stand out in Vietnam War history. Colonel Heinie Aderholt (later brigadier general),[2] commander of the 56th Air Commando Wing, provided the same level of inspirational leadership to the Air Commando (Special Operations) forces operating out of Nakhon Phanom RTAFB that Colonel Robin Olds (later brigadier general) provided to the F-4C Phantom fighter pilots operating out of Ubon RTAFB, Thailand. Those unconventional, but incredibly effective, combat leaders earned the respect and admiration of every member of their fighting organizations.

The A-26 pilots and navigators who flew in the "Secret War" in Laos had guts. They flew high-risk nighttime dive-bombing missions in aircraft that had no radar, no sophisticated electronic equipment, and no ejection seats. The A-26 pilots and navigators sat side by side in the cockpit, and the navigators also performed copilot duties. Historians acknowledge that the Ho Chi Minh Trail was the North Vietnamese lifeline that enabled up to a million NVA troops, and their weapons and war supplies, to reach combat areas in South Vietnam, and that the outcome of the war depended in the infiltration of North Vietnamese troops, weapons, and supplies through Laos into South Vietnam. Beginning in 1966, almost all of the North Vietnamese supply truck convoy activity on the Trail shifted from daylight operations to night operations in an effort to hide from U.S. air strikes. Thereafter, U.S. nighttime strike aircraft, such as A-26, AT-28, B-57, and AC-130 gunships, became the mainstay of U.S. attack aircraft capability on the Trail at night. The A-26 Nimrod crews arrived on the scene in SEA at exactly the same time that

A-26A parking area at Nakhon Phanom RTAFB, circa 1968–69 (courtesy Al Shortt).

Another view of the flight line at Nakhon Phanom RTAFB, circa 1968–69 (courtesy Al Shortt).

the North Vietnamese military emphasis shifted to nighttime resupply truck convoy operations down the Ho Chi Minh Trail.

Tactics employed by the A-26 crews evolved over time in Steel Tiger and Barrel Roll. Initially, single A-26 aircraft with flare dispensers and bomb loads were relatively free to roam the Ho Chi Minh Trail and the Plain of Jars areas at nighttime in search of targets (A-26 sorties were scheduled about every hour at night). A-26 crews could act as their own FAC, or they could team up with other FACs (air or ground). Because of the large number of AAA sites along the Ho Chi Minh Trail, A-26 crews usually relied upon other FAC aircraft to locate and mark targets (using high-intensity flares descending on small parachutes and incendiary "logs" released from aircraft that burned on the ground). When working with a FAC pilot, the A-26 pilot ensured safe altitude separation and relied upon the FAC pilot for target information (i.e., heading and distance information relative to a specific ground location). When cleared for an attack pass, the

Crews of the 609th Special Operations Squadron in front of an A-26A in 1968 at Nakhon Phanom Royal Thai Air Force Base, Thailand. Note truck "kills" depicted under the cockpit. Lieutenant Colonel John J. Shippey, squadron commander, stands at far right beside nose wheel. *On wing, left to right:* Captain Jay Norton, Captain Thomas Owens, Major Robert Bennett, Major Robert Squires, Captain Thomas Bronson, Major Mark Richards, Captain Frank Nelson, Major Bryant Murray, Major Walter Langford, Captain Michael Roth, Captain Seijun Tengan. *Standing at ground level, left to right:* Major Douglas Carmichael, Major Bobby Sears, Major Loren Gierhart, Lieutenant Colonel Francis McMullen, Major Bernard Disteldorf, Captain Richard Willems, Major Robert Zimmerman, Major Kenneth La Fave (on ascent ladder just below canopy), Captain Michael Henry, Major Bennie Heathman, Major Douglas Hawkins, Captain Bruce Wolfe, Lieutenant Colonel John Shippey (USAF).

Another photograph of the A-26A crews in 1968 timeframe. *Front row, left to right*: Major Delbert Litton, Major Walter Langford, Major Robert Bennett, Major Loren Gierhart, Captain Thomas Bronson, Captain William Cohen, Major Kenneth La Fave, Major Robert Squires, Captain Roger Graham, Captain Lawrence Elliott. *Back row, standing, left to right*: Major Bobby Sears, Captain Don Maxwell, Major Edward Robinson, Major Douglas Carmichael, Captain Ernest Weidenhoff, Major Mark Richards, Captain Leroy Zarucchi, Lieutenant Colonel Francis McMullen, Lieutenant Colonel Robert Brumm, Lieutenant Colonel Atlee Ellis, Captain Michael Roth, Captain Jay Norton, Major Daniel Grob, Captain Chuck Kenyon (USAF).

A-26 pilot concentrated on the proper heading and dive angle and lining up the pipper on the target, and the A-26 navigator concentrated on opening the bomb bay doors, proper positioning of the armament switches, and calling off altitudes in 500-foot increments as the aircraft descended toward the target. Generally, A-26 aircraft initiated a dive-bombing pass on a target some 3,000 to 5,000 feet above the target elevation and initiated the pull-up after bomb release some 1,000 to 3,000 feet above the target elevation. These altitudes could vary very substantially depending on the nature of the target, the type of ordnance being used, the weather, and the level of antiaircraft fire in the vicinity of the target. A-26 crews tended to team up more with other FAC and strike aircraft in Steel Tiger and tended to operate more on their own and with friendly ground FACs (usually Hmong ground troops) in the target areas east of the Plain of Jars. The concentration of enemy AAA sites increased each dry season, leading to the practice of frequently scheduling two-ship A-26 sorties (one A-26 crew provided AAA gun suppression while the other A-26 crew attacked the target). A-26 crews loved to team up with B-57 (Yellowbird and Redbird) strike aircraft in Steel Tiger, but generally had to clear the target area if fast-movers (e.g., F-4 aircraft) needed to unload on the target and return home because of low fuel reserves. During the rainy monsoon season, A-26 crews

Another photograph of crews of the 609th Special Operations Squadron in front of an A-26A (1968). *On wing, left to right*: Captain Chuck Kenyon, Major Dan Grob, Major Walt Langford, Major Del Litton, Captain Roy Zarucchi, Captain Don Maxwell, Major Bob Bennett, Captain Tom Bronson, Captain Lawrence Elliott, Captain Mick Roth, Captain Roger Graham, Captain Jay Norton. *Standing at ground level, left to right*: Captain Ernest Weidenhoff, Major Mark Richards, Major Ed Robinson, Lieutenant Colonel Francis McMullen, Lieutenant Colonel Bob Brumm, Major Ken LaFave, Major Loren Gierhart, Captain Bill Cohen, Major Doug Carmichael, Lieutenant Colonel Atlee Ellis, Major "Pappy" Sears, Major Bob Squires (USAF).

Group photograph of the 609th Special Operations Squadron "Nimrods" at NKP (Nakhon Phanom RTAFB), Thailand, in 1969. Lieutenant Colonel Bob Stout, squadron commander, is standing on fuselage behind nose guns (top center of photo) (USAF).

Lt	Maj	Maj	Maj	Maj	Capt	Capt
Jim	Ken	Joe	Earl	Chuck	Norm	Jack
Collins	Yancey	Jefferis	Milam	Vogler	Wolfe	Bright

Capt	Lt	Capt	Capt	Lt	Maj
Larry	John	Charlie	Roscoe	Rusty	Charlie
Ullrey	Terry	Lews	Roberts	Arbeit	Bates

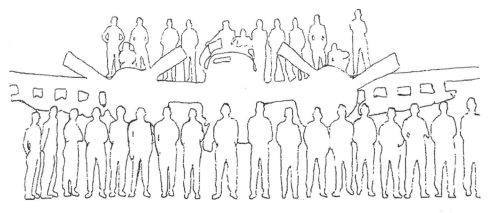

Lt	Lt	Maj	Maj	L/C	Capt	Capt	Maj	Maj
Bob	Tony	Dick	Howard	Bob	Jerry	Larry	Lee	Jim
Skipp	Hotsko	Watson	Andre	Schultz	Meek	Counts	Griffen	Rachael

Maj	Maj	Maj	Maj	Maj	Maj	Capt	L/C	Maj
Bob	John	Jim	Larry	Chuck	Al	Pat	Doug	Elmer
Dixon	Callanan	Fitzgerald	Gierhart	Kenyon	Shortt	Smith	Carmichael	Peters

The Nimrods 1968/1969 (USAF).

flying in bad weather sometimes made straight-and-level bomb drops on targets under the control of U.S. ground radar sites.

Several factors enabled the A-26 crews to be exceptionally effective in nighttime attack operations. First, the A-26 aircraft were armed to the teeth with mixed ordnance loads of incendiary bombs, napalm, hard bombs, frag cluster bombs, CBU cluster bomb units, 2.75-inch rocket pods, and eight machine guns in the nose. The A-26 had enough fuel reserves that it could loiter in target areas some four or five hours and still have enough fuel to get back to NKP. The A-26 crews usually worked with highly proficient FAC crews who located and marked the targets. The A-26 crews generally flew some 150 to 200 combat missions in a one-year tour, so they became very proficient in flying the aircraft, and in finding and attacking targets. Good crew coordination was essential to the success of the missions. Probably the most important factor of all—the A-26 crews made multiple passes (it could vary greatly depending on the mission, but 10 or more passes on targets were common) on multiple targets during each mission, vastly multiplying the destruction rained down on enemy trucks, troops, tanks, and various other targets.

The A-26 Nimrod pilots and navigators returned to the fight night after night in an all-out effort to destroy the NVA supply trucks bound for South Vietnam and Cambodia, and to provide close air support for friendly ground troops. They faced very formidable AAA defenses, and on many occasions lost aircraft and crews.

The A-26 Nimrods were awarded three Presidential Unit Citations during the 1966–69 time period. The Presidential Unit Citation is awarded to units of the Armed Forces of the United States for extraordinary heroism in action against an armed enemy occurring on or after December 7, 1941. In his book review of *The Nimrods*, Colonel (Ret.) Jimmie Butler, an accomplished author and military historian, stated that: "The Nimrods were the best truck killers in South East Asia until the AC-130s became fully operational in the late 1960s." That's a real compliment coming from a fellow combat veteran who flew 240 FAC missions in O-1s and O-2s, mostly over the Ho Chi Minh Trail in Laos.

Ilustration by Cliff Prine (courtesy *Air Force Magazine*).

NIMROD—King of the Trail[3]

Capt. Michael J.C. Roth, USAF

In 1966, the first A-26s—Call sign "Nimrod"—began operating out of Thailand's Nakhon Phanom Air Base against the Ho Chi Minh Trail. A former A-26 pilot of the 609th Air Commando Squadron tells of his experiences in this sturdy Douglas light bomber, a machine that first saw combat in World War II, was dusted off for Korea, and now has served with distinction in Southeast Asia—a truly remarkable retread…

The author, Capt. Michael J.C. Roth, is a 1963 graduate of the Air Force Academy. Following pilot training, he served for three years as a SAC KC-135 crew member. In 1967 and 1968, Captain Roth flew A-26s in Southeast Asia. After two years as a graduate student in management at the University of Southern California, he was stationed in Japan as a WC-135 pilot and as transportation officer at Yakota AB. He has recently been assigned to the Systems Program Management office at Wright-Patterson AFB, OH.

One day in the spring of 1964 we had an unscheduled arrival at Williams AFB, Ariz. I was then about halfway through basic pilot training in the T-38, and this stranger on the ramp aroused my curiosity. It was a Douglas B-26—the World War II "Invader," known until 1948 as the A-26—on its way to the bone yard at Davis Monthan AFB. The poor old girl couldn't quite make it all the way to her final resting place.

At the time, I was occupied with things like afterburners and flight director systems. I looked on this surprise visit as one, perhaps only, chance to get a close-up look at a disappearing species. It would have surprised me to learn that, as I looked over this old prop-driven airplane, forty other B-26s were being completely rebuilt by the On Mark Engineering Co. of Van Nuys, Calif. And it would have been an even bigger surprise to know that four years later, I would be returning from Thailand, utterly convinced that this aircraft, which I had by then flown in combat, was a magnificent machine.

As I looked over the B-26 at Williams that day, I recalled some of the things I'd heard about it. There was the story of a B-26 in Korea pulling up on the wing of a Mustang, feathering an engine, and staying right in formation with the F-51, though the fighter pilot had his throttle firewalled.

And there was one about the B-26 pilot who had run a North Korean truck over a cliff at night by coming in on the deck with his landing lights shining into the truck driver's eyes. Were the stories true? I couldn't say for sure. But they did give the airplane a certain aura. By 1964, however, that aura was tarnished by stories of B-26s losing wings in flight, and there was little doubt in my mind that the airplane was finished.

A Shock to a Jet Pilot

Then in June 1967, I stood on the ramp at England AFB, LA, and looked at the airplane I had just been assigned to fly: the On Mark-modified B-26K, which had been redesignated the A-26. I quickly found out that this was not the speedster from Korea. Though it was claimed to have a top speed of 305 knots with external armaments (which in itself was somewhat less than a firewalled Mustang), the airplane actually cruised at a little over half that speed. The reason was some of the modification done on the old B-26: a beefed-up wing, permanent wingtip tanks, greater internal fuel capacity, and increased armament capability.

The inner workings of this airplane were a real shock to a young captain who had nothing but jet experience. The main compass was similar to that used as a second backup on the KC-135 I had been flying. The instruments in front of the right seat were vacuum driven, something that had been mentioned back at Williams only as an interesting historical note. The oxygen regulator was the oldest type I had ever seen, but I was reassured on that point. The oxygen system purged and never used. And there was one distinctly disturbing thing about the airplane—no ejection seats. To bail out, you simply jettisoned the canopies and dived over the wing.

Perhaps most bewildering of all to a jet pilot, used to only throttles, was the array of levers to control props, mixtures, and carburetor heat. I remember so well some of the early questions like, "What's a jug?" and, "If I want to go fast, what do I push?"

The program at England AFB answered those, but raised one other big question that took a long time to answer. The airplane was slow, but stable. It maneuvered decently if you supplied the muscle. If you exerted all of your strength and got an assist from the navigator, you might even be able to pull the maximum allowable Gs. So the big question became, "Why this airplane at this time?"

To SEA in the A-26

In eight weeks at England AFB I learned to land the A-26 decently and to deliver ordnance with it passably. I was then sent to the 609th Air Commando Squadron at Nakhon Phanom Royal Thai Air Force Base, familiarly known as NKP. This organization had brought the first A-26s to Southeast Asia in 1966, and began using them in one of the most demanding missions in the history of aerial warfare—interdicting the Ho Chi Minh Trail. The 609th adopted the permanent call sign "Nimrod."

The Nimrod mission was unusually demanding because of the combination of obstacles it had to overcome. The Ho Chi Minh Trail itself was—and is—a vast network of vehicular roads, footpaths, and staging areas. It comes out of North Vietnam in a number of places from Mu Gia Pass down to the DMZ, winds through Laos, and enters South Vietnam in the vicinity of Khe Sanh and several more southerly points.

The terrain through which it runs is spectacular. Rugged, 5000-foot mountains are interspersed with wide river valleys. From the floors of those valleys jagged limestone formations, called karst, rise hundreds of feet straight up. And covering it all is a dense rain forest that in some places is triple tiered. The main roads, with a few exceptions, are visible from the air, but the footpaths and way stations are hidden under the forest canopy.

This road network was protected by an array of antiaircraft guns that ranged from 12.7 mm up to 57 mm. Here was a partial answer to my big question. For some reason, up until I left the Nimrods in 1968, the Communists never brought SAMs or radar-controlled guns into the area. Since the vast majority of traffic moved at night, all A-26 missions were flown in the dark. This gave us a sporting chance to survive in a gun environment that would have been disastrous in daylight. But the darkness was a two-edged sword. It greatly complicated our search for targets.

In September 1967, when I arrived at NKP, there were no operational strike aircraft equipped with night target-detection devices such as those on the AC-130 and AC-119 gunships now flying the Trail. The problem of pinpointing and hitting targets on the Trail at night was solved by teamwork between the FACs in O-2s, C-123s and C-130s, and the strike aircraft.

The equipment used by the FACs enabled them to visually spot truck on the roads, even on the darkest nights. Truck sightings by our FACs numbered well into the thousands each month during the dry season, from October through April, and included some vehicles as large as moving vans.

Teamwork on the Trail

When the FACs picked up a target, they had to reference its position on the ground to something that could be seen and identified in the dark by a strike pilot's unaided eye. Flares were used frequently to illuminate targets, but most pilots preferred the protection afforded by the darkness. The reference was usually a fire—perhaps one left from a previous strike or from a marker dropped by the FAC. This required precise communication, and FACs frequently met with strike crews to work out exact descriptive wording.

Once the strike pilot was satisfied that he had sighted the reference that the FAC was describing and could locate the target, he would launch a strike. After the first strike, the FAC could guide the strike pilot further by making corrections from the point of the initial strike.

And here was the rest of the answer to my big question: "Why the A-26?" Under prevailing conditions, the A-26 could run through this process with better results than any other airplane the Air Force could put into the air.

The reasons are not mysterious. The airplane was equipped with eight external ordnance pylons, a large bomb bay, and eight .50 caliber machine guns in the nose. It could carry a maximum armament load of 11,000 pounds and had a combat radius of 575 miles, which allowed an hour and a half over the target and a half hour of reserve fuel. Since most of the Ho Chi Minh Trail is within 200 miles of NKP, the time on target could be considerably over an hour and a half.

Because of the airplane's low speed and adequate maneuverability, the Nimrod pilot could cruise at a low enough altitude to easily pick out reference points the FACs were using, go from there to his target, and roll into his attack pattern from that same low altitude.

The A-26 was also an extremely stable platform, which made for very good bombing and strafing accuracy. And, finally, the airplane was rugged. I know of A-26s that took hits in the props and engines and still managed to land with both engines running.

A Big Night for Nimrod

Of the 146 missions I flew, I think perhaps the one that best demonstrated the great value of the airplane took place on April 5, 1968. On that night I was assigned to work with an O-2 FAC on a short stretch of the Trail about sixty miles due east of NKP.

As often happened, we searched for a long time without sighting a single truck on the road. The movement of trucks usually took place in short spurts of activity, and trucks seldom, if ever, made the entire trip from North to South Vietnam in one night.

A little over an hour after arriving on station, my FAC sighted two trucks on the road. He dropped a flare and marked them with a rocket. I made two passes with hard bombs. The FAC then confirmed that I had destroyed one of the trucks, but, before he could determine the exact whereabouts of the other, he began to have airplane problems, and had to return home. A radio check with other FACs at different locations on the Trail revealed that there was no other activity. So I began an unaided visual search of my assigned road section.

At this point, I should say that a more proper pronoun to use in referring to the A-26 is "we." Each airplane carried a pilot in the left seat and a navigator in the right. My navigator, Lt. Col. Francis L. McMullen, is one of the finest men it has been my privilege to know in the Air Force. His navigation duties were minimal, since he had no tools other than a map.

TACAN was the primary method of navigating, and the pilot was able to operate that alone. The navigator's main job, according to the checklist, was to operate the armament and fuel systems. In the course of their tours, however, our navigators actually became second pilots. Every one of them, I believe, was capable of flying the airplane home and landing it. Two A-26 navigators that I knew are now pilots—one in F-4s and the other in B-57s.

Jackpot

After our FAC returned to NKP that night, we spent another half hour searching over our assigned area before sighting something. That "something" was a 37-mm anti-aircraft gun that fired two clips at us.

I was able to pinpoint his position in the dark because of three small fires on the ground that surrounded him, probably unknown to the gun crew. We flew high over the gun's position to get a TACAN reading and then checked it on our map. It was well off any road, and in an area where there were no known villages.

Colonel McMullen gave me the elevation of the terrain at the gun position and figured out the best heading for a pass on it. Through we carried flares, we knew it was to our advantage to attack a gun in the dark. We rolled in and laid CBUs (cluster bomb units) across the triangle formed by our three reference fires.

One of the bomblets scored a direct hit on some munitions that flared into an intense pinpoint of white fire, sending rays of light through the trees almost like a spotlight. Colonel McMullen saw three more guns come up during our first pass, but we chose to ignore them and concentrate on the fire we had started.

After climbing back up to our base altitude, we informed the nearest FAC, a C-123, that we had a good target for him to look over, He started for our position, bringing with him the A-26 with which he was working. Since we had already been out for more than three hours and fuel was beginning to become a problem, we decided to lay more ordnance around our first strike rather than wait for the C-123.

Three more passes on the target with fire bombs turned the area into an inferno.

We could see secondary explosions every few seconds, and our incoming friends had no trouble finding their new target. We remained in the area while the C-123 made a pass over the growing fire.

His observer shouted over the radio, "My God, you found a truck park!" He counted eight burning trucks and said that the secondary explosions were coming from oil drums and crated cargo laid out on the ground. As we departed for NKP we heard him begin to brief his A-26 on the target.

This was a particularly good mission because of the target we had found—the truck park. The objective of interdiction is, of course, to stop the enemy's supplies from reaching him. We learned that destroying trucks on the Trail and putting craters in the roads made the enemy's logistics operation more difficult, but was not coming close to achieving the objective. Obviously the Communists were getting enough supplies down the Trail to support a very large war in South Vietnam.

Bombing the road system itself was an almost futile exercise, because of the many bypasses and alternates available and because of the large labor force permanently stationed on the Trail. Thus, it was especially satisfying to find and hit one of the large caches of supplies destined for South Vietnam. We found them occasionally, but not often enough.

Magnificent Airplane

The A-26 was a magnificent airplane. It did its job better than any other could have, and I'm sure that any pilot could share my attachment to the Nimrod. But, I also have tremendous admiration for the other aircrews and airplanes that worked the Trail. The FACS, whether in O-2s, C-123s, or C-130s, were the indispensable eyes of the team. Un-armed or lightly armed, they braved all the gunfire that came up at us. I never saw a FAC get chased off a target by ground fire.

The other members of the strike force are equally deserving of praise. During the early part of my tour, we frequently worked with T-28s, whose call sign was "Zorro." I was told at one of my early briefings at NKP that "if a Zorro can find a truck, he'll get it every time." I soon learned that this was true. The Zorro pilots finally wore out their T-28s, and near the end of my tour reappeared on the Trail in A-1s, as deadly as before.

Another group of pilots I really respected were our friends in the B-57s, out of South Vietnam. The B-57 came closest to matching the capabilities of the A-26 for this mission, and it was always a pleasure to team up with one. The B-57 crews I saw were all gutty, excellent marksmen.

The F-4s that worked the Trail with us were obviously a different class of airplane from those I've mentioned. Their greater speed, wider patterns, and higher roll-in altitudes were all drawbacks for night strikes. Even so, I saw many F-4 pilots lay their ordnance exactly where the FACs wanted it.

But for me, the Nimrod will always be King of the Trail. I feel fortunate to have had an opportunity to fly it. It made me a part of something I thought I could only look at—like a museum piece—as I did that day in 1964 at Williams AFB. Nimrod was a mighty hunter and its crews, proud men.

Forward Air Controller Perspective

NKP Combat Operations

Jimmie Butler

Lieutenant Colonel Pallister (left) and Captain Jimmie Butler (FAC pilot, right) (courtesy Jimmie Butler).

Beginning in February 1967, I was a USAF forward air controller (FAC) flying unarmed Cessna O-1s and O-2s out of NKP. We patrolled the Steel Tiger section of the Ho Chi Minh Trail through central Laos. Our basic mission was to search for targets and to direct airstrikes against those targets.

A FAC's main job was to *know*: to know and understand the enemy's actions and capabilities and to know our capabilities to respond. Therefore, when an experienced FAC expresses an opinion about his areas of responsibility, that opinion carries some weight. In that year as a first lieutenant, then captain, I had more authority and responsibility daily than I could expect in my next 10 years in the Air Force.

About 10 percent of my 240 missions were at night over the Trail in the 10th month of my combat tour. Our basic night tactic out of NKP was as a hunter/killer team. The hunter was a FAC and an observer with a Starlight Scope looking for trucks out of the right window of an O-2. The killer was an Air Commando flying an armed T-28 (Call-sign Zorro) out of NKP. We also controlled airstrikes by any other aircraft sent to us.

O-1 Bird Dog (FAC aircraft) in flight (courtesy Jimmie Butler).

While I did not get to work a lot with the Nimrods, I was happy whenever Alley Cat gave us an A-26 with its large armament load and night-savvy crew.

I remember two missions.

On 29 October, our assigned sector included Foxtrot, the best interdiction point in central Laos. Route 911 emerged from the jungle and was in the open for three miles on the hillsides west of the Xe Namkok River. Unlike most of the Trail where jungle was within a hundred yards, there was no place to hide in Foxtrot.

A one-lane road. No guard rails. No U-turns.

Consequently, the jungle-covered hills above the road and the large meadow on the east side of the river had many, many 37-mm antiaircraft artillery (AAA) weapons—the primary aircraft killers at that time in Steel Tiger—and antiaircraft machine guns. Nearly 35 years later, I stood on the road through Foxtrot. I told our little group of travelers that in certain seasons of the year, men fought and died here almost every night.

My observer immediately located 11 trucks with their lights on coming into Foxtrot. I called Alley Cat for ordnance. The controller said an A-26 had just taken off. He said I would have the Nimrod in 20 minutes and assigned a strike frequency. While we kept the trucks in sight, I talked to the A-26 pilot as he got closer. He said if the trucks still had their lights on, he wanted to make a blacked-out, head-on pass without us marking the target or dropping a flare. That is how open Foxtrot was during that time period.

Within 15 seconds, all 11 trucks turned off their lights.

Communications security was a major problem over Laos with the enemy listening in whenever they chose.

Instead of the Nimrod's innovative tactic blocking the road with the first truck near the south end of Foxtrot, we did not get them stopped before they disappeared into the jungle.

Interdiction Point Foxtrot, Ho Chi Minh Trail (courtesy Jimmie Butler).

When I got back for debriefing, I was still angry. Using strike frequencies routinely monitored by the enemy was ridiculous. However, technology did not support the overall battlefield command and control system by having regular frequencies that could not be monitored. Higher headquarters could not make up and distribute new frequencies to be used every day.

Nevertheless, maybe we could make up different strike frequencies to be used each night. FACs were trained to solve problems.

Each night, the crews of NKP's little hunter/killer force of Nail FACs, Zorros, and Nimrods received our mission briefings in the same briefing room—with the same chalkboard on the wall. I suggested that the first FACs of each night make up two frequencies for each of the three communications radios on the O-2 and write those frequencies on the chalkboard. The briefers each night would tell the following crews to copy down those frequencies.

My notes from a mission briefing about two weeks later include:

A. 231.6	C. 118.9	E. 46.5
B. 255.5	D. 124.7	F. 50.2

Here is how that little NKP-based scheme worked over the Trail. Whenever Alley Cat assigned us a Nimrod or a Zorro, they assigned a normal strike frequency. In a minute or two, the strike pilot would check in on that frequency. I would say something like, "Roger, this is Nail 12. Let's go up Alpha." We would both change to 231.6.

There was a slim possibility that 231.6 would be someone else's active frequency. If so, the FAC might say, "Let's go up point 2." Both aircraft would switch to 231.8.

This little scheme worked surprisingly well. I did not see anyone on the ground ever react again to anything we said during airstrikes. This was just one example of the close cooperation among NKP's people to get the mission accomplished.

On 18 November in the jungle north of Foxtrot, we had better luck with one of the Nimrod's "funny bombs." A convoy scattered under the jungle when we dropped the first flare. A funny bomb covered a large area with fire, and the Nimrods in their low-level attacks out of the darkness were more accurate than any of the jets dropping from much higher.

After two or three passes by the Nimrod, we let the jungle go dark again, except for the fire. Even without a Starlight Scope, I saw enough to credit the Nimrod with four trucks. (We only declared a truck kill when a truck was burning, so the Nimrods undoubtedly killed more trucks than we could ever give them credit for.) I saw four brightly burning rectangles in two rows of two where they had taken cover near the road.

A big thing I loved about Nimrods: As long as we had trucks, they had ordnance.

In my 11 months at NKP, the Nimrod squadron lost five aircraft and four crews. (Normal squadron complement of 12 aircraft.) Night flying for a full tour was a challenging and dangerous assignment.

While at the Air War College, I did extensive research on air interdiction over the Ho Chi Minh Trail. For example, in December 1966, during the Nimrods' first dry season over the Trail, they flew 7 percent of USAF sorties in Steel Tiger and claimed 80 percent of trucks destroyed or damaged. Not everyone's mission was to kill trucks, but killing trucks was the reason NKP's fliers went to the Trail each night. I concluded from research and personal experience as a FAC that the Nimrods were the best truck killers in Southeast Asia until the AC-130s—with all their electronic wizardry and firepower—became operational in the late 1960s.

This small group of brave aviators, flying their somewhat updated aircraft from World War II, destroyed huge amounts of weapons and munitions headed for the battlefields of South Vietnam. One price of their bravery is that 22 Nimrod names are engraved on the Vietnam Veterans Memorial in Washington, D.C. If not for the bravery of all the Nimrods, that memorial wall would be larger.

Memorable Flight of Nimrod 31

Jimmie Butler

The successes of the Nimrods were not without costs. In the early evening of December 14, 1966, Nimrod 31 was attacking a target near Tchepone when automatic weapons fire from a ZPU-2 struck the aircraft. Although his aircraft was hit in the right wing and the left engine, Lieutenant Colonel Albert Howarth rolled the A-26 back in and dropped CBU-14 across the gun position. Pulling up off the target, the crew jettisoned the rest of the ordnance and headed for NKP. The left engine, however, had developed an uncontrollable fire.

A few miles west of Foxtrot, Colonel Howarth ordered the crew (Captain Jack Bell and Captain Harold Cooper—both navigators) to abandon the A-26. The first navigator had no trouble getting out of the aircraft from his position in the copilot's seat. The other new navigator, occupying the cramped seat located directly behind the copilot's seat, did encounter some difficulty. As he tried to move his large frame from the cramped position, his parachute harness tangled on some of the aircraft equipment.

A newspaper article on the mission described Colonel Howarth's heroism in the following way.

> Despite the critical situation and diminishing chances of his own survival, Colonel Howarth, while maintaining firm control of the aircraft, physically assisted the remaining navigator in getting disentangled, and only after insuring his safe egression did he parachute to safety.

All three crewmen landed near the southern end of the jungle-covered ridgeline known to NKP's crews as the Big Rooster Tail. Another Nimrod responded to the Mayday call. Well after dark, that A-26 was joined by a search and rescue team consisting of an HH-3E Jolly Green, two UH-1Fs Hueys, and four A-1E Skyraiders. The area was essentially undefended, and the ridge line was relatively smooth with no jagged peaks, so the SAR commander decided to attempt a night rescue. Jolly Green 55, piloted by Captain Oliver O'Mara, picked up two of the downed Nimrods, while Captain Frederick Yontek's Huey (UH-1F) rescued the third crewman. This rescue mission was credited as one of the first, if not the first, night combat saves of the war.

The courageous actions during the ill-fated flight of Nimrod 31 were judged by a review board as the most meritorious flight of 1966. For his "exemplary courage and airmanship" during that dark night over the Ho Chi Minh Trail, Colonel Howarth earned the highly coveted Mackay Trophy for 1966.

(Note: During extensive research at the Air War College, I became familiar with the story above. I composed this story based on information and quotes from an article in the 9 August 1967 issue of *NKP News*, the base newspaper at Nakhon Phanom Royal Thai AFB, and from the December 1966 edition of the Summary of Air Operations Southeast Asia, produced monthly at PACAF Headquarters. Jimmie H. Butler, Nail 12.)

February 1967
A Sad Month for NKP

JIMMIE BUTLER

Arriving at your first combat base is a personal experience. Most who survive a combat tour will remember those early days.

The Nimrods had deployed as a squadron to a very primitive airfield in the jungle at NKP almost a year earlier. U.S. Army and Marine Corps personnel usually deployed to SEA in large units. Most U.S. Navy personnel arrived and departed together on their ships.

I was one of four replacement forward air controllers (FACs) who reached NKP on the Klong Shuttle from Bangkok on 7 February 1967. The 23rd Tactical Air Support Squadron (23rd TASS) was down to under 40 pilots for 32 sorties per day. Since the beginning of the year, three FACs were shot down in their small, unarmed Cessna O-1s over Laos and North Vietnam.

We knew even less about what we were getting into than most. We had gotten refresher training for a few days in the O-1 Bird Dog in South Vietnam. The instructors, who knew about NKP, said in hushed tones that they could tell us no details about what we would be doing. They knew we would be flying over the heavily defended Ho Chi Minh Trail in the secret war against the North Vietnamese invasion of neutral Laos. We did not know until 7 February.

NKP was the smallest of the major U.S. airfields in Thailand. Korat, Takhli, Udorn, Ubon, and U-Tapao all had long, concrete runways with several large USAF units flying mostly jets. NKP had a shorter, metal runway that was slick when wet—and a forecast rainfall of 80 inches during the summer monsoon in May through August. And, the relatively few aircraft we had in the 56th Air Commando Wing, the 23rd TASS, and the detachment from Udorn's Air Rescue Squadron all had propellers. Most other Thai bases made headlines for their missions deep into North Vietnam. NKP's fliers seldom made headlines in our 24-hour-a-day fight in the secret war.

February 1967 was not a good month to arrive at NKP. My review of USAF casualties for February in SEA showed the Air Force lost 11 aircraft in combat with 14 crewmen killed in action in USAF aircraft. Another USAF pilot was lost on a U.S. Navy F-4B.

Of those 11 aircraft lost and 15 fliers killed in February, four aircraft and six crewmembers made their final takeoff from NKP. Those deaths came on two days in February 1967.

The 56th ACW and the 23rd TASS flew about 50 aircraft. Detachment 1 of the 38th Aerospace Rescue and Recovery Squadron kept two HH-3E Jolly Green Giant helicopters and four A-1 Skyraiders on alert at NKP. In real numbers, our losses would have been called small by the bureaucracy at higher headquarters—but there were not a lot of us flying across the river every day into enemy territory. Nevertheless, with the arrival of the Nimrods in the spring of 1966, that little force of old, propellor-driven aircraft became the USAF's most effective force at night against the enemy flooding the Ho Chi Minh Trail through central Laos.

* * *

The 6th was NKP's deadliest February day. Captain Lucius L. Heiskell, Nail 65, flew his O-1 deep into the Mu Gia Pass, the deadliest target area in central Laos. Fighter pilots who flew missions over the concentrations of antiaircraft artillery (AAA) in Mu Gia would recognize immediately what a ridiculous mission that was for a Bird Dog flying at about 100 knots. Heiskell was shot down by 37-mm AAA while he directed an airstrike about three miles across the border in North Vietnam. He parachuted from his O-1, then established radio contact saying he was trying to evade nearby enemy troops.

A rescue force of Jolly Green Giant helicopters and A-1 Skyraiders launched immediately from NKP. They were unable to make contact before low clouds moved in over Heiskell.

Weather improved in the afternoon, and Jolly Green 05 picked up Captain Heiskell. Almost immediately, a 37-mm gun firing down on the helicopter from higher on the side of the pass shot down Jolly Green 05. Major Patrick H. Wood, Captain Richard A. Kibbey, and Staff Sergeant Donald J. Hall of the 38th Aerospace Rescue and Recovery Squadron died along with Captain Heiskell.

The crew's pararescueman, Airman 1st Class Duane Hackney, was the lone survivor. He had just picked up a parachute before being blown out of the helicopter when it was hit. His parachute opened up enough for him to survive before he went into the jungle. The second Jolly Green rescued Hackney shortly thereafter. For his extraordinary heroism that day, Airman Hackney became the first living enlisted man in USAF history to be awarded the Air Force Cross. He also was awarded the 1967 Cheney Award.

NKP was a small base few heard about within the big war that was growing in 1967. Yet, in less than two months, the A-26 squadron commander, Lieutenant Colonel Albert Howarth, earned the Mackay Trophy for 1966, and Airman Hackney earned the 1967 Chaney Award, both highly coveted, USAF-wide honors.

February 7 was a grim day to arrive at the 23rd TASS for our first combat assignments. We attended a rather heated pilots' meeting that evening. After three quick losses, it was obvious that 23rd TASS FACs were not going to survive flying at the same altitudes flown by in-country FACs.

Not a good introduction to the start of a combat tour.

In two weeks, I got another firsthand introduction to the hazards facing NKP's fliers. At breakfast that morning, I learned two A-26s had crashed during the night just east of the base. I have details, but I defer to Jim (Lee) McCleskey's firsthand report of being one of the two survivors.

By 22 February, I had finished my combat training missions. Walking to the intelligence center for mission briefing, I was on my way to my 13th combat mission from NKP, my first as solo lead where I would be directing the airstrikes. The route to briefing from my living quarters passed the dispensary with the two, big ambulances parked in front. As I approached them that morning, corpsmen were removing two sheet-covered stretchers. A grim reminder, indeed, of the risks facing NKP fliers.

One of our assignments for the mission was to spend time afterward over the crash site so my wingman's photographer could get aerial photographs. I guess he got some good ones, but as we circled, I did not see anything I could recognize to tell me two A-26s had crashed there.

August 1967 would be the next bad month for the Nimrods.

* * *

NKP was a base where the few who wore flight suits and flew across the river received sharp salutes from the many in their fatigues who supported us. As a FAC who flew small, unarmed Cessnas, I knew that anytime I crossed the river, I might not be coming back. I am guessing most of the fliers in the Air Commando Wing and the rescue detachment lived with the same understanding.

February 1967 taught some of us that reality. All fliers assigned to NKP understood the dangers. Yet, whenever our names showed up on tomorrow's schedule, day after day, night after night, we saddled up and flew across the river to face whatever fate awaited.

I share great pride, along with many others, in the daring accomplishments of that small group of fliers.

Trouble Over the Trail

James "Lee" McCleskey

My navigator, Captain Mike Scruggs, and I were scheduled for an A-26 Barrel Roll mission in northern Laos with a takeoff around 0100 on 22 February 1967. As we were leaving the Tactical Units Operations Center (TUOC), we were told that a reconnaissance jet had reported many, many trucks rolling down the roads in Steel Tiger (central/southern Laos). We also received information that HQ 7th Air Force in Saigon was directing NKP to put an increased effort out into the area to stop those trucks. It seemed logical to divert us from the Barrel Roll mission, and, in the interest of time, to take the load already on the aircraft. Furthermore, we were to delay our takeoff slightly so that we could be joined by a returning A-26 (crewed by Captains Dwight Campbell and Bob Scholl) as soon as their aircraft was turned and ready to go. The thinking was that the double load of flares on our aircraft would work for both of us and it would be much faster to load the other A-26 with just bombs, rockets, bullets, and gas.

After all the hoop-jumping by the superb armament and other ground crews, we took off less than five minutes apart and headed out to an area a few miles south of the Mu Gia Pass in central Laos to search for targets. We didn't see "many, many trucks," but we did find a convoy of six or eight south of the pass and just north of Interdiction Point Delta. I told Dwight that we would provide flare light and flak suppression while he and Bob attacked, and then we could trade off. He stopped the convoy and started additional passes while Mike and I kept the flare light on the scene and made an occasional

A-26A (B-26K) with full load of ordnance flying in the vicinity of NKP (1967). Note that only the code "TA" and the serial number (671) appears on the vertical tail section. No U.S. insignia was depicted on these U.S. Nimrod aircraft because the aircraft were part of the "Secret War in Laos" (USAF).

drop on some of the AAA sites that were providing "moderate and close" defensive fire. After numerous passes, Dwight was getting low on weapons, except for the guns, so we swapped roles (except that we still had to keep the flares going). Even though the gunners on the ground were bothering us, their fire was not so close as to be much of a danger, especially when one of us would divert from time to time from the trucks to hit the gun positions, causing them to put their heads down a little. There was, however, one gun in the trees in direct alignment with the convoy on the road. Because both Dwight and I were making most of the passes along the road, vice across it, we kept getting fairly close to the stream of tracers from that gunner, especially during pullout from the passes. Meanwhile, about five miles to the south, a 37-mm AAA position began firing in our general direction, adding to the fun. We didn't see him as too much of a threat due to the time of flight of his rounds, and the fact that his big orange tracers clearly showed where the danger was.

On one of our strafe passes, the gunner in the trees was getting closer and closer to us, although he was having trouble adjusting to the fact that we were diving instead of going in a straight line. I got enough of that and, on the next gun pass, I allowed the pipper to drift right up into the trees where he was, and then sprayed the entire area by using a little pressure on the rudder pedals. I think that took care of him as he did not shoot at us on the next pass. However, when we pulled off to the left after that pass, the 37-mm gunner to the south was ready to try again. As he watched to his north, he probably saw a big, black A-26 silhouette against the flare light and he fired off another clip of seven rounds. One of those rounds impacted the bottom of the right wing in the vicinity of the right main fuel tank. It may have been somewhat tangential to the tank because it didn't cause the wing to fail. It did cause us to immediately lose 250 gallons of fuel and it started a small fire in the aft part of the wing/engine nacelle area. I knew it was a solid hit, so I turned toward the west, jettisoned everything off the wings (all internal bombs had already been expended), and started climbing for home while checking the condition of the aircraft. It was about this time that the right engine started to fail and the fire, as reported by Dwight and Bob as they escorted us, was growing. I feathered the engine and fired the fire suppression bottle into it. Dwight immediately reported that "You almost got it." At that point, we had to decide whether to fire the second bottle or to wait in case it got worse. We didn't have to wait long before Dwight advised that the fire was growing, so I fired the second bottle. Dwight came back with his then-classic line of "You almost got it."

By this time, we were somewhere around 3,000 feet and in reasonable flying condition on one engine and pointed toward Thailand and NKP. We heard the right main tire explode as the fire continued to grow. I was not thrilled with the possibility of a belly landing on the pierced steel planking runway at NKP. But since I couldn't get the gear down anyway, it would still be preferable to bailing out. I did, however, take the precaution of going over bailout procedures with Mike and reminding him to be sure to pull the "D ring" on his parachute. That latter part was more for my benefit, as Mike had always flown with a manual parachute in large aircraft and I had always flown jets with an ejection seat and automatic parachute deployment. The electrical system was being affected by the fire and the lights and radio were somewhat erratic. During this time, with things getting more and more exciting, I heard a very clear voice say that "*It is going to be OK!*" It was a very calming voice and there has never been any doubt in my mind that it was God speaking directly to me right then.

While Bob and Dwight continued escorting us back by flying to the rear and somewhat off to the side, we were joined by a C-130 flare ship overhead. We were approaching the Mekong River (the Laos-Thai border) and started feeling some more significant explosions while the flames seemed to be growing rather rapidly. I could see light from the flames through the small glass plate in the floor of the cockpit and heard the nose tire explode. Just as I reached up and jettisoned the canopies, I heard Dwight say, "You're coming apart … get out of it!" By that time, Mike had turned around and was having trouble diving over the side of the cockpit because the wind blast had forced him down onto the back of his seat. I let go of the controls and tried to help him get up and out but happened to sense that the aircraft appeared to be going out of control in the pitch-black nighttime darkness. This required me to return to flying the aircraft with one hand, while helping Mike with the other. He was able to exit shortly afterwards, and I immediately turned and dove over my side of the cockpit. Sometime between the time I left the cockpit and the opening of my parachute, the aircraft turned into a fireball. I say this because I looked for it right away and it was not there. The escort C-130 started putting out flares to aid us and to help the recovery helicopters in finding us. The NKP wing commander, Colonel Aderholt, had launched two CH-3E "Jolly Green Giants" to go get us in one of the first night pickups of the war. I estimate that we were about 300 feet above the ground when we went out. The time was roughly 0300 hours in the morning. There was not much time to think about making a good PLF (parachute landing fall) as the ground came up rather quickly. My own touchdown was more like a PFL (poor frapping landing).

Mike and I landed in rice paddies about a mile apart and we were recovered by separate helicopters. Mike had suffered a broken foot when he hit the cockpit on the way out of our aircraft. I broke an ankle landing in the rice paddy, probably because it was the dry season and the ground was extremely hard. I had also apparently ripped the leg of my flight suit from top to bottom as I left the cockpit and my left leg struck the horizontal stabilizer on the aircraft tail section. (I learned later that a navigator at Hurlburt Field had lost a leg a few years earlier when his leg hit the tail section after he had to bail out.) The black rubber residue on my calf was clear evidence that the deicer boot on the leading edge of the tail was what struck my leg. The blow damaged all the ligaments in the ankle and caused the leg to turn black from knee to toe in one huge blood clot. Mike and I were medevacked by C-130 the following evening to the big Air Force hospital at Clark Air Base in the Philippines. He was there about four weeks and then was released to a new assignment in Rescue C-130s in California. After six weeks, I returned to NKP and resumed flying a week or so after that. I finished my tour in November 1967 with 151 combat missions, 75 of which were over North Vietnam.

The sad, sad part of this story is that our good friends Dwight and Bob either flew through our exploding aircraft debris or possibly experienced a sympathetic explosion of some of the ordnance they still had on board. The C-130 crew reported that their aircraft took on a strange glow, went into a shallow glide, and crashed into one of the few trees in the area. They were both killed in the crash.

Every Pilot's Nightmare

James "Lee" McCleskey

During much of the rainy season in 1967, the main Nakhon Phanom runway was closed while the engineers converted it from pierced steel planking (PSP) to anti-skid aluminum planking. Combat and support operations continued by using the parallel PSP taxiway and edge of the aircraft parking ramp as the interim runway. This mission was with Jim Whipps as my navigator and we were scheduled for the Steel Tiger area of Laos. We taxied to the far end of the slippery PSP taxiway and turned around in the pouring rain for a takeoff to the east. The time was around 0300 or 0330 hours and it was really dark outside. The small "beanbag" lights along the edges of the substitute runway didn't do much for the visibility either. The tower cleared us for takeoff and we began the roll that turned into every pilot's nightmare. The instruments indicated we were getting full power from the engines and acceleration felt normal. I slowly raised the nose, and just as the aircraft lifted off, the left engine failed. (Subsequent investigation revealed that the duct providing air to the carburetor had collapsed internally and closed off almost all of the air.) All instruments showed that the engine had quit and I realized that I had to feather it quickly to have any hope of continuing flight. As I reached for the emergency T-handle to start the feathering and shutoff process, the aircraft's automatic feathering feature (designed for precisely this type of emergency) kicked in just ahead of me to start the sequence. Jim was working closely with me to keep maximum power on the good engine and helping me monitor the airspeed. We had to momentarily delay the jettisoning of all the armament and flares under the wings because our Tactical Units Operations Center (TUOC) was just ahead and slightly left of the nose. In spite of leveling off at a very low altitude, we were so heavy with ordnance and fuel that the airspeed was getting dangerously low. As soon as I could, I pushed the jettison button and everything on the wings fell away into the murk. We had the gear coming up and, when the gear doors closed, we felt a bit of acceleration, giving us hope that the bird was going to fly after all. We still had two 750-pound bombs in the bomb bay, but I couldn't see trying to drop them. The significantly increased drag from the open bomb bay doors would have been too large a penalty to pay.

Recovery at NKP in the rain and darkness on the slippery pseudo-runway was not an option, so we immediately headed west toward Udorn Royal Thai Air Force Base, a friendly jet base about 150 miles away. The runway there was concrete, wide, and long … much more appealing. It was necessary to run the right engine at near METO (maximum except for takeoff) power to try to climb a bit and to keep up our speed. This put a great deal of stress on the good engine and both of us worried about it lasting long enough to get us to Udorn. Eventually, the rain slacked off, the clouds started thinning, and Jim was able to establish radio contact with Udorn tower. Things were looking up— we thought. Tower cleared us for a long straight-in approach to the nearest runway. I delayed lowering the gear until we were closer to the field than normal. When I did put it down, the gear indicators in the cockpit showed only two green lights. The nose gear indicated unsafe. As Jim and I discussed this additional challenge, he made the valid point that, if the nose gear really was unsafe and collapsed on touchdown, the two big bombs behind us would immediately move forward and be right in the cockpit with us. He strongly recommended we go around and try a manual extension of the nose gear. His point was well taken, but my worries about the reliability of the right engine to operate much longer at such high power caused me to decide to go ahead and land, hoping for the best. I carefully eased the aircraft down onto the big concrete runway just as we both heard a distinct "thunk" sound. I glanced down at the gear lights and saw three green. Rollout and clearing of the runway were very normal and relaxing.

A Dangerous Hunt and a Close Call

James "Lee" McCleskey

My navigator at the time (I believe it was Jim Cavell) and I flew a series of missions into Barrel Roll in northern Laos, just southwest of Hanoi. On two successive missions, we had spotted a very large truck working his way through the mountains west of Sam Neua. Weather was a factor for us, but it had emboldened the driver so that he was running with his lights on both times. However, as soon as we dropped a flare, he shut off his lights and we lost him in the terrain and clouds. Jim and I schemed a way to finally get him before he got away. On the third trip to the area, we had agreed to shoot him in the dark with the guns, hopefully stopping him on the road so we could then flare and finish him off.

It was shortly after we arrived in the area that we spotted the big, loaded truck coming around the mountain, again with his headlights on. The clouds were quite low, but it appeared we had room to begin the attack with a strafe pass, so that's the way we lined up. I knew we had only that one pass to stop him, so I flew a rather long final approach to make sure we got it right. Bear in mind, we were looking at a single set of headlights through total darkness with intermittent rain and clouds. For those who have been there, I'm sure you can grasp what is happening. When I finally squeezed the trigger, the time of flight for the bullets was very short and the impact was on the hillside above the truck. I also realized we were faster in the dive than I had planned. I "bunted" (pushed the nose down slightly) momentarily, and then realized we were far too close to the target. My navigator realized we were too low, too fast, and needed to do something quickly. He and I both pulled back on the sticks simultaneously, and as we zoomed up into the clouds we were braced for impact. Fortunately, it appears that God does look after dummies (this dummy in particular) and we cleared the terrain and made a steep climb recovery on instruments in the dark and clouds. We never saw the truck again, but I sure relearned a lesson about something known as "target fixation."

A-26s—How We Kept Them Flying

Jim Galluzzi

During the hot and humid days and nights at NKP in June and July of 1967, we started to have some problems with low BMEP and low manifold pressure on takeoff roll. A dangerous situation, especially on a short PSP runway and with a heavy bomb load. This serious problem resulted in a much higher abort rate than usual.

What was the problem? All of us maintenance types were scratching our heads! Why? Because, during the morning hours, the problems with the aircraft that had aborted the night before could not be duplicated. We could not find a problem with engine performance during the run-up checks when they were performed by our engine mechanics. As the flight line maintenance officer, and having been checked out in the aircraft, I would perform a "high-speed taxi check." In performing the check, I would simulate a takeoff roll down the active runway (no bomb load of course), to check out engine performance and to try to duplicate the low BMEP and low manifold pressure instrument readings. However, during these checks, the engines developed the proper power and performed to specifications. I would sign off the aircraft and it was "returned to service." Unfortunately, in several instances, the same aircraft that had checked out okay during the morning check run would later cause an abort, on takeoff roll, for a night combat mission with a full bomb load. Needless to say, this situation caused a lot of concern, not only with the flight crews, but also on the maintenance side—and my ass was on the line—in front of Colonel "Heinie" Aderholt (the wing commander), wanting to know what the hell was going on!

Well, I managed to convince him and the DCM (Colonel Jug Hess) to give me some time to try and figure out what we could do to solve the problem. (At the expense of my

Crucial and challenging engine maintenance, circa 1968 (USAF).

Air Force career I might add). Working with the Maintenance Records guys, we managed to narrow down the problem to about six aircraft. We took those aircraft off the line for a more exhaustive engine shake down.

During the de-cowling process on one of the affected aircraft, an engine mechanic noticed that the hard rubber "boot" which connected the top half of the cowling to the to the carburetor appeared to be too soft. On the top of the cowling, starting from the leading front edge, there was a covered air passageway (intake), the length of the cowling, which provided proper airflow, through the "boot" directly into the carburetor. After mulling the soft boot situation over for a while, we collectively concluded that on takeoff roll, with hot and humid conditions, and the "hot" airflow pressure flowing to the carburetor through the boot, the boot was probably collapsing enough to restrict the proper amount of airflow to the carburetor during high power demands on the engine.

The question: how to fix the probable cause of the problem?! We checked the "supply house" and there were no spare boots. Well, in a combat zone, you do what you have to do to fix a problem! Again, we collectively came up with a "Commando fix" (unauthorized and without the tech order paperwork). We managed to stiffen the boot by riveting and securing two pieces of aluminum, about 4" wide, against the top and bottom surfaces of the boot, thereby preventing it from collapsing at high power settings. We did this on both engines.

I did a thorough run-up and taxi check down the runway—about four times. Everything checked good. The acid test came later—on a combat mission. I told our QC flight test pilot what we had done to fix the problem. After he and I had a consultation with the DCM and then Heinie to explain the "fix," Heinie agreed that we could schedule the modified aircraft for a combat mission that night. Since the QC pilot was authorized to fly combat missions, it was agreed that he would fly the mission. I also volunteered to fly the right seat, but I was denied.

We all watched: the flight line guys, the engine mechanics who worked on the engines, the sheet metal tech who fabricated the fix, the DCM, and Heinie. We watched intently as power was applied on takeoff roll. The "Commando modified" aircraft flew beautifully and returned from its mission without a write-up! Did we find the *fix*?

Well, one modified aircraft—and one mission in which the aircraft performed and didn't abort! Maybe that's just luck! Heinie was happy; he gave the DCM instructions to try the mod on a couple of more aircraft to see if we had really solved the problem. We complied—and the problem appeared to be successfully solved—so we modified all the aircraft and never again had low power and BMEP problems.

Not the end of the story! Being a good DCM (SAC trained, but a great guy), Jug decided he should notify the depot responsible for the A-26 and explain to them the problem and what we did to fix it. They immediately responded with, "You can't do that—that's an unauthorized modification to an aircraft—we will ground all the aircraft." Jug quickly told them that "if they could come up with a better fix—have at it. We're in a combat situation and need flyable aircraft. We are going to continue flying the aircraft as they are." Within a week, two engineers from the Sacramento depot descended upon us at NKP to investigate. Happy to say they were "all right" guys who understood the problem and the necessity of our improvised fix.

After a week of observing our operation (and happy to be collecting combat pay), they were satisfied the "Commando modification" would work, and it would be okay until a permanent fix could be engineered. About two months later the "real" fix was engineered and published. All aircraft in the inventory were to be modified accordingly—starting with the aircraft at NKP. The permanent fix entailed eliminating the air duct (air passageway from the front of the cowling and the rubber boot to the carburetor) and replacing it with an "air scoop" about 6" high above the carburetor to provide unobstructed airflow to the carburetor. It worked! We never had the problem again! Eventually, all aircraft were modified, including #679, the only flyable A-26A (B-26K) left in the world!

Just Another Day at NKP

Jim Galluzzi

I started my association with A-26 aircraft at Hurlburt Field, Florida, in 1965. I was only there a short time when the wing was transferred to England AFB, Louisiana in 1966. At England AFB, I became the 850th OMS commander, and as such I was responsible for all flight line operations and aircraft. The wing had some unique flying slots for people other than pilots and navs. Since I had previous flying experience, including pilot training for 11 months before washing out (another story—there was a general USAF pilot surplus at the time), and my maintenance experience, I was selected to become "right seat" qualified in the A-26. Over the years, I accumulated more than 650 hours of

A-26A Counter Invader ready for another combat mission; note wing flare racks (courtesy Joe Kittinger).

Farm Gate crew: Jack Mezzo (top) and Woody Halsey (courtesy Maury Bourne).

"right seat" time flying mostly test flights, including 185 hours in Southeast Asia at NKP (Nakhon Phanom RTAFB, Thailand).

One day, in June or July of 1967, I got an unexpected opportunity to land an A-26 at NKP from the right seat on a 5,000-foot PSP runway. Woody Halsey (our quality control pilot) and I were up flying a test flight for an engine change. As was the procedure, we climbed to 10,000 feet before "punching" off the new engine and running the checklist. When we completed what we had to do, Woody told me to bring us back to NKP and go ahead and "shoot" an approach before landing. Previously, I had flown many test flights with Woody, so he knew that I could handle the aircraft, and he also knew about my pilot training experience.

Much to my delight it was a chance to impress Woody with my flying skills. So, without hesitation I made a "Commando" approach to the runway, dropping several thousand feet in a very short time! To the surprise of both of us, Woody suffered a severe and painful sinus block. He was very much "out of it" and incapacitated. He managed to tell me to declare an emergency and land the aircraft as soon as possible, which I did without further incident. Upon landing, I taxied off the active runway at the south end of the runway where all the emergency vehicles met us. I quickly shut down both engines and tried to help Woody. Among the group that gave us a real "VIP" welcome was Colonel Harry "Heinie" Aderholt, the wing commander. After the medics took care of Woody and things quieted down the focus by Heinie was—*Who landed the aircraft?* Smiling, I said, "I did!" Somewhat surprised, he put his arm around me and said, "You deserve a medal, and a big thank-you."

Needless to say, that landing was the talk of the day at NKP and a gratifying event in my life. Woody eventually recovered and everything went back to normal on the flight line—just another day at NKP!

"Maintenance Meanies"—12, "Flight Crews"—6

Mike Packard

In 1931, my dad dropped out of high school during his senior year (Salem, Oregon) to join the Army Air Corps. "Blind as a bat," he couldn't be a pilot so he chose aircraft maintenance. He would spend the rest of his 60-plus years around airplanes; the day before he died he had been tinkering with a friend's Cessna 172. Most of Dad's adult working life was spent with Lockheed Aircraft, the last 20 years as a C-130 tech rep. Reading this book makes the chances of your having flown in a C-130 fairly good.

As a product of New Mexico State's AFROTC program, I also wound up in aircraft maintenance. The genetics simply ran too deep for me to do otherwise. Although I learned how to fly a Cessna 140 during college, my eyes, too, failed me so the decision was essentially made for me. Nine months at Chanute Field learning the composition of an airplane set me up to become an aircraft maintenance officer for a squadron of C-130s at Pope AFB, North Carolina. I recall the most important discussion of my short four-year Air Force career taking place a week before I graduated from Chanute. It happened at the same place a lot of other significant discussions have and will continue to take place, the "O Club" bar. One of my instructors, a captain, approached me and asked if I had a moment. I did, of course. He said, "Lieutenant, you are about to take on a huge responsibility at Pope." I countered that I was lucky to have a father that was a C-130 tech rep. His response was something to the effect that was all well and good but that I was going to spend seven days a week overseeing 60–70 sergeants and airmen, all of whom knew a lot more about their jobs than I did, and that the smartest thing that I could do was to keep my mouth shut, listen, and observe. That captain's advice was a huge reason for my ultimate success as an officer.

I was not married during my Air Force tenure, and as a result I often volunteered for TDYs (temporary duty assignments) to allow my fellow married officers the opportunity to remain with their families. I spent late 1965 and early 1966 in the Dominican Republic to assist the 82nd Airborne and the OAS quell a communist attempt to overthrow the Dominican government. That was one of America's finest hours, yet like Grenada and other relief efforts around the world by our military, that great effort seems to have been forgotten by the media. In late summer of 1966, I volunteered for an extended TDY to Mildenhall, England. Oh well, someone had to go! During that opportunity, I assisted with two NATO exercises: one at Rhein Main, Germany, and the other a German air base near Munich. The first exercise involved my only real "screwup" as a maintenance officer. Keeping airplanes in the air is the primary goal of aircraft maintenance. With a C-130 grounded due to a broken propeller, and my ground crew without a propeller sling to remove and replace it, I ordered the first one I could find. When the sling was delivered we found it to be for an A model C-130 instead of the B models we were servicing. My dad, "the C-130 tech rep," never let me live that one down.

After too many months of fun (121 days to be exact) in England and "the Continent," I finally went home to Pope. In early 1967, I volunteered for Vietnam, not only to save a married maintenance officer from the grief of spending a year away from his family but because I knew for career advancement, it was simply the right thing to do.

In June of 1967, I received orders for an Air Commando Squadron at Nakhon Phanom (NKP), Thailand. I remember the briefing I received before my departure about the fact that I was to be involved in a clandestine operation. The briefing team was able to give me some information; however, it was not until my first day at NKP that I found out the truth about a "secret war" that I would help support for the next 12 months. On that day I also received my requisite "bush hat" and "jungle boots" that I would wear consistently for the next year. I was assigned to a two-man bungalow where my roommate was Captain Steve Powers. Steve was a great maintenance officer and would one day be promoted to O-6 (colonel).

I was to become the officer in charge of aircraft maintenance for the A-26 Nimrod squadron whose primary mission was to destroy trucks on the Ho Chi Minh Trail in Laos at night. For the first two months, I worked under Captain Jim Galluzzi, who was the OIC for A-26 maintenance. I learned a lot from Jim (who, by the way, eventually left the Air Force, becoming a wine distributor in Florida and a 20-plus-year NHL referee) as I had never seen an A-26 twin engine assault bomber before I arrived at NKP. Jim taught me how to "crank up" the airplane, which was not easy to do, plus everything about its mechanics. I found soon that parts for the airplane were a valuable commodity and that unfortunately several airplanes had to be taken out of service so that we would have enough spare parts for the remaining aircraft. Those aircraft were simply cannibalized or "cannon balled," per the slang translation.

Sometime after I took on Captain Galluzzi's duties, it became all too apparent that meeting the nightly sortie requirements that our mission demanded was going to be a challenge. Far too many sorties were aborted every night due to maintenance issues. Thanks to a great boss in Colonel "Jug" Hess, a superb first sergeant in E-9 Roger Smith,

60–70 airmen who understood the need to work "12 on and 12 off," six days a week, and my decision to micromanage the whole effort, we got "things turned around." Not only did aborted sorties diminish, I recall one 31-day stretch where we had zero aborts. That resulted in my buying beer for everyone once a week every week we had zero aborts for "jobs well done."

Since the mission of our A-26 aircraft was primarily to destroy trucks, our maintenance guys painted a truck on the side of our flight crew's airplanes after they notched a truck kill.

A typical day for me was to go to the flight line midmorning and to return when the last sortie returned later that night. However, rarely did I miss a stop at the "O Club" on the way back to my barracks. I can still remember the heat and humidity that our maintenance personnel dealt with during the day. There were a few months in the winter when the days got a bit cooler but not much. I can remember requesting an electric blanket from home and using it for those months.

Early on, I came to recognize that a genius had tapped the greatest aircrews in the Air Force to fly, navigate, and act as spotters on these incredible airplanes. I was fortunate to know most all crewmembers and unfortunate to suffer along with them when we lost crewmembers and their planes. Pilot Major Carlos Cruz sought me out early on and made it clear how much he appreciated the hard work and dedication of our maintenance team. At his request, I flew with him after an engine change to check out the new engine. For the uninitiated, the true test for whether a new or rebuilt engine will work or not is to have that engine fly the airplane while the other engine is "feathered" (not operating). After the checkout, Carlos flew that airplane in ways not many other A-26 pilots ever did. He spun the airplane, chased sampans on the Mekong and water buffalo through fields. To this day, I have never had a more exhilarating experience.

We lost Carlos Cruz and his crew, Bill Potter, navigator, and Paul Foster, "spotter," shortly thereafter. He was a super pilot, simply fearless. Carlos was Puerto Rican by birth; Puerto Rico would be proud of their hero. Fortunately, the daughter of Carlos Cruz, Carla, has "appeared" after many years and many Air Commandos have gotten to know her; importantly, she attended the A-26 reunion in 2009.

Colonel John Shippey, the A-26 squadron commander, was a hero to me for numerous reasons—most of all for his quiet leadership style. John Shippey was the person everyone looked up to. Unfortunately, he suffered a tragedy on a mission one night when his navigator, Bo Hertlein, was killed by a 50-millimeter shell while on an assault on trucks. Bo's father was a Georgia legislator and Bo would often brag about how many votes his dad would garner if he should be killed in action.

Major Pietsch and his navigator, Louis Guillermin, and I had lunch together the day they were shot down over Laos. Major Pietsch left a wife and four children. He and Louis were two superfine people. This was to be their last mission before returning to the States.

Although most of the year all of us spent at NKP was a lot of work, and little "play," there were some bright spots. Bob Hope and his entourage, including Raquel Welch, provided us with a great show over the 1967 holiday period. That certainly didn't hurt morale. I do not remember whether that night resulted in a "stand-down" for missions or not. To my delight, Ms. Welch rode in my jeep, although I was not her escort.

Billy Casper also made an appearance and hit dozens of balls into the jungle while providing golf lessons some of us wouldn't be able to use for a long time.

Ironically, over the 1967 holiday season, Colonel Gerry Larson, who would one day be promoted to major general and work for me many years later during our civilian years, landed a wounded F-105 on our aluminum airstrip. General Larson's "claim to fame" was that he was a Thunderbird pilot in the early 1960s, flying the solo position.

Unfortunately, there were too many sad events that took place during that year in addition to our lost Nimrod comrades. I recall an A-1E returning from a daytime sortie in the middle of a monsoon rain and flipping on its back and then into a culvert that had filled with rainwater. I do not remember whether the pilot's cause of death was due to the landing trauma or drowning. I also witnessed a Thai Air Force T-28 explode on impact, and "sappers" attempting to disrupt our flight line one afternoon. They were quickly dealt with by our MPs.

Sadly, one evening an inebriated airman thought he would fly our "base C-47" home; he got the airplane airborne but not for long. He was killed and we lost a valuable aircraft.

The Navy joined us at NKP in early 1967. Their mission was to drop listening canisters in Laos from P-2V aircraft. Unfortunately, they lost many crews and eventually their mission was aborted.

I also remember a "Jolly Green Giant" helicopter bringing in a group of Green Berets that had been rescued from a hilltop in Laos. At least four of them were hanging on for their lives on a rope looped from a side cargo door. There was also a successful wheels-up landing by an O-2 one day. The runway had foam applied to it to cushion the landing.

Snakes, very bad ones, were common in Thailand, and in fact all of Southeast Asia. I came out to my jeep early one morning to find out I had run over a krait snake the night before. A bite from one of those guys would ruin your whole day; it is one of the deadliest snakes in the world.

I remember the aircraft at NKP made the "base" appear to be right out of World War II. A-26s (originally the B-26), A-1Es, and T-28s were certainly from that era, and the C-119 came not too much after the end of World War II. We also had O-2s and "Jolly Greens," and for a while the Navy P-2Vs.

I received the proverbial "Dear John" letter from my college girlfriend, who had met the love of her life at Baylor about halfway through my tour. Her soon-to-be husband would eventually receive his PhD in economics at Baylor and remains today as a professor of economics at that university. Although the news was very tough for me at the time, it worked out best for both of us. I ended up with a truly super wife, Jeri, who has managed to put up with me for many years.

I remember occasional trips to the town of Nakhon Phanom in my jeep. The clock tower presented to the town by Ho Chi Minh, and the fact that it was located next to the Mekong River, was the town's claim to fame. I frankly preferred being back at the base with my people.

The Thai people that worked at our base were simply unique. They were always happy and proficient. One never had to worry about getting your money's worth along with a smile from the local Thai people. I often wondered how such a peaceful folk reconciled our "mission," or if they even understood it.

As my year wound down, I was confronted with a tough decision. Colonel Hess offered me a regular commission and a shot at below-the-zone major if I would remain another six months at NKP. He did sweeten the offer with a promise of a 30-day leave before I undertook the next six months. I had many positives come my way during my decision-making process. Colonel Shippey gave me a painting of an A-26, the same one he provided to all A-26 aircrews, an honor that I will never forget. Sergeant Smith, on his departure about two months before I left NKP, shared some very positive thoughts with me about my job performance. He had experienced 30 years in the Army Air Corps and Air Force serving in World War II, Korea, and now the Vietnam conflict. E-9 Roger Smith would retire once he returned to his home in South Carolina as truly one of the finest NCOs ever. We were both recommended for the Bronze Star, which we received on our return to the States.

I ultimately turned Colonel Hess's offer down. I truly loved the Air Force and the opportunities it provided me. A "nonrated" officer (not a pilot or navigator) was/is somewhat of a second-class citizen in the Air Force and deservedly so. Aircrews put their lives on the line whenever they fly a mission in a wartime setting. They more than deserve their place on the pedestal. I, however, felt the need to pursue a career where I would not have a ceiling in terms of opportunity. There are very few "nonrated" generals, so the decision for me was inevitable.

In early 1968, either an aircrew member or a maintenance guy challenged the other to a touch football game of Maintenance versus Aircrews. Someone came up with the name of "Maintenance Meanies" (don't look that up in your dictionary!) in order I assume to intimidate the "Flight Crews" team. It must have worked because the Maintenance Meanies won 12–6. In retrospect, we had a lot of fun but we didn't feel any "meaner" after the game than we did before the game. We went right back to maintaining our A-26s, just as we had done only a few hours before.

A Night Flight with Saint Elmo

Jack Krause

One late summer night, my navigator and I launched from a remote jungle airfield west of the Mekong River for an interdiction mission over a large expanse east of that large river. We were flying a renovated A-26, twin-engine, fully loaded attack bomber modified for special operations, and were headed out to find and destroy enemy trucks, cars, bicycles, and water buffalo headed from north to south with strategic supplies for the enemy. The terrain we operated in was akin to the foothills of the Cascades north of Mt. Rainer. At night. Under flares.

We had been advised at our briefing of a line of thunderstorms running east and west that bisected the operational area. No problem, since we were going to be working the southern half anyway.

As we crossed the Mekong River heading east, we made contact with the airborne controlling agency and were vectored south to search out targets. It felt good to put the roiling storms behind us with all that lightning visible for miles.

However, a short time into our flight we received an urgent call from the airborne controller telling us to head north to help out a ground installation that was under enemy attack. That meant we would have to fly right through that ugly line of thunderstorms. If I had been texting back then, my response would have been, "OMG!!!" But what the heck, this is what we were getting the big bucks for, right?

We did a "180" turn, tightened down our seat belts, secured everything in the cockpit, and headed north. Hey, when somebody was in trouble, you just have to go help.

(It should be pointed out that although thunderstorms in the part of the world where this event took place are not as severe as those in the Southwest and Southeast U.S., this experience *should not* be taken as a suggestion by anyone that it is okay to fly into *any* thunderstorm on purpose. There are too many grave markers to prove it shouldn't be done.)

As we entered the towering columns of clouds partially illuminated by the rapidly recurring lightning, things began to get bumpy. And bumpier! And!! … Yikes!!! With my regular nav on leave, I had been paired for this flight with an older navigator who had once been a pilot officer during World War II and had more pilot time than any of us "youngsters." He had been recalled before the Korean conflict and was now a navigator. It was a comfort to have him along. For example, until that night, I had never utilized a "thunderstorm light" that many models of airplanes had in the cockpit in that era for negating the blinding flashes of lightning. In fact, I forgot we even had one until he turned it on. I appreciated his experience.

Things began to "intensify" as we proceeded into the jaws of this maelstrom. Sometimes we were mere passengers, and other times we actually got to steer the machine. One thing I will always remember is how much the wings actually flexed. What was worrisome is I didn't realize until that moment that the wings actually did flex on this airplane. Moreover, this model airplane had been removed from combat a couple of years prior because it had a tendency to shed wings. (It was eventually reworked and, obviously, put back into service.)

Then St. Elmo made his appearance. The windshield started glowing and sparkling a pale blue all around the edges. Then the side windows started to dance in blue. It was an intensity that I had never before experienced despite many hours flying in bad weather, including the far north, where St. Elmo hung out quite a bit. I peeked out at the wings and saw huge blue bow waves formed on the tip tanks. These fan-shaped apparitions stuck out at least five feet in front of the tanks. Then the armament under the wings began to glow with huge fan-shaped arcs of blue leading them. Then the propellers began to produce thick blue corkscrews that trailed back over the wings and trailed back into the darkness. Meanwhile, we were being thrown around inside the cockpit with disturbing intensity.

The finale occurred when a string of softball-sized globules of blue formed at the apex of the windshield and rolled down between our seats and into the bomb bay. This was mesmerizing to say the least. I actually tried to catch one, but there was nothing there.

Two more "terrifying" thoughts entered my mind about then. One was the effect of what all that static electricity was having on the fuses in the armament we were carrying. The other was how well we must be illuminated for those gunners on the ground. Just like a slow-moving meteor.

After about 25 minutes we popped out into a clear, smooth, star-illuminated black night. Phew.

After a sigh in relief, we made a call to the controlling agency in that sector to tell them that we were there and ready for action. You will never believe what they said. But here it is anyway. They asked, "What are you guys doing up here?" That is the truth. They advised they had nobody in trouble, no targets, and that we may as well go home.

Uttering another "OMG," we turned and headed for home. You may ask why we just didn't land up there and wait out the storm. Good question, except the wait would probably be in a bamboo cage chained to a hardwood pallet eating rice once a day for several years. We decided on the thunderstorms.

St. Elmo soon joined us again as we reentered the storms. The show was just as spectacular, but my arms were getting mighty tired. As we approached our airport, we were told that the weather was deteriorating badly, and that we should "hurry." We hurried and were soon on the GCA (PAR) final approach to our steel plank runway with the airplane's hydraulically operated windshield wipers humming at super speed. When my nav said we were at treetop level, and with no runway in sight, I added power and headed for our alternate about 90 miles west.

It was very early in the morning as we touched down, parked, and made our way to the operations center. It had been about a four-hour flight, and I found the latrine facilities first before going to be debriefed. Now may the Chief Pilot in the Sky strike me down if this isn't a true story, but as I stood there, I looked up to see that someone had scrawled in large letters on the wall over the urinals the following: *WILBUR, CALL HOME. I HAVE A GREAT IDEA. ORVILLE.*

Ferrying an A-26 to Nakhon Phanom RTAFB, Thailand

Bob "Pappy" Sears

George Bernhard ("Bo") Hertlein III and I were asked to ferry an A-26 from England AFB, Louisiana, to Nakhon Phanom RTAFB, Thailand. We were to depart on Monday, 20 November 1967, three days before Thanksgiving Day. We were under the control of the Ferry Command, Langley AFB, Virginia (that was a joke). Because we had limited navigation aids, and no overwater nav aids, we were scheduled to have an escort from San Francisco, California.

The A-26 aircraft was prepared for the long flight with extra fuel tanks and an oil tank. The oil tank was a 30-gallon tank and it was located behind the copilot (Bo's seat) and equipped with a wobble pump. The fuel tanks were two pylon tanks and a bomb bay tank. As we taxied for takeoff, we checked fuel flow for each added tank. The bomb bay tank would not feed, so we returned to the maintenance ramp. The flex line was being pinched by the bomb bay tank. We thought the problem was fixed. Fuel flow checks were made and the checks were okay. We departed on the main tanks and after reaching cruise altitude we started using fuel from the added tanks. We used fuel from the pylon tanks for a while, then changed to the bomb bay tank. After about 20 minutes, this tank stopped feeding. We were flying the southern route to California, then north to McClellan AFB, California. After crossing into Arizona, we lost fuel flow from the right pylon

Armed A-26 at NKP (USAF).

tank. We notified air traffic control of this event. Because we could not get fuel from the bomb bay tank, we were having a problem with the center of gravity. We called air traffic control and requested a flight plan change to land at Williams AFB, Chandler, Arizona. Then we called Williams for landing instructions. They wanted to know if we were declaring an emergency. We told them "no" but we asked if they could have an empty fuel truck meet the aircraft. During landing, we had to carry extra power and land hot, but this was no problem because of the length of the runway. After reaching the parking area, we were met by a fully loaded fuel truck. We told the driver we had plenty of fuel but needed to move the fuel to other tanks. We arrived at McClellan later than scheduled without further problems. Because McClellan had to order a pylon tank, which would take a couple of days, our departure would be delayed. The fact that McClellan did not work on Thanksgiving Day helped to lengthen the delay. We notified the ferry command of our delay and told them we would keep them up to date. We did not transfer oil from England AFB to McClellan AFB. When we landed at Williams AFB, we checked oil usage and it was very minimal. We were able to make the entire trip without pumping oil from the onboard tank.

We were able to depart for Hawaii the following Monday, 27 November 1967, after a morning weather delay. We were able to meet our escort, an Air-Sea Rescue C-130, near San Francisco, California. The C-130 continued to change heading from left to right back of our position so Bo and I decided to hold our planned heading. After about 40 minutes, the C-130 pilot told us we had to return to McClellan because he was having engine problems. We told him we were not returning. After some heated discussion, he returned to his station and we continued to Hawaii. We were not concerned because halfway to Hickam AFB, we located a Navy ship and determined that our planned heading was good. At the appropriate time, we made radio contact with the Navy and learned that their radar was inoperative so they could not give us a fix. We continued to fly our planned heading and hoped to meet our escort out of Hickam on time and on course. There was a 3,000-feet overcast but clear above. We could see commercial aircraft coming from different directions but converging at one point. We thought that was good because the point was off our nose. About two hours after making radio contact with the Navy, we made contact with our escort out of Hickam. He had our position directly in front of his position. After about 15 minutes, we saw a C-130 pass directly over our position at 18,000 feet. Bo gave him a call and he fixed our position off his tail. He was not catching up but as we were approaching Hawaii we could see some rough weather ahead so we slowed down until the escort caught up. We flew very close to the tail of the C-130 and he vectored us through little turbulence but a lot of rain. After landing at Hickam, we called the ferry command. They could not have an escort for several days.

I had been stationed at Goodfellow AFB with the Hickam Air-Sea Rescue Commander so I called to see if he had a mission scheduled toward Midway the next day. He said he would schedule a training mission and escort us toward Midway. We departed Hickam the next day and after we all determined we were flying a good course, the C-130 returned to Hickam and we continued on to Midway. After landing, we called the ferry command and after some heavy discussion about how we got to Midway, we learned (once again) that they would not have an escort for several days.

Before leaving base operations, we saw a C-124 land. We decided to wait and talk to the crew. After they arrived at base ops, we learned that they were going to Clark Air Base, Philippines. We asked if we could fly with them. They said it would be okay but wanted to check with their command. They were given the okay as long as they were not responsible for our safety. That was okay with Bo and me so we departed base ops with the understanding that we would meet again 10 hours later (after dinner and rest). As agreed, we met the C-124 crew (all captains and enlisted personnel) and prepared for our flight to Clark. After reviewing flight plans, Bo and I decided to depart one hour ahead of the C-124 because of the difference in ground speeds. The C-124 crew agreed. We departed Midway and after several minutes of flight we caught up with the C-124. It was a beautiful clear night and we saw the lights of the C-124. After reaching the C-124, our planned heading was on course so we continued on to Clark ahead of the C-124. After landing at Clark AB, we called the ferry command to let them know we were in the Philippines. The conversation was very short.

After crew rest, we departed for Nakhon Phanom RTAFB. This was a very short leg compared to the others so we decided we could make the remaining trip without an escort. When we were about 100 miles from the coast of South Vietnam, we were able to navigate on our own using TACAN navigation aids. The flight went well until we reached the coast of South Vietnam. At that point, we flew into some very rough thunderstorms. We were off course after reaching the other side of the storm. We were able to get back on course and land at Nakhon Phanom RTAFB, Thailand. Mission complete.

Loss of Carlos, Bill, and Paul[4]

Roger D. Graham

On the night of December 29, 1967, the unthinkable happened. We lost Captain Carlos Cruz (pilot), Captain Bill Potter (navigator/copilot), and Staff Sergeant Paul Foster (scope operator). Carlos and Bill had flown over 100 combat missions and were recognized by all Nimrods as being the best of the best. Sergeant Paul Foster, only 22 years old at the time, volunteered during that mission to occupy the gunner's position in the fuselage of the aircraft, which enabled him to observe the enemy truck traffic along the Ho Chi Minh Trail that night using a Starlight Scope (night vision scope). Paul could see the trucks using the night vision Starlight Scope, mark the target, and enable Carlos and Bill to roll in and attack the target at night. Normally, we did not fly with anyone occupying the gunner's position, but occasionally, we would fly with a volunteer non-commissioned officer (NCO) qualified to operate the handheld Starlight Scope. Paul didn't have to fly on that mission, but like Carlos and Bill, on the night of December 29, 1967, had a rendezvous with destiny. Incredibly, for me personally, it had only been 25 days since I flew my first combat familiarization mission with Carlos and Bill. As Pappy and I heard the radio call on the night of December 29, 1967, that Carlos, Bill, and Paul were down, my first combat familiarization ride on December 4, 1967, seemed like a lifetime ago.

At the time, Carlos was Captain Carlos Cruz, a 29-year-old U.S. Air Force pilot originally from Arroyo, Puerto Rico. He was one of the most aggressive and effective combat pilots I had ever met. Bill was Captain William Joseph Potter Jr., an uncommonly calm and effective navigator/copilot from Ambridge, Pennsylvania, 32 years of age, and a dedicated professional who had volunteered for a six-month extension of his almost complete one-year combat assignment. Paul was Staff Sergeant Paul Foster, age 22, night vision scope operator and a true patriot from Knoxville, Tennessee.

The night before, Pappy and I had flown another horrendous mission. No sooner had we reached the Steel Tiger area of operations than we were directed to orbit over a downed F-4C. The F-4C crew had been shot down with .23-millimeter ZPU antiaircraft fire. Both F-4C pilots had managed to eject successfully just before their aircraft impacted with the ground. I could hear both of them plainly on the ground—they were talking to us with their survival rescue radios. The aircraft commander was okay but the backseat pilot's chute was hung up in the cliff-like karst, and he had sustained a head injury. Pappy and I orbited over the area for over two hours while rescue helicopters and "Sandies" (A-1E single-engine attack aircraft) attempted to rescue the two F-4C pilots. Despite "all-out" rescue efforts, the operation had to be called off until sunrise because of intense AAA and darkness. Pappy and I were forced to return to NKP. To our great joy, we learned after landing that both F-4C pilots had been rescued. For us, the rescue celebration was short-lived. The very next day brought another mission and the loss of Carlos, Bill, and Paul.

I was in shock and denial—my guess is that Pappy felt the same way. On the night of December 29, Pappy and I took off about 30 minutes after Carlos and his crew took off. Pappy and I were only about 15 miles north of them in Steel Tiger when we heard the radio report that they had been hit by antiaircraft fire. We heard Carlos's radio report stating that they had been hit by AAA fire, that they were just over treetop level, and that they could not get out. Then the radio communications with Carlos and crew went silent. Pappy and I immediately turned and flew to their last known position. I distinctly remember looking down as we approached that position—as we approached, there was a large area of fire and smoke on the ground that appeared to be the crash impact area. We could not establish radio contact with Carlos or Bill. We orbited the area for a long time hoping to establish contact with Carlos, Bill, or Paul. It did not happen. We felt so helpless and we were in such pain. Finally, we had no recourse other than to fly to a different location, strike the enemy with our remaining ordnance, and return to base. We subconsciously flew our A-26 aircraft on the return trip home. We were somewhat numb, but the loss made us even more determined to win the war.

Loss of "Bo" Hertlein—Spirit of the Nimrods[5]

ROGER D. GRAHAM

This is one of the most painful points in this story. I need to try to tell you about the loss of Captain George B. Hertlein III, FV3102462. His middle name was Bernhard, but for a long time, I thought it was Beauregard. He was from Decatur, Georgia. In my recollection, he was the spirit of the Nimrods. We all called him "Bo" (at the time, I mistakenly thought of him as "Beau"). How can you go on if you lose your spirit? Upon reflection, we certainly did lose Bo in combat on the night of April 24, 1968, but I believe we were able to go on because we didn't really lose his indomitable spirit. His fighting spirit never left us.

I need to reflect back now, to think back, and to focus on my first meeting with George B. Hertlein III. We first met during A-26 combat crew training in 1967 at England AFB, Alexandria, Louisiana. My first impression was that Bo was a very likeable person. He loved to fly. He loved to laugh. He had a wonderful Southern accent. He was full of life and we loved him. I don't know how it happened, but during A-26 training at England AFB, Bo and Lieutenant Colonel John Shippey became a crew. My next recollection concerning Bo is that he and Major Bobby (Pappy) Sears ferried an A-26 aircraft to NKP, Thailand, after combat crew training in Louisiana. An A-26 ferry flight from the States to Thailand was a major accomplishment in itself. I had the good fortune to be crewed with Pappy at NKP. He remains my hero and good friend to this day. But I digress … those early impressions didn't begin to do justice to Bo.

My next memory of Bo took place after I arrived at NKP, Thailand, in November of 1967. It is difficult to describe, but I would like to try to describe the scene to you. In November of 1967, I had just arrived at NKP after the pain of leaving Dianne and Kimberly back in West Virginia. I was definitely suffering from culture shock as I arrived at NKP and renewed friendships with fellow crewmembers. I ran into Bo soon after arrival at NKP. I recall looking directly into Bo's bright blue eyes. Bo was wearing a dark green "many times washed" USAF flight suit with dark black rank insignia. Bo stood about 5 feet 10 inches tall, he was sporting a huge Southeast Asia "curled" mustache, and he was beginning to suffer from a thinning hairline. Bo was smiling, he had a huge contagious twinkle in his eyes, and right in front of me, he lifted his arms and hands to tweak his mustache. Can you see him??? I can still see him. Bo impressed me as being a warrior from the ages. I can attest that Bo had a spirit of the ages. Bo's spirit, whether it was from the ages, or from the South, represented the true fighting spirit of the Nimrods.

I recall many times being airborne on a mission and hearing Bo and Colonel Shippey report in to Alley Cat, the C-130 Airborne Combat Control Center, as we flew various missions. Bo frequently handled radio communications for their crew. His voice was always loud and clear—and there was no mistaking his accent. He always made you feel like the USA flag had just been unfurled and that he and Colonel Shippey were ready to lead yet another charge directly into the face of the enemy. His voice inspired you to gather your courage for yet another night of combat. Bo's spirit was … and simply is … unforgettable.

On April 24, 1968, Bo was killed in combat. My diary says that Lieutenant Colonel Shippey and Bo's aircraft was hit with five or six rounds from a 12.7-millimeter anti-aircraft gun. They were hit as they made a dive-bombing pass on a target. My diary says, "One round came through the front of the canopy on Bo's side and impacted his shoulder." My recollection is that Colonel Shippey came back and told us that Bo had been hit and was lost in combat … we were numb with denial! Colonel Shippey had a shocked expression in his eyes. John Shippey was one of our very best … and he had just lived through the nightmare of losing Bo … his good friend and fellow crewmember. It's a real tribute to Colonel Shippey that he was able to regain control of the aircraft and make it back to NKP for a landing despite the horror of Bo bleeding to death right beside him in the aircraft, and despite the damage to the aircraft.

I did not immediately visit the aircraft containing Bo's body, but I heard a lot of people talk about the antiaircraft bullet hole in the front of the canopy of the aircraft. Sometime later, I visited the aircraft to see for myself. There was, in fact, a hole in the right side of the canopy directly in front of where Bo was sitting on the night of that fateful mission. As Colonel John Shippey and Captain Bo Hertlein bravely and aggressively made yet another nighttime dive-bombing attack on the enemy below, the horrible event actually occurred. We all knew that this same result could happen to any given crew on any given night. We had seen too many tracers race by the canopy as we dived into yet another target area. Even if the enemy didn't have radar-guided antiaircraft guns to hit us at night, they had an ever-increasing huge inventory of Russian and Chinese World War II–era antiaircraft guns on the Trail to throw up huge barrages of antiaircraft fire as we attacked the targets. The enemy gunners could hear the different sounds our aircraft made as we nosed over into a dive to attack targets—they responded by throwing up a huge barrage of antiaircraft fire over the target area. Somehow, on the night of April 24, 1968, the bullets from one of those antiaircraft guns ripped through Colonel Shippey and Bo's aircraft as they pressed the attack.

On April 26, the entire squadron attended a memorial service for Bo at the base chapel. Chaplain (Major) Cole presided at the service. The cover of the Memorial Service program showed a picture of the cracked U.S. Liberty Bell, flanked on each side by a United States flag, and above the Liberty Bell appeared a quote by Richard Powell: "Freedom is a light for which many men have died in darkness." The service was brief but it was a dignified and impressive tribute to Bo—we will never forget him.

How can you kill the spirit of the Nimrods? How can you kill George B. Hertlein III? The truth is that you can kill an individual (at least as far as our time on Earth is concerned), even a key individual like "Bo," but you can never kill the spirit of a true combat organization unless you kill everyone in the organization. That's what happened in the Vietnam War. We lost key individuals, but we continued to fight. We discovered a strength that we didn't know we had. As it turned out, Bo's spirit had not been killed at all—his spirit stayed with us and made us a far better combat organization.

The Lima Site 85 Mission with Colonel Learmonth[6]

Roger D. Graham

On the night of March 10, 1968, Lieutenant Colonel Allen Learmonth and I unknowingly flew a historic mission. I knew that Lieutenant Colonel Learmonth was a heavyweight as far as officers were concerned at NKP. He was the vice commander of the 56th Special Operations Wing, and he was already on the promotion list to be promoted to full colonel. It was my good fortune to be assigned to fly with him from time to time. He was much like Lieutenant Colonel Farmer and Lieutenant Colonel Shippey—senior combat officers who were true professionals and who had the respect of all of the officers and enlisted personnel at NKP. Colonel Learmonth had some mixed gray hair in his sideburns, he was a calm and collected gentleman (calm blue eyes), he knew how to hit the enemy where it hurts, and he was a true professional A-26 pilot flying combat missions out of NKP.

As we pulled up the gear and flaps and took up a northwesterly heading toward Barrel Roll on the night of March 10, 1968, Colonel Learmonth and I had no idea what was in store for us. We checked in with Alley Cat, acknowledged the assignment that we were to proceed to Lima Site 85, and adjusted the throttles, RPM levers, and mixture levers as we climbed to our cruise altitude of 11,000 feet. I can clearly recall the sensation of departing the airfield at NKP, turning northwest toward the Barrel Roll area of operations, and sitting back in the seat at an elevated angle as the engines and props labored to climb out to cruise altitude. Imagine for a moment that you are there with us. The engines and the propellers are roaring with great determination. The instrument panel in front of us is alive with instrument displays, colors, and key airspeed, heading, and altitude information. As we look out at the wings, the faint light from the moon and stars illuminates the whirring propellers, the wings, and the wing fuel tanks on the extremities of the wings. As we reach the cruise altitude of 11,000 feet, we retard the throttles, RPM levers, and mixture levers for maximum fuel efficiency. Less than an hour later, we arrive in the vicinity of Lima Site 85. We are poised to attack.

Once at Lima Site 85, all hell broke loose. Lima Site 85 was a very important site in northern Laos. Not only was it a TACAN navigational site, it was also a classified radar

Lima Site 85, perched on the top of Phou Pha Thi, was situated in the part of Laos where the enemy was the strongest. The mountain was 15 miles from the Laos–North Vietnam border and fewer than 30 miles from Sam Neua, the capital of the Pathet Lao (*Air Force Magazine* map by Zaur Eylanbekov).

site for bombing targets in North Vietnam. Lima Site 85 was literally located on the top of a remote mountain called Phou Pha Thi. A picture is worth a thousand words. The aerial photograph of Lima Site 85 in northern Laos is an incredible photograph.

How could such sophisticated radar bombing and navigational aids have been constructed on that remote mountaintop in 1967–68? Only our top-level political and military leaders know. As a navigator-bombardier, I knew that Lima Site 85 was a key navigational aid, and I also knew that the classified bombing radar site meant that Hanoi was only 160 miles from the site and vulnerable to precision radar attack around the clock and in all types of weather. Colonel Learmonth and I found out on the night of March 10 that the communists also understood the importance of Lima Site 85.

As Colonel Learmonth and I flew into the vicinity of Lima Site 85 that night, we saw an impressive display of enemy firepower. The NVN and Pathet Lao forces were mounting a full-scale attack on Lima Site 85. We observed a multitude of muzzle flashes, tracers, and incendiary trajectories indicting that enemy troops were firing small-arms fire

Three sides of Phou Pha Thi were nearly vertical; the fourth was heavily fortified. Lima Site 85 perched on the very top of the bluff. Imagine U.S. military personnel under attack at night at such a site; imagine U.S. aircrews conducting close air support missions at such a site at night (USAF; photograph by Lt. Col. Jeannie Schiff).

and mortars and small rockets into the friendly forces at Lima Site 85. The weather was terrible. Thunderstorms and lightning were everywhere. We were in and out of rain and lightning. I remember being tossed about in the cockpit. In that cauldron of light and shadows, we communicated as best we could with our fellow American fighting men below. We made repeated dive-bombing attacks on the enemy units that were firing at Lima Site 85, unloading all of our ordnance directly into the midst of the enemy troops below. At the end of our attacks that night, the enemy troops simply stopped shooting. Unfortunately, that is not the end of the story.

According to my diary, we learned the following day that the enemy troops overran Lima Site 85 just before sunup and killed at least 12 Americans—helicopters managed to rescue several men from the site. Unofficial records state that this was the largest single ground combat loss of USAF personnel during the Vietnam War. Colonel Learmonth and I were stunned to hear the bad news, and NKP went into mourning. (For an outstanding article that tells the incredible full story of the fall of Lima Site 85, see Correll, John. T., "The Fall of Lima Site 85," *Air Force Magazine*, April 2006, p. 66.) Chief Master Sergeant Richard Etchberger, a senior radar technician at the site who lost his life while defending and rescuing fellow airmen, was posthumously awarded the Air Force Cross (later upgraded to the Medal of Honor) for his extraordinary heroism on that fateful night.

Friends for Life

Roger D. Graham

My first recollection of seeing Bob Sears was at the flight crew briefing room at England AFB, Louisiana. We were in a group of pilots and navigators who had just arrived at England AFB for A-26 transition training before being assigned as A-26 crewmembers at Nakhon Phanom Royal Thai Air Force Base (NKP), Thailand. All of us had received our orders for a one-year Vietnam War combat assignment, but few of us had ever flown in an A-26 before. When I first noticed Bob Sears, the pilots and navigators were sitting in separate sections. Bob appeared to be in his mid-thirties, and unlike the others, had considerable gray in his salt-and-pepper short hair. I was a 25-year-old B-52 navigator at the time. Something about his demeanor caught my eye, and he impressed me as a man I would like to fly with in A-26 aircraft. At the first break, I summoned my courage, introduced myself, and asked him if he might want to fly with me as his navigator. I recall him looking me over but he made no commitment. However, shortly after that, we started flying A-26 training missions as a crew. I could not have been happier. That was one of the most fortunate turning points in my life.

Sometime during our A-26 training, Bob Sears picked up the nickname "Pappy." Obviously, he picked up that nickname because of his premature gray hair. Bob was a major at the time, and I was a captain. I felt a lot more comfortable calling him Pappy, and he did not seem to mind. So from then on, he was Pappy and I was Roger. From the beginning, Pappy was a joy to fly with in A-26s. I did not learn until later that Pappy had been an IP (instructor pilot) in B-25 aircraft. The transition from being a B-25 pilot to an

Captain Roger Graham (left) and Major Bob (Pappy) Sears, NKP, 1968 (USAF).

A-26 pilot appeared to be a piece of cake for him. The transition from being a B-52 navigator to an A-26 navigator was a bit more challenging for me. The pilot and the navigator sat side by side in the A-26. In reality, the navigator served in more of a copilot capacity than a navigator role. The pilots trained us to be copilots. Our primary means of navigation was using VORTAC navigation aids. The pilots did not need the navigators to do that; they did need the navigators to perform certain copilot duties.

The A-26 training period for our group of pilots and navigators lasted about two months (August–October 1967). During that time, we became familiar with the aircraft handling qualities, the engines, and the bombing and nose gun firing systems. We practiced dive-bombing and strafing runs on a nearby bombing range. One airborne incident stands out in my memory. On one training flight, Pappy was in the left seat, Major Joe Maynard was instructing from the copilot seat, and I was observing from the jump seat behind the copilot seat. Shortly after takeoff, Pappy informed Major Maynard that we had a generator overheat warning light on the left engine. Emergency checklist language stated, "Turn off the affected generator, and if the light does not go out, shut down the engine." After the left generator was turned off, the light did not go out, so the left engine was shut down and an emergency was declared with England tower. If that was not challenging enough, the tower informed us that the field was now IFR (instrument flight rules). The ceiling was about 500 feet with half-mile visibility. Major Maynard briefed Pappy to continue flying the aircraft, to maintain 125 knots on final, and to make the landing unless a "go-around" became necessary. Major Maynard later commented, "It was a textbook approach, and doggone it, if he didn't fly and land the plane as well as I could have done it myself." That was high praise from a fellow pilot. Maynard further stated, "Bob Sears was without a doubt the best and smoothest student pilot I had ever flown with in either the A-26 or the C-123."

Another strong memory from A-26 training was a cross-country flight from England AFB to Eglin AFB, Florida. We charted a navigation route across northern Mississippi and Alabama, and then south down to Hurlburt Field and Eglin AFB near Fort Walton Beach, Florida. The primary means of navigation was using VORTAC stations as specific points along the route, dead reckoning, and map reading. The flight took place in the autumn of 1967. The color in the trees was beautiful and the weather was sunny and mild. It was turning dark as we approached Eglin, and the lights of the base and surrounding area seemed almost magical. That was one of the most enjoyable flights I have ever experienced.

While in Florida, we gained valuable experience by dropping live bombs on the bombing ranges. The strongest memory from that experience was dropping live napalm canisters on the Eglin ranges at night. The entire night sky lit up behind the aircraft shortly after we released the napalm. That was our graduation exercise. We were now

This photograph captures the exhilaration of flying the A-26A Counter Invader (USAF).

ready for our combat assignment at NKP. Pappy and Bo Hertlein ferried an A-26 from England AFB to NKP (a huge adventure in itself). Dianne, Kim, and I drove to Princeton, West Virginia, where Dianne and Kim would stay with her mother while I was away for a year in the war. Ironically, I flew to Southeast Asia via commercial airlines.

After completing jungle survival school at Clark Air Base in the Philippines, Pappy and I arrived at NKP in October 1967. Following three or four familiarization flights, Pappy and I immediately began flying combat missions as a two-man crew. One question was immediately answered. There really was a war going on, and we had our work cut out for us. Flying dive-bombing missions at night in rugged terrain, and often in thunderstorms, is some of the most challenging flying that exists. Add intense levels of antiaircraft artillery (AAA) fire, and you have a most dangerous situation. Pappy and I quickly adapted to these new challenges and became an even more closely knit crew. I appreciated Pappy's expert piloting skills and his unwavering courage in attacking targets. He consistently demonstrated the optimum balance of aggressiveness in attacking targets with good judgment in knowing when to avoid taking too many chances. Our general mindset was that we wanted to do our part to help win the war. I believe that all of the A-26 crews shared that view.

There are some missions with Pappy that stand out in my memory. The first one was a mission in Steel Tiger when we heard a radio call that Carlos Cruz's aircraft had been by hit by AAA and they could not get out of the plane. Pappy and I immediately flew to that location but could not contact Carlos, Bill Potter, or Paul Foster by radio. If they had managed to bail out, we were hoping they could use their survival radios to communicate with us. Unfortunately, all communication efforts failed. We observed one area of fire on the ground that was the likely crash site. Carlos, Bill, and Paul had just lost their lives in combat. That was a shocking and very sobering experience. My first A-26 orientation ride at NKP, only a few weeks earlier, had been with Carlos and Bill. Suddenly, the war had become very personal. Another shocking mission involved Lieutenant Colonel John Shippey and Bo Hertlein. During a dive-bombing pass, AAA rounds came through the front of the canopy and struck Bo in the shoulder. Colonel Shippey was able to regain control of the aircraft, but Bo died from loss of blood before Colonel Shippey had time to return to NKP and land. Although Pappy and I were not flying that night, we certainly felt and shared Colonel Shippey's shock and pain at losing Bo. Colonel Shippey was our squadron commander; he had the deep respect of every member of the 609th Air Commando Squadron. Bo personified the spirit of the Nimrods. May he rest in peace.

Pappy and I flew so many missions against trucks, truck convoys, and gun positions that they almost became a blur. I recall bright orange tracers flying all around the aircraft, supply trucks and fuel trucks burning on the ground, and the constant radio chatter coordinating airstrikes with FAC crews. During one mission we observed a huge red tracer tumbling end over end directly over our cockpit, and on another mission, we narrowly evaded a midair collision with a FAC aircraft that suddenly appeared directly in front of our aircraft as we were making a dive-bombing pass on a target. We flew roughly 100 missions together as a crew, and many other missions with other pilots and navigators. During the dry season (November through April), the level of truck traffic down the Ho Chi Minh Trail was at its highest. During that time period, the forward air control (FAC) pilots and crews almost always had targets waiting for us as soon as we arrived in Steel Tiger. Steel Tiger was a large geographical area in eastern central Laos containing much of the Ho Chi Minh Trail and truck traffic south of the North Vietnam

Another view of an A-26A Counter Invader in the vicinity of NKP (1968) (USAF).

border and the Mu Gia Pass. On most nights, even before we arrived in the combat zone, we could see and hear intense combat activity. AAA tracers filled the sky over hot choke points, and flashes from detonating bombs covered the road structure. We methodically took our turn making multiple passes on the targets below. One mission with Pappy in that environment that stands out in my memory was a mission in April 1968 near Mu Gia pass in which the FAC pilot credited us with destroying 10 trucks. When possible, we loved to team up with other A-26 or B-57 crews to take turns attacking trucks and gun positions. While one crew was attacking trucks, the other crew flew overhead and was poised to roll in on firing gun positions. That tactic worked. We had the highest respect for other A-26 and B-57 Yellowbird and Redbird crews whose courage and bombing accuracy were simply astounding.

Another memorable mission with Pappy took place in the Barrel Roll area of northern Laos. That night in July 1968, Pappy and I provided direct air support to General Vang Pao and the Hmong mountain tribesmen near the Plain of Jars. After coordinating our strikes with a FAC ground controller, Pappy and I expended our ordnance on opposing communist forces below. What happened after that was most unusual. Unlike most nights, there were three other A-26s and a C-130 operating in that same general area that night. Since the sky was just starting to light up in the early morning hours, we communicated with the other aircraft and decided to join up for the flight back to NKP. As we were joining up, another A-26 crew (Jay Norton and Roy Zarucchi) decided to roll in and check out what appeared to be some kind of searchlight on the ground. At that moment, the entire area burst into the most intense barrage of antiaircraft fire that any of us had seen before. Tracers filled the sky and ground gunfire flashes could be seen everywhere. I estimate that 100 or more AAA sites were firing at us. It is a miracle that none of our aircraft were shot down. That incident taught us that the unexpected can happen, and that you can never let your guard down in a combat zone.

One last mission merits mention. It is what happened on the ground, not in the air, that is so memorable about that mission. The mission seemed routine up through starting the engines and taxiing to the end of the runway in preparation for takeoff. I remember Pappy going through the normal engine run-up checks and obtaining clearance from the NKP tower for takeoff. I also recall Pappy pushing the throttles forward and starting a turn onto the active runway. That is when the unexpected happened. Suddenly, the aircraft made a hard lurch to the left and we could not believe what we were seeing and hearing. The noise from the left engine and propeller was deafening, but the sight of a huge ball of sparks flying in front of the cockpit and around napalm canisters on the wings was even worse. Our immediate response was to set a record shutting down engines and departing the aircraft. It is a miracle that the aircraft did not catch on fire, and that none of the ordnance exploded. We learned later that the left main wheel assembly sheared off as we made the turn onto the runway. That caused the left propeller to dig into the pierced steel planking taxiway, causing the huge shower of sparks in front of the aircraft. After that scare, I thought we might get the night off. Wrong. Not an hour had passed before Pappy had another loaded A-26 for us. We preflighted and took off for another mission over the Trail.

Pappy recalls two more missions of interest. One of them occurred in the aftermath of the fall of Lima Site 85 in northern Laos. Lima Site 85 was an important radar and VORTAC navigation aid site located high on a rugged mountaintop in northeast Laos, very close to the North Vietnam border. The radar equipment located at the site enabled U.S. aircrews to accurately bomb targets in Hanoi, and the response of the North Vietnamese Army (NVA) was to mount a major offensive on the night of March 10–11, 1968, to take down the site. Despite airstrikes from A-26 and F-4 aircraft, the site was overrun by the NVA and the surviving U.S. personnel had to be rescued by helicopter. After the site was totally evacuated and abandoned by U.S. authorities, Pappy recalls being tasked to make repeated A-26 napalm passes to destroy what was left of the site to keep U.S. equipment from falling into the hands of the enemy.

The second mission involves one of Pappy's favorite stories. One night after completing another demanding mission, a seemingly routine landing turned into a screaming emergency. When Pappy engaged prop reverse on the two engines, only one propeller went into reverse thrust. The result was a spinning aircraft on the runway that ended up with the nose of the aircraft pointing 180 degrees in the opposite direction from the intended landing. Someone in the NKP tower quickly came on the radio and stated, "Nimrod 35, what are your intentions?" Pappy immediately replied, "We are trying to figure that out right now, and as soon as we do, you will be the first to know." That story still makes me laugh.

In August of 1968, after eight months of combat, Pappy and I were more than ready to meet our wives for some rest and recuperation. Actually, we managed to get two weeks' leave, and we made arrangements to meet Elaine (Pappy's wife) and Dianne (my wife) in Honolulu, Hawaii. That was two of the best weeks that all four of us ever experienced. Pappy and I took military hops to Hickam Air Force Base, and Dianne and Elaine booked commercial flights to Honolulu. For the first few days, all four of us stayed in two cottages on the beach at Bellows Air Force Station, located within view of Diamond

Head northeast of Honolulu. Being together with our wives again was like heaven on earth. The beach there is absolutely beautiful. After resting for a few days, we toured the entire island of Oahu, including Sea Life Park, the Polynesian Cultural Center, pineapple plantations, and a sailplane airstrip. After touring the island, Dianne and I checked into the Outrigger Hotel in Honolulu for the remainder of the trip, while Pappy and

Friends for Life Bob (Pappy) and Elaine Sears (left) Dianne and Roger Graham (right) (courtesy Roger D. Graham).

Elaine checked into their own hotel. Of course, all too soon, the joy of being together had to come to an end. Pappy and I had to return to the war to finish our tours, and Dianne and Elaine had to return home to children and job responsibilities. The parting was painful; however, there is no doubt that the two weeks in Hawaii had made all four of us friends for life.

In due course, Pappy and I completed our A-26 combat tours and returned home to the United States. I was assigned as a B-52 navigator at March AFB, California. Pappy was assigned to a military airlift organization in Illinois, but before he had a chance to settle in he received orders to return to NKP on a temporary duty (TDY) basis because there was a shortage of A-26 pilots. Pappy thought one of his best A-26 pilot friends (Buck Bennett) was pulling a joke on him and did not make any preparations to return to the war. The reason Pappy thought a joke was being played on him was that he had played a similar joke on Buck Bennett before leaving NKP. Pappy knew that the last assignment Buck wanted when leaving NKP was to be assigned to SAC (Strategic Air Command), so Pappy had fake orders made up stating that Buck had been assigned to an SAC unit. It wasn't until Pappy's wing commander in Illinois had two burly air policemen escort Pappy to the wing commander's office that Pappy realized the assignment back to NKP was no joke. Like a good soldier, Pappy then departed for NKP and completed the TDY tour.

Pappy, Elaine, Dianne, and I stayed in close contact over the years. Pappy and I completed our Air Force careers, and both of us were fortunate to retire as full colonels. I transferred to the judge advocate field, and Pappy remained in flight operations. We attended numerous A-26 reunions together at Hurlburt Field, Florida, and stay in close contact by phone. Pappy is a Texas Tech graduate, and I am a WVU law graduate. We love to follow football and basketball games involving those two teams. Dianne and Elaine loved their visits together to catch up on news concerning children and grandchildren. Unfortunately, Elaine became ill and passed away on January 17, 2020. She was buried near Dallas, Texas. Pappy and Elaine lived at Marble Falls, Texas. They were married for 68 years. We remain friends for life.

A-26 Flight Across the Pacific

Frank Nelson

On the evening of September 8, 1967, Juni Tengan and I were scheduled for two check rides in the A-26. On the first mission I was being evaluated by Major Oncay. I was in the right seat while Major Oncay was squeezed in behind me in the jump seat position. Juni was in the left seat. It was the quickest check ride of my Air Force career. We took off, went to the Claiborne Range, dropped a couple of flares, made several dive-bomb runs, and flew back to England AFB. Our second flight was a check for Juni so Frank Gorski took the right seat and I had to wiggle into the jump seat. This mission was pretty much a repeat of the earlier one and one hour later we were approved to go to war.

At the time, the normal routine for crews going to Southeast Asia (SEA) was to take

Major Seijun (Juni) Tengin and Captain Frank Nelson (courtesy Frank Nelson).

a few days leave, then travel to the Philippines for the jungle survival school, then on to your assigned base. A couple of days after our check rides, I was at the squadron taking care of some out-processing items. Juni was also there and he asks me about flying one of the A-26s over to Thailand. I had not even considered such a thing, but it turns out that Juni (being from Hawaii) had been lining this up for some time. I immediately said yes. I assumed that we would be part of a flight of several A-26s with some type of escort aircraft. The next day I learned that we would probably be going across by ourselves.

Being an ex–KC-135 navigator, I thought about how I would navigate across the Pacific with the A-26's minimum equipment. I wasn't concerned about finding Hawaii but getting to Midway and Wake Island could be a challenge. I thought as long as the TACAN system worked it shouldn't be a problem.

On the 5th of October I arrived at McClellan AFB and met up with Juni and our crew chief. Unfortunately over the years I have forgotten our crew chief's name. We were going to be flying aircraft 651 and it would be ready for us in several days. On the morning of 9 October 1967, Juni and I took 651 up for a functional check flight. The airplane seemed to be in great shape; we had no problems. Most of the time was spent with me learning how to fly it, since we planned to take turns flying at one-hour intervals. Upon landing, we checked the oil consumption. We used this information to determine how much oil to pump to the engines. We would have a small barrel of oil tied in behind the right seat. A crank-type pump would be used to pump the oil to each engine.

The morning of 11 October was a beautiful autumn day. We received our weather briefing and it looked very good. En route winds were forecast to be relatively light and mostly out of the northwest. In order to keep things simple, I broke the mission into three sections, computing a heading for each leg. I also computed a point of no return, just in case things did not go as planned. Climbing out from the Sacramento area, we leveled off at 8,000 feet and headed for San Francisco. About 30 miles from San Francisco we could clearly see the Golden Gate Bridge—and beyond it, the Farallon Islands. Although Juni and I had both flown this same route in the KC-135, there was a different feeling about this trip. Maybe it was the lower altitude, the slower speed, or the noise from the two Pratt & Whitney R2800 engines. Whatever it was, this seemed like more of an adventure than any of those crossings in the KC-135.

Shortly after we passed over the Farallons, Juni turned to me and said it was my turn to fly the aircraft. While I was flying the aircraft on our earlier test flight, it seemed relatively easy. This was not the case, however, now that we were much heavier with a full fuel load. Holding the correct heading didn't seem to be very difficult but altitude control was another matter. We were supposed to be at 8,000 feet but for that first hour I was usually somewhere between 7,500 and 8,500 feet. Juni didn't say much; he just let me struggle with it and by the end of the hour I was starting to get a better feel for it. When I wasn't flying the airplane, I would get on the HF radio and make a position report; otherwise, there was not a whole lot to do. All the aircraft's systems were functioning perfectly—next stop Hawaii!

At the midpoint of the route we would be passing near a Coast Guard cutter known as *Ocean Station November*. I made radio contact with the cutter and requested a verification of our position using their radar. The operator reported that their radar system was inoperative but he would attempt to use a backup system. A minute or two later he came on the radio and reported that he could hear us just to the north of their position. The backup system being his ears! We said thanks and pressed on. As we got closer to Hawaii we were to contact an SA-16 aircraft with the call sign Duckbutt. We did make radio contact with him and attempted some DF steers to get visual contact but never did get a visual sighting on Duckbutt.

By this time, we had climbed to an altitude of 13,000 feet and it would not be long before the Hawaiian Islands would become visible. We got a TACAN lock-on 90 miles out. I estimated we were four to five miles north of our intended course so we made a correction to the heading and contacted air traffic control. We flew in just south of Diamond Head and turned northwest for our approach and landing at Hickam AFB. Total flying time was 10 hours 30 minutes.

As we taxied in, a "follow me" truck guided us to our parking spot where a blue Air Force bus was already waiting. Much to my surprise, as we shut down the engines, Juni's family started coming off the bus with flower leis in hand. It was a wonderful ending to our flight. In short order, Juni, myself, and our crew chief had three or four leis around our necks. All in all, it was a real Hawaiian welcome that I will always remember.

We had the following day off, which gave Juni a chance to visit with his family. That evening we all attended a wonderful banquet with many of Juni's family members and relatives.

The next morning, October 12, we departed Hickam AFB for Midway Island. Many of Juni's family members were there to see us off. The flight to Midway was to be just under six hours. It was a perfect day, clear and sunny. We just followed the reefs and islands of the Hawaiian archipelago to Midway Island. We enjoyed a relaxing evening on Midway, a nice place to visit but not a place I would like to stay for a year.

As we prepared to leave Midway, we had a short delay for some repairs. While doing the preflight inspection, I found an exhaust stack on #2 engine had broken. Fortunately, our crew chief had packed a spare one. He completed the repair in short order and we were off to Wake Island, a little over 1,000 miles away. The flight to Wake Island went smoothly and by now I had no trouble flying the aircraft on the correct altitude and heading.

We departed Wake Island for Guam the next morning. The weather was forecast to be VFR conditions our entire flight. The flight to Guam was 5 hours 40 minutes and once again aircraft 651 performed flawlessly.

As we were taxiing to the transient aircraft parking area, Juni remarked that there were no other aircraft on the ramp.

After parking and going into base operations, we found out why. The base was under an alert for an approaching typhoon and any aircraft that could not be secured in a hangar had been evacuated to Japan. It was decided that we would ride out the storm. The weather forecasters thought that the base would not get a direct hit from the typhoon. The plan for us was to be on alert that night and if the wind started to blow more than 30 knots we would have to go to the aircraft, start the engines, and keep the nose headed directly into the wind as the storm passed.

The command post contacted Juni and me about midnight and said we would have to go to the aircraft as the wind was building rapidly. Our crew chief had obtained a pickup truck so he came by the BOQ to get us and we then proceeded to the flight line. By now it was raining heavily and wind gusts were above 30 knots. We climbed into the cockpit while the crew chief took off the tiedowns. After the engines were started, our crew chief headed for the pickup while Juni started aiming 651 into the wind. As the storm increased in intensity, all manner of debris flew by. As we sat there watching the airspeed indicator work its way up to 70–80 knots, we were amazed that we had not been hit by pieces of trees, barrels, sheet metal, and other junk going by.

By daybreak things were starting to settle down and we were able to shut the engines down. Other than being very wet, everything was okay with us. Unfortunately, there was a fair amount of damage on the base, and several days passed before things started getting back to normal.

We finally departed Guam on the 20th of October and headed for Clark AB in the Philippines. The route to Clark was just over 1,400 miles and would take about 6½ hours. We had just passed the halfway point on our route when our first systems problem started. The fuel pressure gauge for #2 engine began dropping and eventually got to zero. The engine seemed to be running fine and I could not see anything abnormal. The crew chief suggested we swap the fuel pressure gauges, thinking that maybe it was a gauge problem. After doing that we still had zero pressure for #2. Since we still had several hours to go before reaching Clark, we decided to keep the engine running even though the checklist recommended the engine be shut down since a fuel leak could lead to a fire. Once we were established on approach to Clark, Juni elected to shut it down and he made a fine single-engine landing. Later that evening, maintenance told us they found the problem and we would be okay to depart for our final destination (Nakhon Phanom) the next morning.

The morning of October 21 we received our weather briefing and it looked like we could possibly have another encounter with a typhoon. The storm was located in the middle of the South China Sea, slowly moving to the north toward Hong Kong. We departed Clark AB, climbing to 10,000 feet. Our planned route would take us over Da Nang, on the Vietnam coast, then due west into Thailand. It wasn't long before we began to see the building clouds of Typhoon Dinah. Before long we were well into the storm and the rain was extremely heavy; in fact, we could not even see the wing tips. The cockpit canopy leaked badly and before long we were soaking wet. Juni asked me to get on the radio and request a climb to 13,000 feet. After transmitting several times on the HF radio attempting to reach the en route control agencies, we began to suspect the radio was not working. By now we were getting buffeted by the winds, the rain continued to be very heavy, and Saint Elmo's fire was glowing around the entire airframe. About that time, Juni tells me he has vertigo and for me to take over the controls. While I was doing my best to keep us upright, Juni tried working the radios but had no contact. By this time we knew we should be close to Da Nang. We could see a few breaks in the weather, to the north, so we decided to get into VFR conditions, establish our position, and try to get into Da Nang. As we got a little further north, we spotted an aircraft carrier and several other navy ships.

We then realized we were close to the area known as Yankee Station. Turning to the southwest, we headed to the coast and started to look for Da Nang Air Base. At this time we discovered that the VOR/TACAN systems were not working. We were unable to see Da Nang, so we stayed VFR and headed south along the coast. Eventually, we found Cam Ranh Bay Air Base, made a pass over the field, got a green light for landing, and brought this flight to a close.

However, there was a bright side to this episode. My brother, Steve, was in the Army and had recently been assigned to duty at Cam Ranh Bay as a transportation officer. After a few phone calls, I was able to make contact with him. Steve was able to join Juni and me later that evening at the officers' club. The next morning, he met us on the flight line and saw us off. Actually, there were a number of people there to watch us taxi out. Word had gotten around about the A-26 on the flight line. The maintenance folks had gotten all our comm/nav equipment dried out and we were ready for the final leg to

Capt. Frank Nelson (right) and brother Steve Nelson, Cam Ranh Bay Air Base, South Vietnam, October 22, 1967 (courtesy Frank Nelson).

A-26 #17651 departing Cam Ranh Bay AB, South Vietnam on final leg of flight from McClellan AFB, California to Nakhon Phanom, Thailand. Pilot, Capt. Seijun "Juni" Tengan, and navigator, Capt. Frank Nelson, October 22, 1967 (courtesy Frank Nelson).

Nakhon Phanom. After a smooth, uneventful flight, we landed at Nakhon Phanom Air Base. The date was October 22, 1967. Our total flight time for the trip was 40 hours and 25 minutes. Seven days later, I squeezed into the jump seat behind Bill Potter and Carlos Cruz for my introduction to the Ho Chi Minh Trail.

Juni and I flew together until August 1968. He returned to duty in Hawaii flying KC-135s and I continued flying with the Nimrods until the end of September 1968. My next assignment was a C-130 squadron at Dyess AFB, Texas. Juni and I stayed in touch over the years and I visited him and his family several times. In July 2007 I spoke to him about attending the Nimrod reunion. Unfortunately, he said he was unable to attend. In late October I called to tell him about the reunion. I also sent him a copy of Roger Graham's book *The Nimrods*. A few weeks later his wife, Chuck, notified me that Juni had passed away on November 24, 2007.

A-26 #651 survived many missions over the Trail, eventually ending up in the "boneyard" at Davis Monthan AFB. Today, it is on display at the Korea Aerospace Industries (KAI) Museum in Sacheon, South Korea.

Khe Sanh Day Mission

Frank Nelson

Of the 185 missions I flew out of Nakhon Phanom, only one was flown during daylight hours. As a result, this particular mission remains vivid in my memory. During February 1968, Juni Tengan and I were one of four crews assigned to provide close air support to the Marines at the Khe Sanh Combat Base.

Located in the northern part of South Vietnam, Khe Sanh had come under constant attack by North Vietnamese troops since late January. For several days, rainy weather and fog had hampered much of the air support that the Marines needed to defend the base. It was thought that the Nimrods, with the A-26, could be effective in this situation.

I remember our pre-mission briefing being short and to the point. After getting into the Khe Sanh area, we were to contact a forward air controller (FAC) for specific targets. Since there were several thousand enemy troops surrounding the base, we could expect almost anything in the way of antiaircraft weapons.

Upon our arrival in the Khe Sanh area shortly before noon, we made radio contact with the FAC. Finding a break in the clouds to the west of the base, we descended to a lower altitude. We could now see the base and several hilltops where the Marines had established outposts.

I remember thinking here we are under all these white clouds with an airplane painted black on the underside. What a nice target for enemy AAA crews. The FAC described our target area, which was on the very edge of the base perimeter close to the opposite end of the airstrip from our position. He said there was a concentration of enemy troops digging ditches up to the edge of the base. Just on the other side of the wire some Marines were dug in observing this activity.

Our bomb load was 4 × 750-pound finned napalm and 4 × 500-pound unfinned napalm on the wing pylons plus some fragmentation bombs in the bomb bay. Juni was concerned about a bomb going into the Marines' position: he turned to me and said, "We need to go in low for this and use the four 500-pound napalms." He then started a dive and leveled off just above the tops of the trees and bushes along the base perimeter. As we were doing this, the FAC was on the radio yelling, "Nimrod, Nimrod, you're going too low, Pull up! Pull up!"

As we flew along the edge of the base you could clearly see the bunkers that the Marines were in. All of a sudden we see one Marine jump up on top of a bunker. He had his weapon above his head waving us on. I remember he had his helmet on but no shirt. You would have thought we were at a football game going for a touchdown!

About the time we passed our cheering Marine, I set up the armament switches and Juni started firing all eight of our guns in hopes of keeping the enemy troops heads down. As we got closer to our target area, I glanced out about 11 o'clock and saw four or five troops trying to move some type of gun, on wheels, across a small clearing. They did not pay any attention to us. Juni then did a quick pop up to about 200 feet and I selected up the outboard pylons in quick sequence, stringing the napalm along a 100-yard line. As the area erupted in fire, the FAC was ecstatic, saying our drop was perfect.

We pulled up to the base of the clouds and the FAC began directing us in on several artillery positions and enemy bunkers to the north of the base. We made four attacks using the finned napalm, then finished up by dropping the fragmentation bombs. Several times during these attacks the FAC said we were being shot at but neither Juni nor I saw any tracers.

When we arrived back at NKP and did a post-flight check of the aircraft, we found several holes in the aft fuselage area. One bullet had gone right up through the middle of the bomb bay.

Later, in talking about the mission, Juni and I both decided that flying at night had its advantages.

Joining the Air Commandos by Volunteering for Graduate School

WILLIAM "BILL" COHEN

By the time I got into the Air Commandos, we were in a war with enemy guerrilla insurgents and the North Vietnamese conventional forces too. We were not just supporting friendly insurgents behind enemy lines. Air Commandos were fighting large numbers of troops, supported by major powers, wherever they were found. The difference was that the Air Commandos, like their counterparts in the other armed services, were specially trained for a unique type of warfare, which was quite different from the work done by regular Air Force commands. Air Commandos were not focused on flying higher and faster or a nuclear holocaust, like SAC, or a strategic war of attrition as eventually fought against North Vietnam by our jets, but flying and fighting with mostly World War II and Korean War–era aircraft over the jungles of North Vietnam and Laos. Although the Air Commandos did their share of night close air support of friendlies in North Vietnam and elsewhere, their primary battles involved night interdiction of supplies running through the Ho Chi Minh Trail. The Trail was a vast logistics network, winding through the mountainous karst formations throughout the jungles of North Vietnam and Laos into South Vietnam, built and maintained to resupply the enemy guerrillas and regiments fighting our troops in South Vietnam.

Consequently, many World War II aircraft were brought out of storage and many were updated and modified for this new type of warfare. New Air Commando units were activated. This got publicity within the Air Force, which asked for volunteers from all commands.

I kept up with development of the Air Commandos in the Air Force, especially when 40 A-26 World War II attack planes were pulled out of the desert where they had been stored after the Korean War. The A-26s were modified by On Mark Engineering Company in California, updated with new features (such as strengthened wings, increased ordnance and fuel capacity, navigation aids, and auto-feather and reversible props), and turned over to the Commandos. Finally, after much thinking about this, I decided to give it a shot. My thinking was along the lines of "We were now in a shooting war and my duty under the circumstances was to volunteer."

Of course, the idea of actually going into battle under these circumstances was a little disquieting. First, they did not call it "special operations" for nothing. I was in correspondence with a West Point classmate who was, at the time, in the squadron I wanted join, but in another modified aircraft, the single-engine T-28. It was something of a mismatch. The Air Commando aircraft had mostly World War II technology. However, the AAA used by the North Vietnamese, which opposed us, embodied the latest technology. My classmate said that things were getting "a bit sporty" in their work. Before my arrival, losses caused us to fly at night only, and forced the T-28s to be withdrawn from the area of heavy concentration of enemy fire. Finally, the squadron was split. The T-28 flyers got a newer airplane, the A-1, and the A-26 flyers became the 609th Air Commando Squadron.

In addition, although I did not know it at the time, I would be entering combat fresh off my honeymoon as a newlywed. I had met a beautiful Israeli girl while in graduate school and we were soon married. And yes, 53 years and several wars later, we are still married.

Successful in my career in Strategic Air Command, I had been an instructor and standardization navigator and acquired about 3,000 hours flying time in the jet-engined B-52. It was a first-rate outfit, with risks and challenges of its own. Still, I submitted my paperwork and volunteered for the Air Commandos. I had flown for several years for SAC and it was SAC's decision whether to let me go or not. SAC said I was needed in B-52s, and I was turned down.

Having been raised in the Air Force, I did have some personal contacts. Several months after volunteering and being rejected, I decided that I should try to do something on my own to get into the Air Commandos.

A friend of the family, Harry Coleman, was a full colonel in Tactical Air Command. "How are you, boy?" he asked when I called. "I haven't seen you since West Point. How are you doing?"

I told him, "Sir, I'm doing fine, but I volunteered for Vietnam hoping to get A-26s, but I'm unable to get the assignment because I'm in B-52s. I'd like to join the Air Commandos. Is there anything you can do?"

"We're sending some of our best young officers to Vietnam," replied Colonel Coleman. "Where are you and what is your unit assignment? I'll see what I can do." I told him and he told me that the general officer commanding my unit several levels up was a classmate of his from flying school and that he would call him to see what if anything could be done.

With a full colonel supporting me, I thought that I would be able to go with no problem, but I was wrong. Two weeks later, I got a telephone call from Colonel Coleman. "Bill, I wouldn't have believed it but I can't do anything. I talked to the general who is in your chain of command and told him about your request." He said, "If we let that young man go to Vietnam, they'll all want to go."

The military is like all organizations in some ways: the old boy network can help if you are asking for something in the Air Force's interest, but in this case, though it was in Colonel Coleman's organization's interest, it was not in my general's. I understood perfectly.

By 1965, I had another plan. The Air Force had come to the decision that they wanted all of their officers to get graduate degrees. So when I first was commissioned I was told that after I'd finished flying school and five years of flying duty they wanted to send me to graduate school.

Five years were just about up. My plan was to go to graduate school as the Air Force wanted, and then volunteer for A-26s in Vietnam again. I would be out of SAC and not one of their assets. That is pretty much what happened. I was very fortunate in being able to go the University of Chicago for a master's degree and because of my involvement in advanced methods of navigation, with Captain PVH Weems, USN ret., and "the Father of Air Navigation," I was slated for an assignment in research and development. However, on getting my degree I called Air Force personnel and volunteered for assignment to A-26s as an Air Commando in Vietnam. Personnel did not want to send me at first but they finally agreed.

On my graduation from the University of Chicago in September of 1967, I received my orders to A-26 school in Alexandria, Louisiana. I was scheduled for Jungle Survival School in the Philippines at Clark Air Force Base before reporting to Nakhon Phanom Royal Thai Air Force Base in Thailand as an Air Commando. But I encountered more problems.

I was stopped at Travis Air Force Base in California. They could not find me listed on the roster for transportation to Jungle Survival School in the Philippines. There was no Cohen, William A., on the roster. They told me that I would be on a waiting list, and I might have to hang around Travis for several weeks. I checked in at the BOQ and went back to the man with the transport list early the next morning. I figured it out. I told them to look for William, Cohen A., on the list. Hooray, they found it, and I was off.

That was not the end. I was stopped again. This time in Jungle Survival School. They had transport issues too. They solved it by priorities. Priority 1 was fighters, Priority 2 was bombers, Priority 3 was recon aircraft and forward air controllers, Priority 4 was transport aircraft, and Priority 5 was everything else. Air Commandos was not listed so I was in the last priority, and they even wanted to give me a desk job! I told them that Air Commando priority was included in the fighter category. The scheduling officer just shook his head and gave me the priority I demanded. I found this generally true in the whole Southeast Asia area. If you wanted to get things done, just tell them you are an Air Commando!

After I returned to the States, I was sometimes asked if I "enjoyed" high-risk flying in World War II airplanes during the Vietnam War, using essentially obsolete equipment from World War II against abundant and more modern AAA used by our enemies. A-26s did not even have ejection seats. If we had to leave the aircraft suddenly because of battle damage, our instructions were to jettison the canopy, climb out of the cockpit, and bail out over the wing. Since among other things, we had no autopilot, the chances of that being successful were slim.

We rarely thought about it. What we did think about is the pride of being a member of 609th Air Commando Squadron, and the job we were doing. An example is expressed in my book, *The Art of the Leader* (Prentice-Hall, 1990).

How I Learned What It Means to Be an Air Commando

In the Southeast Asian conflict, I was an Air Commando. I flew as a member of the 609th Air Commando Squadron, flying A-26s at night, and attacking truck convoys in a heavily defended, mountainous area.

Flying low on a night interdiction mission, these mountainous formations called "karst" were particularly dangerous. The enemy used every weapon they could get their hands on, from small-caliber ZPU machine guns to 37-mm and 57-mm guns, and possibly to radar-controlled 85-mm AAA guns. Yet in the Air Commandos, we flew an old World War II aircraft that the old Army Air Force used for the first time in 1944. This was 1968! The 609th Air Commando Squadron won the Presidential Unit Citation for its gallantry in combat. The price was possibly the highest per sortie aircraft loss rate in the Vietnam War.

What made us do this? On our flying suit we wore a special insignia patch that proclaimed us a "Nimrod." This was also our radio call sign. Nimrod, in the Bible, was the first hunter. This patch said that its wearer had over 100 missions in the aircraft: all night strikes. We wore it proudly.

When I returned to the States, my assignment was to Wright-Patterson Air Force

Base, at Dayton, Ohio. I had a job as a program manager in charge of development of aircraft life support equipment. Once a month I would put on my flying suit and fly to maintain flying skill.

A few months after I returned, I was walking along in my flying suit on my way to the flight line. A car suddenly stopped directly opposite me across the street. The driver, another officer with his wife next to him, called out, "Could you come over a minute, Captain?"

I went over to the car, and the officer introduced himself. He had flown another type of aircraft in another squadron from my base. However, he was not thinking about himself, or what he had done. Instead, he turned to his wife and pointed to my "Nimrod" patch with respect. "Honey, this is one of the fellows I was telling you about. This is an Air Commando. He's a Nimrod."

The Mysterious Silence of Zorro 23

William "Bill" Cohen

You may wonder about what a "Zorro" has to do with a story about A-26s and Nimrods, but as you will soon discover, there is a connection. Early in the secret war over North Vietnam and Laos, "Zorros" and "Nimrods" were both in a single Air Commando squadron. Of course, in those days, Zorros were flying AT-28s, a two-place training plane that had been modified for combat and ground attack missions. But lest you think a training plane didn't have the punch, it had performance characteristics and power that was similar to some of the best World War II fighters. However, 25 years after the war ended, technology had marched on, and it had become more difficult for both the A-26 and the AT-28 to survive in the daylight combat environment of the late 1960s.

As a result, the Nimrods in the A-26s were relegated to night attacks, and the AT-28s to a working area, which while still dangerous, consisted of mainly small-arms fire and not usually the 23 mm and 37 mm, which populated the Ho Chi Minh Trail. With this split in mission and target area, the Nimrods and Zorros were separated into two separate squadrons, although both were part of the 56th Air Commando Wing (later the 56th Special Operations Wing), which was based at Nakhon Phanom Royal Thai Air Force Base not far from the Mekong River, the border with Laos, a country in which the enemy was very active.

The next major change you need to know about to set the stage is that things got even hotter for the AT-28. And so the Zorros eventually transitioned from the AT-28 modified trainer into the post–World War II, but still non-jet, A-1 Sky Raider. This was through the courtesy of this aircraft's original owners, the U.S. Navy. Like the AT-28, the A-1 had but a single engine, as opposed to the A-26 with two.

With the arrival of the A-1, the Nimrods and Zorros not infrequently worked together over the heavily defended Ho Chi Minh Trail, where nightly convoys of trucks, well-guarded by many, many large-caliber antiaircraft guns, made their way south from North Vietnam to supply enemy forces fighting us and our allies in South Vietnam.

One night as we went to operations to brief and fly, I saw the movie star William Holden. At least, it looked like William Holden. His hair was neatly combed above his handsome face. He was wearing a Zorro patch on a neat flying suit, which while not starched, was certainly well-ironed and pressed. He reached out his hand to introduce himself. I expected him to say, "Hi, I'm Bill Holden." He didn't. His real name doesn't matter. The William Holden look-alike was obviously a "new guy" although he held the senior rank of lieutenant colonel. He told us that he was a newly arrived Zorro flying his first solo night combat mission in an A-1, having just completed the Zorro's combat checkout program. In the Zorro A-1 checkout flights, he had always flown with an experienced combat pilot sitting in the right seat of the two-seat A-1E. Now he was flying the single-seat A-1H and his call sign for the evening was Zorro 23.

We chatted briefly and I told him that we'd see him on the Trail. Intel briefed us on the latest situation in our working area. Then we were taken to base supply, where we picked up our helmet and drew our other flying gear: parachute, survival vest, emergency radios, and a .38 revolver and ammunition. I always loaded it with three rounds of ball ammunition and three rounds of tracer. My theory being I didn't know which might be more important if I had to bail out and fight my way until rescue on the ground. I also stuffed my pocket with a small bag of spare ammo. You never know.

Then we were driven to our A-26 in a van by a Thai driver. We preflighted the aircraft, started the engines, taxied, and after clearance from the tower, took off. "Invert," Nakhon Phanom's radar control, immediately sent us to the radio frequency of "Alley Cat," an orbiting C-130 that controlled all the aircraft on the Trail at night. Alley Cat told us that a "Nail" had some trucks at the Delta 79 choke point near an enemy airfield at Tchepone, in Laos. Delta 79 was rumored to be associated with a gunnery school nearby, because while there always seemed to be a particularly large concentration of antiaircraft gun activity near Delta 79, the AAA gunners at Delta 79 didn't seem to be as accurate as gunners elsewhere along the Ho Chi Minh Trail.

A Nail was a small military version of a twin-engine Cessna aircraft which functioned as forward air control (FAC) on attacking targets on the Trail. We transferred to "Nail's" radio frequency and checked in. Using his Starlight Scope, he could see the activity on the ground even though it was pitch-black. He had spotted a convoy of nine enemy trucks moving along the Trail. Zorro 23 checked in shortly afterwards and was flying to the same action.

Zorro was at a lower altitude and carried less ordnance, so we decided that he would attack first, making the necessary number of passes at the target until the truck convoy was destroyed or Zorro ran out of ordnance. Meanwhile, we would suppress enemy fire from the guns that were certain to open up on him. The defending AAA (antiaircraft artillery) always created a fascinating but deadly display in the night sky. The stream of blue tracers from the ZPUs, the clips of seven rounds of orange 37-mm fire, and if working that night, the non-tracer, radar-controlled, popcorn-like puffs of high-velocity 23 mm exploding at altitude. Since we flew at night, the bad guys couldn't see us coming and so fired mostly at the sound after we struck and were climbing back to our orbit altitude. All of this enemy fire converged, creating a cone focused on the withdrawing aircraft. We "jinked," that is executed violent maneuvers left and right as we attempted to avoid getting hit and struggled for altitude. The enemy's AAA fire gave the appearance of many fire hoses trying to wet down the withdrawing aircraft, and in our jargon, we called it "getting hosed down."

We usually wouldn't waste our valuable napalm, high-explosive iron bombs, fire bombs (called "funny bombs"), or even CBU (cluster bomb units) in suppressing the AAA fire. We reserved those weapons for use against our main target: the trucks. Instead, we would use our eight .50-caliber machine guns mounted in the nose of the A-26, which worked just as well and maybe even better for flak suppression. After Zorro had expended all of his ordnance, we would assume the lower orbit position and make our own attacks. Then "William Holden," or whoever we were partnering with, would return the favor and fly flak suppression for us using his guns.

Nail dropped a "log," a pyrotechnic device which burned with a blue light. It was easily seen from the air, but hard to see if you were on the road, since it fell in the jungle. The Nail gave William Holden instructions on where to put his first nape (napalm) from the "log." "Put 'er just due north of the log," he told the Zorro. "The lead truck is almost abeam of that position."

"Roger," responded Holden in Zorro 23. "Rolling in."

We got ready to roll in ourselves when the guns opened up on the A-1. Strangely, that never happened. Some time elapsed. Suddenly, there was a huge explosion on the ground. "Hold off, Nimrod," the "Nail" shouted over the radio. Not a gun fired from the ground.

"Zorro," he called over the radio. "Zorro 23."

No response.

He tried again. "Zorro, Zorro 23, do you copy? Check in."

Nothing. There was dead silence.

I don't remember who I was flying with that night. Although in the A-26s, we had teamed up in two-man crews, about half the time we might fly with someone else. In any case, in the dim light of our instruments we looked at each other. Both of us knew what the other was thinking. William Holden had augered into the ground. That was the big explosion on the ground. "Nail" kept trying to call "Zorro," but there was no answer.

"Nail" made one final try. "Zorro 23, Zorro 23, come in please."

This time he got a response—not much of one, but a response nevertheless. The voice sounded desperate and frightened: "Stand by one, stand by one."

"Zorro, Zorro, are you okay?"

The same response: "Stand by one, stand by one."

A couple minutes went by. Then William Holden came on the radio again. His voice was much calmer, but having experienced more than a hundred combat missions, we could detect the strain and the fear. "Nail, I'm back at altitude," he reported.

"Roger, Zorro, what happened on that pass?"

"I'll tell you on the ground. My ordnance is all expended. I'll yo-yo with Nimrod, and he can go after the convoy." Zorro had made only a single pass at the target. This was highly unusual, but we knew now that this was the reason for the big explosion on the ground. He had expended all of his ordnance on this single pass. We went to the west and descended to Zorro's former altitude, while he headed east and climbed to the altitude we had formerly occupied. Looking through his "Starlight" scope, Nail announced that Zorro hadn't hit any of the trucks. Never mind, we got all nine when we made eight passes putting out a nape or an iron bomb on each of the first six and then one each "funny bomb" from our small bomb bay on the last two. We used our CBU as decoys, putting out a little just before we rolled in. The CBU fell and went off just about the time that we struck, and it always seemed to confuse the gunners and lessen the strength of their hosing. Still, the guns didn't call a truce on our attacks and we got hosed down plenty good. Zorro did his duty, used his guns, and suppressed the flak as best he could.

Nail gave us our BDA (bomb damage assessment) and we headed home to our base at Nakhon Phanom. Our A-26 cruise speed was somewhat higher that of the Zorro's A-1, so we landed earlier than the Zorro, turned in our equipment, and were in the process of debriefing when a figure approached. It was William Holden, but he was barely recognizable. His hair was matted. His face no longer looked so relaxed or handsome. He was perceptibly thinner. He looked haggard. The neatly pressed flying suit was thoroughly soaked with moisture and was in disarray. The thought crossed my mind that maybe his squadron mates had mistaken him for someone completing his tour of combat duty rather than just starting it. The practice was to get fire hoses and wet down the survivor of a year's tour of duty thoroughly before allowing him to debrief, and then escorting him to the club to celebrate his survival with a small party. But I never heard of a mistake like that before.

"What in hell happened to you? … Sir," I asked. I was only a captain at the time, but I was an old guy in combat time. I was still respectful, but my questioning of a new guy wasn't entirely out of line.

"It was that pass I made," he answered. "I rolled in and descended in a steep dive. The only thing was I made a mistake. I forgot to switch fuel tanks. In an A-1 we burn off the centerline tank that contains extra fuel and it is mounted outside the aircraft. However, we're not supposed to strike while burning fuel from that tank. We're supposed to switch to our mains, which are inside the aircraft. Then on the way home we switch back to centerline again and bring the empty tank back home. It's no big deal. The airplane flies the same either way. However, tonight I found out why we have this policy."

"I aligned my piper (on his gunsight) just north of the log, and when I had it in solid I pressed the button to release a single nape. But, the damn nape was stuck. It didn't come off the aircraft. I shook the airplane, but it just wouldn't separate."

Now, nobody brought back napalm hanging outside on the wing. If it broke loose while landing and was armed, it had a tendency to roll forward, not backward. This was true in an A-26 or an A-1. The airplane then would disappear in a holocaust of flame and it would ruin your whole evening. Zorro had good reason to be worried.

"Still in a dive, I decided the only thing to do was to pull the jettison switch and clean the wing of all of my nape. I reached forward under the instrument panel and grasped the jettison T-handle and gave it a good yank. What a shock! I forgot that three inches from the emergency jettison T-handle to clean my wings of ordnance was another emergency jettison handle, almost the same size. That one was used to jettison the centerline fuel tank in an emergency. I had made another mistake and pulled the wrong T-handle! Not only did my nape not separate, but my centerline tank jettisoned and my engine quit. It was dark, I still had a hung nape, I was in a steep dive, over mountainous karst in enemy territory, and my one engine wasn't running because I had just cut off its source of fuel."

"I got very, very busy. I pulled the right jettison handle and cleaned my wings. Then as the altimeter unwound and I headed straight for the ground, I tried to restart my engine. It coughed and didn't start at first. Finally on the third try it did. I managed to pull out just in time before hitting the ground."

"But your flying suit is really wet. I didn't think anyone could sweat that much."

There was a mysterious silence from Zorro 23. He looked at me ashamedly. Finally, he explained: "I also wet my pants … a lot."

I didn't say anything. What could I say? But I thought to myself: "That's nothing to be ashamed of, Mr. Holden, any of us might have done the same."

A Short Visit to an Enemy Gunnery School

William "Bill" Cohen

On Saturday night, May 11, 1968, my fellow Nimrod Ken La Fave and I took off in our A-26 for what was to become an exciting mission from which we almost did not return, a fact of which was due partly to my faulty analysis of the situation, but disaster was avoided due to his good piloting and a last-minute act on my part.

A Saturday night mission was usually all the same to us. I didn't even realize what day it was. It was just another armed recon sortie over the enemy-controlled area called "Steel Tiger" looking for truck convoys traveling the heavily defended Ho Chi Minh Trail. The Trail was the main attraction for us.

We launched eight aircraft spaced about an hour apart every night. We were Nimrod 36 that night. The Trail wound its way south into South Vietnam through the jungle which spread over North Vietnam and Laos, but it really wasn't a trail. It was more of a rough highway through the jungle with numerous enemy strongpoints, choke points, and AAA defenses throughout and protecting the entire route. The headquarters building of the enemy's 559th Engineering Corps responsible for "the Trail" was itself huge. It was 200 meters long and housed offices, a staff of about 100, and included even a fully operational and up-to-date telephone switchboard system. The power of the enemy's AAA was self-evident. At one well-known choke point alone, the Mu Gia Pass, more than 50 of our aircraft had been downed, including A-26s. All this was because it was the North's main artery of supply and infiltration leading into South Vietnam.

Our job was to interdict or at least slow down the massive traffic of armament supplies and troops that were rolling south nightly to supplement the growing army of invaders which were fighting the ARVN (Army of the Republic of Vietnam) troops supported by several hundred thousand Americans. That should give you some idea of the size of the enemy force already in-country killing and harassing the local inhabitants. Eventually, of course, we pulled our troops out and the ARVN, standing alone against the Northerners, were overwhelmed, and South Vietnam fell to the enemy despite our extraordinary efforts at preventing it. But armies can do nothing without the political will of the people from which they spring.

When available, we teamed up with a FAC (a forward air controller) flying in a small unarmed O-2 aircraft. Its crew of two consisted of the pilot and a navigator with a handheld Starlight Scope who doubled as copilot. Their role was to supplement our unaided night vision and to help us stop this traffic. The Starlight Scope allowed the FACs to see in the dark and locate enemy truck convoys, which they would then mark for us to strike. We also sent sorties up across the mountains in northern Thailand, bordering the Plain of Jars in Northern Laos and Vietnam, to give close air support to friendly tribesmen and others who opposed the regime up north and supported our efforts. There was no supply line like the Ho Chi Minh Trail for us heading north. Maybe there should have been. Some of our senior generals thought that to build our own trail and take the fight into North Vietnam was the only way to win this war, and maybe it was. But our efforts did succeed in draining the resources of communist countries in the area and stopping the further spread of communism in Asia.

The Pre-Mission Briefing

The briefing before takeoff was that there wasn't a lot of action on the Trail that night. So once airborne, we would be calling the C-121 communication aircraft known as "Alley Cat." It orbited the area and monitored and controlled U.S. military aircraft flying into, out of, and attacking the Trail in Steel Tiger or heading further north into North Vietnam.

As reported by our crews that had already been there that evening, it was generally quiet although the guns at Choke Point Delta-11 (D-11) remained active and aggressive. Heck, the guns around D-11 were always aggressive, frequently shooting wildly at anything that moved.

There were a lot of them, and they shot a lot, but they never seemed to hit anything flying around D-11, which of course, was okay with us. We thought that maybe they belonged to a gunnery school whose graduates defended the entire Trail. D-11 was close to the town, really just a large village, called Chepone, also known as Xépôn, Tchepone, and Sepon, in the Sepone administrative district of Savannakhet Province.

During the 1950s, the French military built a military airfield about a mile northwest of the village. It was the largest airfield in Savannakhet Province, and the second-largest airfield of any in the nearby South Vietnamese provinces. The bad guys took over when the Royal Laotian Army pulled out in 1961 and built a substantial military complex. In any case it was located not far from a critical juncture on the Trail.

Alley Cat Sends Us to Chepone and the Nail Finds a Target

As soon as we were clear of Invert Control at NKP, as copilot, I called Alley Cat and checked in. Things were still quiet, but Alley Cat directed us to D-11, where a Nail (call sign of the O-2 FAC aircraft supporting us) thought he might have seen some activity on the Trail earlier.

As we climbed out, we altered course about 40 degrees to the right towards D-11. Ken made contact with the Nail who thought he saw some ground activity and got fired at by a 37 mm. Easy to tell the 37 mm. It fired a stream which included a clip of seven bright orange tracer shells which we could see and other non-tracer shells which we couldn't see unless we were hit. The ZPU fired a stream of blue tracers, which was longer and the number of individual tracer shells uncountable. Once in the area of D-11, the Nail gave us some general orientation and instructions but didn't drop a flare on this occasion. Ken was able to identify the target from the Nail's instructions. I told the Nail the direction we were coming from and intended withdrawal. Ken, meanwhile, instructed me, "Give me a nape."

The armament panel was exactly in front of the copilot's position controlling the armament of the four wing stations on either wing. I gave him the outermost finned napalm on the port (left wing) and responded, "You've got one nape from the port wing," and Ken began a steep dive concentrating on the target through the piper gunsight mounted in front of him. I looked for early fire during the attack phase when the gunner couldn't see us but if this happened it was generally at dawn or dusk when we flew earlier or later missions and it was easier for the gunners to spot us. I also glanced at my altimeter and called the altitude out verbally as we descended.

As the target began to fill the windscreen, Ken punched the nape off, stopped our descent, and began to climb while jinking the aircraft. The jinking maneuver was rapid and varying changes of direction to avoid the AAA fire from the numerous defending guns, which immediately opened fire as soon as they saw the flash as we dropped our ordnance or fired our guns. Meanwhile, I focused on the duplicate instruments on my side of the cockpit, monitoring the altitude and the aircraft's attitude and ready to assume control if Ken got spatially disoriented, which happened occasionally with everyone at night, and especially when jinking to avoid enemy gunfire in a darkness broken only by hundreds of bright tracers.

The pilot who was focused on avoiding the flak and regaining a safer altitude from which to begin another run on the target would sometimes lose orientation as to which way was up and could be jinking and heading for the ground at high speed at night without realizing it. Then the copilot would announce, "I've got it," and take control until the pilot got his bearings. Ken did not become disoriented on this flight. He was doing a fine job of avoiding the flak and we were almost back at pre-attack altitude when there was a loud bang and flash on my side of the cockpit at about shoulder height. Needless to say, I was startled by the explosive impact as shrapnel flew by my face and imbedded itself in my instrument panel.

Heavy vibration started almost at once. Ken told me that the airplane was responding and that he still had control. He then called the Nail and told him we'd been hit and asked for clearance to make another pass and drop our remaining ordnance on the target, fending off further questions from him as to our status, except to say that we were hit but were okay.

We made this one additional pass and got rid of our ordnance and I gave Ken a heading for NKP. Meanwhile I talked to NKP and told them we had battle damage but were okay and were on the way home.

This part was a little confusing as everybody seemed to be on the radio and there was some external noise from the shrapnel hole. Of course, NKP had their own checklist to run on this situation, which always includes the question, "How many souls on board?" and I was tempted to ask if they thought we had taken on any hitchhikers but did not. I was too scared to be flippant as I sometimes was over interphone.

Once we had given NKP our status and declared that we were on the way home, we began to think about the vibration again and speculated about the cause. Clearly, it had something to do with the starboard engine and Ken wanted to shut it down. I was against it and that's where I almost got us both killed. I think now that he had expected me to agree with an engine shutdown. We had engine problems during a mission a month or so earlier with the same starboard engine. We shut her down, feathered the prop, and brought the airplane back with no problems at all.

I think what I said surprised him: "I think that whatever hit us has already done its damage and right now we've still got a flyable airplane. We don't know the damage and if we change anything, we don't know what is going to happen." However, I probably said that mouthful a lot quicker. Ken seemed to make up his mind right away, but I don't think that he agreed with my analysis. However, he could see that the close explosion of the 37-mm shell and the resulting shrapnel had shaken me up a bit, because the conversation he started next was a little bizarre. So not shutting down the engine might have been to humor me.

He asked me if I had been hit. When I answered, "No, I'm fine," he continued, "Well, be sure. You know it's a Purple Heart medal if you're wounded, no matter how slight the wound." It sounded inane since we were both clearly concerned with the engine and maintaining control of the airplane while talking to NKP and heading toward that base, which we could see in the distance. At the same time, I was thinking about how we might need to jettison the canopy and climb out over the seat and bail out over the wing. That was not our first choice. Manually bailing out of an A-26 at night, with a lot of cumbersome gear, is definitely a last-resort option.

To prove I could be just as inane, I responded, "Well, I'll check myself over when I take a shower on the ground and let you know." At first, Ken didn't understand, and I repeated my statement. How's that for a conversation during a rather sporty in-flight emergency in combat?

Anyway, before long we were on final and it was clear we were probably going to make it without something bad happening, although the vibration was still pretty intense. Shortly before touchdown, I went to "Props Full Increase." The already considerable vibration got considerably worse. I may be stupid, but I'm not a complete idiot!

I brought the props back to cruise configuration instantly and we landed that way. By then, Ken was engrossed on landing and probably didn't even notice, but it was lucky that I did. On the ground they discovered that only one bolt held that thousand-pound engine to the wing. If it had failed, it would have fallen off the aircraft, causing a significant weight differential, and an uncontrollable roll, which would have ruined our friendship and left both of our wives as widows.

Debriefing with intel was a blur. Intel at 7th AF at Tan Son Nhut in South Vietnam confirmed later that it was a 37 mm that had hit the prop and sent the shrapnel my way. The photo lab gave us 8×10 glossies of our beat-up A-26 featuring the prop with its shortened blade prominently displayed. Ken and I flew the same airplane a week or so later. It was completely repaired. We had full confidence in the job the maintenance crews had done; as always, they didn't let us down.

Ken left NKP early several months later before a year's tour was up. He didn't have to fly a full year because he had already flown in Vietnam, I think in C-47s, in the early days and received credit for the time.

I lost contact with Ken until about 10 years later. In the interim I had become a navigator instructor, and squadron training officer in the 609th ACS; had served in research and development for two years at Wright-Patterson AFB in Ohio, resigned my commission, and helped develop Israel's first home-manufactured jet fighter; helped design a militarized version of the Arava STOL and demo it to the Luftwaffe in Germany; and fly combat in the Yom Kippur as a member of the IAF in 1973. I had returned to the U.S., was recommissioned, and was getting checked out in C-141s. I ran into Ken in an Air Force base coffee shop in Alaska while the airplane was being refueled. We only had a few minutes, but Ken bought me a cup of coffee and welcomed me back to the U.S. Air Force. He also gave me some good advice about restarting my career. We reminisced a bit about our time together at NKP. However, I didn't remind him of his near-death experience at my hands after our night visit to the enemy gunnery school at Chepone back in 1968.

Batman and Robin Attack a Cave

AL "BATMAN" SHORTT

Captain Larry Counts (Robin) and Major Al Shortt (Batman) (courtesy Al Shortt).

On a night with a typical load on our A-26 (eight finned napalms on the wing stations; eight 50-caliber machine guns in the nose; and a miscellaneous load of munitions in the bomb bay), Al "Batman" Shortt, pilot, and Larry "Robin" Counts, navigator, headed out for what turned out to be anything but the typical "road-recce" mission for trucks and antiaircraft gun suppression.

Earlier in the day, a FAC spotted activity near the bottom of a mountain, but high enough on the side to preclude normal high-angle bombing. Other "slow movers" (prop attack aircraft) had attempted to hit the camouflaged cave, but nothing had hit the opening. When we got in the area, our FAC asked if we had ordnance that could somehow strike the opening and we responded "affirmative." Luckily, we had finned napes versus unfinned napes (unfinned napes were good for dispersion against trucks, but not for having a predictable flight pattern).

We arrived in the area and saw many small fires near the target, but the ground was barely distinguishable due to only a partial moon. The FAC tried to explain the exact location of the cave by giving directions in regards to the fires—not very scientific, but a good starting point. When we felt we knew the location he was directing us to, I felt it would be a good choice to fire a short burst of our guns to see if we were on the same page. The .50-cal rounds would "sparkle" when they hit the rocky area to indicate the impact area relative to the target.

The big difference in this mission was that we were flying low over rough terrain (Larry gave me the "don't go below" altitude). We were flying a very low angle of descent into a target that was difficult to see other than the fires, and we had to do some "Kentucky windage" to know how close, at what airspeed, and at what approximate altitude would be correct to release a napalm canister and have time to maneuver away from the mountain.

Our first nape fell short; the second pass was better but still not high enough. We decided to fly faster and a couple hundred feet higher. Success! The nape appeared to hit right at the edge of the cave, with half the fire going inside. By the time we made our hard climbing turn and looked back, some mini-explosions were seen coming out of the opening. The FAC was ecstatic! We were ecstatic too!

We struck a few trucks that night with our remaining ordnance, but nothing made us feel as good as hitting that cave on the side of a mountain. After debriefing, we went to the club for a few beers, and when a later mission crew came back and told us it was still exploding, we really felt good! "Batman and Robin" had a good ride!!!

Almost Toast—B-52 Attack

Al "Batman" Shortt

Batman (Al Shortt) and Robin (Larry Counts) had a close call while working the Ho Chi Minh Trail. It wasn't from the 37-mm or ZPU gunners. It was from our own B-52s!

Our FAC (forward air controller) had found some Trail activity where reconstruction of the road was underway with bulldozers and trucks. We were having an uneventful (minimum AAA resistance) sortie when suddenly the Trail just south of our position started to light up as if another strike was being focused on a target. We soon changed our thinking. The "strike" kept coming toward us very rapidly!

It soon became obvious that this was *big* and not an ordinary fighter or Air Commando strike. We realized that this had to be an arc light (B-52) bombing that had not been coordinated with our FAC. We immediately "hauled ass" away from the Trail as the bombs were exploding almost under our position, which meant the bombs were coming right through us! (The A-26 wasn't the speediest plane so we couldn't separate ourselves from the

Major Al Shortt under "Funny Bombs" (courtesy Al Shortt).

Trail as fast as we would have liked—to say the least!) In other words, we almost became part of the target, which had to be further destroyed on that part of the Trail. I must admit, I was *very* impressed with the devastation the B-52 could do with its bomb load!

That was about as close as we ever came to becoming a statistic! All because of the lack of coordination and communication from headquarters, which should have made that target "off-limits" for everyone except the B-52 strike. I couldn't get to a telephone fast enough to debrief some colonel in headquarters. I never "chewed out" a superior before, but I let it all hang out in that confrontation! Nothing is worse than getting killed by "friendly fire," and that would have qualified in what almost happened on that particular night.

What a f---ed-up war!!!

My A-26 Time at NKP

Leon "Crazy" Poteet

I arrived at NKP on 6 January 1969 after completing "Snake School" (Jungle Survival School) in the Philippines. My first A-26 flight at NKP was on 13 January 1969 with Jack Bright, after orientation rides in the C-123, OV-10, and O-1. I flew 147 combat

Leon "Crazy" Poteet (left) and Paul Marschalk (courtesy Franklin Poole).

missions until our squadron was deactivated, with the last flight being on 9 November 1969. I was a navigator and my first assigned pilot was Neal Monette. We flew our first mission together on 22 January 1969. Shortly after that, Neal's father died and Neal took compassionate leave to go home. He came back to NKP in early March, and shortly after that, he and John Callanan were killed in an A-26 crash near the end of the runway. The cause of the crash was fuel starvation on the right engine just as power was applied to go around. I was supposed to be on that flight, but as fate would have it, the schedule was changed to assign an instructor navigator (John Callanan) in my place.

My next assigned pilot was Chuck Kenyon, who I believe wrote the Dash 1 for the A-26. I learned a lot from him. On our first flight, he drew a line with his hand down the right side of the center of the cockpit and said everything on the left was his and everything on the right was mine. Of course, as time went on, we each violated that rule somewhat just to have fun. We got along very well. Around June 1969, Chuck's tour was over, and I was crewed with Paul Marschalk for the remainder of the tour. We worked well together, and he felt comfortable with me flying the aircraft from time to time (we had flight controls on both sides).

We flew in Barrel Roll, Steel Tiger, and a few missions in Cambodia. Parrot's Beak, the Chokes, Ban Laboy (Mu Gia), Ban Karai, are all prominent location names that come to mind. ZPU, 23 mm, 37 mm, 57 mm, and an 85 mm just across the border at Mu Gia, are all antiaircraft guns that come to mind. The 85 mm would lob shells across the border if we were working in the area close to it. We were shot at on most missions if the weather was good, and there were many missions when the shots came so close we could smell the cordite. We bombed trucks, suspected truck parks, and roads on the Ho Chi Minh Trail in Laos and Cambodia, and enemy troops-in-contact in Steel Tiger and Barrel Roll (even just across the Mekong River not far from NKP). We also supported Lima Sites in northern Laos when enemy troops were threatening. A memorable mission was on 30 May 1969, with Batman, I believe, where we made numerous passes, dropped all ordnance and fired the guns until empty, and killed five trucks, with everything shooting at us except the 85 mm. This may have been in the Chokes area. Paul and I also had some good missions where we killed several trucks with napalm, hard bombs, and .50-cal machine-gun bullets, and took a lot of incoming fire from ZPU, 23-mm, 37-mm, and 57-mm antiaircraft rounds thrown at us. On the way back to NKP on our last mission, we did a barrel roll with the A-26 to celebrate our last combat mission.

Most A-26 crewmembers had a handle, or nickname. Paul was "Hulk" (he was a big man) and I was "Crazy." My name came from a game of jarts (lawn dart game) because I put a dart in the ring on just about every throw, even when drinking in a party mood. Lee Griffin commented that this guy is crazy, and from then on, I was "Crazy."

When the 609th was deactivated in November 1969, Paul and I were the first crew to start bringing the A-26s back to the States. The first stop was at Clark AFB, Philippines, where we were ready with our Nimrod stencil and red paint to leave our trademark all over the Pacific on our way home. From there, with a Navy C-131 providing navigation assistance, we flew to Guam, Wake, Johnston Island, and Midway (cannot remember the order), before arriving in Hawaii, leaving our red Nimrod aircraft symbol across the Pacific. After a few days at Hickam in Hawaii, we departed for McClellan AFB in Sacramento, California. However, shortly after takeoff, some pins in my parachute came loose and we had to return to Hickam. This really pissed off the C-131 crew. Finally, without any more problems, we arrived at McClellan. As soon as we shut down and got out of our A-26, we went over to the C-131 and sprayed our Nimrod symbol on the side of it. The C-131 crewmembers were gone but they must have been surprised the next day. We never saw them again. After a couple days at McClellan, Paul and I took turns at the flight controls flying our A-26 to the boneyard at Davis Monthan Air Force Base, Arizona. It was a sad ending for a magnificent combat aircraft.

Paul and I got together many times after that, mainly at A-26 reunions at Hurlburt Field, Florida. If you wanted to say anything to the group at reunions, you had to stick your hand in an ice bucket and keep it there while you spoke (keeps speeches short). Paul always had something to say, and he is famous for always ending our reunions by dumping the ice bucket on his head. Sadly, Paul passed away in January

Paul Marschalk ending a reunion by dumping an ice bucket on his head, 2005 (courtesy Al Shortt).

2013. He is survived by his loving wife, Sue Marschalk, who lives in Tennessee.

For me, looking back, since I came back alive, flying the A-26 at NKP was the most fun I ever had in the Air Force.

Unforgettable Nimrod Missions

TIM BLACK *and* BRUCE "GUS" GUSTAFSON

Lucky Night in Barrel Roll

Bruce Gustafson ("Gus"), navigator, and I were an A-26 crew at NKP in 1969. On one of our missions, we were working with an air FAC in northern Laos, the Barrel Roll region. Our weapons load consisted of six napes and two pods of rockets on the wings, our standard load of .50 cal, and an internal bomb load of 72 fragmentation bombs. The FAC had been using our nape on a road junction area. He had told us to watch our area boundaries as there were other fighter aircraft working target areas close by. After expending the napes, Gus and I were asked to use our rockets. The FAC gave us the target brief and we set up to roll in to expend the rockets. As we were going down the chute, Gus was calling out the altitudes and I was focused on putting the pipper on the target. As I was about to press the rocket button, an F-4 came flying through my pipper, so we immediately came off the pass without expending. As we pulled back up to the base

Capt. Bruce Gustafson (left) and 1LT Tim Black (right) (courtesy Tim Black).

altitude, we told the FAC what had happened. He said he had seen the F-4 just at the last minute as he flew through our target area. He was supposed to be working another valley over but must have strayed into our area on one of his passes. If it had happened one second later, the F-4 would have had an aircraft full of 7.62 rockets. This was his, and our, lucky night. After the F-4 passed back into his area, we went back to work.

Tank Attack in Barrel Roll

On another mission, Gus and I were the number two Nimrod in the flight. We were always number two since I was the youngest pilot there at that time. Gus was a little older … but smarter … but, I digress. This mission was to support friendly troops which were in contact with the enemy. According to our initial brief, the friendly position was being overrun. Our target was in the PDJ (Plaines des Jarres) of northern Laos. We had been expending our napes and hard bombs (500-pounders) on the area where the FAC said the enemy troops were. After we had made several alternating passes trying to stem the ground attack on the friendly forces, the FAC called out that he had an area off to the side of the immediate target. The FAC had a Starlight Scope with which to view the target area at night. The FAC said he could see an area that looked like the enemy forces were refueling their tanks. So he gave us the target brief on the exact location and asked for us to use a 500-pound bomb. Gus armed up the outboard station for the 500-pound bomb, and we rolled in from our base altitude. As Gus called out the altitudes, I focused on my drop parameters. (In the A-26, the pipper placement for dropping a bomb or nape using a 30-degree dive angle could not be displaced to where the center of the gunsight was right on the target when you released. A pilot had to let the target go under the nose of the aircraft and use a "wag" to accurately release the bomb. My particular "wag" was to count one potato, two potato, release.) At release altitude, I hit the release button and we started our pull-off zooming back up to our base altitude. As we did on almost every pass, either dropping nape or hard bombs, I rolled the aircraft up on its wing so we could see where the bomb hit. There was a tremendous explosion on the ground and then a fireball climbed straight up into the night sky as if it were chasing us up. The FAC got very excited over the radio and told us it looked like the 500-pound bomb had gone right down the open turret of a tank being refueled. I don't really know if this is what happened, but needless to say, Gus and I thought that was pretty cool. Gus kept telling me to tell the FAC that we were the first team, so what would he expect. (As I recall, I did mention to the FAC that we were the first team.) Apparently, after our two-ship finished working the target over, the enemy forces broke off the attack.

One Over the North by Mistake

We did have one mission where Gus and I could have gotten our names in the newspapers, but, fortunately we didn't. Otherwise, I don't think I would have had a successful 25-year Air Force career. On that particular night, we were again number two, and we had one of the later scheduled missions. We were scheduled to "arm recce" Rt. 7 from the M in the river in central Laos over to the Fishes Mouth at the border of NVN. That night there was a lot of weather over all of Laos, so after we got our intelligence briefing, we just sat around the operations area waiting for the weather to break. After several hours, our flight lead decided that we probably weren't going to fly, so we headed out to the aircraft to get our parachutes and survival vests, which we had already placed in the aircraft. As we were up on the wing, the navigator from the lead aircraft came running over to us and said they told us to go. He was in a fit because they wanted us airborne ASAP as it was beginning to get light and he had left his maps in the briefing room. As we were number two, Gus said to take his maps and we'd just follow them. We took off ASAP and headed up to Barrel Roll to perform our mission. There were a lot of clouds around and weather, but we were able to pick our way to the target area. As we did, however, it did get light. Once on Rt. 7, we separated and began an in-trail zigzag formation looking for any enemy activity. As we were proceeding east (toward NVN), we thought we spotted activity and called lead. Both of us did a turn around the point looking for signs of the enemy. Apparently, there was nothing there, so we continued our turn around to head east again, believing lead was doing the same thing behind us. However, he only did a 180-degree turn and headed west back toward the M in the river. We did a 360-degree turn and headed back toward the east expecting lead to do the same thing, except that we would be in front now. We proceeded for some time and Gus became antsy about our position. He thought we were getting close to NVN. I told him not to worry, lead was right behind us and he would keep us straight. After more time passed, Gus was really getting antsy, so to calm his fears, I said lead was right behind us, but to prove it, I did a banked turn to the right to show him lead was right there. However, there was no aircraft. So I did a big, banked turn to the left so I could show him lead was on that side. No lead. No bomb craters under us either. So I called lead over the radio and asked for his position. He said (very faintly) that he was over by the M in the river. He asked where we were, and I said we'll be there shortly. Doing a high G turn back to the west, I told Gus to arm up all our stations and if we got shot at, we would release all our napes and bombs on them, put the aircraft on the deck, and beat feet. After several minutes, actually long minutes, we arrived over the M in the river and rejoined with lead. Adventure over! Once back on the ground, we very rapidly headed over to the map room to see where our flight had taken us. I won't say exactly, but if you continue past the Fishes Mouth along Rt. 7 and draw somewhat of a straight line, you come to Vinh, the airfield in NVN. So I guess had we continued east, and made it back alive, someone really high up the chain of command would have been asking a lot of questions. We did have a patch made up that said, "One Over the North by Mistake."

At this point, I'd like to have Gus relay what he was thinking on this mission:

I remember being concerned—after we made our orbits looking for activity—that lead had left us. I remember saying to my fearless leader, "How can the other A-26 be lead if we are in front?" Of course, Tim had an answer, which was something like "because he's lead Rundunk." I knew we were headed east but I didn't know who we were following. When we left all the bomb craters on the ground and found ourselves looking down at basically fresh green rolling hills that had experienced little "traffic or attention," I began to look for interceptors … and not ours. After Tim did a couple of turns into or away from lead, who was supposedly just behind us with the maps, and could not see him, we turned back eastbound. Something in the back of my mind said, "East is least and west is best," and I started to think we might get some air-to-air action. I had full confidence if we could see any enemy aircraft that Tim would get the bead on him and that at our slow speed we could out turn any jet. After we could faintly hear lead over the radio way back at the M in the river, he made a call to the airborne command post and said we were wondering if they happened to have our position on radar. They responded with a statement something like "Turn to a heading of 270 and call us back in about 15 minutes." My thought at that time was it would be just our luck not to see some MiG at our six-o'clock position. It was hard enough to see our five- or seven-o'clock position. I also was looking pretty hard to see some bomb craters again but I think we both were relieved to join up again with lead over by the M in the river. We wondered if we showed up on their NVN radar, and if so, what was going through their minds. We also wondered if the airborne command post would report our "radar contact" to NKP. There are only two people I know who wear a "One Over the North by Mistake" patch.

Bar Talk Story

This mission was our normal night two-ship formation with us as number two. The pilot and navigator in the lead aircraft were two majors, just as a sidenote, but that had no bearing on this flight. Our mission that night was in southern Laos, the Steel Tiger area of operations. We got our FAC brief and began working the target area, a suspected truck park. Nimrods usually dropped a single nape or hard bomb at a time so as to be as accurate as we could and to give the FAC as much time on station as we could. This usually meant our missions were one to two hours long or more. After many passes and expending all our wing and bomb bay ordnance, the FAC asked if we had any further napes, bombs, or other ordnance left. Lead told him we had our .50 cal remaining. The FAC said he had a favorite target he liked to expend ordnance on if we had the time. Of course lead said yes, because no Nimrod wanted to bring any munitions back to NKP after a combat sortie. So we proceeded down the trail to the FAC's new target for us. As we were approaching the target area, it began to get light. The FAC gave us the target description and cleared us in "hot." As lead was pulling off his pass, Gus and I noticed ground fire, probably a ZPU 23-mm gun, firing at him. So we called we were in on the ground fire. As we pulled off this strafing pass, the FAC said there were two gun positions now firing at us. Lead made another pass on the gun positions, and upon pulling off, another gun came up. Now there were three. As lead got back up on the perch, he said he wasn't going to make any more passes. Gus and I, being true warriors, said we were in again. Now it was one v. three. We made a couple more passes with each one getting more violent in maneuvering as we tried to avoid the ZPUs. We were rolling in, jinking like a fighter while going down the chute, rolling wings level just long enough to fire our .50s, and then jinking like crazy pulling off. On one of the next passes, as I was pulling off, I noticed Gus looking out his side window. No matter what the situation, we always bantered back and forth. I said something like, "Here I am doing all the work over here and you're just riding along sightseeing." He said, "I'm just watching the tracers going between the wing and the tail." At that moment, we looked at each other and thought, this is one of those "bar talk" stories from the old heads. We remembered being told one night from an old head, "Do not take on a gun with a gun in the daytime." Reason, they can see you, but you probably can't see them. So at this time, we decided that discretion was the better part of valor and said we weren't making any more passes either. We returned to NKP with both aircraft intact. We relearned a lesson that night. When the old heads tell you something at the bar, it's usually best to listen to them.

Just a Little Fire

A story from Gus. We were a single ship for some reason, sent north to Barrel Roll to meet up with a Thai or Laotian ground FAC who had been planted near enemy forces. When we were near his location, Tim called on the assigned frequency for our check-in. The FAC said, in broken English, that he could hear our plane and to continue our heading, that when we got a little closer he would wave his flashlight at us. (Of course I thought, "Fat chance seeing a little flashlight at midnight through the forest from a DR [dead reckoning] heading.") About two minutes later he said, "You are close, I wave flashlight." Well, eagle eye Tim said, "I see your flashlight," and the FAC said he was talking softly because he was very close to the enemy, laying in a ditch beside the road. He wanted us to drop a bomb (some one or two klicks to the north of his position and he would correct from that). I don't know how Tim got the 26 turned around in 360 degrees so precisely but that is his skill and talent. He used his one potato, two potato technique, keeping an eye on where the ground FAC was laying in the ditch, and punched off a 500-pounder. As Tim pulled off, he said, "Uh-oh, that's a little long." We watched the bomb explode as we pulled back up to our base altitude. Not hearing anything from the FAC, we made a couple of radio calls to him. No contact. After some long moments, the next thing we heard on the radio was a loud "Ooeeo that too close Nimrod, you 'bout knocked me out of ditch." He said he would give us another chance, but to start farther back and he would work us in closer to the target. On our pull up and turn back for another pass, and an extra potato three, we saw a small fresh fire in the woods about a mile to the Northeast. Tim informed the ground FAC and asked permission to go check it out. The FAC said he could see the reflection and asked that we drop a bomb on it. I don't know if he just wanted us a little farther from him or if he had a similar hunch. So away we go to the little fire that had gotten a little bigger and Tim makes his dive and release and on the pull out we see a very large explosion and then several more. I don't remember much more about the drop zone and our activity. I know I wanted to go drop another bomb, but it seems we had to RTB back to NKP. We informed the FAC of the multiple explosions and fires. I think he said he could see it from his position in the ditch. He said something like "Velly, velly good" or "You did good" or "You number one bomber." Tim and I were pretty elated with the results. We checked the BDA figures the next day and it reported many tanks destroyed or damaged and at least 175 enemy casualties with lots of resources being used to clean up or relocate the storage area. I wondered why it wasn't retargeted for the Nimrods, but maybe it was for another unit. My assumption was that someone was refueling and when our first bomb went off the refueler or one of his helpers did something that ignited the first little fire.

Too Close for Comfort

It was a really terrible weather night for flying, with near pitch-black conditions punctuated by rain, thunder, and blinding flashes of lightning. Tim had his hands full maintaining our assigned altitude due to the turbulence. The instrument panel resembled a blurred, bucking bronco. To make matters even more challenging, we were stacked in a holding pattern over a target area that night with two A-26s, 2 A-1s, and the night FAC. One of the A-1 pilots made a radio call to let everybody know he was having a very difficult time staying anywhere near his assigned altitude. He said he had up and down drafts causing a fluctuation of altitude of a thousand feet or more. We were all supposed to be maintaining an altitude separation of 1,000 feet. About 10–20 minutes later, I had my eyes on the instrument panel trying to see if anything would come in focus and to try to be of some backup if we got upside down. We too had 500–1,000-foot deviations from our assigned altitude. Tim had his head glued to the instrument panel and was doing everything in his power to keep our aircraft at its assigned altitude. All of a sudden, I heard a loud radial engine directly overhead. I immediately looked up and out my right-side front window into the pitch-black darkness and saw (from the light in our cockpit) the tail wheel of an A-1 aircraft that appeared to be about 18 inches in front and about two feet above the top of the right side of our canopy. From that angle, it looked like the A-1 had passed over us from about the seven-o'clock position to the one-o'clock position relative to our aircraft, and that it was in a high Vy to Vx pitch attitude … and of course was gone in a split second. I'm not exactly sure what I said but it was something like, "Woooahh!!! Did you see that tail wheel? It was right in front of the canopy. Did you hear the engine?" To hear the A-1 single engine over both of the always loud close engines of the A-26 would have put it pretty close. I can remember having some other lucky times as I grew up and my mother said to me during one of our great visits after retiring from the Air Force that I had worked my guardian angel pretty hard. Well, that night both Tim and I worked a couple of guardian angels pretty hard.

Ferry Flight Back to the Boneyard

The Duckbutt C-130 met us a couple of hours after leaving Hawaii for McClellan AFB, California, for the purpose of correcting our navigation track. Tim Black (pilot) and I (navigator) were number two in the A-26 three-ship formation (not lead). We did not have any nav aids aboard the A-26 that were designed for flights across an ocean. Hence, we had been flying a dead reckoning (DR) heading since leaving Hawaii, and we needed a navigation assist from the C-130 crew. The C-130 navigator proceeded to give us a 10-degree correction to the right for our "updated" heading. I questioned his correction. Several years earlier, when I was a second lieutenant, an old-head SAC roommate had told me about a radio station in San Francisco that was very powerful. The radio station was KGO SF @ 590 on the dial. I had tuned it in about an hour after takeoff from Hickam AFB, and the ADF needle was pointing about two degrees left (the same as our planned flight heading). Tim and I were not lead, and as you might guess, nobody else questioned the 10-degree right heading correction received from the C-130 navigator. I finally jumped on the radio and asked him if he would double-check his suggested heading. He came back in five minutes and said affirmative 10 degrees right. I fumed inside a little and asked him to recheck, which he did, and he again said 10 degrees right. Now I was really getting concerned: (1) We were not lead; and (2) What are the other five Nimrod crewmembers in the other two A-26s, and Tim, thinking about me questioning the C-130 navigator? How or why would Old Gus (me) have any reason to question the C-130 with its superior navigation equipment? Anyway, I asked the C-130 nav to check again because the heading didn't agree with the heading I thought was correct. He came back in 10 minutes and said he still computed 10 degrees right, but "confirm your destination as Los Angeles." I replied that "Our destination is McClellan AFB at Sacramento." He came right back and said, "Oh, three degrees left." Because Los Angeles is so far southeast of Sacramento, our A-26 aircraft would have run out of gas. We only had 30–45 minutes of reserve fuel for Sacramento.

Leaving Our Mark

Just a note about flying the A-26s back to the boneyard in January 1970. We flew nine aircraft in three cells of three aircraft, island hopping across the Pacific. A favorite memory of these flights was that before we left the Philippines, each crewmember and crew chief was given a silhouette of an A-26 and two cans of red spray paint. Well, you can guess what happened. All the way across the Pacific, we left our mark. There were red A-26s on anything that looked appropriate, or inappropriate, from Clark AB, Guam, Wake Island, Midway, Hickam AFB, and all the way to Davis-Monthan AFB, where we took the aircraft. I would bet that one could find some red A-26s still painted on things across the Pacific. However, don't ask Gus or myself who spray-painted the

First Lieutenant Tim Black (left) and Captain Bruce Gustafson (courtesy Tim Black).

glass doors on the DV lounge at Hickam AFB, or the chrome bumper of the wing commander's staff car.

Concluding Thoughts

Upon arrival at England AFB in 1969 for our A-26 training, we were told that during our classes we should decide who we wanted to be paired up with as a crew. After a couple of days being together as a group, I knew that I wanted to be paired with Gus. Maybe it was the "twinkle" in his eyes or his attitude about flying that impressed me, but I just knew that we would get along fine. Our instructor thought so too, if the two of us could keep from getting killed. There is no finer person than Bruce Gustafson to fly with. On many missions, I placed my life in his hands and even to this day, I would gladly do it again. When we get together now, we're not in our 60s or 70s. We're in our 20s … but, maybe just a little bit slower.

The whole time, the entire time, I have shared with Tim has made my heart soar like an eagle. I feel very fortunate to have shared the airplane with him and to appreciate his talent and humor. At 73 years young, I still get to fly several times a week as director of pilot operations and check airman of our Lane Community College Flight School. I have been there over 22 years. We launch 20–30 flights a day that I get to watch out my flight line window. I have a picture of our NKP crews on the A-26 on the PSP ramp at NKP. It is on my office wall and the students drool at the cool picture, but I recognize it is "history."

Last A-26 Flight Out of NKP

Jim Blanchard

My logbook shows that Ed Parris and I flew A-26 aircraft number 644 to Clark Air Base in the Philippines on 16 November 1969, and that we flew an FCF (call sign list 70) on it the day before (flight times of 5.7 hours and 1.3 hours, respectively). If my memory is correct, I believe 644 had maintenance problems and couldn't fly with the main squadron gaggle of A-26 aircraft being ferried from NKP to Clark on 13 or 14 November 1969. Ed was held back because he was FCF qualified, which means I was held back too because I was his navigator. After the maintenance work was completed on 644, we flew an FCF and subsequently departed on 16 November 1969 for Clark as part of a three-ship A-26 formation.

Based on the above, and considering that there were no A-26 aircraft left at NKP beyond 16 November 1969, I believe being number three in the Nimrod 13 flight placed Ed Parris and me in the position of being the last takeoff of an A-26 Nimrod from NKP, closing a very significant chapter in A/B-26 history. I spoke to Ed and his memory is the same as mine.

After our A-26 assignments, Ed continued his career in multi-engine recips and jet aircraft. Following Air Force retirement, he had a successful career as an airline pilot and retired from American Airlines. I returned to the States to become an instructor at undergraduate navigator training (UNT), became a weapon systems officer (WSO), and flew as a WSO in F-4s at Kadena Air Base, Okinawa, and Kunsan Air Base, Korea. I also served in two staff position assignments at Tactical Air Command headquarters, Langley AFB, Virginia.

Needless to say, like all Nimrods, I have very strong memories of flying A-26 combat missions out of NKP. I think the last Nimrod takeoff from NKP has a significant

SO T-3714, HQ 56TH COMBT SPT GP (PACAF), APO SAN FRANCISCO 96310, 12 Nov 69

MAJOR	KELLER, RICHARD G.	609SPOPSQ	TS
MAJOR	KOSTAN, JAMES A.	609SPOPSQ	TS
MAJOR	KOYN, DANIEL W.	609SPOPSQ	TS
MAJOR	LORIMER, WILLIAM H.	609SPOPSQ	TS
MAJOR	RILEY, FRANCIS E.	609SPOPSQ	TS
CAPT	BAME, KARL T.	609SPOPSQ	TS
CAPT	DEMARCO, JOSEPH R.	609SPOPSQ	TS
CAPT	HOTSKO, ANTHONY M.	609SPOPSQ	TS
CAPT	MARSCHALK, PAUL M.	609SPOPSQ	TS
CAPT	PARRIS, EDDIE L.	609SPOPSQ	S
CAPT	PETERSON, PETER F.	609SPOPSQ	S
CAPT	POST, DELBERT A.	609SPOPSQ	TS
CAPT	POTEET, LEON J.	609SPOPSQ	TS
CAPT	RUSSELL, RAYMOND E.	609SPOPSQ	TS
CAPT	SCHMIDT, NOLAN W.	609SPOPSQ	TS
CAPT	SCHULZ, RONALD E.	609SPOPSQ	S
CAPT	WAYMIRE, LESTER D.	609SPOPSQ	TS
CAPT	ZAISER, ALAN R.	609SPOPSQ	TS
1/Lt	BERNHARDT, THOMAS R.	609SPOPSQ	TS
1/Lt	BLACK, RALPH P. JR.	609SPOPSQ	S
1/Lt	BLANCHARD, JAMES R.	609SPOPSQ	TS
1/Lt	CUTLER, RICHARD R.	609SPOPSQ	S
1/Lt	HICHLY, EDWARD M.	609SPOPSQ	TS
1/Lt	HOWE, PAUL S.	609SPOPSQ	TS
1/Lt	TALBERT, DAVID P.	609SPOPSQ	TS
1/Lt	TUTHILL, LANNY Y.	609SPOPSQ	TS
1/Lt	VANETTEN, PETER (NMI)	609SPOPSQ	TS

handwritten: SSN's DELETED

2

Opposite: USAF Order Dated 12 November 69 authorizing Lieutenant Colonel Jackie Douglas and Squadron pilots and navigators to Ferry 609th Special Operations A-26 aircraft from Nakhon Phanom RTAFB to Clark Air Base, Philippines. *Above:* Continuation age for USAF order described above listing more names of pilots and navigators involved in ferry flight to Clark Air Base, Philippines.

FLIGHT ORDER

(If more space is required, continue on reverse, identifying items by number)

1. CREW MEMBERS LISTED BELOW WILL PROCEED IN AIRCRAFT INDICATED AND UPON COMPLETION OF FLIGHT WILL RETURN TO PROPER STATIONS.	2. EFFECTIVE ON OR ABOUT 14 NOV 69	3. RETURN ON OR ABOUT N/A

4. FROM: (Place flight will originate) NAKHON PHANOM RTAFB, THAILAND	5. TO: (Itinerary, list complete address, variations in itinerary authorized) CLARK AB, PHILLIPINES

6. MISSION

FERRY

7. CREW NO.	8. TAKE-OFF TIME	9. DURATION OF FLIGHT	10. SECURITY CLEARANCE FOR PERIOD OF FLIGHT DUTY	11. SPECIAL INSTRUCTIONS
N/A	0900L	5+15	TOP SECRET	NONE

12. CREW (See AFTO 00-20-5 for position codes)		13. NAME (Last, first, middle initial, AFSN; indicate commander of aircraft by placing asterisk next to his name.)	14. ORGANIZATION AND MAJOR COMMAND (If not issuing agency)	15. AIRCRAFT		
NO. A	POSITION B			TYPE A	SERIAL NO. OR TACTICAL CALL SIGN B	FUEL LOAD (Lbs/Gals) C
	PP	*KELLER, RICHARD G. OFR		A-26A	NIMROD 13	
	NN	BERNHARDT, THOMAS R. V				
	PP	*LORIMER, WILLIAM H., JR. FV		A-26A	NIMROD 14	
	NN	TALBERT. DAVID P. FV				
	PP	*PARRIS, EDDIE L. FR		A-26A	NIMROD 15	
	NN	BLANCHARD, JAMES R. FV				

16. RESERVE PERSONNEL NOT ON EXTENDED ACTIVE DUTY, ARE SUBJECT TO THE PROVISIONS OF THE UNIFORM CODE OF MILITARY JUSTICE WHILE PERFORMING THIS DUTY.	17. DATE OF ORDER 18 Nov 69	18. ORDER NUMBER 609SOS-005

19. DESIGNATION AND LOCATION OF HEADQUARTERS DEPARTMENT OF THE AIR FORCE 56th Special Operations Wing (PACAF) APO San Francisco 96310	20. FOR THE 609th Special Operations Squadron 21. SIGNATURE ELEMENT OF ORDERS AUTHENTICATING OFFICIAL. JACKIE R. DOUGLAS, Lt Colonel, USAF Commander

AF FORM 615   PREVIOUS EDITION OF THIS FORM WILL BE USED

Copy of USAF flight order dated 18 November 69 authorizing three A-26 crews (including navigator James Blanchard and pilot Eddie Parris) to ferry A-26 aircraft to Clark Air Base, Philippines.

56th SOW
Change of Command
5 October 1969

Change of command ceremony, 1969 (courtesy Jimmie Butler).

A-26 Nimrod squadron deactivated, November 1969 (USAF).

place in the history of both the aircraft and the Nimrods. The TDY orders dated 12 November 69 (see below) associated with ferrying the A-26 aircraft from NKP to Clark AB are an interesting part of this history. Those TDY orders include the names of the 30 Nimrod pilots and navigators who flew the aircraft to Clark. Also, the flight order dated 13 November 69 (see below) includes the names of the three crews involved in the last three-ship flight out of NKP.

"ODE TO A NIMROD"

Anonymous

The sleek black beauty sits on high
Frothing vengance from the sky.
A nimble candle lights a light,
The enemy convoy comes into sight.
The marks are placed, no more to say,
That valiant bird is on his prey.
With nerves of steel he makes each run
The guns are up but this is fun.
His load is gone, his guns are dry
The weary Nimrod relieves a sigh.
Now the time has come and he must go
But God, he's been a fearless foe.
His wings are clipped, he'll cease to soar
That mighty hunter we'll hear no more.
But in our hearts they'll live again,
For we'll have known we've fought with men.

Notes

1. See Karnow, Stanley, *Vietnam: A History*, pp 332–34, New York: Penguin Books, 1984.

2. For an excellent discussion of Brigadier General Heinie Aderholt's distinguished Air Force career, and his many outstanding leadership contributions to Air Commando combat operations, see *Air Commando One: Heinie Aderholt and America's Secret Wars*, written by Warren Trest and published by Smithsonian Institution Press, 2000.

3. From "Interdiction on the Ho Chi Minh Trail," Air Force Magazine Online, October 1971. Reprinted by permission from *Air Force Magazine*, published by the Air Force Association.

4. Reprinted from *The Nimrods*, Bloomington, Indiana: AuthorHouse, 2007.

5. Reprinted from *The Nimrods*, Bloomington, Indiana: AuthorHouse, 2007.

6. Reprinted from *The Nimrods*, Bloomington, Indiana: AuthorHouse, 2007.

CHAPTER 4

Rosters and Squadron History Documents[1]

Roster of Rated Officers
of the Original
JUNGLE JIM Organization
4400TH COMBAT CREW TRAINING SQUADRON (TAC)
United States Air Force
Eglin AF Auxiliary Field Nr 9, Florida

SPECIAL ORDER 3 August 1961
NUMBER P-10

Under the Provisions of Paragraph 7 Section V, Chapter 2, AFM 35–13, the following named Officers, this squadron, this station are placed on Unconditional Flying Status Code 1, Effective 1 Aug 61.

COL BENJAMIN H KING
LT COL ROBERT L GLEASON
LT COL CHESTER A JACK
MAJ RICHARD N BROUGHTON
MAJ JOHN L DOWNING
MAJ HOMA B STILLWELL
CAPT THOMAS L BIGGERS
CAPT HERBERT W BOOTH JR
CAPT GEORGE F BRENNAN JR
CAPT HARRY J BROWN
CAPT JACK H CAPERS
CAPT HOMER J CARLILE
CAPT JOHN D CARRINGTON
CAPT BILLY J CHANCELLOR
CAPT FRED C CLOW JR
CAPT JOHN S CONNORS
CAPT WILLIAM R DAVIS
CAPT SIEGEL M DICKMAN
CAPT PAUL G DONNER

CAPT DANIEL F GROB
CAPT GERALD S HAMMER
CAPT JAMES M HARRIS
CAPT DAVID E HENRY
CAPT KEITH H HILL
CAPT HENRY L KARNES JR
CAPT IRA L KIMES JR
CAPT GEORGE R KIRBY
CAPT JAMES A KOSTAN
CAPT ROBERT A LAMBERTON JR
CAPT JEAN D LANDRY
CAPT RICHARD F LEGEZA
CAPT JESSE E LEWIS JR
CAPT ARTHUR G LIMPANTSIS
CAPT LAWRENCE L LIVELY
CAPT THOMAS C MCEWEN
CAPT JOHN R MCGAVIN
CAPT LORIS R MILLER
CAPT HERMAN S MOORE

CAPT WILLIAM E DOUGHERTY

CAPT MARVIN A FITTS

CAPT DONALD L GEPHART

CAPT LEROY E GLIEM

CAPT RUBEN H PATTERSON

CAPT JOHN L PIOTROWSKI

CAPT ARTHUR W PITTMAN

CAPT RICHARD J RICE

CAPT EARL D RICHARDS

CAPT JOHN M ROWAN

CAPT RICHARD W SANBORN

CAPT MARTIN G SAUNDERS

CAPT PAUL E SHEPARD

CAPT RICHARD N SMITH

CAPT HENRY B STEIDL

CAPT IRWIN C SWETT

CAPT THOMAS H TEMPLE JR

CAPT GERALD F TEWES

CAPT ARNOLD A TILLMAN

CAPT EUGENE J WALDVOGEL

CAPT LUTHER A WEBB

CAPT WILLIAM R WILLIAMSON

1ST LT EDWARD J AHERN

1ST LT JOHN R ALBRECHT

1STLT JOHN W BRIGGS

1ST LT CHARLES R CARROLL

1ST LT THOMAS B CARTER

CAPT DAVID L MURPHY

CAPT AARON L NILES JR

CAPT FRANKLIN G OWENS

CAPT JOHN R PATEE

1ST LT WILLIAM G CASTLEN

1ST LT JOSEPH J CONDE JR

1ST LT ROBERT F DAVIS

1ST LT ROGER S EDWARDS

1ST LT LOYD L ENNIS

1ST LT RANDALL EVERETT III

1ST LT CHARLES W FISHER

1ST LT MAURICE S GASTON

1ST LT CHARLES R HARPER

1ST LT JAMES L HARPER

1ST LT WALTER K HENNIGAN

1ST LT JOHN A HOPE

1ST LT CLYDE L HOWARD JR

1ST LT DUDLEY J HUGHES

B. H. KING

Colonel, USAF

Commander

WARREN V. TRENT

Captain, USAF

Administrative Officer

* * *

SPECIAL ORDER 4 August 1961
NUMBER P-11

Under the Provisions of Paragraph 7 Section V, Chapter 2, AFM 35–13, the following named Officers, this squadron, this station are placed on Unconditional Flying Status Code 1, Effective 1 Aug 61.

1ST LT ANDREW T JESSUP

1ST LT EDWARD K KISSAM JR

1ST LT ROBERT L LESCHACK

1ST LT JACK D LETOURNEAU

1ST LT JOHN H LIVESAY

1ST LT ROY I LEWIS

1ST LT RONALD G PHILLIPS

1ST LT DEXTER F POTTER

1ST LT BOBBY K REYNOLDS

1ST LT RICHARD A RUSSELL

1ST LT CARMEN T SCARPINO

1ST LT PAUL E SCHUELER

1ST LT ROBERT F MAHEU

1ST LT CLYDE E MARTINEZ

1ST LT RICHARD A MATHISON

1ST LT DONALD J MAXWELL

1ST LT JOHN D MITCHELL JR

1ST LT JIM A MOORE

1ST LT RALPH M NADDO

1ST LT HILLARD J WALLACE

1ST LT PAUL R WINDELL

1ST LT GLYNDON V SCOTT

1ST LT WILLIE L SEIRER

1ST LT RONALD L SELBERG

1ST LT RICHARD G SEMPLE

1ST LT JOHN P SLAUSON

1ST LT RICHARD C TEGGE

1ST LT LORENZ J WALKER

1ST LT THOMAS R WHITE

BIG EAGLE ROSTER
USAF Operations Plan 5–66, 1966
(Original A-26 Deployment to NKP)

1. Colonel Curto, Domenico A.
2. Lt. Col. Howarth, Albert R.
3. Major Duke, George G.
4. A1C Fowler, Kenneth E.
5. A1C Taylor, George L.
6. SSgt Toms, Richard L.
7. MSgt Christian, Carlous L.
8. A1C Smith, Peter, Jr.
9. A2C Collard, Patrick C.
10. SSgt Thomas, Edward
11. SSgt Owens, Norman C.
12. A1C Young, James H
13. Major Piper, Charles W.
14. SSgt VonRyik, Walter
15. A1C Potter, Robert E.
16. Major Welch, Henry C., Jr.
17. Major Kittinger, Joseph W., Jr.
18. Capt. Dudley, Charles G.
19. Capt. Gorski, Frank J., Jr.
20. Capt. Maynard, Joe E.
21. Capt. Rowland, Alva G.
22. Capt. Geron, Richard P., Jr.
23. Capt. Mitchell, John C.
24. Capt. Dutton, Robert C.
25. Capt. Green, Billy L.
26. Capt. Howard, Clyde L., Jr.
27. Capt. Wolfe, John W.
28. Capt. Blum, Franklin E.
29. 1LT Blount, Jack R., Jr.
30. 1LT Dimaggio, Peter S.
31. 1LT Hanley, Paul J.
32. Capt. Hayes, Francis W.
33. 2LT Albee, Harlan G.
34. 1LT Cavalli, Anthony F.
35. 1LT Tidwell, Robert L.
36. 1LT Tuttle, William C., Jr.
37. 1LT Riddle, Clarence H.
38. 2LT Bell, Jackie O.
39. Capt. Tanimoto, Miles T.
40. 1LT Rosa Gonzales, Jose
41. MSgt Boehme, Melvin E.
42. MSgt Gustin, Geoffrey O.
43. SSgt Reamer, Earl H.
44. A1C Smith, Oris A.
45. TSgt Piontek, Stanley, Jr.
46. TSgt Day, Charles E.
47. TSgt Hunter, Eldon L.
48. TSgt Floyd, Kenneth G.
49. TSgt Miner, Lloyd
50. SSgt Allanbrand, Glenn E.
51. SSgt Bennett, Charles W.
52. SSgt Wilson, Harry R.
53. SSgt Lay, Robert E.
54. SSgt Hunt, Lamar L.
55. A1C Jackson, Lindsay J.
56. A2C Richard, Cavio C.
57. TSgt Hartford, Jackie L.
58. A1C McNamara, Donald P.
59. A1C Henderson, Kenneth M.
60. A2C Clark, Gilbert R.

61. A3C Schodorf, Charles J.
62. A1C Jordan, Walter L.
63. A3C Adams, Guy M.
64. A3C Bass, Eddie C.
65. TSgt Sherwood, Ralph
66. SSgt Chastain, James W.
67. A1C Mitchell, Barry P.
68. A3C Hendrix, Bruce E.
69. SSgt Lucas, Herbert R.
70. A1C Terech, Edward J.
71. SSgt Haught, Herbie B.
72. A1C Frisbee, Lynn A.
73. A2C Trotter, Sammie C.
74. A3C Lambert, David G.
75. SSgt Holder, James H.
76. A1C Pasena, Sidney W.
77. SSgt Stockton, James T.
78. A1C Carpenter, Larry O.
79. A3C Rutman, David W.
80. TSgt Laxee, Paul B.
81. SSgt Miller, Ralingh B.
82. A1C Sapesnik, James R.
83. A1C Taylor, James B.
84. A2C Rodgers, Augustin M.
85. A1C Bixby, William O.
86. A2C Currier, John P.
87. SSgt Duedler, Donald C.
88. A2C Olson, Maynard C., Jr.
89. A2C Walker, Wingred R.
90. A1C Sutton, Arthur L.
91. SSgt Bowling, Edward M.
92. A1C Werner, John P.
93. A1C Allen, Howard K.
94. MSgt Howard, Lawrence L.
95. SSgt Tobey, Paul A.
96. SSgt Dietrich, Eugend
97. SSgt LaBarge, Harold L.
98. SSgt Plant, Joseph B.
99. SSgt Carter, Howard E.
100. SSgt Shepard, Donald B.
101. SSgt Hanley, Gilbert A., Jr.
102. SSgt Wintle, Walter Mr., Jr.
103. A2C Jay, Richard O.
104. A2C Brant, Roger W.
105. A2C Lint, Lyle O.
106. A2C Martinez, Jose E.
107. A2C Allen, Thomas B.
108. A1C Nordman, John M.
109. A1C Salasar, Gerald L.
110. A1C Ong, James R.
111. SSgt McCarthy, John B.
112. A1C Brenizer, Raymond L.
113. A2C Lovell, Frederick C.
114. A2C Ryman, Randolph B.
115. A2C Land, Walter F.
116. A2C Stamm, Elder L.
117. A3C Danielowiez, Thomas E.
118. A3C Mengwasser, Kenneth J.
119. A3C Smith, Gerald B.
120. A3C Mitchell, Gerald N.
121. A3C Poynter, Porter L.
122. A3C Ray, Robert A.
123. A3C Richardson, Gary J.
124. 1LT Frye, Donald E.
125. A2C White, Robert J.
126. A2C Moreland, Brian S.
127. A1C Schroeder, Charlie O.
128. A2C Ellwood, Wade H.
129. TSgt Adkins, Russell, Jr.
130. SSgt Jewell, William H.
131. A1C Stout, Roger L.
132. TSgt Boyd, Clarence R.
133. A1C Everson, Burgess L.
134. A1C Mahurin, Joe C.
135. 1LT Wishart, Ronald K.
136. A1C Petersen, Gary A.
137. A2C Brook, Dustin V.

<u>HISTORICAL DATA RECORD</u>	FROM: 1 Oct 67
(RCS: AU-D5)	TO: 31 Dec 67
FROM: 609th Air Commando Squadron	APO 96310

I. MISSION
    a. To conduct combat operations as directed
    b. To fly night armed reconnaissance, flare support and FAC missions to disrupt and harass enemy lines of communications by attacking or directing attacks on preselected targets and targets of opportunity in Laos and North Vietnam.

II. PERSONNEL STATUS (AS OF 31 DEC 67)

	Officers	*Airmen*	*Civilians*	*Total*
Assigned	43	81	0	124
Authorized	40	113	0	153
Attached	0	0	0	0
MIA	2	0	0	2
KIA	0	0	0	0

III. EQUIPMENT STATUS (AS OF 31 DEC 67)

Nomenclature	*No. Assigned*	*Gains*	*Losses*	*Reasons*
A-26A	13	6	1	Combat Loss
½ ton Pickup	1	0	0	
Metro Van	1	0	0	

IV. SIGNIFICANT STATISTICS
    a. Total Combat Hours—2058+35 hrs
    b. Number Combat Sorties Scheduled—766
    c. Number Combat Sorties Flown—739 (25 MND, 1WX, 1 Ops CNX)
    d. Munitions Expended –

CBU14	2,267	M31/M32	1641
MIA2/MIA4	2373	MK82	553
M28	516	M47	150
.50 Cal	164,460 rds	LAU54 Rockets	17
BLU1B/BLU27B Fire Bomb	148	M117	233

    e. Targets Struck

Truck Parks	133	Guns	209
Barges	3	Troops/Storage areas	46/94
Roads, Bridges, Fords	56	Trucks	1,920

    f. Strike results—

Secondary fires	1074	Guns destroyed	83
Secondary explosions	983	Guns silenced	50
Trucks destroyed	628	Roads interdicted	16
Trucks probably destroyed	102	Trucks damaged	73

V. Narrative

There were no mission changes during the quarter the A-26 scheduled sorties went from 6 a night to 9 a night. This was possible because of a gain of crew strength, maintenance skill level, and 2 more aircraft.

Lt. Col. Learmonth, Allen F., FR17682, assumed duties as Operations Officer 1 Dec 67.

Maj Robinson, Edward M., FV1858858, served as Operations Officer through October and November.

As of 1 Oct 67 the squadron was C-4. Caused by the rotation of combat ready crews and the replacement with non-combat ready crews. With a comprehensive training program the squadron was C-3, 8 Nov: C-2, 28 Nov; and C-1, 10 Dec. As of 31 Dec 67, the 609th had 17 combat ready crews with 18 crews authorized.

During the quarter A-26s suffered 8 aircraft with battle damage, one aircraft lost in combat with the crew missing in action.

October saw the coming of the dry season with the expected increase of men and materials moving through Steel Tiger to stagings in the south. Truck traffic has been heavy and is increasing. With the increase of traffic, the Nimrod truck kill has increased, i.e., 40 in October, 324 in November, 264 in December. The truck kill rate has increased for the following reasons: (1) more trucks sighted, (2) Use of starlight scope both in a FAC aircraft and in the A-26, (3) Better FAC-strike coordination. The nail 0–2 FACs and the candlestick UC-123 FAC-Flare ship have been particularly outstanding in finding, marking and directing attacks, (4) Use of area weapons. The M31/M32 incendiary bomb cluster has proved particularly effective against trucks, (5) Better weather.

As the truck traffic has increased the enemy has reacted by protecting the lines of communication with AW and AAA positions. To survive, the A-26 Nimrods, when possible, have flown in teams with another Nimrod, or a T-28 Zorro, or a B-57 Yellowbird or Redbird. Any combination of the 3 strike aircraft has proved effective in discouraging enemy defenses and increasing the truck kill.

We expect the truck kill to increase through the rest of the dry season if Steel Tiger remains relatively permissive with adequate FLAK Suppression.

VI. Commanders Conclusions

During our first quarter of operation as a squadron we have been able to surpass existing records in truck kills. This has been due largely to the use of area type weapons such as the M-31 & M-32 incendiary clusters. During December, these weapons also became in short supply, and we had to switch to MK82, GP bombs. The decrease in truck kills was directly proportional to the decrease in M-31 and M-32s carried.

Personnel manning of our combat crews lagged behind the rotation of crews to the ZI. Our personnel status went from C-1 in August, to C-4 in October. However, by mid–December we were C-1 again. We were somewhat hampered in our theater indoctrination program by crew members arriving singly. The result was that the various required briefings had to be presented an exorbitant number of times.

Our forecast crew inputs indicate that during the next 2 quarters, we will be considerably over-manned with crews, and will have far too many pilots in relation to the number of navigators. Since we fly as crews (pilot and nav), crew coordination will be disrupted by the interchange of navigators.

The manning of our flight line maintenance section remains critical. Approximately 70 percent of the authorized slots are manned. The grade structure and skill levels are also incompatible—too few sergeants and too many 3-levels. The net result has been that the line crews have had to go to two twelve hour shifts, six days per, to provide the required manhours. The assignment of two NOA coded aircraft, raising our total aircraft to 14, did not help this situation any.

OJT training has also suffered. All of the airmen tested failed their tests. There just aren't enough hours in the day for the airmen to study effectively and also work 12 hours. The maintenance supervisors have taken some steps that may help, but the crux of the problem is that a combat theater is just not the place to provide upgrade training. It is not fair to the airmen, and it imposes an unnecessary load on the combat organization.

VII. Roster of Key Personnel
    Commander—Lt Col Farmer, Howard L., FR42005
    Operations Officer—Lt Col Learmonth, Allen F., FR17682
    Administrative Officer—Major Hawkins, Douglas W., FR65649
    First Sergeant—MSgt Dalrymple, Bobby, AF16201563
    NCOIC Maintenance—MSgt Docherty, James A., AF42222161
    NCOIC Armament—SMSgt Machamer, William F., AF239975344

VIII. Supporting Documents
    56ACW Weekly Activities Report—56ACW Hq Operations Report—4
    TUOC

THOMAS E. OWENS, CAPTAIN, USAF   ALLEN F. LEARMONTH, Lt. Col. USAF
Historical Officer Operations   Officer, 609th ACS

HISTORICAL DATA RECORD	REPORTING PERIOD
(RCS: AU-D5)	From: 1 April 1968
	TO: 30 Jun 1968
FROM: 609th Air Commando Squadron	TO: 56 ACW (DXI)
APO San Francisco 96310	

I. Mission
    a. Primary : To conduct combat operations as directed.
    b. Secondary: To fly armed reconnaissance, flare support and FAC missions to disrupt and harass enemy lines of communications by attacking or directing attacks on pre-selected targets and targets of opportunity in Laos and North Vietnam.

II. Presonnel Status (as of 30 Jan 1968)

	Officers	Airmen	Civilians	Total
Assigned	42	117	0	159
Authorized	40	113	0	153
Attached	0	0	0	0
MIA	2			
KIA	1			

III. Equipment Status

Nomenclature	No. Asgd	Gains	Losses	Reasons
Truck, Multi-stop	1	-	-	

Nomenclature	No. Asgd	Gains	Losses	Reasons
4×2				
Truck, Pickup	1	-	-	
3 Pass.				
A-26 Aircraft	13	-	1	Combat

IV. SIGNIFICANT STATISTICS

- a. Total Combat Flying Hours   1,958:15
- b. Total Combat Sorties Scheduled   793
- c. Total Combat Sorties Flown   713
- d. Sorties Cancelled Due Adverse Weather   55
- e. Ground Aborts   12
- f. Maintenance Non-Delivery   8
- g. Sorties Canx by Higher Headquarters   5

MUNITIONS EXPENDED

Description	Amount
MK81 (250 lb. Gp Bomb)	366
MK82 (500 lb. Gp Bomb)	409
M117 (750 lb. Gp Bomb)	108
MIA4 (Fragmentation Bomb Cluster)	1,724
M28A (Fragmentation Cluster)	415
BLU-10 (250 lb. Unfinned Fire Bomb)	152
BLU-1/B (750 lb. Finned Fire Bomb)	64
BLU-23 (500 lb. Unfinned Fire Bomb)	464
BLU-27 (750 lb. Finned Fire Bomb)	561
BLU-32 (750 lb. Finned Fire Bomb)	480
M31, M32 (500 lb. Incendiary Bomb Cluster)	1,261
CBU 14/A (Cluster Bomb Unit)	1,938
CBU 25 (Cluster Bomb Unit, Foliage Penetrating)	10
CBU 29 (750 lb. Cluster Bomb Unit, Delay Fused)	18
CBU 24 (750 lb. Cluster Bomb Unit, Impact Fused)	132
LAU 54 (2.75 "HE/WP Rocket POD")	1
50 Cal. Armor Piercing Incendiary Ammunition	157, 835 rds

TARGETS STRUCK

Description	Amount
Trucks Destroyed	831
Trucks Probably Destroyed	128
Trucks Damaged	11
AAA Guns Silenced	123

Description	Amount
AAA Guns Destroyed	27
Secondary Fires	1,343
Secondary Explosions	1,495
Road Interdictions	7
Boats Destroyed	2

AIRCRAFT STATUS

	April	*May*	*June*	
OR	75.5%	76.9%	76.7%	(July–Dec 67)
NORM	23.5%	23.0%	22.0%	(62.9)

V. NARRATIVE

During the period of 1 April 1968 through 30 June 1968 the 609th Air Commando Squadron continued its combat operation of interdiction on enemy supply routes in Steel Tiger, Tiger Hound and Barrel Roll Operating Areas of East—Central and Northern Laos. The majority of 609th ACS sorties delivered their ordnance in attacks upon truck convoys moving through the infiltration routes commonly known as the Ho Chi Minh Trail. Flying nine sorties a night the aircrews of the 609th ACS compiled a record number of truck kills during the quarter.

The average 609th ACS sortie logged a total flight time of 2.7 hours with 1.7 hours being spent over the target area. The primary method of striking trucks was dive-bombing either by visually acquiring the headlights of the trucks or striking a point defined by a FAC aircraft such as the O2A/B, C-123 or C-130. In almost all cases bomb damage assessment (BDA) was given by these FAC aircraft using light amplification devices which enabled their viewing of the strike results under night conditions. In addition to striking truck convoys the 609th ACS aircrews often aided high performance jet aircraft in target acquisition by making the initial strike on a target. A-26 crews also frequently supplied FLAK suppression against the numerous 37 mm, 14.5 APU and automatic weapons employed to defend the road complex against air attack. Due to the extended loiter capability offered by the A-26 aircraft, 609th ACS crews were able to accomplish this task and then proceed with their own strikes against trucks.

Typical of this action was a strike accomplished by Captain Jay L. Norton, FR63672 and Captain Thomas E. Bronson, FR3160694 while flying mission Nimrod 39 on the 7th of April. Captain Norton stopped a 20-truck convoy by placing a napalm strike on the lead trucks and then pulled off the target to attack 4 37 mm gun positions while 3 B-57 "Yellowbird" aircraft destroyed 16 of the trucks using Captain Norton's well-placed strike as a marker. This teamwork action initiated by individual crews has taken place many times and earned the 609th ACS Nimrod crews many plaudits from other tactical units. (Atch 1 & 6)

Truck movement on the Ho Chi Minh Trail complex was heaviest during the month of April; during this period Nimrod crews attacked a total of 1,285 trucks. There were numerous outstanding sorties flown by the 609th ACS crews during the month and the flowing narrative of Nimrod sorties obtained through intelligence and operations debriefings indicates some of the destruction the 609th ACS crews brought to the enemy's supply system. On the 2nd of April Lt. Colonel Allen F. Learmonth, FR17682, pilot and Captain Roger D. Graham, FR70029, navigator, flying sortie Nimrod 31 attacked and destroyed 6 trucks and obtained 6 secondary fires. During the night of the 4th the activity continued the tempo as Captain Michael J.C. Roth, FR70258 and Lt. Colonel Francis L. McMullen, FV2215574 pilot and navigator respectively, attacked 9 trucks moving into a parking area on route 911. While under the continuous fire of 5 37 mm AntiAircraft position, they were able to destroy all the trucks, silence one of the 37 mm positions and hit a POL Dump which resulted in ten large secondary fires and 73 explosions. A total of 25 trucks were destroyed by Nimrod crews on the night of the 4th. The enemy continued their efforts as the days passed and the night of the 5th saw Major Richard J. Mendonca, FV3035471 and Major Robert C. Zimmerman, FR61238, striking a convoy on route 911 at interdiction point Foxtrot. Striking under the heavy fire of 5 37 mm gun positions they were successful in destroying 7 trucks and obtaining 3 secondary fires. Shortly thereafter Captain Seijun Tengan, FR72019 and Captain Frank W. Nelson, FR313297 flying Nimrod 38 struck in the same area and destroyed 5 more trucks. Despite the constant nightly attacks by USAF aircraft, supply trucks continued their runs and Major Kenneth E. La Fave, FR60712 and Lt. Colonel Francis L. McMullen flying Nimrod 39 on the 12th of April attacked a large convoy destroying 8 of the trucks, probably destroying 3, in addition to 8 secondary fires and 22 explosions.

Antiaircraft fire remained heavy to moderate along the route 911 complex during these strikes, and 609th aircrews attempted to work with each other or "Yellowbird" B-57 aircraft in order to have FLAK suppression. However, often times aircraft for FLAK suppression were not available and the crews were called upon to attack truck convoys while under the fire of 8–14 37 mm positions and numerous 14.5 ZPU and automatic weapons. On the 24th of April Nimrod 32 with Lt. Colonel John J. Shippey, FR39944 as pilot and Captain George B. Hertlein III, FV3102462 as navigator was attacking a convoy of trucks on route 911 when their aircraft was hit by ground fire. Although damage was received to the cockpit and rudder control was lost Lt. Colonel Shippey managed to recover control, and land at Nakhon Phanom. The hits had taken their toll however and 609th personnel were grieved to learn that Captain Hertlein was killed as a result of the hits in the cockpit of the aircraft. Nimrod 37, flown by Major Edward M. Robinson, FV1858858 and Major Walter M Langford, FR47973 was hit by 37 mm fire on the 29th but managed to land safely at Nakhon Phanom Air Base with no injury to either crewmember. On the 30th of April the threat of the heavy ground fire was one again realized with the loss of Nimrod 34 during his first pass. The pilot, Captain Robert E. Pietsch, FR67605 and the navigator, Captain Louis F. Guillerman, FV3150435 are listed as missing in action.

During the final week of April truck movement along the "Trail" remained at a very high level and the Nimrods continued their unparalleled success. The night of the 23rd saw 15 trucks destroyed, 2 37 mm gun positions destroyed and 2 silenced. Captain Michael J.C. Roth, FR70258 and Lt. Colonel Francis L. McMullen, FV2215574 flying Nimrod 31 continued the good hunting on the 24th by destroying 8 trucks. Captain Roth and Lt. Colonel McMullen reported intense ground fire in the area of their target, from 12 37 mm positions. Nimrod 31 had a high degree of success again on the 25th and 6 trucks were destroyed and one 37 mm position silenced. Major Robert F. Bennett, FR60166 and Major Douglas W. Hawkins, FR65649 were the crew on Nimrod 31. The high score for the activity on the 26th again when to Nimrod 31 this time the sortie was flown by the 609th ACS Commander Lt. Colonel Robert E. Brumm, FR17717 and Lt. Colonel Francis L McMullen, FV2215574. Lt. Colonel Brumm was credited with destroying 10 trucks and obtaining 25 secondary explosions. During the final four days of April the traffic slowed somewhat but the Nimrods accounted for 45 destroyed trucks. The BDA for the final 7 days was 103 trucks destroyed and 16 probably destroyed. In addition 9 37 mm and 1 145 ZPU gun position was silenced.

For the complete month of April the 609th ACS Aircrews had compiled the impressive record of 459 trucks destroyed, 60 probably destroyed, 627 secondary fires, 541 secondary explosions, 73 antiaircraft gun positions silenced and 15 destroyed.

The first week of May saw a rapid decrease in the number of truck sightings as compared to April. During the first 12 days of May, Nimrod crews struck at 124 trucks and destroyed a total of 36, in addition to 12 probably destroyed. Although few truck sightings were made, antiaircraft defenses continued to remain very active and two 609th A-26s suffered battle damage. On the 6th of May Nimrod 30, crewed by Major Daniel F. Grob, FR45960 and Major Bryant A. Murry, FR42531 was hit by a 14.5 ZPU weapon and sustained major damage to the vertical stabilizer and right horizontal stabilizer. On the 11th, Nimrod 36, crewed by Major Kenneth E. La Fave, FR60712 and Captain William A. Cohen, FR55438 was struck by a single 37 mm shell. Explosion of the projectile caused extensive damage to the right propeller, right engine nacelle, right wing, and forward fuselage area. There were no injuries sustained by the crewmembers on either Nimrod 30 or 36. Due to the fact that five aircraft had been hit by ground fire during the period 24 April to 11 May the 609th again reviewed its combat tactics. In order to increase effectiveness and decrease vulnerability tactics are constantly reviewed and aircrews advised of the results of the review. In the case of the five battle damaged aircraft during the period 24 April–11 May no pattern of vulnerability could be established. Three aircraft were hit while pulling off target at altitudes in excess of 5,000 ft. AGL, one aircraft was hit, and lost, on its first pass and another was hit while about 3,500 ft. AGL. A 14.5 ZPU gun appeared to be responsible in four cases but in each instance only one or two guns were firing. The only commonality in the hits appeared to be ZPU with unusually deadly accuracy. All crews were briefed that they should experiment with releases up to 6,000 ft. AGL and to pull off the target if heavy or accurate ground fire was encountered and call for FLAK suppression or select another target for their strike. Information gathered from this review and correspondence with 7th Air Force resulted in the establishment of a minimum release altitude of 5,000 ft. AGL and a maximum of 6 passes for dive bombing. (Attach 3)

On the 7th of May 609th ACS aircraft did not fly any missions due to maintenance being performed on the runway at Nakhon Phanom Air Base. With the resumption of flying on the 8th 609th crews reported very few trucks moving on the roads and only one was destroyed. Activity continued to ebb and on the 10th no truck kills were reported by 609th crews.

During this period the 609th ACS initiated correspondence to the 56th Air Commando Wing in order to discontinue the "Alert" Status of Nimrod 35, 36 and 38. Records showed that the aircraft were expedited only 9 times while on alert and after being airborne were directed to perform a normal armed reconnaissance mission in their regularly fragged operating area. The alert status was discontinued on the 15th of May. By the 15th of May traffic upon the roads had begun to increase and Nimrod 32 with Lt. Colonel Howard L. Farmer, FR42005 as pilot and Captain Thomas E. Owens, FV3133367 as navigator struck a convoy of 10 trucks, destroying 7 of them and silencing a 37 mm gun position which was defending the area. By the 22nd of May the flow of trucks had begun a rapid increase and 609th crews accounted for 22 trucks destroyed. Nimrod 31 initiated the evening's activity by destroying 7 trucks. Pilot and navigator aboard 31 was Major Richard A. Schramm, FV2225538 and Captain Roger D. Graham, FR70029. Within an hour of Nimrod 31's strike Captain Charles A. Kenyon, FR51001 and Major Donald J. Maxwell, FR3072009 attacked another convoy and destroyed 6 trucks. The activity continued that night until approximately 2400 hours when a heavy undercast cloud condition developed and obscured most of the road complex from sight. As a result of the unfavorable weather conditions Nimrods 37, 38, and 39 were unable to deliver any ordnance. By the 26th truck movement approached that of April and Nimrod 36 crewed by Major Bobby J. Sears, FR47177 and Captain Roger D. Graham, FR70029 destroyed 10 trucks. The crew also debriefed that 5 37 mm positions fired upon them continually during their attacks. During the period 20 thru 26 May, 609th ACS aircrews attacked 578 trucks, destroying 136 and probably destroying 7. Additionally, 136 secondary fires and 139 secondary explosions were obtained. Following the activity of the 26th traffic began to decrease once again and only 43 trucks were destroyed from the 27 thru 29 May.

The first four days of June were largely hampered by weather and 13 sorties were cancelled. Several of the sorties that did take off were forced to utilize ground controlled radar drops (Combat Sky Spot). Activity throughout June slowed in comparison to April and May. A great deal of northern route 911 was reported to be covered with water from the monsoon rains and as a result an increasing number of trucks were noticed on Route 912. The majority of trucks destroyed by 609th crews during June were struck on Route 912 or the southern portions of Route 911.

Although truck sightings were few, Captain Bruce R. Wolfe, FR77247 and Captain Laurence J. Elliott, FV3150643, flying Nimrod 36, on the 3rd, did account for 6 trucks destroyed and 27 secondary explosions. This strike was unusual in that Captains Wolfe and Elliott encountered no ground fire during their strike. Several other Nimrod sorties accounted for 6 additional destroyed trucks night although adverse weather caused Nimrod 39 to be cancelled.

Although the weather and a general slowing of the traffic hampered the 609th's hunting the Nimrods accounted for 57 trucks destroyed during the first 14 days of June. Crews reported that the trucks were found moving singularly or in groups of 2 or 3, thus it was relatively easy for them to escape detection by turning off their headlights or moving off the road into heavy foliage. On the 19th of June Major Delbert W. Litton, FR47196 and Major Loran W. Gierhart, FR30028 destroyed 5 trucks and obtained 6 secondary explosions. Major Litton and Gierhart encountered only light 37 mm ground fire during this strike. Weather however continued to hamper operations during the final days of June and on the 28th 6 sorties were cancelled due to weather although Nimrod 32 crewed by Major John A. Parrish, FR47852 and Captain Frank W. Nelson, FR3139297 destroyed 7 trucks and probably destroyed 2. The following night the only trucks destroyed were those 3 attacked by Lt Colonel Robert E. Brumm, FR17717, 609th ACS Commander, and Captain Roger D. Graham, FR70029. Nimrod 33 through 39 were cancelled on the 29th due to poor weather over the target area. Strikes on the 30th of June were also troubled by heavy weather and 4 sorties were cancelled, while Nimrod 37 was forced to deliver ordnance on a truck park via Combat Sky Spot.

The aircrews of the 609th ACS were awarded numerous decorations for their combat operations during this and previous periods and a total of 17 Silver Stars and 41

Distinguished Flying Crosses were approved during this quarter for the deeds performed by Nimrod crews. Lt. General William W. Momyer, Commander 7th Air Force, visited Nakhon Phanom Air Base on the 25th of June and presented Sliver Stars to Major Edward M. Robinson, FV1858858, N. Disteldorf, FR58260, Major Donald J. Maxwell, FR3072009 and Captain Richard L. Willems, FR3151684. The outstanding efforts of the 609th aircrews were also recognized by General Momyer in a message on May 14th to Commander of 56 ACW, Colonel Roland K. McCoskrie. (Atch 2) Further commendation was received from Lt Colonel Lloyd R. McKeehen, Commander of C-130 mission, APO SF 96304 (Atch 6) and also from Lt Colonel Richard A. Grant, Commander of 606 ACS at Nakhon Phanom (Atch 7).

During the months of April and May the 609th ACS Maintenance Section held a 100% manning status with an adequate number of trained and experienced personnel. During the month of June however manning dropped to only 72% of that authorized. Further complications evolved due to many of the experienced personnel having rotated from their S.E.A. tour, leaving many 3 level personnel to replace the various positions. On the Job Training was intensified at this time and under a program outlined by NCOIC of training, Sgt. Melvin C. Duncan, Jr., AF13434284, a total of 19 personnel were tested for a higher skill rating. 17 personnel were raised from 3 level to 5, while one was advanced from 5 level to 7 level.

Maintenance on the A-26 aircraft is hampered due to only one hanger being available. The majority of work must be performed on the flight line under hot, dusty conditions. With the onset of the monsoon season, during late June, work will be further hampered by frequent rain. An interview with NCOIC of Maintenance, SMSgt James W. Pitsonberger, AF16381907 has indicated that equipment and tools are in good supply and that the supply pipelines for A-26 parts have greatly improved over the past quarter. Despite the several adverse conditions mentioned the 609th Maintenance was able to deliver aircraft for all but 3 of the scheduled sorties.

Ordnance supply for the 609th ACS was good during the past quarter and the problem of a lack of area coverage weapons such as the M31 and M32 incendiary cluster bombs was not encountered as it had been during the January–March period of this year. A minor problem was encountered in the "Flashing" of old .50 caliber API ammunition. A decision to use later dated ammunition in preference to older supplies seamed to reduce the amount of "Flashing" during the firing of the A-26s guns. (Atch 8)

Aircrew manning for the period was adequate although navigators were required to fly several additional sorties per month as compared to the pilots. The pilots averaged 13 sorties per month while navigators flew an average of 15.

The "C" rating for the 609th ACS remained at C-1 throughout the quarter. 609th ACS aircrews encountered few difficulties in operating in the Steel Tiger and Tiger Hound Areas. In as much as the entire area is within the range of various radio navigation aids (TACAN) and there are numerous FAC aircraft to direct the various strike aircraft against lucrative targets. Operations in the Barrel Roll Area however were troubled by the tremendous difficulty of finding the roads without any accurate navigation aids and the problem of positively identifying a target upon acquisition of the general area. Accurate weather reports of the area were also not generally available until the first Nimrod sortie for the area had actually flown across the target. As a result, of 16 sorties flown to Barrel Roll during April, 13 reported no visual results while 3 sorties obtained several fires and explosions during a strike against a military storage area.

During May, activity in Barrel Roll was quite slow although the 609th ACS was called upon to strike several large troop encampments. During June slightly more success was enjoyed however, and Nimrod 32 destroyed one truck on the 14th while on the 20th Nimrod 32 was credited with destroying 4. On the 21st Nimrod 33 destroyed one truck while working with a road observation team on route 7. Those sorties working in the Barrel Roll area during June worked in conjunction with a C-130 flareship and a radar picket College Eye aircraft which was able to assist us in locating the roads and target areas.

VI. COMMANDER'S CONCLUSIONS

The 609th Air Commando Squadron was highly effective during this period because of the excellent coordination between the FAC and the 609th A-26 crews, resulting in rapid orientation of the crews as to the exact point on the ground that they must hit. The use of the M31 and M32 incendiary cluster bomb was a second key point to the effectiveness of the 609th. Because of the "Football Field" area that this weapon covers and the extreme heat generated by the bomblets absolute pin-point accuracy was not necessary against a moving truck. The skill and judgment of the combat crews in the extremely hazardous area was the final factor causing the high rate of effectiveness. Praise is due the armament and maintenance crews assigned the 609th ACS for the many long hours that they worked under the adverse conditions of weather. Maintenance aborts and armament malfunctions were at a minimum during this period because of their efforts. Finally, the excellent support furnished by the 56th Air Commando Wing must also be commended.

VII. ROSTER OF KEY PERSONNEL

Commander: Robert E. Brumm, Lt. Col, FR17717
Operations Officers: John J. Shippey, Lt. Col, FR39944
Administrative Officer: Kenneth E. La Fave, Major, FR60712
First Sergeant: Bobby Dalrymple, MSgt, AF16201563
NCOIC Maintenance: James W. Pitsonberger, SMSgt, AF16381907
NCOIC Armament: William F. Machamer, SMSgt, AF23975344

VIII. SUPPORTING DOCUMENTS

1. Nakhon Phanom RTAB Form 20 (Pilots Mission Debriefing Form, 609ACS Records).
CONFIDENTIAL
2. 609ACS Weekly Summary Reports. April, May, June.
3. 609ACS Flight Orders. (609ACS Records)
4. Attachment—1. Letter of Appreciation from Commander, 8th TAC Bomb Squadron.
5. Attachment—2. Letter of Commendation from Commander, 56th Air Commando Wing APO SF 96310, 15 May 1968.
6. Attachment—3. Combat Tactics Directive, 609ACS, 9 June 1968.
7. Attachment—4. Request for Discontinuation of A-26 Alert Commitment, 609ACS to 56ACW (DOO). 15 May 1968.
8. Attachment—5. Request for Discontinuation of A-26 Alert Commitment, 56ACW to 7AF/DO. SECRET, 16 May 1968.
9. Attachment—6. Letter of Commendation from Commander, C-130 Mission APO 96304. 8 April 1968.
10. Attachment—7. Letter of Appreciation from 606ACS Commander, Lt. Colonel Richard A. Grant. 15 May 1968.

11. Attachment—8. Communication concerning .50 caliber API Ammunition. Colonel Neal A. Hess, DCM 56ACW, to 609ACS. 2 May 1968.

FRANK W. NELSON, Captain,
FR3139297

ROBERT E. BRUMM, Lt Colonel,
FR17717

609th Air Commando Squadron
Historian
    18 July 1968

609th Air Commando Squadron
Commander
    18 July 1968

FROM: 8 TBS (C)

SUBJECT: Letter of Appreciation

TO: Commander 609th Air Commando Squadron
    APO 96310

1. The aircrews of the "Yellowbird" squadron have nothing but praise for "Nimrod" aircraft and crews. The crews are continually commenting on the professional competence and bravery exhibited by your personnel in your daily operation.

2. It was recently brought to my attention that a specific instance of this dedication is truly worthy of noting and is typical of the attitude displayed by your personnel.

At 0400 on the morning of 21 Feb 1968 Yellowbird 54 was tasked to work with Candlestick 02. While inbound to the target area YB54 tuned into Candlesticks frequency to establish contact and monitor any work he was doing. Candlestick 02 was preparing to run Nimrod 34 against a convoy of 15 to 20 trucks which he had detected. YB54 advised Candlestick that he would arrive shortly and assist with FLAK suppression if desired.

When YB54 arrived over the target, Nimrod 34 had stopped the convoy by 2 well placed bombs and several trucks burning. Despite ground fire from several 37 mm gun positions, Nimrod continued to press the attack at low altitude. Coordinating directly with Nimrod, YB54 was able to attack one of the 37 mm sites while it was firing. As a result the remainder of the attacks on the convoy were made without AAA interference. Nimrod displayed outstanding aggressiveness by making repeated low passes over the entire target area, attempting to draw AAA fire, and when he had expended everything but his guns he continued to fly cover while YB54 struck the trucks. Because of this YB54 was able to give full attention to directions of Candlestick 02 on the placing of bombs, resulting in the destruction of eight trucks. This degree of success would not have been possible if Nimrod 34 had not first stopped the convoy and then stayed around to neutralize the antiaircraft gunners.

3. Coordination such as was exhibited on 21 February has not been isolated but has taken place on numerous instances. For this reason on behalf of the 8th Tac Bomb Sqdn and the Crew of YB54 I wish to say "Thanks, for a job professionally done," to Nimrod 34.

PATRICK H. KENNY, Jr., Lt Col, USAF
Commander, 8th Tac Bomb Squadron

Atch 1

DEPARTMENT OF THE AIR FORCE
HEADQUARTERS 56TH AIR COMMANDO WING (PACAF)
APO SAN FRANCISCO 96310

REPLY TO:
ATTN OF:

15 May 1968

SUBJECT: Letter of Commendation
To: 609th Air Commando Squadron (C)
    APO 96310

1. It gives me a great deal of pleasure and pride to forward the following message from General William W. Momyer, Commander, 7th Air Force:

"Personal for McCoskrie from Momyer. It has come to my attention that the 609th Air Commando Squadron destroyed more trucks in April than the entire 56th Wing in November of last year, which was a record high. The destruction of 459 trucks was a tremendous achievement for the month of April. The Contribution made by the 609th Squadron in interdicting enemy supply movements has been in the finest tradition of the Air Force. Their operations require great personal courage, dedication, and professional skill. I want them to know I am proud of their accomplishments and the role they have played in achieving the highest truck kill rate of the war. We have hit the enemy where it hurts. To the men of the 609th, I want you to know as Commander of the 7th, I am proud to have such an organization in my command. Continued good hunting"

2. I add my personal commendation to the observations of General Momyer. The "Nimrod" crews and all who support them have done and continue to do an absolutely superior job.

ROLAND K. MCCOSKRIE, Colonel, USAF
Commander

Atch 2

DEPARTMENT OF THE AIR FORCE
609TH AIR COMMANDO SQUADRON (PACAF)
APO SAN FRANCISCO 96310

Jun 09 1968

REPLY TO: 609ACS (O)
SUBJECT: Combat Tactics
TO: All Aircrews

1. Recent correspondence from 7th Air Force indicates that to reduce the possibility of combat damage or loss due to opposing ground fire, strike aircraft tactics should be modified as necessary. To accomplish this and still permit an effective operation the following limitations in combat tactics will be adhered to:
    a. Minimum release altitude will be 5,000 Ft. AGL.
    b. The normal maximum number of passes will be limited to 6. This does not apply to gun passes.

c. Gun passes for flak suppression will be initiated high enough to terminate at 5,000 Ft AGL. Gun passes will be made for flak suppression only under the most optimum conditions, i.e., when in a two ship operation, when gun positions are firing away from the aircraft intending to use .50 cal for suppression, when the area is not defended by enough gun positions to make such tactics unreasonable.

JOHN J. SHIPPEY, Lt Col. USAF
Commander

Atch 3

15 May 1968

FROM: 609th Air Commando Squadron (C)
        APO San Francisco 96310
SUBECT: Discontinuation of A-26 Alert Commitment
TO: 56th ACW (DCO)

1. Since 4 April 1968, three Steel Tiger A-26 Sorties per night have been committed to a ground alert of approximately three hours duration. We were informed initially that the alert would continue for a three week test period, and that its purpose was to provide a capability to scramble the aircraft ahead of normally take-off times against lucrative targets.

2. We are now into the sixth week of this three week test period, and, in my opinion, the results do not warrant continuation. We have had only 9 sorties scrambled during the entire period, and none since 26 April 1968. In most cases, those scrambled were within 30 minutes of their scheduled take off times, and could have been expedited from their normal briefing times. Also, when airborne, all of the scrambled sorties were directed to their fragged target by ABCCC, not to a special target. Presently, continued poor weather in the operating area limits visual acquisition of lucrative targets.

3. Request that action be taken with higher headquarters to relieve the 609th of the alert commitment.

ROBERT E. BRUMM, Lt. Colonel, USAF
Commander

Atch 4

16 May 1968

FROM: 56AIRCOMMANDOWG NAKHON PHANOM APRT THAI
TO: 7AF/DO (TACT)/TAN SON NHUT AB RVN
INFO: TASK FORCE ALPHA (MESSENGER)
SUBJECT: Discontinuation of A-26 Alert Commitment (U).

Request the requirement for A-26 alert commitment on NIMRODS 35, 36, and 38 be cancelled as of 16 May 68. The alert requirement no longer appears valid. No alert status NIMROD has been launched since 26 Apr 68 and in view of the current rainy season affecting the primary target area, the low probability of requiring scrambled sorties does not warrant continuation. In the few cases that alert NIMRODS were scrambled, they were directed by ABCCC to proceed to their previously fragged targets. The continuing poor weather in the operating area usually limits visual acquisition of lucrative truck targets. Actual results during the alert test phase have not justified maintaining an alert status. Should special or emergency situations dictate an earlier than scheduled takeoff, we will make every effort to launch NIMROD aircraft prior to scheduled TOT. Gp4

Major BLACK	FRED R. HENDERSON JR, Colonel, USAF
Chief, Current Operations	Deputy Commander for Operations

Atch 5

FROM: C-130 Mission APO 96304 8 April 1968
SUBJECT: Letter of Commendation
TO: 56 ACW (C)
    APO 96310

1. On 6 April 1968, Nimrod 35 and Nimrod 36 struck under the Forward Air Control of Blindbat 01 and Lamplighter 01 respectively.

2. From the Aircraft Commander's mission reports read "Nimrod 35 outstanding work" and "Nimrod 36 outstanding job of bombing." Their efforts resulted in six fires, nine explosions, two probable trucks and ten trucks destroyed. This ordnance was delivered in an area of "heavy-accurate" antiaircraft fire.

3. Once again, the Nimrods have proved their superior airmanship and judgment in their role. This is so exemplary of the performance of your aircrews. My thanks to you and your unit for their continued good work.

LLOYD R. MCKEEHEN, Lt Colonel, USAF
Commander

Atch 6

FROM: 606 ACS (C) 15 May 68
SUBJECT: Letter of Appreciation
TO: 609th ACS (C)

1. I wish to express my appreciation for the outstanding professionalism and devotion to duty displayed by the crews of the "Nimrod" Squadron in their work with the C-123 "Candlestick" Section of this unit from 1 October 1967 through April 1968. Due to the dedication, skill, courage, and determination of the officers and men of the 609th Air Commando Squadron in pursuing aggressively and relentlessly the hostile opposing forces in the unfriendly environment of our area of operation, an outstanding successful record of accomplishment has been built by your organization.

2. Through their tenacity and raw courage, the Nimrod crews have repeatedly been observed to fly through the heaviest and most accurate hostile fire to attack hostile gun positions and destroy the trucks which constitute lines of communication. In strike after strike their determination and cool, professional capability has been a source of inspiration and wonder to the Candlestick crews. The feeling of sustained, expert accomplishment of a difficult and extremely dangerous mission must be a source of continuing pride and joy to you.

3. For the sacrifices made and losses you have sustained, we grieve with you knowing that the valor and courage and gallantry of these men will be sorely missed. Their dedication and ultimate contribution of life itself must always be a source of inspiration to those who follow in their footsteps. The proud tradition that they have helped so much to make will always reflect a great contribution to the United States Air Force.

4. As your results of the past month have indicated, your unit has continued to accelerate its efforts to force an unacceptable loss rate on the present foe and bring about what we all so fervently desire: an honorable and lasting peace. From the "Candlestick" crews who have been associated with you in the mutual effort to bring about this result, a fervent and sincere "Well Done!"

RICHARD A. GRANT, Lt Col, USAF
Commande

Atch 7

HISTORICAL DATA RECORD

(ROS: AU-D5)

FROM: 609th Special Operations Squadron (OPS)

REPORTING PERIOD

From: 1 Jul 1968

TO: 30 Sep 1968

TO: 56 SpOpWg (OPS)

I. Mission

a. Primary: To conduct combat missions as directed.

b. Secondary: To fly armed reconnaissance, flare support, and FAC missions to disrupt and harass enemy lines of communications by attacking or directing attacks on pre-selected targets and targets of opportunity in the Steel Tiger (including Tiger Hound) and Barrel Roll areas of Laos.

II. Personnel Status: (as of 30 Sep 1968)

	Officers	*Airmen*	*Civilians*	*Total*
Assigned	40	115	0	155
Authorized	41	100	0	141
Attached	0	0	0	0
MIA	0 (This reporting period)			
KIA	0 (This reporting period)			

III. Equipment Status

Nomenclature	*No. Asgd*	*Gains*	*Losses*	*Reasons*
Truck, Multi-Stop 4×2	1	-	-	-
Truck, Pickup, 3 pass,	1		-	-
A-26 Aircraft	14	2	-	(1 of 14 assigned Undergoing repairs— Landing accident)

IV. SIGNIFICANT STATISTICS

a.	Total Combat Flying Hours	1958 + 50
b.	Total Combat Sorties Scheduled	865
c.	Total Combat Sorties Flown	756
d.	Sorties Cancelled Due to Adverse Weather	55
e.	Sorties Cancelled Due to Maintenance	15
f.	Sorties Cancelled Due to HHQ	19

MUNITIONS EXPENDED

Description	Amount
MK81 (250 lb GP Bomb)	409
MK82 (500 lb GP Bomb)	54
M117 (750 lb GP Bomb)	52
M1A4 (Fragmentation Bomb Cluster)	5,290
BLU-10 (250 lb Unfinned Fire Bomb)	130
BLU-27 (750 lb Finned Fire Bomb)	214
BLU-23 (500 lb Finned Fire Bomb)	70
BLU-32 (500 lb Finned Fire Bomb)	2,344
M-31, M-32 (500 lb Incendiary Bomb Cluster)	236
CBU 14/A (Cluster Bomb Unit)	1,295
CBU 25 (Cluster Bomb Unit, Foliage Penetrating)	128
CBU 29 (750 lb Cluster Bomb Unit, Delay Fused)	8
CBU 24 (750 lb Cluster Bomb Unit, Impact Fused)	60
LAU-3 (Rocket Pod)	42
50 Cal. (API Ammunition)	167,050

TARGETS STRUCK

Description	Amount
Trucks	925
AAA Guns	105
Road Segments	10
Troop Concentrations	63
Troop/Storage Area	132
Truck Parks	183
Boats/Barges	7/9
Bulldozer	1

STRIKE RESULTS

Description	Amount
Trucks Destroyed	287
Trucks Probably Destroyed	29
Trucks Damaged	6
AAA Guns Silenced	53

Description	Amount
AAA Guns Destroyed	4
Secondary Fires	1,632
Secondary Explosions	580
Road Interdictions	6
Boats/Barges Destroyed	9/1

AIRCRAFT STATUS

	July	*August*	*September*
OR	75.7%	55.5%	62.8%
NORM	24.3%	44.5%	37.2%
NORS	LESS 5%	LESS 5%	LESS 5%

V. Narrative:

During this quarter, Nimrod crews of the 609th Special Operations Squadron, flying A-26 Attack Bomber aircraft, continued their night armed reconnaissance operations in the Steel Tiger/Tiger Hound areas of east-central Laos and in the Barrel Roll area of Northeast Laos. Crews of the 609th were restricted from flying missions into the southern panhandle of North Vietnam, and were prohibited from violating a ten-mile buffer zone along the North Vietnam border north of 19 degrees latitude in the Barrel Roll area. The high level of supply truck movement along the Ho Chi Minh Trail of last quarter was significantly reduced during this quarter, the primary cause being the heavy rains associated with the Southwest Monsoon. Weather personnel recorded a total of 42.92 inches of rain during this three-month period, which damaged certain route segments to the extent that truck traffic was either impossible or greatly hindered.

As in the past, Nimrod crews operating in the Steel Tiger/Tiger Hound areas concentrated on destroying moving supply trucks bound for enemy North Vietnam and Viet Cong military forces in South Vietnam; and in the case of crews operating in Barrel Roll the primary effort was still to destroy moving supply trucks heading for enemy North Vietnam and Pathet Lao forces which are mainly concentrated in the Plaines Des Jarres region of Northern Laos, but which are also encountered in various locations depending on rapidly changing enemy military objectives in that region. Nimrod crews abandoned their primary effort of destroying moving enemy supply trucks only to come to the aid of friendly Royal Laotian ground forces that were either under direct attack by North Vietnam and/or Pathet Lao units, or if it was determined that attack on friendly forces was imminent. Secondary targets included AAA positions, road interdictions, and intelligence pre-briefed truck park/storage areas. As a last resort, ordnance was dropped under the direction of ground radar sites (Combat Skyspot) when weather prevented visual target acquisition.

Although Nimrod crews have the authority to FAC themselves in on target strikes, their ability to do so is limited because of the lack of A-26 electronic aids; they have neither light amplification devices (Starlight Scopes) nor radar, but must rely on visual target acquisition from flare light, or in some cases by moonlight. As a result of those limitations, A-26 crews are almost completely dependent upon specialized FAC crews, such as the C-123 Candlesticks, the O2A/B Nails, and the C-130 Lamplighters and

Blindbats, who do have the capability to acquire and mark targets by using light amplification devices and radar (O2A does not have radar). Nimrod crews have no doubt that their success is heavily dependent on close coordination with FAC aircrews who locate and mark targets. In some cases, primarily in Barrel Roll, target strikes result from coordination with friendly ground teams who patrol the roads and call in strike aircraft if they are able to spot moving trucks.

During this quarter, a total of 756 combat sorties were flown by 609th crews. Of that number, 537 were flown in the Steel Tiger/Tiger Hound areas and 219 were flown in Barrel Roll. The average sortie flying time was 2.6 hours, and the average time-over-target was 1.4 hours. Truck sightings, and consequently truck kills, were significantly reduced from the previous quarter. During the previous quarter (April–June), 831 trucks were destroyed by Nimrod crews. In comparison, only 925 trucks were struck during this quarter (July–September), and 287 of those trucks were destroyed. The 287 kills were either confirmed by FACs with Starlight Scopes or by ground teams. As was previously stated, this reduction in activity was a direct result of the heavy monsoon rains. However, the level of truck movement and associated AAA defensive reactions greatly surpassed that of the July through September period of 1967. In fact, based on the experience of the July–September period of 1967, crews of the 609th expected truck movement and AAA reactions to come to a virtual standstill during July–September of this year. Such was not the case.

Route 912 from the North Vietnam border to where it intersects Route 911 at D-68 remained open to truck traffic almost constantly. Also, Route 911 from D-68 south to D-11 where it intersects Routes 9 and 914 remained open most of the time, as did Routes 9 and 914 from D-11 southeast to Khe Sanh in South Vietnam and south to the Cambodian border area. This route complex made up the main artery of enemy truck supply movement through the Steel Tiger/Tiger Hound areas of Laos south to South Vietnam.

Route 911/23 from the Mu Gia Pass south to D-68, which was heavily travelled during the dry season, was almost completely abandoned as a supply route during this quarter. The damage to supply routes in Barrel Roll by heavy rains and flooding was negligible because of the rugged, mountainous terrain of the region. In Barrel Roll, Nimrod crews concentrated on destroying trucks along Routes 6, 7, and 61 (See Attachment #3 for location of Steel Tiger/Tiger Hound, Barrel Roll, and their associated routes).

The heaviest activity of this three-month period occurred in July. Although there were few truck strikes and associated AAA reactions during the first week of July, the tempo of activity of the last three weeks picked up considerably, which indicated that many forces were in urgent need of more supplies in South Vietnam. This push to resupply occurred despite the 12.21 inches of rain that fell on the dirt roads of the Ho Chi Minh Trail during July. Some of the outstanding missions flown by Nimrod crews are listed below. (1) Nimrod 35 on 14 July (Pilot—Capt. Michael J.C. Roth, FR70258 and Navigator Capt. Roger D. Graham, FR70029) destroyed six trucks while under fire from 4 × 37 mm and 2 ZPU (14.5 mm) guns. (2) Nimrods 35 and 37 on 19 July (Pilots were Major Mark R. Richards, FR32062 and Capt. Charles A. Kenyon, FR51001, and the Navigators were Capt. Leroy D. Zarucchi, FV3129566, and Capt. William A. Cohen, FR55438) each destroyed 4 trucks. Nimrod 35 had 4 secondary fires and 2 secondary explosions, and Nimrod 37 had 1 secondary fire and seven secondary explosions. Their strikes occurred in the same area and about the same time. A total of 6 × 37 mm guns fired at them during the strikes. (3) Nimrods 31 and 32 on 22 July (Pilots Lt Col John J. Shippey, FR39944, and

Capt. Bruce C. Wolfe, FR77247, and Navigators Capt. Leroy D. Zarucchi, FV3129566, and Capt. Lawrence J. Elliott, FV3150643) each destroyed 6 trucks. Nimrod 31 was fired at by 3 AAA positions and Nimrod 32 noted 7 AAA positions active in his area. (4) Nimrod 32 on 24 July (Pilot Major John A. Parrish, FR47852, and Navigator Capt. William A. Cohen, FR55438) destroyed 5 trucks and had 2 secondary fires while being shot at by 1 × 37 mm. (5) Nimrod 31 on 26 July (Pilot—Major John A. Parrish, FR47852, and Navigator Capt. Frank W. Nelson, FR3139297) destroyed 4 trucks and had 3 secondary fires and 5 secondary explosions while being fired at by 1 × 37 mm. (6) Nimrod 32 on 31 July (Pilot—Lt Col Atlee R. Ellis, FR18377, and Navigator Capt. William A. Cohen, FR55438), destroyed 1 × 37 mm and silenced 2 × 37 mm positions out of a total of 5 × 37 mm positions that were firing at them. They also noted 4 secondary fires and numerous secondary explosions.

A total of 84 trucks were confirmed destroyed during August, which was a significant reduction from the 136 truck kills during July. Little truck movement was observed during the first three weeks of August, mainly due to the 14.55 inches of rain that fell during the month. However, clearing weather the last week of August prompted another push by the enemy, especially along Route 912 of Steel Tiger. A tropical storm during the second week of August forced HHQ to cancel 25 missions. Only one truck was struck that week and none was destroyed. In general, crews were forced to increase the number of strikes on truck parks, either visually or under ground radar control (Combat Skyspot).

Some of the outstanding missions during August are as follows:

(1) Nimrod 38 on 27 August (Pilot—Major Lee D. Griffin, FV3034963, and Navigator—Capt. Ernest J. Wiedenhoff, FV3101926) destroyed 6 trucks and had 32 secondary fires and 6 secondary explosions. (2) Nimrod 33 on 28 August (Pilot Major Elmer E. Peters, FV3025999, and Navigator—Capt. Thomas E. Bronson, FR3160694) destroyed 4 of the 5 trucks they were attacking and had 1 secondary fire. A total of 4 × 37 mm positions fired at them during their strikes. (3) Nimrod 32 on 28 August (Pilot Major John A. Parrish, FR47852, and Navigator—Capt. Lawrence J. Elliott, FV3150643) destroyed 4 trucks while under fire from 2 × 37 mm positions.

Truck movement during September was lower than any other month of this reporting period, and lower than any month of the previous 12 months. Heavy typhoon rains fell on the enemy route structure during the first two weeks of September, but the weather gradually began clearing up the later part of the month indicating that the Southwest Monsoon was drawing to a close. A total of 16.16 inches of rain was recorded by weather personnel during September. However, Nimrod crews managed to destroy 67 trucks during the month despite poor weather conditions, and despite the fact that they were forced to work with reduced ordnance loads from the 5600 ft. parallel taxiway while the main 8000 ft. runway was being repaired. Three outstanding missions during the month are listed below: (1) Nimrod 32 on 7 September (Pilot—Lt Col Robert L. Schultz, FR42560, and Navigator—Capt. Jerry L. Meek, FR82966) destroyed 2 trucks in Barrel Roll and probably destroyed 2 more. (2) Nimrod 36 on 11 September (Pilot—Major Mark L. Richards, FR32062, and Navigator—Capt. Leroy D. Zarucchi, FV3129566) destroyed 9 boats and 1 large barge loaded with POL; there were 15 secondary fires which burned for more than 45 minutes after the strike, and there was one secondary explosion. They were fired at by automatic weapons. (3) Nimrod 31 on 19 September (Pilot—Major Albert Shortt, FR53228, and Navigator—Capt. Lawrence

J. Counts, FR3129974) destroyed 4 trucks and observed one secondary explosion while being fired at by 1 × 37 mm.

VI. Tactics

Since the subject of tactics is too broad in a report of this type, only the basic tactics used by Nimrod crews will be covered here. Night dive-bombing combat missions in rugged terrain, and often in inclement weather, demand the highest level of pilot skill and pilot/navigator crew coordination. A crew must constantly be aware of their location, altitude, and the terrain elevation below. The 609th has continued the policy of making a maximum of 6 passes and releasing ordnance 5000 AGL when in high threat areas. Although all AAA defenses were lighter this quarter than during the previous three quarters, none of the 609th aircraft received battle damage during this quarter, which attests to the validity of this policy. Nimrod crews concentrated on killing trucks but made every reasonable effort to provide flak suppression for other aircraft. However, Nimrod crews have learned through experience that no matter how good their tactics and coordination with FAC crews are, their effectiveness is dictated by the type of ordnance they have available. Specifically, the most effective ordnance for night strikes, because of the large area coverage obtained, are incendiary bomb clusters of the M-31, M-32, and M-36 variety. Regrettably, this type of ordnance was in short supply this entire quarter and probably will be for the foreseeable future.

Two crewmembers, Major Daniel F. Grob (Pilot) and Major Robert W. Squires (Navigator), are assigned the additional duties of being Squadron Tactics Officers. They monitor tactics of the 609th, and about once a month squadron meetings are held to bring all crewmembers up to date on current tactics.

Lt. Col. Atlee R. Ellis, Squadron Operations Officer, attended a tactics conference at Bangkok on the 9th and 10th of September. Representatives of combat units from all over SEA who are directly involved in night combat operations were present at the conference. The purpose of the conference was to evaluate past night tactics and to come up with more effective tactics to be used in the coming dry season, which resulted in the drawing up of Operations Plan "Commando Hunt." Listed below are the basic points which Lt. Col. Ellis brought up at the conference:

1. Incendiary ordnance preferred for night truck strikes (M-31 and M-32).
2. Need more strike aircraft and more FACs.
3. Need improved airspace control.
4. Need more flak suppression.
5. Expedite FAC supply of large Starlight Scopes.
6. Request approval for hot pursuit of trucks across Route 912 at NVN border.
7. Suggest B-57s use NKP for turnaround.
8. Suggest firecan (radar) warnings be broadcast over guard frequency the same as MIG calls.
9. Update photos of route structure every 30 days.
10. Suggest timely BDA photographs be available to FAC aircrews.
11. Eliminate coding of delta points to decrease confusion.

VII. Maintenance

Interview with the Squadron Maintenance Officer, 1st Lt James M. Collins, FV3180154, and the NCOIC of Maintenance, SMSGT James W. Pitsonberger,

AF16381907, disclosed that 13 of the 14 A-26 aircraft are available to accomplish the mission. One aircraft (Tail #677) is out of commission as the result of a landing accident on 31 August. The pilot encountered a propeller reverse malfunction on a wet, slippery runway and was unable to keep the aircraft on the runway during the landing roll. The gear, nose, and propellers were damaged to the extent that this was considered a major accident. The pilot and navigator escaped injury, but approximately 5000 man-hours will be required to make the aircraft operationally ready again. Only 15 sorties out of a scheduled 865 were cancelled because of maintenance, which is an outstanding record considering the fact that there were 50 percent turnover of maintenance personnel during this quarter. Maintenance was required to provide operationally ready aircraft for 9 sorties a night up until the last half of September when the requirement was raised to 10 sorties a night.

The major maintenance problem encountered during this quarter was the lack of specialists: there are 140 aircraft on base, but there are only enough specialists to take care of fewer than 100 aircraft. To help alleviate this problem, the 609th formed a five-man engine team under the supervision of SSgt Lankford, which decreased the out of commission time because of engines by about 80 percent. Faulty electrical and comm-nav components, caused by rain leaking into the aircraft, was another major problem. Every attempt was made to keep the aircraft cockpit covered when the aircraft was not being flown. Certain parts, such as fuel flow transmitters, and BRIC units, were in short supply this quarter but this situation is improving.

VIII. Training

A-26 aircrews received the bulk of their training at England AFB, Louisiana, but are required to complete a checkout program after they arrive at Nakhon Phanom RTAFB. The checkout program is controlled by the squadron commander and operations officer and is monitored by Capt. William A. Cohen, the 609th Training Officer. Pilots get an average of 7 checkout rides with instructors, and navigators get an average of 6 rides. There are 7 instructor pilots and 7 instructor navigators in the squadron who actually conduct this training. (See Attachment 2 for names of IPs and INs).

The squadron combat safety ready status has remained at C-1 during this quarter except for two brief periods when the PCS rotation temporarily dropped the rating to C-2 until additional crewmembers were checked out. At the end of this quarter, the rating was C-1 with 15 crews in combat ready status.

IX. Armament

1st Lt Robert Skipp, FV3180519, the 609th Armament Officer, provided the information that follows. The base has only about 250 M-31/M-32 bombs in stock and there are only about 700 bombs of this type scheduled to be delivered in the future. This is the best truck killing ordnance that Nimrod crews have used because of the large area coverage and intense heat of the weapon. A 750 lb version of this bomb, the M-36, is scheduled for production but will not be available in the near future.

Dud rates were low during this quarter except for BLU-23 napalm bombs (1 out of 4 were duds). The ingredients of this bomb were discovered not to be properly combined and this problem has been corrected. The flare (M-24) dud rate has been greatly decreased by utilizing the SUU 25 B/A flare dispenser. Special emphasis has been placed on increasing the efficiency of the eight 50 caliber guns, i.e., they are cleaned and oiled daily and the fire-out rate has increased considerably.

A noteworthy change of procedure was initiated by armament personnel this quarter to increase safety. To prevent inadvertent firing of guns or release of ordnance the procedure of disconnecting batteries prior to loading and pulling the master arm circuit breaker was established.

X. AWARDS AND DECORATIONS

A total of 13 Silver Stars and 21 Distinguished Flying Crosses were presented to Nimrod crewmembers during this quarter (See attachment 2 for names of recipients). Other medals have been presented prior to this quarter, either at Nakhon Phanom RTAFB or at the crewmember's next PCS station.

The large majority of medals presented to date were awarded for missions flown during the past dry season, i.e., November 1967 through May 1968. The Silver Stars were presented by either General Nazzaro, General Momyer, General Gideon, or General Brown, during various visits to Nakhon Phanom RTAFB in this quarter. The Distinguished Flying Crosses were presented by Colonel McCoskrie, 56th Sp Op Wg Commander, or by a member of his staff.

Major Kenneth E. LaFave, FR60712, was awarded the Thirteenth Air Force "Well Done" plaque for his outstanding performance of duty as an A-26 pilot on 11 May 1968. On that date, Major LaFave's aircraft took a 37 mm hit while he was striking a truck convoy, but he managed to successfully fly the seriously crippled aircraft back to Nakhon Phanom RTAFB for a safe landing. (See Attachment #4.)

XI. COMMANDER'S CONCLUSION

I, Lt Col John J. Shippey, FR39944, replaced Lt Col Robert E. Brumm, FR17717, as the Squadron Commander of the 609th Air Commando Squadron on 18 July 1968. (See Attachment #5.) On 1 August 1968, the 609th Air Commando Squadron was redesignated as the 609th Special Operations Squadron. (See Attachment #6.) The squadron effectiveness has remained high due to many factors. Continuing emphasis is placed on training of newly arrived crewmembers, as well as improving tactics for all. The imposition by the 56th Sp Op Wg of a 5000 ft minimum release altitude for ordnance delivery in high threat areas caused some difficulties for a short period, but modified tactics were rapidly adopted by all crews and our bombing accuracy was not significantly degraded. Adverse weather conditions prevailing throughout the reporting period due to the Southwest Monsoon season drastically reduced truck movement and opposing gunfire, however, this has still been the most active monsoon season reported since the A-26s began working in our operating area.

Improved FAC'ing has been continually provided, primarily by the "Candle Sticks," the C-123 FACs of the 606th Sp Op Sq.

The limitations imposed in the Barrel Roll area, i.e., no strikes within the 10-mile buffer zone, being fragged only to limited areas of the Bravo and Cocoa areas (Routes 7, 6, and 61), and the fact that TACAN is available as a navigational aid only approximately 50 percent of the time when in the area, caused some decrease in our effectiveness in the northern area.

Maintenance difficulties were a major source of concern throughout the period, caused primarily by a severe shortage of qualified technicians. Flight line personnel absorbed a great deal of work normally accomplished by specialists, which prevented the loss of many missions. The flight line personnel, both maintenance and munitions loading, worked many hours of overtime under the worst possible conditions to continue our effort at a maximum rate. They are to be very highly commended for an outstanding job.

Our squadron OJT Program improved drastically, due primarily to the efforts of TSgt Duncan, the Squadron Training NCO. Through his training program and the efforts of supervisors within the organization, 11 individuals of 13 tested, passed.

/S//S/

JOHN J. SHIPPEY, Lt Colonel, USAF
Commander

ROGER D. GRAHAM, Capt, USAF
Unit Historical Officer

SUPPORTING DOCUMENTS

    1. Nakhon Phanom RTAFB Form 20 (Pilot's Debriefing Form, 609th Sp Op Sq Records). Confidential.

    2. 609th Sp Op Sq Weekly Summary Reports. July, August, September of 1968.

    3. 609th Sp Op Sq Flight Orders. (609th Sp Op Sq Records).

    4. Attachment 1: Roster of Key Personnel.

    5. Attachment 2: Roster of 609th Crewmembers.

    6. Attachment 3: Familiarization Map of Laos.

    7. Attachment 4: Thirteenth Air Force "Well Done" Award.

    8. Attachment 5: Special Order #14.

    9. Attachment 6: Special Order G-167.

ATTACHMENT 1
ROSTER OF 609TH KEY PERSONNEL

Squadron Commander	Lt Col John J. Shippey
Operations Officer	Lt Col Atlee R. Ellis
Administrative & Executive Officer	Major Kenneth E. LaFave
"A" Flight Commander	Major Robert F. Bennett
"B" Flight Commander	Major Daniel F. Grob
"C" Flight Commander	Major Douglas W. Carmichael
Maintenance Officer	1st Lt James M. Collins
NCOIC Maintenance	SMSGT James W. Pitsonberger
Armament Officer	1st Lt Robert Skipp
NCOIC Armament	MSGT Clarence H. Turk
Squadron 1st Sergeant	TSGT James M. Spivey

ATTACHMENT 2
PILOTS

Bennett, Robert F., Major, FR60166	(IP)	DFC
Bright, Jack W., Capt., FR62533		
Brumm, Robert E., Lt Col, FR17717	DFC	
Carmichael, Douglas W., Major, FR44621	(IP)	DFC
Disteldorf, Bernard N., Major, FR58260	(IP)	

Continued: Attachment 2 Pilots...

Ellis, Atlee R., Lt Col, FR18377	DFC	
Fitzgerald, James C., Major, FR56827		
Grob, Daniel F., Major, FR45960	(IP)	SS, DFC
Griffen, Lee D., Major, FV3034963		
Kenyon, Charles A., Capt., FR51001	(IP)	
LaFave, Kenneth E., Major, FR60712	SS, DFC	
Litton, Delbert W., Major, FR47196	(IP)	
Norton, Jay L, Capt., FR63672	SS	
Parrish, John A., Major, FR47852	SS, DFC	
Peters, Elmer E., Major, FV3025999		
Richards, Mark R., Major, FR32062	SS, DFC	
Roth, Michael J.C., Capt., FR70258	(departed PCS August)	
Sears, Bobby J., Major, FR47177	(SEFE/IP)	SS, DFC
Shippey, John J., Lt Col, FR39944	SS, DFC	
Shortt, Albert, Major, FR53228		
Tengan, Seijun, Major, FR72019	SS	(departed PCS August)
Vogler, Charles C., Major, FR53888		
Wolfe, Bruce R., Capt., FR77247	DFC (departed PCS August)	
Yancey, Kenneth E., Major, FR65191		

NAVIGATORS

Bowman, Peter R., Major, FR72766		
Bronson, Thomas E., Capt., FR3160694	(IN)	DFC
Cohen, William A., Capt., FR55438	(IN)	DFC
Counts, Lawrence J., Capt., FR3129974		
Elliott, Lawrence J., Capt., FV3150643	DFC	(departed PCS Sep)
Gierhart, Loren W., Major, FR30028	(IN)	
Graham, Roger D., Capt., FR70029	SS, DFC	

Henry, Michael D., Capt., FV3118238

Langford, Walter N., Jr., Major, FR47973   (SEFE/IN)

Laws, Charles P., Capt., FR57922

Meek, Jerry L., Capt., FR82966

Nelson, Frank W., Capt., FR3139297   (IN)   SS, DFC

Richeal, James E., Major, FV3024881

Squires, Robert W., Major, FR57833   SS, DFC

Watson, Marion R., Major, FR47641

Willems, Richard L., Capt., FR3151684   (IN)

Wiedenhoff, Ernest J., Capt., FV3101926

Zarucchi, Leroy D., Capt., FV3129566   (IN)   SS, DFC

Zimmerman, Robert G., Major, FR61238   SS, DFC (departed PCS Sep)

Wolf, Norman D., Capt., FV3151066

HISTORY
OF
56TH SPECIAL OPERATIONS WING
JULY–SEPTEMBER 1969
VOLUME I

Assigned to:
Seventh Air Force/Thirteenth Air Force, Seventh Air Force
Thirteenth Air Force, Pacific Air Forces
Stationed At:Nakhon Phanom Royal Thai Air Force Base, Thailand

The following pages, from the 56th Wing History, show the operations of the 609th Special Operations Squadron (Nimrods) for July–September 1969. Some of this narrative can also be found in monthly 609th histories written by 1LT Paul Howe.

609th Special Operations Squadron

During the reporting period Nimrod crews of the 609th Special Operations Squadron continued their night armed reconnaissance operations in Southeast Asia. Flying A-26 attack bomber aircraft, these performed in their usual capacity as an interdiction force against enemy supply routes in the north, central and south-eastern areas of Laos.

Normal operations included strikes against: enemy supply carriers such as trucks, barges and pack animals; enemy gun positions and various small arms and automatic weapons; enemy supply storage and redistribution areas and truck parks; bridges, roads and trails used in enemy supply movement; and enemy troop concentrations in situations where close air support was required.

On 8 July, the 609th Special Operations Squadron experienced their only two combat losses of the quarter.

Nimrod 22, piloted by Maj. James E. Sizemore, with Maj. Howard V. Andre, Jr. as navigator, was out on a road reconnaissance mission in the BARREL ROLL area. After one hour Nimrod 22 and his wingman Nimrod 23 began to strike a road segment. Nimrod 22 dropped all of his napalm, frag bombs and flares in this area. Nimrod 23 dropped all of his napalm and flares but retained his frag bombs. Neither aircraft strafed the area.

Before Nimrod 23 had the opportunity to drop his M1A4 fragmentation bombs, the flight received word that Firefly 32 was working troops in contact with a ground FAC. Nimrod 22 flight proceeded to that area to assist with strafe and Nimrod 23's frag bombs.

The flight received a target briefing from Firefly 32, including target elevation of 5,500 feet and high terrain to the south 6,200 feet. The area was readily identifiable by old napalm fires. There had been no ground fire observed directed at aircraft but there was fire being exchanged on the ground.

Nimrod 22 elected to make a strafing pass to insure they had properly identified the target before Nimrod 23 dropped his frag bombs. Nimrod 22 rolled in from 8,000 feet and fired a short burst with the .50 caliber guns. The aircraft then began a pull off straight ahead, but shortly thereafter hit the ground and exploded. There was no further contact with the crew.

A friendly ground team furnished information that no one could have survived the crash. Since the area of the crash was occupied by hostile forces it was impossible for a ground team to reach the crash site. Although remains were not recovered, available information indicated beyond any reasonable doubt that no one survived. Death was apparently instantaneous.

On 12 July, Maj. Robert L. Dixon, and Maj. Earl E. Milan, flying aircraft 660, lost an engine on final approach, attempted a go-around, could not make it, and ended up making a wheels-up landing on the parallel taxiway.

On 23 July, the investigating officer rode with the 609th Special Operations Squadron chief stan/eval on a normal training flight in A-26 SN-17644. At 6,000 feet the instructor pilot demonstrated normal training configurations which approximated the conditions experienced by the pilot during the accident.

The resulting sink rate, airspeed bleed off, power required, and rudder forces confirmed the view that the pilot made the correct choice in electing to make a gear up landing.

Weather during the month of July was very poor, causing a total loss of 55 missions and many drops on "dump" targets due to low scud in the target area.

July marked a very significant month for the men of the 609th Special Operations Squadron. On 19 July, they were awarded the Presidential Unit Citation by Lt. Gen. James V. Edmundson.

Due to the heavy rains during July, the roads in Laos were generally impassable, thereby limiting truck traffic. Also the poor weather, with accompanying low stratus clouds generally obscured visual acquisition of truck traffic by the FACS. Hence, during the month the squadron's strikes against trucks dropped 64 per cent. The lack of truck targets and the poor weather also reflected a large increase in strikes against "hard" targets.

During August, the squadron had some difficulty in working with the Blind Bat FAC aircraft. Since these were only assigned here TDY, there was a high turnover rate. There was also a marked lack of experience in the new crews, which often contributed confusion to the strikes. To help resolve this problem, meetings were held to keep all personnel current on striking methods and operating limitations. Although this helped considerably, the rapid turnover rate still created a problem.

Considerable staffing of the operational requirement versus ordnance and fuel load culminated in the decision in August to reduce take off gross weight and drag profile to the maximum extent possible for the rainy season. Fuel load was reduced from 1100 to 1000 gallons, .50 cal ammunition was reduced from 2400 to 1600 rounds and ordnance profiles have been continually assessed to assure lowest drag possible consistent with available ordnance.

Effective ordnance continued to be a problem during this reporting period. Napalm was in short supply. The ordnance available was relatively ineffective and projected deliveries appeared to be based on past consumption and not necessarily the operational requirement.

The weather in September was a definite improvement over the previous two months. This was reflected in an increase from 80 per cent to 90 per cent in the ratio of sorties flown to sorties scheduled. The number of strikes against trucks began to increase this month as the roads gradually dried out and became passable.

During the month of September, the maintenance section of the 609th Special Operations Squadron experienced a large turnover in personnel. Also during the month, the squadron experienced some difficulty with the operation of the canopy release. Through the efforts of Lt. M.A. Noreen, maintenance officer, and TSgt Silfredo Hernandez, a new phase inspection method was devised for the phase dock, to alleviate this problem.

A total of 2,332.2 flying hours were flown by Nimrod pilots during the quarter. This flying time resulted from 820 sorties being flown out of 985 scheduled. Out of the 163 sorties cancelled, 156 were for weather.

The Nimrods were credited with destroying 19 trucks, one gun position, 41 military structures, one barge, two howitzers and two mortars. Additionally four trucks were damaged, 32 road cuts made, 492 secondary fires and 240 secondary explosions occurred as a result of strikes. The Nimrods were also credited with 1,838 KBA.

HISTORICAL DATA RECORD	REPORTING PERIOD
(RCS:AU-5)	FROM: 01 Nov 69
TO:	01 Dec 69
FROM: 609th Special Operations Squadron	TO: 56th Sp Op Wg (DXI)

I. Mission

    a. Primary: To conduct combat operations as directed.

    b. Secondary: To fly armed reconnaissance flare support and FAC missions to disrupt and harass enemy lines of communications and supply by attacking or directing attacks on pre-selected targets and targets of opportunity in the Barrel Roll, Steel Tiger North, and Steel Tiger South

    c. Areas of Laos.

II. Personnel Status (as of 01 December 1969)

	Officers	*Airman*	*Civilians*	*Total*
ASSIGNED	0	0	0	0
AUTHORIZED	47	0	0	0
ATTACHED	0	0	0	0

All personnel have re-assigned from this squadron due to Inactivation of the squadron, effective 1 Dec. 1969.

III. Equipment Status

Nomenclature	No. Assigned	Gains	Losses	Reasons
A-26A Aircraft	0	0	15	Sent to Clark AFB
Jeep	0	0	2	All equipment recalled
11/2 Ton Flatbed	0	0	2	by the motor
MB4 Tractor	0	0	2	pool due to
Metro Step Van	0	0	3	inactivation of sq.

IV. Significant Statistics

a. Total Combat Flying Hours 242.6

b. Total Combat Sorties Scheduled 90

c. Total Combat Sorties Flown 86

d. Total Combat Sorties Cancelled

   1. For Adverse Weather 4

   2. For Maintenance 0

   3. Total 4

e. Munitions Expended

   BLU 32 500 lb. Finned Fire Bomb 80

   BLU 27 750 lb. Finned Fire Bomb 564

   MLA 41 120 lb. Fragmentation Bomb Cluster 132

   MK 82 500 lb. General Purpose Bomb 116

   .50 Cal API 65,477

   M117 750 lb. General Purpose Bomb 4

f. Strike Results:

   1. Targets Struck

     Trucks 214

     Gun positions 20

     Truck Parks 2

     Storage areas 3

     Road crews 1

     SALOA 2

   2. Results

     Trucks destroyed 29

     Trucks damaged 5

     Guns silenced 5

     Secondary explosions 11

     Secondary fires 66

Continued: 2. Results....

Road cuts	1
RMO	3

NARRATIVE

On 4 November, Nimrod 20, piloted by Major Bates was involved in a highly dangerous situation with a Night Owl F-4. During their strikes against trucks the Nimrods were shot at by an enemy antiaircraft gun position. The Night Owl reacted to the gun without first determining if there were other aircraft already in the area. Consequently the Night Owl started dropping flares directly through the Nimrod strike pattern.

Major Koyn, piloting Nimrod 20, had the best BDA results for the month. On 9 November, Major Koyn destroyed 4 trucks and silenced one 37 mm gun position.

Ground fire directed at the squadron's aircraft increased markedly during the month of November. There was a 250 per cent increase over the totals for the month of October, and the squadron flew only nine days in November.

ATTACHMENT 1

HISTORICAL OVER-VIEW OF THE A-26 and THE 609th SP OP SQ

The Douglas A-26 was developed during World War II. It was designed to incorporate the best features of the Douglas A-20, the North American B-25 and the Martin B-26. The Army Air Corps wanted an aircraft that was fast, highly maneuverable, and had long range. In addition it was to have exceptionally heavy firepower and be capable of efficient operation at both tree top level and at medium altitudes. They got everything they wanted in the A-26.

It proved to be the fastest, most versatile, and deadliest medium bomber developed during the war. After the war, most of the A-26s were put in storage, where they remained until recalled for action in Korea.

Over 1000 A-26s (reclassified as B-26s) were reconditioned and placed in service in Korea, where were used extensively in both day and night operations. The B-26s dropped the first bombs in North Korea and the last bombs of the Korean conflict. Following Korea the 26s were again placed in storage.

Early in 1961, the Air Force began to recondition and deploy the B-26 to Eglin AFB, Florida, Howard AFB, Canal Zone, and in 1962 to South East Asia, for counter-insurgency training and operations. In the spring of 1964 the B-26s were grounded and recalled due to recurring wing spar failure. The aircraft were sent to On Mark Engineering where they were reconditioned and rebuilt. Several modifications were made at this time, including reinforced wing spars, permanent tip tanks, new and more powerful engines, reversible props and increased ordnance capacity. The first few of these B-26s were sent to the Congo to aid in counter-insurgency operations.

In June 1966, 8 B-26s, redesignated as A-26s, were deployed, TDY, to Nakhon Phanom under operation "Big Eagle." Their operations proved so successful that they were kept on a permanent basis. In January 1967 the A-26s were merged into the 606th Air Commando Squadron, and in August 1967 they were formed into the 609th Special Operations Squadron. As their mission grew, the Nimrods gradually acquired more crews and aircraft. By December 1968 the 609th Squadron had a total of 18 aircraft.

The Nimrods lost 2 aircraft in March 1969, one due to groundfire and the other during an inflight emergency. In July 1969 a third Nimrod was lost due to unknown causes during a strafing pass in the Barrel Roll portion of Laos.

The last A-26 missions were flown the morning of Monday 10 November 1969. On 14 November 13 aircraft were ferried to Clark AFB, PI. One of those aircraft No. 64–660 is to be ferried to Davis Monthan AFB, Arizona for storage while the remaining 12 aircraft were placed in flyable storage at Clark AFB. The remaining 2 A-26s left NKP 16 November 69 for Clark AFB where they were placed in flyable storage.

In the slightly more than 2 years of its existence, the 609th Squadron flew 7,159 combat sorties for a total of 19,762.7 combat flying hours. During this period, the Nimrods are credited with destroying 4,268 trucks and damaging 696 more. The Nimrods also destroyed 201 enemy gun positions and silenced an additional 696. The Nimrods have an extremely high truck kill record, averaging slightly better than 1 truck destroyed or damaged for each 1-1/2 sorties flown. This is significantly higher than any other weapon system currently in use in South East Asia campaign.

The A-26 has compiled a long and distinguished career, contributing significantly to the U.S. Air Force's effectiveness through 3 major military conflicts. On 1 December 1969 the 609th Special Operation Squadron was inactivated, so again the A-26s were put to bed. We of the 609th Special Operations Squadron are proud to have been a part of this history.

PAUL S. HOWE, 1Lt, USAF   JACKIE R. DOUGLAS, Lt Col, USAF
Unit Historical Officer Commander

ATTACHMENT 2
ROSTER OF SQUADRON COMMANDERS

Lt Col Howard L. Farmer	Lt Col Atlee R. Ellis
Lt Col Allen F. Learmonth	Lt Col Robert L. Schultz
Lt Col Robert E. Brumm	Lt Col Robert W. Stout
Lt Col John J. Shippey	Lt Col Jackie R. Douglas

ATTACHMENT 3

W VBQ224VV V90624
PP RUSDTG
DE RUSVB 2095 3150110
ZNY SSSSS ZOK JPCC0
P 110029Z NOV 69
FM 7AF TAN SON NHAUT AB RVN
RUSDTG/609SPOPSSQ NAKHON PHANOM RTAFB THAI
BT
SUBJECT: 609 SPECIAL OPERATIONS SQUADRON INACTIVATION
PERSONAL FROM BROWN TO CROSBY AND DOUGLAS.

1. PLEASE CONVEY MY PERSONAL APPRECIATION TO THE MEMBERS OF THE 609 SPECIAL OPERATIONS SQUADRON FOR THEIR OUTSTANDING CONTRIBUTION TO THE SEVENTH AIR FORCE MISSION AND FOR THE

THOROUGHLY PROFESSIONAL JOB THEY HAVE DONE. I WISH GOD SPEED AND CONTINUED SUCCESS TO EACH AND EVERY MAN WHO HAS BEEN SERVING IN THE 609 SP OPNS SQ.

2. THIS MESSAGE MAY BE DECLASSIFIED AFTER PUBLIC ANNOUNCE- MENT OF THIS ACTION IS MADE BY THE U.S. AMBASSADOR

/THAI GOVERNMENT

GP-4

BT

2095F

NOTE

1. Roger D. Graham retyped many of the documents, for the sake of readability, though left most format- ting, abbreviations, and spellings as they appear in the original.

CHAPTER 5

A/B-26 Memorial

IN HONOR OF OUR COMRADES LOST IN THE A/B-26 1961 - 1969

HOWARD F. ANDRE	CLEVELAND GORDON	ROBERT E. PIETSCH
JOHN P. BARTLEY	LOUIS F. GUILLERMIN	WILLIAM J. POTTER
ARTHUR E. BEDAL	GEORGE B. HERTLEIN	HOWARD P. PURCELL
ROBERT D. BENNETT	VINCENT J. HICKMAN	ROBERT L. SCHOLL
GARRY W. BITTON	BRUCE A. JENSEN	JOHN F. SHAUGHNESSY JR.
JOHN V. CALLANAN	JOHN C. KERR	JAMES E. SIZEMORE
JERRY A. CAMPAIGNE	ATIS K. LIELMANIS	FRANCIS E. SMILEY
DWIGHT S. CAMPBELL	LAWRENCE L. LIVELY	JERRY D. STOUT
ANTHONY F. CAVALLI	JOHN H. MC CLEAN	RONALD E. SULADIE
HOWARD R. CODY	JAMES MC MAHON	MILES T. TANIMOTO
CARLOS R. CRUZ	ANDREW C. MITCHELL	WILLIAM B. TULLY
RAPHAEL CRUZ	CARL B. MITCHELL	DAVID H. TYNDALE
ROBERT C. DAVIS	NEAL E. MONETTE	EUGENE J. WALDVOGEL
CHARLES S. DUDLEY	HERMAN S. MOORE	THOMAS R. WHITE
GEORGE "GLEN" DUKE	BURKE H. MORGAN	JAMES W. WIDDIS
PAUL FOSTER	JAMES R. O'NEILL	THOMAS H. WOLFE

In Honor of Our Comrades Lost in the A/B-26 1961–1969 (courtesy Al Shortt).

Howard F. Andre	Cleveland Gordon	Robert E. Pietsch
John P. Bartley	Louis F. Guillermin	William J. Potter
Arthur E. Bedal	George B. Hertlein	Howard P. Purcell
Robert D. Bennett	Vincent J. Hickman	Robert L. Scholl
Garry W. Bitton	Bruce A. Jensen	John F. Shaughnessy Jr.
John W. Callanan	John C. Kerr	James E. Sizemore
Jerry A. Campaigne	Atis K. Lielmanis	Francis E. Smiley
Dwight S. Campbell	Lawrence L. Lively	Jerry D. Stout
Anthony F. Cavalli	John H. McClean	Ronald E. Suladie
Howard R. Cody	James McMahon	Miles T. Tanimoto

Carlos R. Cruz	Andrew C. Mitchell	William B. Tully
Raphael Cruz	Carl B. Mitchell	David H. Tyndale
Robert C. Davis	Neal E. Monette	Eugene J. Waldvogel
Charles S. Dudley	Herman S. Moore	Thomas R. White
George "Glen" Duke	Burke H. Morgan	James W. Widdis
Paul Foster	James R. O'Neill	Thomas W. Wolfe

A/B-26 Losses in the Vietnam War[1]

Date	*Version*	*Crewmembers (Crew Position and Home of Record)*
5 Nov 62	B-26B	Capt. Robert D. Bennett, pilot (Cincinnati, Ohio); 1/LT William B. Tulley, navigator (Maysville, Kentucky); VNAF observer (unidentified); reportedly shot down during napalm run in the Mekong Delta and all KIA.
3 Feb 63	B-26B	Capt. John P. Bartley, pilot (Findley, Ohio); Capt. John F. Shaughnessy Jr., navigator (Houston, Texas); VNAF observer (unidentified); reportedly shot down during strafing run on Viet Cong concentration in the Mekong Delta and all KIA.
6 Feb 63	B-26B	Major James R. O'Neill, pilot (Levittown, New York) (KIA); 1/LT E. Johnson, navigator, and VNAF observer (unidentified) bailed out and were rescued; reportedly crashed after engine failure following AAA hit near Pleiku.
8 Apr 63	B-26B	Capt. Andrew C. Mitchell, III, pilot (Mobile, Alabama); Capt. Jerry A. Campaigne, navigator (Central Valley, California); VNAF observer (unidentified); crew of three KIA during strafing run approximately 33 miles northwest of Pleiku (left wing reportedly came off due to unknown causes).
16 Aug 63	B-26B	Capt. John H. McClean, pilot (New York, New York); 1/LT Arthur E. Bedal, navigator (Tarzana, California); VNAF observer (unidentified); reportedly crashed after wing failure during combat mission in SVN and all KIA.
2 Sep 63	B-26B	Capt. Howard P. Purcell, pilot (Lansdowne, Pennsylvania); 1/LT Neal B. McKinney, intelligence officer (Muncie, Indiana), was assigned to fly this particular mission in the right seat rather than the regular navigator (Larry Granquist); SSgt Raphael Cruz, armament (Stockton, California), flew in the gunner's position; VNAF observer (unidentified) flew in the jump seat; aircraft and crew disappeared on an air cover mission for large ARVN ground operation over Kontum Province, South Vietnam, and never returned to Da Nang Air Base (all four later determined to be KIA).
24 Nov 63	B-26B	Capt. Howard R. Cody, pilot (Gulfport, Mississippi); 1/LT Atis K. Lielmanis, navigator (Quakertown, Pennsylvania); VNAF observer (unidentified); reportedly crashed approximately 24 kilometers south of Ca Mau after being struck by machine-gun fire and all KIA; Capt. Cody and Lt. Lielmanis posthumously awarded the Air Force Cross for extraordinary heroism.

Date	Version	Crewmembers (Crew Position and Home of Record)
7 Jan 64	B-26B	Major Hughie D. Adams, pilot (Houston, Texas); Capt. Cleveland W. Gordon, pilot (Pittsburg, Pennsylvania); both reportedly killed during test flight and crash approximately 10 nautical miles south of Bien Hoa.
14 Jan 64	B-26B	Major Carl B. Mitchell, pilot (Mount Sterling, Kentucky); Capt. Vincent J. Hickman, navigator (Brooklyn, New York); aircraft lost on combat mission over Dong Nai Province, and both crewmembers KIA; Major Mitchell and Capt. Hickman posthumously awarded the Air Force Cross for extraordinary heroism.
11 Feb 64	B-26B	Capt. Herman S. Moore, pilot; Capt. Lawrence L. Lively, navigator; aircraft crashed pulling up from a strafing run during air show at Eglin AFB Range 52 (left wing separated from aircraft, resulting in death of both crewmembers).
28 Jun 66	A-26A	Capt. Charles G. Dudley, pilot (Bozeman, Montana); 1/LT Anthony F. Cavalli, navigator (New York, New York); Capt. Thomas H. Wolfe (FAC pilot) (Monett, Missouri), jump seat; reportedly shot down in Steel Tiger and all KIA.
24 Jul 66	A-26A	Major George Glenn Duke, pilot (Houston, Texas); Capt. Miles T. Tanimoto, navigator (Lawai, Hawaii); following a combat mission, reportedly crashed due to fuel starvation just prior to landing at NKP and both KIA.
14 Dec 66	A-26A	Lt. Col. Al Howarth, pilot; Capt. Jack Bell, navigator; Capt. Harold Cooper, new navigator getting first familiarization "dollar" ride in jump seat behind navigator seat; all three bailed out after AAA hit and all picked up by helicopters.
22 Feb 67	A-26A	Capt. Lee McCleskey, pilot; Capt. Mike Scruggs, navigator; aircraft struck by AAA during strike on Ho Chi Minh Trail and aircraft caught fire; both pilot and navigator managed to bail out (with injuries) and were rescued by helicopter.
22 Feb 67	A-26A	Capt. Dwight S. Campbell, pilot (Fairland, Oklahoma); Capt. Robert L. Sholl, navigator (Kimberton, Pennsylvania); aircraft was escorting damaged McCleskey aircraft back to NKP and crashed shortly after McCleskey aircraft exploded, killing both Campbell and Sholl in crash.
22 Aug 67	A-26A	Capt. John C.G. Kerr, pilot (Miami, Florida); 1/LT Burke H. Morgan (Manitou Springs, Colorado); initially reported MIA in Barrel Roll in northern Laos, and both later reported KIA.
27 Aug 67	A-26A	Lt. Col. Bruce A. Jensen, pilot (Green River, Wyoming); Capt. Francis E. Smiley, navigator (Upper Darby, Pennsylvania); reported MIA in northern Laos, and both later reported KIA. (Lt. Col. Jensen was the squadron commander at the time and flying his next-to-last scheduled combat mission.)

Date	*Version*	*Crewmembers (Crew Position and Home of Record)*
29 Dec 67	A-26A	Capt. Carlos R. Cruz, pilot (Arroyo, Puerto Rico); Capt. William (Bill) J. Potter Jr., navigator (Ambridge, Pennsylvania); A1C Paul L. Foster, combat controller night scope operator (Knoxville, Tennessee); aircraft reportedly hit by AAA during strike in Steel Tiger, and all three reportedly KIA.
24 Apr 68	A-26A	Lt. Col. John Shippey, pilot; Capt. George (Bo) Hertlein III, navigator (Decatur, Georgia); aircraft struck by AAA during strike in Steel Tiger; Capt Hertlein struck by AAA and KIA; Lt. Col. Shippey managed to land damaged aircraft at NKP.
30 Apr 68	A-26A	Capt. Robert E. Pietsch, pilot (Cleveland, Ohio); Capt. Louis P. Guillermin, navigator (West Chester, Pennsylvania); reportedly struck by AAA on strike in Steel Tiger and both listed as MIA and then KIA.
11 Mar 69	A-26A	Capt. Neal E. Monette, pilot (Falls Church, Virginia); Major John V. Callanan, navigator (Orlando, Florida); reportedly crashed at NKP due to undercarriage problems and fuel starvation; both crewmembers KIA.
23 Mar 69	A-26A	Capt. James W. Widdis, Jr., pilot (Newark, New Jersey); Capt. Robert C. Davis, navigator (Burlington, New Jersey); reportedly shot down by AAA during strike in Steel Tiger and both KIA.
8 Jul 69	A-26A	Major James F. Sizemore, pilot (San Diego, California); Major Howard V. Andre Jr., navigator (Memphis, Tennessee); reported lost during strafing run in Barrel Roll and both KIA.

A/B-26 Reunion, Hurlburt Field, Florida, 2011 (courtesy Al Shortt)

A-26A Counter Invader (#676) on display at Wright Patterson AFB, Ohio, was one of the first six A-26A aircraft to arrive for combat evaluation at Nakhon Phanom RTAFB, Thailand in 1966. (National Museum of the USAF).

Cockpit instrument display, A-26A (#676) (National Museum of the USAF).

NOTE

1. For additional information see The Virtual Wall®. Eds. Ken Davis, Jim Schueckler, and Channing Pro-thro. www.VirtualWall.org, Ltd. 1 Jan. 2009, http://www.VirtualWall.org.

CHAPTER 6

Lasting Impact and Legacy

Conclusion of A-26A Combat Operations at NKP

In November 1969, time finally caught up with the A-26A Counter Invader aircraft assigned to the 609th Special Operations Squadron at NKP. Their numbers had been reduced substantially by combat losses, and the remaining aircraft had become increasingly difficult to maintain because of dwindling spare parts, a long logistics trail, and a combat tempo that pushed men and aircraft to the limits. Other significant considerations included (1) AC-130A gunship aircraft operating at higher altitudes were being deployed to Thailand in greater numbers for Ho Chi Minh Trail truck killing operations and (2) AAA defenses on the Trail had become increasingly concentrated and effective, greatly increasing the risk of A-26 low-level bombing operations. The A-26 Nimrod aircrews and support crews never wavered; they were ready for yet another "dry season" of intense combat in Steel Tiger and Barrel Roll as the Trail road structure started drying out in October of 1969. However, an Air Force command decision was made to cease all A-26 combat operations in November 1969. It was a bittersweet moment for the Nimrod community. They had fought the good fight. Their beloved A-26 aircraft had simply flown in combat to the end of their useful lives. The aircraft and crews had established an unmatched record of being the only U.S. Air Force combat aircraft that served in World War II, the Korean War, and finally the Vietnam War.

Because of incomplete records, it is difficult to determine exactly how effective A-26 combat operations were out of NKP. However, the Air Force records that are available (see Squadron Histories in Chapter 5) clearly substantiate that hundreds of trucks were destroyed on the Trail by A-26 Nimrod crews. It is even more difficult to know how effective A-26 attacks were against NVA and Pathet Lao ground forces. On one occasion, General Vang Pao (commander of the Hmong allied forces in Laos) stated that A-26 Nimrod crews had saved the lives of his fighters and his people on many occasions. The following message from General William W. Momyer, commander, 7th Air Force, constitutes concrete evidence of the effectiveness of A-26 crews as a truck killer in the Steel Tiger and Barrel Roll areas of Laos:

> Personal for McCoskrie from Momyer. It has come to my attention that the 609th Air Commando Squadron destroyed more trucks in April [1968] than the entire 56th Wing in November of last year, which was a record high. The destruction of 459 trucks was a tremendous achievement for the month of April. The contribution made by the 609th Squadron in interdicting enemy supply movements has been in the finest tradition of the Air Force. Their operations require great personal courage, dedication, and professional skill. I want them to know I am proud of their accomplishments and the role they have played in achieving the highest

truck kill rate of the war. We have hit the enemy where it hurts. To the men of the 609th, I want you to know as Commander of the 7th, I am proud to have such an organization in my command. Continued good hunting.

The message from General Momyer above was included in a letter of commendation to the 609th Air Commando Squadron from Colonel Roland K. McCoskrie, commander of the 56th Air Commando Wing. Colonel McCoskrie commented: "I add my personal commendation to the observations of General Momyer. The 'Nimrod' crews and all who support them have done and continue to do an absolutely superior job."

Another message dated 9 November 1969 from Brigadier General Bevan to Wing Commander Colonel Crosby and Lieutenant Colonel Douglas memorializes the high regard that senior Air Force leaders had for the 609th Special Operations Squadron and the combat effectiveness of its A-26 crews. That message appears below in its entirety. At the time, Brigadier General Bevan was the director of combat operations, 7th Air Force, Tan Son Nhut Air Base, South Vietnam. Lieutenant Colonel Jackie Douglas was the squadron commander of the 609th when it was deactivated on 10 November 1969.

R 090900Z Nov 69

FM 7AF TSN AB RVN
TO 56SOW NKP RTAFB THAI
BT
FOR COL CROSBY FROM BGEN BEVAN. PASS TO LT COL
DOUGLAS.

    1. THE DAY RAPIDLY APPROACHES WHEN THE 56SOW WILL LOSE ONE OF THE FINEST COMBAT SQUADRONS IN SEA—THE 609th SOS. THE NIMRODS—"A ONE OF A KIND" OUTFIT—PRODUCED BDA UNDER CONDITIONS WHERE OUR MORE SOPHISTICATED WEAPONS SYSTEMS WERE STYMIED. THEIR LOSS, THROUGH DEACTIVATION ON 10 NOV 69, SIGNALS THE END OF AN ERA FOR THE GRAND OLD A-26 AND THE CREWS WHO FLEW IT. THE 609th CAN BE JUSTLY PROUD OF ITS PARTICIPATION IN WHAT HISTORY COULD WELL TERM "THE MOST CRUCIAL CAMPAIGN IN SEA"—THAT OF OUR STEEL TIGER INTERDICTION PROGRAM. THEY LITERALLY "WROTE THE BOOK" ON HOW TO KILL TRUCKS AT NIGHT AND IN THE MOST HOSTILE AAA ENVIRONMENT WE HAVE ENCOUNTERED.

    2. BDA STATISTICS ARE OF INTEREST TO EVERYONE SITTING IN JUDGEMENT OF CONCEPTS, TACTICS, UNITS, AIRCRAFT TYPES, ETC. THE CUMULATIVE TOTALS FROM MAY 68 THRU OCT 69 REFLECT 2053 TRUCKS DESTROYED, 304 TRUCKS DAMAGED, 28 GUNS DESTROYED, 3521 TROOPS KBA. 6655 SECONDARY FIRES AND 7145 SECONDARY EXPLOSIONS FROM A-26 STRIKES. I CONSIDER THESE FIGURES A TRUE MEASURE OF THE DEDICATION AND SKILL OF THE FAMED NIMRODS.

    3. PLEASE CONVEY TO THE 609th SOS MY PERSONAL REGRETS OVER THE DEACTIVATION OF SUCH A PROUD AND PROFESSIONAL ORGANIZATION. THEIR CONTRIBUTIONS TO THE GOALS AND OBJECTIVES OF THE USAF IN SEA WILL BE LONG REMEMBERED.

    GP-4
    BT
    #0172

Lasting Impact on Air Force Special Operations

For the men who flew, maintained, and armed the various models of the A-26 and B-26 in the Vietnam War, the wartime experience of flying and fighting from the air in those magnificent flying machines left a lasting and indelible mark. True to the Air Commando motto of "Any Time Any Place," those veterans of the Vietnam War continued the indomitable spirit of the American Air Commandos who had preceded them in World War II and all prior American wars. Not only did the Vietnam War experience leave a permanent impact on those men, but those men can also rightfully claim that they lived up to the high standards of their Air Commando predecessors, and that they firmly established themselves as a strong link in that continuing Air Commando tradition. The Air Commandos of today, whether they be referred to as "Air Commandos" or "Special Operations Forces," freely acknowledge that they walk and fly on the backs of the Air Commandos who preceded them. The legacy of the Air Commandos who flew in the A-26 and B-26 in the Vietnam War is that they overcame all obstacles and earned their place as highly effective warriors under extremely demanding combat conditions. They formed a combat brotherhood that became ingrained in their lives. That Air Commando spirit was passed on to today's armed forces. Truly, the patriotism and courage of the Air Commandos lives on.

Honors History: A/B/RB—26 Units

Summary of Awards and Citations:

Air Force Outstanding Unit Award to 4400th CCTS: May 1961–May 1962.

Air Force Outstanding Unit Award to 34th Tactical Group: 8 July 1963–31 July 1964.

Presidential Unit Citation (SEA) 1st Special Operations Squadron: 1 Aug 1964–15 Apr 1965.

Presidential Unit Citations to 56th SOW: 1 Nov 1968–1 May 69; 1 Oct 1969–30 Apr 1970.

Presidential Unit Citation to 609th SOS: 1 Oct 1967–30 Apr 1968.

Lasting Impact on Family Members

Wife's Story

Dianne Graham

I first saw Roger, a new student at Athens High School, when he was playing basketball on the outside court in back of the school. He was in the eighth grade and I was a seventh-grader. I had been hearing about the cute new guy for several days. New students were a rare occurrence in the small college town of Athens, West Virginia, and everyone took notice. I still remember the strange feelings I experienced while watching him interact with the other basketball players. He was obviously an outstanding athlete. He was also the cutest guy I had ever seen. Something told me that he would be the man that I would marry.

We didn't become a couple until his senior year. It was one of those stories that you read about: he was captain of the basketball team that won the state championship, and I was a cheerleader. His dream was to attend the United States Air Force Academy and serve his country. Roger graduated from high school in 1959 and began his "Doolie" year at USAFA while I completed my senior year of high school. I graduated from Concord College three years later, the same summer that Roger graduated from the Academy. We were married that October in a military ceremony complete with drawn sabers and the playing of the Air Force Hymn as we left the chapel. Looking back, it truly was "Off We Go" for us and our lives together.

Dianne and Roger, Hawaii, August 1968 (courtesy Dianne and Roger D. Graham).

Roger's first assignment was at Laredo AFB, Texas, followed by assignments in Waco, Texas, Sacramento, California (where our precious Kimberly Anne was born), Merced, California, and Loring AFB, Maine. It was while we were living on base at Loring that Roger received his orders for duty in Vietnam. Roger had to transition from B-52s to A-26s so off we went to Alexandria, Louisiana, for training. When it was time for Roger to leave us, Kimberly and I went back home to live with my mother in Princeton, West Virginia. It was there that my story of what wives experienced during the Vietnam War took place.

Goodbyes are always sad but this goodbye was total pain. Roger was sweetly tender as he sat on Kimberly's bed and told his baby daughter that Daddy had to leave her. He cried as he gently kissed her and quietly left the room. I drove him to the airport and did what I had dreaded for months. I told my love goodbye. Like most Air Force wives, I had a brave "I can handle this" appearance for my warrior. I sobbed all the way back home.

It came as an absolute shock to me that friends, relatives, fellow West Virginians, the news media, Hollywood stars, and even our political leaders did not share my pain. I can still vividly recall the disgust that I felt watching Jane Fonda, an admitted socialist, funding and participating in antiwar demonstrations and rallies, and the shock that I felt watching the news coverage of those demonstrations. But it was a much deeper hurt to know that no one wanted to talk to me about my fears and about what Roger was doing for them and for our country.

It was difficult to find pleasant, encouraging things to tell Roger in my daily letters but that didn't stop me from writing them every day. I sent care packages, pictures, audiotapes, and gifts. I fought fear and loneliness every second of the day and tucked Kimberly into my bed at night. Our sweet little girl helped get me through that year.

It took every ounce of energy that I could muster just to function on a daily basis. Therefore, an event that occurred one evening caused me to come apart. The doorbell rang and as I walked from the back of the house and through the living room to answer it, I saw the outline of two men silhouetted by the streetlights. They were wearing overcoats and flight hats. I fell to my knees and didn't make it to the door. Mother saw what was happening and opened the door. The lack of concern for the war taking place in Vietnam caused them to disregard the fact that their paper hats resembling flight hats, and the fact that there were two of them wearing overcoats resembling military attire, would give them the appearance of the two Air Force officers who would have been sent to tell me that my husband had been a casualty of war. How unthinking and disconnected our nation and our people were!

It was a strange phenomenon that overtook our nation. The men who fought and the wives who waited were treated as if they were diseased. I felt the secret stares of those who knew that I had a husband who was "over there in Vietnam." I was not socially invited into anyone's home—not even by Roger's mother, who lived only seven miles away. Roger's only brother wrote him a letter but the other members of his family seemed to put him, and where he was, out of their minds. My aunt pilfered through my personal belongings, got Roger's address, and had the gall to write and ask him to send her a set of flatware from Vietnam. She seemed to think he was on a vacation.

Although sometimes I wanted to, I didn't become a hermit, hiding in the house. I attended Sunday school and church services on Sunday morning and returned on Sunday and Wednesday evenings for additional services and Bible studies. I was asked to teach math at Bluefield High School. A geometry teacher had resigned unexpectedly and my cousin, an assistant superintendent in Mercer County, phoned and offered the job to me. One of my aunts came and stayed with Mother, Kimberly, and me in order to watch over "Kimmie" while I taught. The same story was true at school. My coworkers showed no interest and expressed no curiosity concerning what Roger and I were going through. I saw apathy toward the Vietnam War from many aspects of society. They didn't want to know what was happening on the other side of the world. They didn't care.

One day, I was surprised by a phone call. It was the wife of an Army soldier who had just been sent to Vietnam. She was experiencing the same feelings of isolation that I was feeling and wanted to meet me for lunch. I gladly met with her. We bonded instantly and shared several hours of memories and worries about our guys. Like me, she also had a baby. Before she left, she asked me if I felt that Roger would come home. I was astonished that she would ask such a question. I immediately replied that yes, I did think he would. She told me that she didn't feel that her husband would make it. Her husband was in the infantry—a very different situation from being in the air. Only a few months passed before I saw a picture of him in the local paper along with his obituary. She had known!

I had asked Roger to plan his "rest and recuperation" from the war to be at a time where I could look ahead and know that the time remaining would not be as long to endure and it had already been. We met in Hawaii and spent two wonderful weeks getting reacquainted, relaxing, touring, and recharging our souls. The time flew by and all too soon we were at the airport. I was catching the plane that would take me home while Roger was heading back to the war zone. It was at the airport that I was told that Roger had been awarded 15 medals, including the Silver Star. I knew then that he had been in far more danger than his letters had told me. He had written newsy letters that never mentioned the terrors of war, the tragic loss of friends, and the fear that had to be overcome each night as those valiant Nimrods climbed into the cockpits and roared off into the black sky in their search for enemy trucks. Those trucks were strongly protected by antiaircraft guns while they traveled under a thick canopy of jungle overgrowth. I didn't know until much later that Roger had kept a complete, descriptive diary of all of the events of his year at NKP. It was extremely difficult for me to read and I could only read a few pages at a time.

Again, I had been the "good military wife" while parting from Roger. Again, I fell apart. The flight attendant came to my rescue and took me from coach to first class. I know that, in part, her action was to help me regain my composure; however, I also know that it was upsetting to other passengers to watch me cry uncontrollably. She gave me a mild tranquilizer and a moist, warm cloth. She came to my much-needed aid. Her concern continues in my memory now because I know that her job of transporting wives back home, after a brief reunion with their husbands, gave her a deeper understanding of the pain and fear we were bearing. She was one of the few who understood and cared about the sacrifice that the wives of our military men were suffering.

One day at a time, I made it through that year. But more importantly, Roger survived his 182 missions in Vietnam.

Thank you, Lord! My Love came home.

The Air Force Academy Plaque Ceremony

Roger D. Graham

On June 6, 2017, I participated in an exceptionally meaningful plaque dedication ceremony at the Air Force Academy near Colorado Springs. The specific location of the ceremony was the Southeast Asia Pavilion on the Heritage Trail, adjacent to Doolittle Hall. The Heritage Trail is one of my favorite places to visit at the Air Force Academy; it is dedicated to preserving the heritage of the Long Blue Line. The purpose of the ceremony was to add our Douglas A-26 Counter Invader plaque to the aircraft plaque wall at the Southeast Asia Pavilion.

Andi Biancur was the moderator for the ceremony. The ceremony program included an opening prayer by Chaplain Harris, followed by attendees standing for the Pledge of Allegiance. Ken Alnwick told the Farm Gate story of B-26 and RB-26 combat operations in South Vietnam in the early 1960s. I told the Nimrod story about A-26 combat operations along the Ho Chi Minh Trail and northern Laos in the late 1960s. Jim Nance, an exceptionally talented sculptor, related the story of how he designed and fabricated the plaque. Carolyn Luck (George Luck's widow) and their son, Mike, officiated at the plaque unveiling ceremony. The ceremony concluded with roll call and the playing of Taps by the Academy bugler.

The A-26 Counter Invader plaque honors all Air Force personnel and family members associated with the Vietnam War. The plaque specifically includes the names of fifteen Academy graduates who flew the aircraft in combat. I look forward to visiting

(Left to right) Ken Alnwick, Roger Graham, and Andi Biancur (courtesy Kenneth J. Alnwick).

Kimberly Graham (daughter), Roger Graham (father), Ryan Graham (son), 2018 (courtesy Roger D. Graham).

the Heritage Trail with my wife, Dianne, and our three children (Kimberly, Kristi, and Ryan). On behalf of the Air Force family, we cordially invite the American public to visit the Academy and walk the Heritage Trail.

A Daughter's Journey to Know Her Father

Carla Cruz-Curtis

Dear Colonel Roger Graham, author of the book titled *The Nimrods*.

A journey of a thousand miles begins with one step. I took one step, and then another, to meet you. The loss of my father, Carlos R. Cruz, in the Vietnam War, was tragic to his family, but you more than anyone would understand. As you too lost your father, Frank J. Graham, at the Battle of the Bulge, at a young age. You too had to be strong for your mother. You too must have heard your father was a hero. It must have been extremely hard, but so natural for you to follow in his footsteps, knowing all the risks you were taking, that you might possibly leave your family to be strong and pass along the story of your life in your absence. And, with the twist of fate, my father might have written a book titled *The Nimrods* to help your children heal the way you have helped me find comfort in my journey to know my father as a man, a hero, and now, your friend.

A26 Invader pilots at NKP 1966–67, (from left to right) Carlos Cruz, Pete Caselle, Bill Potter, Barry Bonwit, Roger Fleishman, John Simon, Frank Barber (USAF)

Yes, you came back from Vietnam. You came back to watch your children grow into adults. Yes, you came back to see your son, in a new unpopular war, walk naturally in your footsteps. Yes, you came home. But, instead of hiding behind the flashbacks of only being 15 miles from the A A A fire that killed my father, instead of focusing on the flames you saw at his crash site in Laos, you engaged your pen to write a way to make sense of it all. You elected to tell your view of the Secret War in Laos that few wanted to remember and most couldn't forget. You eloquently told your story. Some of the same stories my father would have told. When you turned your plane around to rescue him, you couldn't. It was too late. Instead, as destiny will uncover, you told your story to rescue me.

With each complete step I take in this journey, I find the peace of mind necessary to write my story and inspire other sons and daughters of the Vietnam era to share theirs. Hopefully, by consolidating our stories, it will, from lessons learned, help children who have lost their fathers or mothers in the Middle East. There is a new generation of young casualties of war that must not have to learn about their fathers 40 years later. While each situation is different, grieving mothers can find direction on how to approach the loss of a father from those that lost theirs. Silence was an enemy for my family. My mother, by protecting me from the truth, deprived me of knowing myself and of really knowing him. My entire life has been affected from the abandonment I felt as a young child. Yes, each situation is different, but by sharing many stories, I believe there is a common thread to the mentally healthy and a common thread to those that are not.

It is now approaching the eve of Christmas. I am now online again as I recently purchased a used computer so that I could finally type the pencil-scratched letter that I wrote to you a month ago. I wanted to thank you on Veterans Day. Now, I suppose, this letter will arrive as a gift to you near the day of Christ's birth and the death of my father who crashed in Laos that 29th day, December '67.

On Veterans Day, as a nation, we take time to thank heroes of war. On Veterans Day, I wanted to tell you that you were a hero to me. Yes, you came back. You came back to tell a story for those who didn't. Having your book in my hand made me feel so proud. Reading the passage you wrote on the front cover saying, "I have great memories of Carlos Cruz, your father—He was a great combat pilot and a true American patriot." brought chills. I have few memories of him. Then, there it was, right in front of me, "your book." At first, I was afraid of what it might say. I took one step and then another, but once I got started, I was off and running into each chapter until I got to the chapter on the loss of my father, Bill Potter, and Paul Foster. Then, I stepped back again, and plunged forward through its contents, taking in all you had to give. Because of your words and photos, I was able to learn more than you may know. You spoke of my father's determination and aggressiveness to be the best. You spoke of his inner drive to succeed at all costs. Those words made a difference in my life. I know that I am very much like him. The little things meant so much like a photo of the trailers where my father would have lived. The maps where he flew, the runway where he took off on his missions, the O Club where he would join his friends to unwind, and the base exchange where he would have bought supplies, all brought to life the hero inside.

I flew from St. Louis to Fort Walton Beach to attend the October 9 "A-26 Nimrod Reunion," to meet someone who might have known my father. I had never met anyone except immediate family that ever knew him. I knew it was something I had to do. It was like I was pulled towards the light of it all. I knew I had to do it alone. I now know I wasn't alone. My father was with me.

When my son went to Iraq, I regressed to the six-year-old little girl I was when my father's plane crashed. All the feelings came back. I believed that war was a death wish. This fear haunted me in every aspect of my daily routine. I couldn't seem to face the fact that raising a hero was out of my control. The pit was like a cancer forming within. I hoped that by meeting others who did actually "live" that I could find hope in a hopeless understanding of war. So, after reaching out to find a way to mend. I searched online for anyone that might have known my father. That is when I found Donald Vogler, a Nimrod Legacy at http://www.A-26legacy.org. Donald was the son of Lieutenant Colonel Charles C. Vogler, a Nimrod pilot in 1968–69. Donald founded the A-26 Legacy Foundation to restore one of the few A-26 planes left in existence to make a flying museum in memory of his father and other fathers who flew this type of plane. Of course, I wanted to be a part of something so worthy. He told me about the plane my father flew and that my father was a Nimrod. I was shocked that he was calling my father such a thing. It sounded like an insult to me at first until Donald further explained what a Nimrod was. We corresponded back and forth via email for a long time. He helped me to contact other living Nimrods. That is when I was blessed to hear from you for the first time. Unfortunately, my computer obtained a virus and I lost all the letters and contact information I had started to gather. I heard about the reunion two years ago but couldn't go. I just wasn't emotionally ready. I had learned from Donald that a reunion took place every two years. Using a friend's computer, I found Donald's phone number again from his website and gave him a call. He told me when it was, who to contact for more information, and that he would be there with his wife. This time I wasn't going to miss the opportunity to meet him face-to-face. I so wanted to meet someone that knew my father. I wanted to give something of myself, and in return, gain something more than I came with.

The first person I met, at the airport in Fort Walton, was Harry Bright. I heard him talking about the Quality Inn Hotel and the reunion. I walked right up and asked if he would share a ride with me to save taxi fare. He had rented a car and said he would give me a ride. He helped me to put my father's medals and flag in his car. On the way, I told him about my dad. His mouth dropped open with shock. He said, "You're not going to believe this, but…" as he pulled a poem from the back seat of the car "…I wrote this 40 years ago on the night your father's plane didn't come back. I wrote the poem because I couldn't sleep." He was a mechanic on the A-26 that my father flew. He didn't actually know my dad, but he knew Paul Foster, the Starlight Scope operator on the plane when it crashed. I recognized Paul Foster's name because he was buried in the same grave as my father and Bill Potter at Arlington National Cemetery. Their remains were finally recovered in Laos and buried at Arlington in 1991. Harry said that the main reason he took the trip to the reunion from Delaware was to find Paul Foster's address so that he could send the poem to his family. Instead, he felt his destiny was to give it to me. I knew my father was smiling somewhere in the high altitude he loved so much. I hadn't even arrived to the hotel and already my father was leading me to find the answers to heal.

When I arrived at the Quality Inn, people were just starting to arrive. I found the Hospitality Suite, which was, questionably for me, called the "Hostility Suite" by the Nimrods and Farm Gate Commandos. I set up a little memorial to my dad by displaying his medals, flag, a few archaeological remnants from his crash site, photos from his funeral, and other items that I displayed proudly in my home over the years. I placed the memorial in the corner and stood on a chair to hang a POW-MIA flag over it. The flag kept falling down, but I kept putting it back up with tape. I was determined to keep that flag up because I wanted all to know that my father was never forgotten … at least … not by me. One photo that

I displayed was that of my father standing with six uniformed pilots. They were proudly standing in front of an aircraft on a runway. Since I was a little girl, I always wondered who these men were. I knew they would have had to know my father. I was hoping that I might meet someone in the photo at the reunion or be able find someone that might have known any of them. In a way, I thought that by setting up this memorial, it was my way of having him present with me. I'm sure, had he lived, he would have been in attendance.

I called ahead as I really didn't have the money to take the trip to the reunion, but I didn't care. I was going to attend even if I had to sleep on the beach. So, I called both the A/B 26 reunion organizers, Gary Pflughaupt (Farm Gate) and Crazy Leon Poteet (Nimrod), to ask them if I might be able to share a room with someone to help with expenses. They quickly let me know that there would be another girl (now a mature woman) also attending the reunion that lost her father too. Her name was Sheryl Jo Bedal. I was told not to worry about the room charges at the Quality Inn, as an anonymous donor would be paying for the room that would be shared by the both of us. This generosity touched my heart and paved the way for me to go without hardship.

After I created the memorial to my father in the Hospitality Suite, I received the key to the room. Sheryl hadn't arrived yet. Don Voglar and the other legacies (sons and daughters) hadn't either. I was told that the Air Commando Fish Fry (the first activity) wouldn't start for another hour, so, I went to the room to unpack my things. Time passed slowly as I sat in the room making gifts that I intended to give everyone at the banquet. I had rubbed my father's name off the Vietnam Traveling Wall and made 90 copies of Captain Carlos R. Cruz. I drilled a hole in the top of 90 (3"×4") clear baseball card covers and inserted the copies of his name in each sleeve. Then I attached the card cover with a wire to a 33" silver star so that it would make a necklace. My father achieved two Silver Star Medals for heroic service in Vietnam. I thought hanging his name from a silver star bead was appropriate.

Fred Moomau, Carla Cruz-Curtis, and George Matthews (courtesy Carla Cruz-Curtis).

Actually, I packed all this in my suitcase as therapy. As I made each gift, I feared that even if I did not meet anyone that actually remembered my father, I would be satisfied that I did my best to honor his memory. So, by wearing my hero on my neck, and giving it to others at the banquet, he would have not been forgotten at this year's reunion in some way or another.

I went downstairs from my room back to the "Hospitality Suite." I noticed everyone had tickets to eat at the fish fry. I never received any reunion packet, so I asked if there was a ticket or packet for me. I was told that I had to purchase one. I felt so ashamed. I really didn't expect anything. I was so embarrassed. I watched many standing in line for fish. I didn't know anyone. I wasn't even hungry and actually, I didn't even like fried fish. I was starting to feel sick. I walked around the back of the hotel to get away for a moment. It was so overwhelming for me. I walked on the pier to its end crying so hard. It was just me and the view of the bay. I prayed and asked my father to help me with the pain that I was feeling. I kept telling myself … "Stop it…. Stop crying…. Be strong…. You didn't come all this way to break down." I wiped my tears from my face, shook it off, and walked to sit under the tent with strangers. They weren't strangers for long. I just plopped next to a kind face and then another. Leaving all my insecurities behind, I asked questions and listened to the stories of those next to me. I was captivated.

Then, I met my roommate. Sheryl Bedal was the daughter of Arthur E. Bedal. Her father's B-26 crashed with a man that survived but lost his leg in the tragedy. His name was Marice Bourne (Maury). Sheryl flew from California to meet him. He escorted her place to place. He showed her a street on the Hurlburt Air Force Base named after her father. He took her to the Air Commando Association Building to see a brick purchased in her father's name. He gave her his insights to the man that he was in his eyes. She was never alone. He was always waiting for her to go to one place or another. I suppose I felt somewhat out of place. I was so glad that he was there for her, but I went blindly alone to search for my Maury. Maybe I was slightly jealous of the fact that she had someone to help her when I didn't. They were talking about all the places where they went but I had never been. I wish I would have gotten to know her better and am quite sorry that I became distant. We were different personalities, but truly, we had much in common. Later, I did see all the places they spoke of, but it was too late to change the dynamics of our relationship. I didn't have a Maury…. Instead, as I finally discovered, I had many.

That's when I met George Matthews and Larry Williges. George knew my father well and Larry used to debrief him at NKP in 1967. George held the photo of my dad and the other six men in uniform. He laughed as he remembered each of them. Between the two of them, they told me the first and last name of each man in the photograph. They told me about their characters, personalities, and if they were still alive or not. I really liked them. Their smiles lit the room. It was easy to consider that my father would have liked them too.

It was all so emotional for me as one by one, I was greeted by people who either heard of or knew my dad. It was quickly clear to me that my mother wasn't exaggerating. He had always been on a pedestal so high that I often believed the truth might have been stretched over the years like the size of the fish caught so long ago. My father was a hero, was respected, and was a great guy to his peers. I started to get addresses from those who knew him because my state of mind was so overwhelmed that it was keeping me from listening. It was just too hard to take it in all at once.

Then, I met Charlie Williams. He was distributing his father's photo to those attending the reunion. His father, Bruce Williams, Air Force major, crashed in Vietnam on April 16, 1967. His father was in a different unit other than the Nimrods or Farm

Gate. His father was a Spooky. He just wanted to meet someone that knew his father. He was not successful. He traveled all the way from Kentucky to the reunion in Florida to try. I admired his determination. I felt much empathy for him. I was very fortunate to have found so many who knew my dad when nobody seemed to know his. Even though he didn't meet anyone that knew his dad, he did meet me. We have stayed in contact. It is my hope that he will write his life experiences to make a difference for others. It only confirms my belief that the lives of sons and daughters were affected in many different ways by the loss of their fathers. Charlie sells weapons on his website: http://www.mtgweapons.com He assists those who wish to sell their NFA Registered Class III weapons. Seems a little ironic. I sold beads for 20 years. I imported over 1,000 dozen peace sign beads and distributed them all over the world over my websites that are now closed but were http://www.mardigrasbeadstore.com and http://www.sports-beads.com.

Donald Vogler invited the Legacy Sons and Daughters out to dinner. We had a very nice time getting to know one another having steak and a huge dessert. One of the legacies hardly ever left his hotel room. We tried to get him to come, but he just wouldn't leave his room. It was a mystery to me why he would travel all the way to the reunion and stay at the Quality Inn but wouldn't or couldn't for some reason go to the Soundside Club Banquet, the Legacy Dinner, or even the Memorial Service at Hurlburt. Who am I to judge how this experience would affect the kids of those that were lost. I might have elected to jump off the pier at my moment of distress. Each of us handle our emotions differently. I just wasn't going to fly to Florida to at least try to find some meaning in it all. I wish I could have gotten to know him. I hope that one day I will find some peace with his decision to attend but not participate.

Don Maxwell was a fellow Nimrod and friend to my father. I met him after the second day of the reunion. He took me to the Air Commando Association Building. He was the person who bought a brick engraved with my dad's name on the wall of the Air Commando Association Building. Below his name was etched the word "Fearless." Don had purchased the brick many years ago. Watching me view the brick had to bring some closure for him. Who would have ever known that one day, 30 years later, he would witness his comrade's daughter view the brick. It had to be a moment of great pleasure for him. I know it was for me. Years would bring a circle of a lifetime to meet in the middle at that moment. I took pride in the fact that there was someone who thought enough of him to set his name in stone. Later, I ate oysters at the High Tide Restaurant with Don Maxwell. The same place where they ate so long ago. It was so meaningful for me to be with someone who knew my father as a friend. I found my Maury. Don Maxwell shared his insights to the man my father was in his eyes just like Maury did for Sheryl.

The banquet, held at the Hurlburt Soundside Club, gathered a special group of heroes. I placed my star beaded gift by each plate. I was told by many that they would cherish the necklace with my father's name on it. I was also previously told that there would be karaoke at the banquet. So, I was prepared to sing the song "One Tin Soldier" if I had the opportunity. One by one, banquet participants went to the microphone to tell a joke or story. Their hand was placed in a bucket of ice-cold water while speaking so that nobody stayed up there too long. I thought that was pretty funny until it was my turn to freeze my hand to the tune made famous in the movie *Billy Jack*. While singing isn't my talent. I flew to Florida to give something of myself. Singing that song, as bad as I'm sure it sounded, was my way of sharing my soul to the people I admired most. At the banquet's end, I ran back inside to make sure that I didn't leave my father's name behind for the bus staff. Out of 90 made, there were only four remaining on the tables. Knowing that those necklaces are now in the homes of my father's friends and comrades humbles me to no end. I feel like I have many fathers now. I am truly grateful to find strength in this memory.

The Memorial at Hurlburt Air Park was also memorable. I touched my father's name on the plaque near the A-26 plane there. I saw up close the A-26 that he flew. It was an appropriate way to finalize the events. My only regret is that I didn't purchase the photo taken there of the men I will never forget.

At the reunion I met 13 men that knew my dad personally. Don Moody, Bobby Sears, Fred Moomau, Marty Monette, Dave Henry, Charlie Kuczaj, Larry Williges, Robert Zimmerman, Clyde Howard, Don Maxwell, and George Matthews all found time to either share their memories or give me their addresses to contact them to be able to hear more at a later time.

On Monday, October 11, most everyone was leaving. I decided to stay until Tuesday to save $100 in airfare. So, it was my goal to go to the beach once more on my last day in Florida. Sheryl had already left when I saw Maury. I told him what I wanted to do and he said he would go too. The beach was so beautiful. It was nice to finally get to know Maury. His gentle spirit was evident. The water was warm on that sunny day and we swam for hours. As we were leaving, I fell. Actually, I rolled down two flights of stairs. I couldn't believe that I didn't hurt myself more than I did. On the ground, I looked up, and there was Maury asking me if I needed help up. I laugh to this day thinking about that. It certainly shows that a man that lost his leg so long ago helped someone like me to rise to my feet.

I can see me writing with the warm wind of the coastal breeze against my hand as the words crash to the page like the ocean against the shore inspired by the hero in my heart. I do plan to move to Florida and continue to find other sons and daughters who are willing to share their story to make a difference for the new generation of potentially lost souls.

My life experiences have led me to this new step. Teaching inner-city kindergarten/first-grade students in St. Louis Public Schools for 14 years has given me a perspective towards instruction and intervention. Losing a parent should be treated as a handicap; thus, a child with special needs deserves an IEP (individual education program) for that individual child in that individual circumstance. Developing a "parent-based format, for a child in crisis due to the loss of a parent at war, is the primary objective." Because, quite frankly, the surviving parent is so overwhelmed, s/he is not equipped to know how to deal with the issue effectively. This form of counseling is necessary at home and at school. Unfortunately, this was not in place for children who lost a parent in Vietnam. With firsthand experience in this matter, I am certain that after I compile the experiences of other sons and daughters, lessons will be learned through all of us to benefit the children of military families involved with loss. I am sure that there are programs in place now for these new casualties, but those that are closely involved with them will benefit from lessons learned from the stories gathered.

A journey of a thousand miles begins with one step. Another step has been taken. I take these steps with the hope that my father would be proud of the woman I have become and the survivor that I will be.

You, Colonel Roger D. Graham, have inspired me to write again. I would be honored if you would be my mentor to help me towards this goal and provide a connection to your publisher when the time is right to put all this in motion.

> Sincerely,
> Carla Cruz-Curtis

Yes, Dear Lady, I Knew Your Son

HARRY J. BRIGHT

It is the early morning hours of 29 December 1967 at Nakhon Phanom Royal Thai Air Force Base, Thailand. A young airman, just a few weeks shy of his 21st birthday, is working on the engine of an A-1E Skyraider, one of the planes used for close air support over Laos and North Vietnam. A returning flight of A-26 Invaders, having completed their mission over the "Trail," is minus one plane. Quickly, word is received that the missing plane had been shot down, and no sign of survivors was seen. He asks his sergeant how the mother of a lost airman would be notified that her son was gone. The sergeant says usually the unit commander would write some type of letter.

Later, it is learned that one of the crewmembers of the missing plane is a friend of this airman's group of buddies. At the end of his duty shift, the airman goes back to his hooch, cleans up, and tries to sleep. But sleep does not arrive. He cannot stop thinking about his lost friend or the effect that losing a son will have on his friend's mother. He gets out of bed, takes out pen and paper, and writes a letter to the lady. The letter reads:

> Yes, Dear Lady, I knew your son
> But not well.
> I knew him by his name only
> I knew him by his smile and the
> Nod of his head when he walked by me.
> And I knew him by his plane number.
> Not much more.
>
> He was part of a team.
> A team in a small outpost
> In a corner of the world
> That most have never heard of.
>
> Our mission, our job, is never written about.
> This job won't be seen on TV.
> A job using antiquated equipment,
> Stationed in a primitive environment,
> In an ancient land
> Only a few know about.
>
> The mission took your son to a different country.
> A country struggling for its own freedom.
> A country being used.
> A country some do not return from.
>
> Dear Lady, to your son
> Each mission was the most important one.
> Each mission he had to be on.
> Each mission would save someone's life.
> Each mission would help bring freedom.
> This is what your son believed, what he lived.
> And what he gave his life for.
> Yes, Dear Lady, I knew your son.
> I knew his name, his smile, his age.

Major James Sizemore, Nimrod pilot (1969) (courtesy James Sizemore Jr.).

> I knew he missed his home.
> I knew he missed your cooking.
> I knew he missed his father, and you.
> I knew he was of the bravest, of the best.
> I knew him as my friend.
>
> Yes, Dear Lady, I knew your son.
> I knew him well.

Editor's Note: It was never known if Paul Foster's mother received the original letter. Harry Bright's letter was written to comfort Paul's mother, and to honor the memory of Paul Foster, and the pilot (Carlos Cruz) and the navigator (Bill Potter) of that plane.

Letter to My Son

MAJOR JAMES SIZEMORE

4 April 69

Friday Nite
"GOOD FRIDAY"

My Dearest Son, Jeff,

Hi Son, how are you? I'm fine today and I just got your real nice and thoughtful Easter Card. Thank you so very, very much for thinking of and loving me like you do!

I also thank you for praying to our Good Lord for my safety and yes Jeff, when I come home we'll have lots of fun, play golf, ride the bikes, play ball, dig fox-holes, cook steaks, go to the movies, eat popcorn, watch color TV, let you drive the VW like we use to do when we ran errands for Mommy,—Yes, we'll do everything, just like we use too not long ago!

You know Jeff, it's very difficult for a small boy like yourself to fully understand what war is all about. I'm sure it's pretty confusing to you as to why all peoples can't seem to live in peace with one another in the world. You see, Son, there are some men in the world who don't want to see people have their freedom. That

Jeff Sizemore and children (courtesy James Sizemore Jr.).

is the freedom to live as they want to live, go to their own church, believe in their own God, the right to vote for those they want in public office—like our country's President and the state Governors—the right to go to the schools they want to go to—to work in the job of their choice—to marry the woman that they want and on and on.

So Jeff for those people who cherish their freedom they sometimes have to fight those men who try to take freedom away from them! None of us, who are really sane, really like to fight and kill people—but in order for us to persevere our cherished Freedoms—we HAVE TO FIGHT!! This is what Daddy is doing—this is what I CHOSE TO DO! Daddy doesn't want to be killed in a war, but Son, if the Good Lord would will it—that is if he decides it is my time to go to Heaven—then I have no choice! I do hope the War ends soon and that I can come home to all of my loved ones. But Son remember if God wants me then I'll be in Paradise with Him!

Many, many men have given their precious lives for our Country, not only in this War, but many Wars in the time gone past. Jeff, it will be up to men like yourself, and your sons to come someday, to see that these men have not given their lives in vain! Keep your strong faith in God and have courage always. We live in the most wonderful Country in the World and don't let <u>anyone</u> ever forget it!

Daddy flew his 35th Combat Mission last nite. It was a good mission for me—had good weather with a full moon. I could see the ground real good, but the enemy gunners on the ground could see me real good too! I and another "NIMROD" A-26 in my Squadron, attacked a Fuel Storage Area not too far from here. We were able to blow it up with our bombs and I also destroyed a big fuel tanker truck. It sure lit up the sky real good when it exploded as my bombs hit it! My buddy also destroyed a big truck. We were real proud of each other. We did get shot at and a few rounds of fire came pretty close to my plane and my buddy's too! We made bomb drops on the guns and we didn't have any more guns firing at us then! Daddy tries his best to be careful, but in some of the target areas there are quite a few guns and sometimes if it gets too rough we pull out and go to another less protected target. Not that we are "chicken" but it's stupid to let yourself be shot down if you can prevent it!

It's raining real hard outside now. Lots of "thunder bumpers" all around. Looks like the Monsoon's are almost here! I am off tonite so I hope to catch-up my letter writing and sleep. I do hope you have your jungle fatigues by now and that they fit you good. Always try to do your best now in everything you undertake to do! Daddy misses you too, and Son, I love you very much!

> Take care now Much LOVE ALWAYS
>
> Daddy

Note: See comments from James "Jeff" Sizemore, Major James Sizemore's son, below.

I appreciate your sincere offer to take Dad's letter and publish it. This is an incredible moment, to publish what Dad wrote to me, his one and only son. I thought this letter was destroyed; it has been missing for such a long time.

Now that I have rediscovered this letter and the fact that you are publishing letters like mine, I am honored to have your request for this letter in full and for it to be presented to the public. Honestly, this letter can still make me cry. It is a touching letter, full of hope, dreams and plans a dad has for his family and especially his son.

This letter was written "Good Friday" evening, April 4, 1969. It is reproduced as written, with any and all grammatical, punctuation, and spelling errors! It's okay, it was how Dad wrote!

Editor's Note: Sadly, Major James Sizemore, pilot, and Major Howard Andre, navigator, were killed in action on an A-26 mission to Barrel Roll, northern Laos, on July 8, 1969. They were the last A-26 crew lost in the Vietnam War.

"Operation Final Flight"—My Epiphany

Donald Vogler

There comes a time in every son's life when a father/child relationship changes; 1998 was that year for me.

I, like many other military dependents, grew up in a blissfully naive world … always sheltered from the realities of politics and war. My dad, like many other military dependents' fathers, went to work each day … without any of "us kids" really knowing what he did. I knew he was a pilot some of the time … other times doing mysterious things behind what I always thought of as drab military green-blue buildings on a myriad of different Air Force bases. Then in 1968 … he left my life for a period at a very tentative age for me. I was 12/13 … full of boyhood questions … going through puberty. He left for a strange far-off base in Southeast Asia (SEA) … someplace called Nakhon Phanom. I had missed his flight training in Louisiana. My folks sent me off to an all-boys' summer camp where I learned to shoot, sail, and canoe. Was told he would be flying a plane called an A-26 … had no idea what it was or what it looked like. The last thing *I* remember in August 1968 was my mom and dad hugging at Dulles International Airport when he left for that far-off land during the Vietnam War.

My life went on ... sheltered and blissfully unaware of the dangers of his tour. He returned a year later (September 1969). I was so eager to see him again. I remember that I was at our summer home, Mouse Island on Squam Lake, New Hampshire. This was his favorite place. But he was different ... kinda cold ... kinda distant ... almost mean. I ran to his room where he was sleeping and he yelled at me. I remember the hurt and pain that I felt in my heart ... just wanted to give him a hug. I left him to sleep (had no rational conception of time zone changes ... it was bedtime in NKP) ... I ran outside and cried privately. It would be many years before I felt close to him

Don Vogler (courtesy Donald Vogler).

again. Many of my forthcoming 30 years would be spent trying to make him proud of me. Somehow, I felt like I never measured up to his expectations. I even joined the Air Force ROTC program at the University of New Hampshire, my dad's alma mater. But ... even that goal "to be like my dad" was dashed in my senior year. I was diagnosed with diabetes ... and ... subsequently disqualified for a career in the military.

The silver lining in that sojourn was that I discovered flying ... the passion of my life. I was bound and determined to fulfill at least one dream ... and.... soaring became my portal into my Dad's "world." I spent the next 10 years perfecting the art of motorless flight ... earned my commercial glider rating ... logged over 1,500 hours of glider time. Flying became a nonverbal bond between us.

Fast-forward ... 1998. Age and time heals many wounds. My dad and I had grown close. His hard exterior seemed to soften as he aged ... then again ... maybe I had just matured. They say age and wisdom run hand in hand. And ... much to my chagrin.... I discovered how much alike we both really were. Then the other shoe dropped. Seemingly as fast as our bond had formed ... I lost my dad to cancer in 2000. That insidious disease took him away from me before I could ask that myriad of questions about his past. I guess I wanted to find out what made "me" tick and why. That veil of mystery would permeate my life for the next four years.

In the fall of 2003, I returned to flying in earnest. My close friend encouraged me to pursue my single-engine rating. The FAA had relaxed the rules ... and ... would now entertain "controlled" Type One diabetics for powered flight. I headed down to the local "pilots" shop in Nashua, New Hampshire, to pick up the necessary course materials ... when ... I discovered on a shelf *Foreign Invaders: The Douglas Invader in Foreign Military and U.S. Clandestine Service*, by Dan Hagedorn and Leif Hellstrom. I grabbed the book and it fell open to a page that mentioned my dad and "his" plane "Mighty Mouse," named after our summer home on Squam Lake. The chill that ran up my spine was unnerving. It was as though God helped my dad place that book in my hands. My life and world changed that day. I ran home with the book and showed my wife. She went to the computer … typed in "Mighty Mouse" … and an Air Force archive photograph of the plane appeared. The veil was lifting…. I celebrated my dad's birthday on June 30, 2004, by earning my single-engine rating in his honor.

I spent the next six–nine months reading everything I could get my hands on pertaining to NKP and the Nimrods. I tore through my dad's military records and discovered a treasure trove of photos and information relating to his tour in SEA. His collection of military "attic" memorabilia, including a shattered piece of A-26 "greenhouse" canopy … black flight suit … flight logbooks … and … patches, shed a distant torch light on a mysterious, altruistic mission to come. My mother was less than enthusiastic with my interest though … those were long-lost buried periods of her life … not ones she relished. I began to understand why I had felt so sheltered all those years. She, like many other military wives, had been left (by the Air Force) to tend to the brood at home while our fathers served "the greater cause" for our country. Those words sound so harsh to me … but … how those responsibilities were thrust on the moms in the military is another dark world that "us kids" were forever sheltered from too.

My research led me to a "new" close friend, James "Jeff" Sizemore. As I learned … his dad was the last Nimrod pilot to perish in SEA. We spent many hours emailing one another about our misconceptions of our fathers' lives in NKP. And through these conversations … I was introduced to two men who became (and fondly remain) surrogate fathers to me in my quest for information about that lost year in my life back in 1968. Captain Paul Marschalk and Colonel Nolan Schmidt took me under their "wings" and invited me down to the 2005 Nimrod reunion to learn about my dad and his service with the Nimrods.

October 2005 Reunion … my epiphany. I flew down to Fort Walton Beach with my flight instructor (doubled my trip effort with my pursuit of my instrument flight rating). I walked through the door of the "Hostility Suite," the Nimrods' colloquial name for their "party room" at the Air Commando Reunion … and stood there like a deer in the headlights. The eyes of the Nimrods shifted toward me … and … the room went eerily silent. Then…. Colonel Tom Wickstrom approached me and I introduced myself. He stammered for a moment … then … gave me a big hug. He said that he was taken aback because I looked so much like my dad. The weekend was a whirlwind … so much information … so fast. I struggled to take it all in. The Nimrods and their wonderful wives took me in like a long-lost son. I don't remember going to sleep the first night … just the aura of a great awakening surrounding me. The "beer" tales of NKP flowed like an endless stream from a tap at a smoke-filled frat house bar. And … it was there that Tom Wickstrom told me about IF 679's existence … the last flying A-26 Counter Invader in the world.

I returned home to my family in Jaffrey, NH … feeling awed by the shared stories from the men who had known and flown with my dad. I felt proud to be heir to this heroic legacy of airmen. They allowed me to vicariously experience their lives and missions overseas with my father … a rare privilege indeed. They had filled a void that would have otherwise haunted me for the rest of my life. And for that…. I had to do something for them.

In December 2005 … I called Denny Lynch, the owner of IF 679. I told him of my new acquaintance with Tom Wickstrom and the Nimrods … and … let him know that I was interested in acquiring and restoring the aircraft in the name of the Nimrods (as a "flying memorial" to them). He let me know that he was close friends with Tom … and … that the Nimrods had expressed interest in the plane in the past. The cost of operation and ownership impracticality had stalled any "real" ownership change efforts. The plane subsequently succumbed to nature's elemental forces of erosion … and … seemed destined to meet its maker in the aircraft scrapyards.

A month went by as I did some "soul searching" and aircraft finance/acquisition research … only to learn that Denny had passed away over the Christmas holidays. I felt spiritually crushed … my dream of honoring my dad and his squadron seemed to have been dashed before having an opportunity to try. But, mysteriously … the stars aligned again. His son, Randy, found a note in his father's "final" wish list … and … called me to let me know that his father had instructed that IF 679 was to be offered to me (and the Nimrods) under a purchase "right of first refusal." The mission "Operation Final Flight" and the formation of the A-26 Legacy Foundation were born that day.

Research would teach me that only six of the original 40 Douglas A-26s that had been rebuilt for service in Vietnam as B-26Ks by On Mark Corporation, Van Nuys, California, survived the war in Southeast Asia (five of which had already succumbed to age/metal fatigue and were retired to static museum displays around the world … my dad's plane, TA 651 "Mighty Mouse," included). IF 679, the last Counter Invader to come off of the On Mark production line in 1965, was indeed the last flying Counter Invader in the world!

I gathered the support of the sons and daughters (Legacies) of the Nimrods and founded our nonprofit educational organization—the A-26 Legacy Foundation—whose mission Operation Final Flight was to acquire, restore, and operate IF 679 as a "flying" museum … dedicated to our fathers for time immemorial … and to share this historic aircraft with air show visitors nationwide (especially younger Americans) in a tailored aerial educational format designed to raise public awareness of their heroic service to this nation and their plane that flew in the service of the United States Air Force during the Vietnam War *(see www.a-26legacy.org)*. Appropriately named "Special K," IF 679 subsequently became a truly a special plane with a very special mission in its future!

Five years of selfless dedication and perseverance fraught with tears, disappointments, and delays finally paid off in January 2010. We, the Legacies, in partnership with the Pacific Prowler Organization (also a nonprofit educational foundation with a shared vision), Fort Worth, Texas, accomplished the seemingly impossible. Special K was finally ours. She flew from Billings, Montana, to Denton, Texas, … had her paint stripped … and … arrived at the Vintage Flying Museum at Meacham Field in Fort Worth, where she is undergoing complete restoration to her original production glory … completion expected June 2011. Special K will fly to Oshkosh, arguably the world's largest civilian air show, in July 2011; be entered for the "best restoration award" in honor of the Nimrods; and then fly on to Destin, Florida, to meet and appropriately honor our fathers at their 2011 Nimrod reunion at Hurlburt Field … **a long-overdue tribute to these Air Commandos**!

Not a day has passed throughout the course of this mission that I haven't thought about my dad. I miss him so and regret that he won't be there to see the plane in the flesh. I pray that he knows how proud I am of him … and … hope that he and his fallen squadron mates bear witness to Special K as she flies overhead at the Sunday Reunion Memorial Service. May they all provide the lift beneath our wings during *our* flyby ….

Any Time Any Place

Editor's Note: The restoration effort actually took seven years. The restored aircraft was renamed "Special Kay," and it was first featured in an unforgettable flyover at the Air Commando Memorial Service at Hurlburt Field, Florida, on October 15, 2017. Jim Reynolds, and his volunteer restoration team, deserve enormous credit for bringing the "Special Kay" dream to fruition. (See "Callsign: Nimrod," by Frank Church, an exceptionally well-written article [complete with beautiful photographs] appearing in the *Warbird Digest*, Number 80, September/October 2018.)

A Special Day for "Special Kay"

ROGER D. GRAHAM

I can vouch for the fact that Sunday, October 15, 2017, was a very special day for "Special Kay." On that date, the restoration team—for the first time—flew Special Kay overhead during the Air Commando Memorial Service at Hurlburt Field, Florida. For me, and for the A/B/RB-26 family, the flyover of the restored A-26 was the highlight of the Air Commando Reunion in October 2017.

The Air Commando Memorial Service on Sunday always constitutes a most meaningful conclusion to the reunion. Following a presentation of the colors and a prayer by the chaplain, the featured speaker always reminds the participants of the continuing importance of Air Commando operations; always reminds the participants of the importance of patriotism and love of country; and always concludes with calling out the names of Air Commandos who have passed away since the last reunion. The significant addition for the 2017 reunion was that Special Kay flew overhead at the conclusion of the service.

For me, personally, the flyover of Special Kay was even more meaningful than I had anticipated. I realized ahead of time that this would be an incredible moment, but I vastly underestimated the emotional impact the flyover would have on me and all former A-26, B-26, and RB-26 pilots, navigators, maintainers, and armorers (and members of their families). First, I heard the unmistakable roar of the engines, and then, very quickly, I caught sight of the aircraft approaching the Memorial site. The sound and the sight together were overwhelming. I had not seen an A-26 in flight since flying with the A-26 Nimrods at NKP in 1967–68. I could not keep back the tears, and I could not ignore the immense pride in seeing Special Kay in the air.

I am thankful that my wife, Dianne, was with me on that momentous occasion. She has shared every important milestone of my life, so it was most fitting that we were standing there together when Special Kay flew overhead on that unforgettable day.

On behalf of all Air Commandos, I would like to thank Jim Reynolds and his restoration team for making the restoration and flight of Special Kay a reality. I know that it took seven long years, and considerable expense, to make that happen. Jim tells me that he plans to have Special Kay repainted in the summer (combat camouflage pattern), and that shortly thereafter, Special Kay is scheduled to make its first appearance at the Oshkosh air show in the summer of 2018. Jim and his team plan to fly Special Kay to air shows around the country for many years. The Special Kay story will be featured in several *Warbirds* magazine articles. If you ever get a chance, you are cordially invited to attend a local air show that will feature this incredible aircraft.

From Liberty's View

Kristine "Kristi" Graham Visage

I have a vision.
One that is so distant,
But yet is so near to my heart.
Back in what seems another time, I pledged my undying allegiance
To my flag and to my country.
I took an oath to defend
My constitution, my president, and my homeland.
A homeland where the right to freedom
Comes at birth,
And is too easily taken for granted.
I walk the path of those majestic days
In my mind,
While my feet walk the path of a different life.
These barren walls which surround my existence
Teach me the true meaning of freedom and liberty.
A place where hatred, disease, and death
Are my only friends.
The voices of a different tongue
Echo in my ears.
I've lost touch with all time.
The days, months, and years
Have all melted into a vast array of emptiness.
The only means which keep me going
Is a flicker of hope
For a vision
Of a Grand Lady,
Whose shores will bring me back to a homeland,
Where freedom is too easily taken for granted.

Editor's Note: Kristi Graham wrote the poem above in 1986 when she was a 16-year-old junior at West Springfield High School, Springfield, Virginia. Kristi won an award for the poem in a competition sponsored by the National Parent Teachers Association Reflections Program. Her inspiration for writing the poem was a family friend who was shot down on an F-4 mission and endured six long years of captivity in the infamous Hanoi Hilton prison camp in North Vietnam.

Restoration of the A-26A "Special Kay" AF 17679

Jim Reynolds

Concentration. That is what it takes to remember how a vision started 30 years ago at Ellsworth Air Force Base, South Dakota, and the South Dakota Air and Space Museum. I was visiting the museum when I came across an A-26 painted green and white with the number "AF 17640" on the tail. It had wingtip tanks and a gun nose, but there were some signs of an On Mark conversion. On Mark Engineering, located in Van Nuys, California, was well known for converting A-26s into executive transports in the 1950s before the Lear Jet and others were available for business travel. The thought occurred to me that this airplane was one of those conversions, and the museum was just making it appear to be a bomber. The signage next to the airplane indicated it was a B-26K and later redesignated an A-26A but without explanation.

This made me curious about the K model, as I had never heard of it, and I took some pride in knowing my aviation history, having learned to fly at the age of 15 and knowing that was what I wanted to do as a professional career. The internet searches in 1991 were not nearly as good as today, but a reference was found that showed the A-26s were indeed converted by On Mark for the U.S. Air Force as a counterinsurgency attack aircraft in 1964. It did not mention the CIA involvement or the first use of the airplanes in the Congo by the CIA. There was no mention of their use in the Vietnam War, as that was still a classified mission. The last statement in the reference said that all of the aircraft had been scrapped. So that added more confusion to the story because there seemed to be one right next door to Rapid City, South Dakota.

Fast-forward to 2001 and an A-26 sighting at the Billings, Montana, airport. My airline career was well underway by that time, and we had just started service between Phoenix and Billings. As we approached the airport, I noticed three A-26s sitting on a ramp on the north side of the runway. When we got closer, I remarked to the first officer that I sure would like to have one of those aircraft. (By the way, be careful what you wish for!) Being young, he asked what those airplanes were. I asked if he had seen the movie *Always*, about air tankers that had two A-26s in it. He had not, but that movie had gotten me interested in the type. Little did I know that two of the A-26s on the ramp were the same aircraft that appeared in the movie.

Another fast-forward to 2007, when I moved to Montana and made it my mission to go visit the Billings A-26s. That is when I discovered that the two silver airplanes were indeed the *Always* airplanes as supplied by Lynch Air Tankers. Lo and behold, though, the third airplane had camouflage paint, tip tanks, and a gun nose. It was AF 17679, so obviously, not all of the K models had been scrapped. In 2009, a move back to Texas took place, and since I had retired from airline flying, I became involved in a B-25 project called "Pacific Prowler." Shortly after that, I was asked if I knew where any A-26s were that might be for sale. I remembered the three at Billings and passed that along. A buyer wanted an A-26 with dual controls and wanted us to restore it for him. Aircraft AF

17679 fit the bill. The other two A-26s were single-pilot controlled and had already been sold. The deal was made and 679 was fixed up enough to ferry to Texas. But after the new owner got into the airplane, he came right back out with that look on his face that said claustrophobia anxiety. He felt more confined in the A-26 cockpit than he had expected. The project went dead in the water when he said sell it.

The next year, 2011, with hangar rent overdue and a lien on 679, it was looking bad, and a possibility existed that it could be scrapped. By this time, I had attended my first reunion with the A/B-26 veterans at Hurlburt Field, Florida, and learned many of their now unclassified A-26 combat stories from a place called Nakhon Phanom, a.k.a. NKP, Thailand.

The mission became clear: save the airplane and share those stories with the public. We have always felt that the Vietnam veterans did not get the welcome home they deserved, so this was a starting point for us to help change that oversight. As it turned out, one fine day, I had taken the B-25 down the ramp to the Texas Jet FBO at Meacham Airport for display alongside the CAF B-29 "FiFi." As I was giving tours of the B-25 to those who wanted to see it, a man walked up to me in the bomb bay and said that when he was a kid, his uncle (who was in the Air Force) flew a B-25 up to his hometown airport. That made a huge impression on him and when he was old enough, he joined the Air Force and became a mechanic during the Vietnam War. He now wanted to get involved in working on historic aircraft.

We talked a bit more, and soon I invited him to come and see the A-26 that needed a lot of TLC. As it ended up, J.R. Hofmann was just the right man to get the ball rolling. He had several mechanic friends he recruited to take on the project. He also recruited six students who were attending the local junior college A&P course to become mechanics. Then one of the former 301st AF Reserve Fighter Squadron mechanics at Carswell AFB in Fort Worth recruited another batch of his friends. One of the first things we did was clean out and treat the areas where birds had nested during the many years it sat outside in Montana as a bird condo. We started making some traction by 2016. We took apart every landing gear and completely restored the landing gear mechanisms. One engine was sent off for overhaul in Idaho. The props were both overhauled. The other engine needed several cylinders replaced. A lot of the crash damage from a bad landing in Macon, Georgia, in 1977 was still in need of repair. All three landing gears had been ripped out of the nose and the nacelles. All of the ailerons and elevators needed the fabric replaced. The rudder was taken off and serviced. The trim system in the rudder had the same grease inside the gearing, probably since the late 1960s. It smelled terrible. All five control surfaces had the gap seals installed that had rotted away decades ago. There were a lot of sheet metal repairs done on the fuselage and the vertical stabilizer where holes had been punched by flying debris when the left engine was ripped off in the crash.

By 2017, we had the airplane make its first flight since the ferry flight from Montana, but it was not painted yet. We started participating in air shows that year, and most importantly, took her to the Air Commando Association Reunion at Hurlburt Field, Florida, for a flyover of the memorial ceremony with an actual A-26 Vietnam War veteran as a pilot. There were many eyes that got wet when Kay hit her mark over the flagpole at just the right moment. Many in the audience had not seen or heard an A-26 in 50 years or more. It was the highlight of the year.

The year 2018 got even better. Kay received a duplicate of the original paint job she had in 1968 at England Air Force Base, Louisiana, where she served as a trainer for the crews going to NKP. We flew to Seattle in May of that year to participate in a flyover at the Museum of Flight's dedication of their Vietnam Airman's Memorial and Plaza. It was a night to remember as we had taken one of our Vietnam War veterans up there, and he was among the hundred or so who were given a special welcome home at the banquet held in their honor. There were many Medal of Honor awardees and former POWs from the infamous Hanoi Hilton in attendance. The whole crew of four felt so privileged to be with those folks. In July, we flew up to Oshkosh to participate in the Experimental Aircraft Association's annual airshow. Over 500,000 people and 10,000 aircraft attended. Kay was awarded the "Best Bomber" and Silver Wrench Restoration Awards in recognition of the hard work that went into her rebuilding. Again, we had a Vietnam War veteran pilot and his original navigator fly Kay in the warbirds portion of the airshow.

Kay was featured in the "Warbirds in Review" segment on the warbird ramp with David Letterman interviewing our two Vietnam War veteran crewmembers (Tim Black and Bruce Gustafson), along with J.R. Hofmann and Scott Carson, who was an ordnance loader at NKP on A-26s. Scott is a retired Boeing Commercial Aircraft president and has been very helpful in raising funds for the restoration. We are very grateful to him and all of the other donors who have helped along the way. Most notably, the Thomas Haas Foundation has been a solid supporter.

Restoration team members: *Back row, left to right:* Larry Buchanan, Ed Manning, Scott Hines, Jim Reynolds, Lefty Brandon. *Front row, left to right:* Brian Barnett, Chuck Kennedy, J.R. Hofmann (holding Silver Wrench Restoration Award plaque), Jim Stevenson, and Juan Lopez. Many volunteer restoration team members could not be included here (courtesy Jim Reynolds).

Special Kay before-and-after photos. Top photograph shows aircraft after restoration but before paint job. Second photograph above shows restored Special Kay after new camouflage paint job (courtesy Jim Reynolds).

Stunning aerial photograph of Special Kay, complete with camouflage paint and ordnance (courtesy Jim Reynolds).

We had our biggest air show schedule with Kay in 2019. Two of the many shows that stand out to us were the Barksdale AFB, Louisiana, "Defenders of Liberty" show, where our crew was treated like rock stars. They took really good care of us. The other one was the "Spirit of St. Louis" show where we got to lead the warbird parade. Behind us was a B-25 and a B-17 with a Spitfire, a P-51 Mustang, and a Corsair fighter flying top cover. The year 2019 ended with an appearance at the Veterans Fund Raiser and Banquet of Honor at Dallas-Fort Worth Airport.

We started our usual winter maintenance program in December 2019, and then got hit hard by the coronavirus shutdowns. Progress has been slow in getting Kay ready to go again. Besides the direct impact of CDC guidelines, most of the air shows in 2020 and the first part of 2021 were canceled. Our income has been drastically reduced just at a time we need it for finishing the next phase of the restoration of Special Kay.

To date, more than 65 people have worked on Kay, close to 25,000 man-hours of volunteer time devoted to the effort, and well over $1 million spent on the restoration. A special note of appreciation goes to the Special Kay volunteer team for their hard work and dedication. Without them, none of this would have been possible.

Several people have asked, why was so much time and money invested on what would normally be a $150,000 airplane? The answer is simple. The U.S. Air Force Vietnam War veterans who flew and worked on this airplane deserve it. It is not just an airplane. It is their story. It is a symbol of the dedication to their squadron mates and to the mission they accomplished. They didn't let us down. We will not let them down ever again.

Editor's Note: Franklin Poole, associated with Jim Reynolds and the Special Kay restoration team, has made numerous outstanding videos showing various stages of the Special Kay aircraft restoration process, and video interviews of several A-26 pilots and navigators who flew with the A-26 Nimrods in 1966–69. To access those videos, readers can visit youtube.com and use the search terms "Franklin Poole Nimrods." Franklin Poole has also made these videos available to the public at https://vimeo.com/channels/nimrods.

Epilogue

With the passage of time, past events become more clear, and take on added meaning. In the early stages of the Vietnam War, the United States was well prepared to deter or fight a nuclear war, but we were not well prepared to fight limited wars in faraway countries involving counterinsurgency operations. Following the end of World War II, the United States and Western allies became involved in a protracted "Cold War" with the Soviet Union, and in a more opaque way, with its mysterious ally, Communist China. After Premier Nikita Khrushchev announced that the Soviet Union would support "wars of national liberation" on a worldwide basis, the stage was set for the conflict in Vietnam. In the early 1960s, President John Kennedy ordered the initial contingent of U.S. military forces to deploy to South Vietnam to assist that beleaguered country to resist communist aggression from North Vietnam. The Air Commandos, based at Hurlburt Field, Florida, were a part of that initial effort (Operation Farm Gate), deploying to Bien Hoa Air Base near Saigon, where B-26 bombers, T-28 fighter-bombers, C-47, and C-130 aircraft provided the main combat support. The B-26 crews were "gung ho" and very capable, but their aircraft, in reality, were aging aircraft in poor mechanical condition. Despite those challenges, the B-26 crews played a vital role in providing fighter-bomber escort protection for U.S. Army helicopter assault operations, protection for South Vietnam "strategic hamlets" when they came under attack from communist forces at night, and for general combat operations supporting the South Vietnam government. Only after B-26 aircraft and crews were lost due to wing failure were the B-26 aircraft grounded: the Air Force response was to "remanufacture" 40 B-26 aircraft into the updated A-26A Counter Invader configuration that operated out of Nakhon Phanom Royal Thai Air Force Base (NKP) from 1966 to 1969. The initial six-month combat evaluation phase for the remanufactured A-26 aircraft flying out of NKP was called Project Big Eagle, leading into the A-26 Nimrod combat phase from 1966 to late 1969.

The military record of the A-26 aircraft and crews operating out of NKP was most impressive. They operated mainly at night, because that was when the North Vietnamese supply truck convoys operated along the vast Ho Chi Minh Trail complex in eastern Laos. The combat action was especially fierce during the "dry season" in the September to April time frame when the truck convoys were operating at full capacity to resupply communist forces operating in Laos, South Vietnam, and Cambodia. The A-26 crews were also very effective in providing close air support to Hmong and Royal Laotian forces in northern Laos. General Vang Pao, the legendary leader of the Hmong mountain tribesmen, stated the A-26 Nimrods saved him and his people from communist forces on many, many occasions.

Despite the heroism of U.S. combat forces, history reflects that North Vietnamese communist forces invaded and took over South Vietnam in 1975, two years after the withdrawal of U.S. military forces pursuant to a "peace treaty" agreed to in 1973. There are many "lessons learned" from the Vietnam War, but from a military perspective, the lessons are relatively straightforward. Lesson One: U.S. military fighting men (and women) make up a patriotic and unrelenting force that can be counted on to be courageous and to "want to win" for freedom and U.S. principles and values. Lesson Two: the U.S. needs to provide effective political (government) and military leadership if U.S. military forces are to prevail on world military battlefields. Lesson Three: U.S. military forces must be provided with the best training and with the best and most technologically advanced weapon systems in the world.

Since constant limited wars have become the norm in the 21st century, particularly in the Middle East, the need for significant numbers of relatively inexpensive U.S. attack combat aircraft seems obvious. From an air war perspective, the U.S. did not have enough tactical aircraft with A-26 capabilities during the Vietnam War. The A-26 aircraft and crews were highly effective for several important reasons: (1) large ordnance and ammunition loads; (2) long time over targets because of large fuel capacity; (3) highly trained two-man crew; (4) flew low and slow enough to acquire and take out targets; and (5) worked effectively with forward air controllers (FACs) in the air and on the ground to strike and destroy targets as part of a team effort. What A-26 aircraft and crews lacked was today's technology advancements in target acquisition and tracking, and today's advanced munitions featuring "smart bomb" technology. Today's A-10 attack aircraft appear to be the closest operational attack aircraft fulfilling many of the ideal attack aircraft capabilities. Unfortunately, some ill-informed politicians want to shut down A-10 operations to reduce military spending. Just the reverse is really needed. The A-10 squadrons should be maintained as long as possible, and development efforts for relatively inexpensive follow-on attack aircraft should be accelerated.

Fortunately, top U.S. Air Force leaders have recognized the urgent need for the U.S. and allies to evaluate the capability of new light attack aircraft (such as Textron Aviation's AT-6 Wolverine and the Sierra Nevada/Embraer A-29 Tucono). The acquisition of such inexpensive "high tech" attack aircraft would constitute a sound national investment. The establishment of a least one light attack "Armed Overwatch" aircraft operational squadron at Hurlburt Field, Florida, would be a logical addition to existing U.S. Air Force Special Operations capabilities. The number of such light attack squadrons could be multiplied if needed in the future.

According to a July 22, 2021, story published by Daily Report (*Air Force Magazine*),[1] U.S. Special Operations Command (SOCOM) wants four "Armed Overwatch" squadrons, with one squadron always deployed. In testimony to the House Armed Services subcommittee on intelligence and special operations, Army General Richard D. Clarke said he wants to buy 75 Armed Overwatch aircraft to meet a growing need for intelligence, surveillance, and reconnaissance. The Air Force Special Operations Command supports that requirement and wants to start procurement in fiscal 2022. Those are promising developments. On a worldwide basis, we need to be ready to defeat terrorism and win the limited wars to come. The stakes could not be higher. The U.S. must remain the vigilant leader of the free world.

The men who flew, maintained, and armed the B-26, the RB-26, and the A-26 in the Vietnam War were true patriots who had the courage to fly and fight for freedom. Not all their stories appear here—there are many more—but enough of their stories are included in this book to give the reader a real sense of the thoughts and actions of Air Force veterans who fought in that long and controversial war. The stories of family members are important too. What could be more tragic, and long-lasting, than the loss of a beloved family member in war? In contrast, what could be more joyous than the survival of a loved one in a war? We are proud to be Americans, and we are thankful to be free. We are also confident that the men and women serving in our U.S. armed forces today are just as determined to protect and defend the citizens and the values of the United States of America.

Any Time Any Place

NOTE

1. See Armed Overwatch news item written by Brian W. Everstine, Daily Report, *Air Force Magazine*, July 22, 2021.

About the Contributors

Harlan "Gene" **Albee** completed navigation training and was assigned to A-26 aircraft flying combat missions out of Nakhon Phanom RTAFB, Thailand. He was part of Project Big Eagle in 1966 that evaluated the suitability of A-26 Counter Invader aircraft to attack enemy truck convoys on the Ho Chi Minh Trail in Laos. After completing 100 A-26 missions, he was reassigned as an F-4 navigator. Following his Air Force service, Gene worked for Boeing Aerospace for 20 years. He now lives in Crossville, Tennessee.

Kenneth J. **Alnwick** graduated from the Air Force Academy in 1960. After pilot training, he flew the C-121 and C-135 before transitioning to the B-26 at Hurlburt Field, Florida, the birthplace of the Air Commandos. Upon arrival in Vietnam in 1963, he assumed the RB-26 mission and flew high- and low-altitude reconnaissance missions and conducted various tests of new and emerging technologies such as such as shoran and night infrared imaging. Ken retired in the rank of colonel, having held increasingly more responsible positions as a planner, educator, and war game designer. He currently resides in Alexandra, Virginia.

Andrew "Andi" **Biancur** graduated from the Air Force Academy in 1960. His classmates elected him president of the Class of 1960. Following pilot training, Andi served a combat tour in 1963 with the Air Commandos as a B-26 pilot at Bien Hoa Air Base, South Vietnam. In 1966, he served a combat tour with the F-105G wild weasel program, and in 1970, he served as a ground forward air controller. In 1986, Andi retired from the Air Force as a colonel after a 26-year career. In his later years, Andi devoted much of his time to enriching the Air Force Academy's honor and heritage programs. Andi passed away on January 10, 2021. His widow, Carole, resides in Colorado Springs, Colorado.

Tim **Black** graduated from pilot training in 1968 and completed two tours in the Vietnam War. During his first tour, as a first lieutenant, Tim was a C-7 Caribou pilot, and during his second tour (1969–70), he was an A-26 pilot at Nakhon Phanom RTAFB, Thailand. During his 25-year Air Force career, Tim also flew T-38, C-12, and A-10 aircraft. He was an A-10 squadron commander. Tim flew 1,600 hours combat time, and his awards and decorations include the Silver Star, Legion of Merit, Distinguished Flying Cross, and six Air Medals. Tim retired as a colonel, and Tim and his wife, Grizel, currently reside in Austin, Texas.

Jim **Blanchard** completed navigation training and selected the A-26 as his first operational assignment. He was not disappointed. Jim and his pilot flew the last A-26 out of NKP when the 609th Special Operations Squadron was deactivated in November 1969. He later flew in F-4 aircraft as a weapons systems officer, and had two tours at HQ TAC, but the A-26 assignment was the most interesting experience of his 20-year Air Force career. Jim and his wife, Trina, currently reside in Crestview, Florida.

Maury **Bourne** joined the U.S. Air Force in 1960 and completed navigator training. In 1963, he volunteered for the First Air Commando Wing and was deployed to Bien Hoa Air Base, South Vietnam. Maury was assigned to the Douglas B-26 (a two-man attack bomber) and flew 70 combat missions. In December 1965, he was forced to bail out of a B-26 on a bombing range at Elgin

AFB, Florida. He lost his right leg in the incident. His pilot, Captain Thomas R. White, died in that crash. In July 1965, Maury was fitted with an artificial leg and given a medical discharge from the Air Force with the rank of first lieutenant. Maury now lives on the same farm where he grew up in Marquez, Texas.

Harry J. **Bright** was serving as a 21-year-old airman who repaired aircraft engines at Nakhon Phanom RTAFB, Thailand, on December 29, 1967. On that date, he learned that his friend Sergeant Paul Foster was killed on an A-26 combat mission over the Ho Chi Minh Trail. Also killed were Captain Carlos Cruz (pilot) and Captain Bill Potter (navigator). Following news of the crash, Harry could not sleep, so he wrote a poem to Paul Foster's mother, to let her know that he had known her son. Harry now lives in Townsend, Delaware.

Jimmie **Butler** was a USAFA cadet at 17 in the Class of 1963, a colonel at 39, and retired as chief of staff of the Air Force Space Division. Beginning in February 1967, he flew 240 forward air controller missions as a lieutenant/captain, mostly over the Ho Chi Minh Trail through Laos. Being a FAC was his most formative experience leading to a successful USAF career. He is an author, photographer, and patriot living in Colorado Springs, Colorado.

William "Bill" **Cohen** is a West Point graduate with 3,000 hours as a B-52 navigator/bombardier (select crew and instructor). During the Vietnam War, he served as an Air Commando A-26 navigator/copilot and instructor, flying 174 combat missions as a captain in 1968. Thereafter, he resigned his commission and joined the Israeli Air Force. After the Yom Kippur War, he rejoined the U.S. Air Force. His awards and decorations include the Distinguished Service Medal, the Legion of Merit, the Defense Meritorious Service Medal, and the Distinguished Flying Cross with three Oak Leaf Clusters. He retired from the U.S. Air Force as a major general and currently resides with his wife in Pasadena, California.

Carla **Cruz-Curtis** (now Carla Cruz-Craker) is the daughter of Captain Carlos R. Cruz, an A-26 pilot who was killed in action on December 29, 1967, during a nighttime bombing mission over the Ho Chi Minh Trail. Carla was only six years old when her father was lost in combat. Carla's story in *Fly By Knights* is a poignant letter recalling all of the people she met, and valuable information she learned, during an Air Commando reunion at Fort Walton Beach, Florida. Carla is a self-described survivor who wants to help other children who lose their fathers (or mothers) in war. Carla currently lives in Cotopaxi, Colorado.

Robert B. **Denny** is the son of On Mark Engineering Company founder Robert O. Denny. He grew up around On Mark and flew the A-26 as a teenager with his father and others. He was awarded a master's degree in electrical engineering and went on to become an avionics engineer and software developer. More recently, he served as an armed and uniformed volunteer for the Maricopa County (Arizona) Sheriff's Office for 18 years, with the last five being a tactical flight officer and certificated second pilot in the Bell 407 helicopter. Bob currently resides in Mesa, Arizona.

Jim **Galluzzi** was the flight-line maintenance officer at Nakhon Phanom Royal Thai AFB (NKP) in 1967–68. He previously flew as a pilot, having been grounded after completing pilot training. Jim frequently flew maintenance test flights with A-26 pilots at NKP. He was a captain at the time. Following the NKP assignment, Jim continued his career as a maintenance officer and retired from the Air Force in 1980 as a lieutenant colonel. In civilian life, Jim owned and operated a wine importing business in Florida. Jim passed away on September 17, 2019. His widow, Ilene, resides at Merritt Island, Florida.

Dianne **Graham** graduated from Athens High School (West Virginia) in 1960. She graduated from Concord University in 1963, with a double major in math and English. She met Roger Graham in junior high school, and they were married after college in 1963. A career teacher, Dianne has taught math and English in high schools and middle schools across the country. A true American patriot, Dianne supported Roger throughout his Air Force career. Dianne and Roger have three children (Kim, Kristi, and Ryan), and three grandchildren (Colette, Averi, and Chase Visage). Kristi is married to William "Bill" Visage. Dianne and Roger currently reside in Acworth, Georgia.

Roger D. **Graham** graduated from Athens High School (West Virginia) in 1959. He graduated from the U.S. Air Force Academy in 1963, and married Dianne that same year. Roger flew in B-52 and A-26 aircraft as a navigator-bombardier, flying 182 A-26 combat missions in the Vietnam War in 1967–68. Roger was a captain in the Vietnam War, and flew most of his missions at night, over the Ho Chi Minh Trail, with Major Bob "Pappy" Sears (pilot). Roger obtained law degrees from WVU and George Washington University and finished his Air Force career as a judge advocate with the rank of colonel. Roger and Dianne have three children and three grandchildren, and currently reside in Acworth, Georgia.

Bruce "Gus" **Gustafson** completed navigator-bombardier training at Mather AFB, California, in 1961. He volunteered for an A-26 combat tour at Nakhon Phanom Royal Thai AFB in 1969. Gus was a B-52 crewmember during Linebacker II nighttime concentrated Hanoi bomb runs in December 1972 that led to American POW release. He flew 270 combat missions in the Vietnam War; his awards and decorations include two Distinguished Flying Crosses, a Bronze Star, 11 Air Medals, and seven Vietnam Service Medals. Gus accrued 6,000 flight hours in T-29, C-118, A-26, and B-52 D, G, and H model aircraft, and he retired from the Air Force as a major. He currently resides in Eugene, Oregon.

Charles H. "Chuck" **Holden** graduated from navigation school with the Aviation Cadet Program. In 1963, he was assigned as a B-26 navigator at Bien Hoa Air Base, South Vietnam. During a horrendous B-26 combat mission on October 13, 1963, an enemy soldier firing a .30-caliber weapon wounded Chuck in the left foot. Chuck remembers that life-changing mission in his story in this book and relates how that mission had a direct bearing on his progression to becoming a pilot and a full colonel during his Air Force career. Chuck currently lives in Las Vegas, Nevada.

Lindsey **Jackson** was a member of the Air Commandos from 1963 to 1967. During his assignment at Nakhon Phanom Royal Thai AFB, he served as an A-26 aircraft mechanic and non-commissioned-officer-in-charge of the arming/de-arming area. Following active duty service, Lindsey joined the Air National Guard in 1973, working in the areas of security, electronic power production, corrosion control, and recruiting. Lindsey retired as a master sergeant (E-7) in 1995. He continues to be an active member of the Civil Air Patrol (30-plus years). Lindsey and his wife (Maxine) currently reside in San Antonio, Texas.

Joe **Kittinger** is a legendary Air Force fighter pilot who flew A-26 and F-4 aircraft in combat in the Vietnam War. From an early age, Joe loved adventure and flying. As a test pilot, Joe made a parachute free fall from 102,800 feet (high-altitude balloon), during which he achieved a speed of 614 miles per hour. In 1964, Joe flew the B-26 out of Bien Hoa Air Base, South Vietnam, and in 1966, Joe flew the "remanufactured" A-26 out of Nakhon Phanom Royal Thai AFB, Thailand. Later, Joe was shot down during an F-4 mission and was released from a North Vietnam POW camp in 1973. His autobiography, *Come Up and Get Me*, was published in 2010. Joe retired from the Air Force as a colonel, and currently resides with his wife, Sherry, in Altamonte Springs, Florida.

Bruce **Kramer** completed navigator and bombardier training as an aviation cadet. In July 1963, he was part of the B-26 Air Commando deployment to Bien Hoa Air Base, South Vietnam. Following his B-26 assignment, Bruce was assigned to a B-57 unit that flew combat missions throughout Vietnam. Next came pilot training, and an assignment as a T-37 instructor pilot in an allied German Program. Bruce then left active duty but continued his military flying career in the Reserves. Bruce currently lives in Portland, Oregon.

Jack **Krause** graduated from West Point with the Class of 1954. Earning his pilot's wings in 1955, Jack had a career as an interceptor pilot, ground attack pilot, aide-de-camp, and staff and maintenance officer assigned to more than a dozen units, several commands, and USAF Headquarters. In 1967, he completed 150 Air Commando night interdiction missions in Laos flying A-26 attack aircraft for which he was awarded two Distinguished Flying Crosses. Retiring as a lieutenant colonel in 1979, he led a four-ship formation of single-engine jet aircraft in a flyby at his own retirement ceremony. Jack passed away on March 9, 2020. He last resided at Shelton, Washington.

James "Lee" **McCleskey** is a 1961 graduate of the Air Force Academy. After graduating from pilot training in 1962, Lee became an instructor pilot at Laughlin AFB, Texas. From 1966–67, he flew combat missions as an A-26 pilot at Nakhon Phanom Royal Thai AFB, where his battle-damaged aircraft exploded just after he and his navigator successfully bailed out at low level. Lee's numerous decorations include two Silver Stars, two Distinguished Flying Crosses, and a Purple Heart. He retired as a colonel in 1991 and has long been associated with the ROTC Program at Texas A&M University. Lee and his wife, Joani, currently reside in College Station, Texas.

Frank **Nelson** was promoted to captain in 1968 after completing navigator training and A-26 transition training. On October 11, 1968, Frank and Captain Juni Tengan (pilot) departed McClellan AFB, California, on their A-26 flight across the Pacific to Nakhon Phanom Royal Thai AFB, where Frank flew 185 A-26 combat missions with the 609th Air Commando Squadron. He then received a C-130 assignment. Subsequent assignments included serving as an instructor navigator at Mather AFB, California, and assignments to F-111D and F-111E units. Frank retired from the Air Force as a major and currently resides in Lincoln, California.

Mike **Packard** graduated from New Mexico State University in 1964. An ROTC graduate, Mike was commissioned as a second lieutenant in the U.S. Air Force. He served on active duty from February 1965 to February 1969. Mike was also a graduate of Aircraft Maintenance Officer School, serving as the officer in charge of A-26 aircraft maintenance at Nakhon Phanom Royal Thai Air Force Base, Thailand, from August 1967 to August 1968. He was a captain at the time, and he was awarded the Bronze Star Medal. His subsequent civilian career entailed 40 years as an executive in real estate management. He currently resides in Carlsbad, California.

Ed **Parker** was an Air Force flight engineer during the Vietnam War, serving combat tours from 1967 to 1969 in Vietnam, Thailand, Laos, and Cambodia. He was an A/B-26 crew chief and flew some 130 missions on EC-47 aircraft. His highest rank served was staff sergeant (E-5), and among his awards and decorations are the Distinguished Flying Cross and four Air Medals. Ed survived a forced landing after taking accurate ground fire, and experienced TET 1967 and 1968. He is active in veteran affairs, and currently lives in Peoria, Arizona.

Jimmy **Phillis** served as an aerial photography specialist in 1963 flying in RB-26 and T-28 aircraft out of Bien Hoa Air Base, South Vietnam. As a young airman, he volunteered for the "Jungle Jim" Program and became an air commando. From his crew position in the RB-26 (behind the bomb bay), Jimmy experienced combat while operating camera systems. He was discharged from the Air Force on October 7, 1963, and he passed away on October 7, 2010. Jimmy's widow, Ruth, resides in Pawnee, Illinois.

Leon "Crazy" **Poteet** served 21 years in the U.S. Air Force as a navigator. Initially, he was a B-52 crewmember at Altus AFB, Oklahoma, and then was assigned as an A-26 navigator/copilot at Nakhon Phanom Royal Thai AFB in 1969. He flew 147 combat missions over Laos and Cambodia. He then flew as an F-111 crewmember at Nellis AFB, Eglin AFB, and Upper Heyford, England, where he was a flight commander in charge of units flying NATO exercises. He obtained a master's degree in engineering administration at Southern Methodist University. After retiring from the Air Force as a major in 1984, he moved to Texas and worked for 22 years at Tracor/BAE Systems. Leon currently resides in Bastrop, Texas.

Jim **Reynolds** is a former science teacher and airline pilot who lives in Fort Worth, Texas. He is a member of the Commemorative Air Force, the Civil Air Patrol, and the Experimental Aircraft Association-Warbirds. He has been flying since 1960 and has over 20,000 hours in the air. He is type-rated in 14 aircraft, including the B-25 and A-26. Jim led the restoration team that rebuilt "Special Kay," the A-26A lone survivor that is still airworthy, based at the Vintage Flying Museum at Meacham Field, Fort Worth. Jim has three daughters, four grandkids, five grand dogs, one grand kitty, and a squadron of 15 volunteers who work on Special Kay and a T-33 as PGM Aviation nonprofit.

George **Rose** graduated from East Carolina University in 1955. He was commissioned a second lieutenant and completed navigation training at Ellington AFB, Texas, in 1957. In 1964, he completed a tour as a B-26/C-47 navigator-bombardier with the 34th Air Commando Group at Bien Hoa Air Base, South Vietnam (awarded three Air Medals). In 1965, he completed a tour as a B-57 navigator-bombardier with the 8th Tactical Bomb Squadron at Bien Hoa Air Base and Da Nang Air Base, South Vietnam (awarded five more Air Medals). George retired from the Air Force as a major in 1976 and worked in management analysis with the U.S. Navy civil service, Norfolk, Virginia, for 20 years. George passed away in September 2015, and his widow, Kathleen, currently resides in Williamsburg, Virginia.

Capt. Michael J.C. **Roth**, USAF, graduated from the U.S. Air Force Academy in 1963. In his First Class (senior) year at the Academy, he was the cadet wing commander. After pilot training, Mickey flew KC-135 and A-26 aircraft. He flew 140 night bombing missions over the Ho Chi Minh Trail in the A-26 Counter Invader, and his numerous decorations include the Silver Star. Following his Vietnam War service, Mickey joined USAA and became the inaugural president of the USAA Investment Management Company. Mickey passed away on January 23, 2021. His widow (Jutta) resides in San Antonio, Texas.

Randy **Ryman** served in the U.S. Air Force from 1965 to 1969 as a munitions/armament specialist. In 1966, he participated in the first deployment of A-26 Counter Invader aircraft to Nakhon Phanom Royal Thai Air Force Base, Thailand. He served with the 603rd Air Commando Squadron under the code name Project Big Eagle. Randy and his wife currently reside in Loris, South Carolina.

Bob "Pappy" **Sears** graduated from Texas Tech University in 1954. He entered the Air Force and graduated from pilot training in 1955. He served as an instructor pilot in B-25 and T-29 aircraft, flew A-26 aircraft in combat out of Nakhon Phanom RTAFB (188 combat missions from 1967 to 1969), and flew DC-9 aeromedical aircraft from 1969 to 1973. He served as the commander of the Military Airlift Center Europe at Ramstein, Germany, and the inspector general of the San Antonio Texas Air Logistics Center. Sadly, his wife of many years, Elaine, passed away on January 17, 2020. Colonel (Ret.) Sears currently lives at Marble Falls, Texas.

Al "Batman" **Shortt** served as a career U.S. Air Force fighter pilot. He flew F-80, F-86 (Korea), F-102A, and F-4E fighter aircraft. Al says that his most rewarding and memorable Air Force experience was being the operations officer and pilot, as a major, flying the A-26 on combat missions out of Nakhon Phanom Royal Thai AFB in 1968–69. He flew 194 A-26 combat missions and was known as "Batman." His navigator, Captain Larry Counts, was known as "Robin." Al retired as a fighter pilot with the rank of lieutenant colonel. Al and his wife (Dottie) currently reside in Lynn Haven, Florida.

Major James **Sizemore** was an A-26 pilot flying combat missions with the 609th Special Operations Squadron when he was killed on a combat mission in northern Laos on July 8, 1969. His navigator, Major Howard Andre, was also killed in the crash. Prior to that fateful mission, Major Sizemore had written a poignant letter to his son, "Jeff" Sizemore, which appears in this book. Major James Sizemore was from San Diego, California.

Tom **Smith** was a captain and a B-26 pilot flying combat missions with the 1st Air Commando Group in the early 1960s, the earliest deployment of U.S. Air Force counterinsurgency units in the Vietnam War. He became an American Airlines pilot in 1965, and concurrently flew F-100 and F-105 aircraft with the District of Columbia Air National Guard. Tom retired from the Air Force in 1980, and later retired from American Airlines in 1995 after 30 years as an airline pilot. Tom currently resides in Emerald Isle, North Carolina.

John **Sodergren** soloed in an Aeronca Champ as a teenager in 1953 and received his Air Force pilot wings in 1958. John checked out in the B-26 at Hurlburt Field, Florida, in 1963. He flew B-26 combat missions out of Bien Hoa Air Base, South Vietnam, from July 1963 to January 1964. In 1965, John started a 30-year career as a pilot for American Airlines. During his time in the Air

Force, John also flew the B-25 and the C-46. However, John says he still loves the A/B-26 above them all. John currently resides in Killingworth, Connecticut.

Kristine "Kristi" Graham **Visage** graduated from West Springfield High School (Virginia) in 1987. She graduated from the University of Virginia in 1991, with a major in government and foreign affairs and a minor in French. She obtained a law degree from Georgia State University in 1999. She married William "Bill" Visage in 1994 and has three children (Colette, Averi, and Chase). Kristi and Bill currently reside in Acworth, Georgia.

Donald **Vogler** is the son of the late Lieutenant Colonel Charles Vogler (A-26 Nimrod pilot 1968/1969). He founded and chaired the A-26 Legacy Foundation, a nonprofit organization (including other sons and daughters of Air Commandos) dedicated to the concept of restoring and operating an A-26A/B-26K Counter Invader as a flying memorial to their fathers' Air Commando service in the Vietnam War. That concept gained support and was brought to fruition in 2018 when award-winning "Special Kay" was presented at the EAA AirVenture national air show in Oshkosh, Wisconsin. Donald currently resides in Jaffrey, New Hampshire.

Jack **Williams** enlisted in the Air Force in 1960. He completed navigator training at James Connally Air Force Base, Waco, Texas, in 1961, and completed the Electronic Warfare Course at Keesler AFB, Mississippi, in 1962. He was assigned to the 306th Bomb Wing (B-52) McCoy AFB, Florida, prior to being assigned to the 1st Air Commando Group. He completed A/B-26 transition training in 1963, followed by a six-month B-26 assignment with Detachment 2A to Bien Hoa Air Base, South Vietnam. He resigned as a captain in 1964 and became an FBI agent. He also worked with American Airlines. Jack and his wife currently live in The Villages, Florida.

Index

Numbers in **bold italics** indicate pages with illustrations

277